W9-CNW-358

Université d'Ottawa
BIBLIOTHÈQUES
LIBRARIES
University of Ottawa

Issues and Developments in Public Management

Survey 1996-1997

ORGANISATION FOR ECONOMIC CO-OPERATION AND DEVELOPMENT

ORGANISATION FOR ECONOMIC CO-OPERATION AND DEVELOPMENT

Pursuant to Article 1 of the Convention signed in Paris on 14th December 1960, and which came into force on 30th September 1961, the Organisation for Economic Co-operation and Development (OECD) shall promote policies designed:

- to achieve the highest sustainable economic growth and employment and a rising standard of living in Member countries, while maintaining financial stability, and thus to contribute to the development of the world economy;
- to contribute to sound economic expansion in Member as well as non-member countries in the process of economic development; and
- to contribute to the expansion of world trade on a multilateral, non-discriminatory basis in accordance with international obligations.

The original Member countries of the OECD are Austria, Belgium, Canada, Denmark, France, Germany, Greece, Iceland, Ireland, Italy, Luxembourg, the Netherlands, Norway, Portugal, Spain, Sweden, Switzerland, Turkey, the United Kingdom and the United States. The following countries became Members subsequently through accession at the dates indicated hereafter: Japan (28th April 1964), Finland (28th January 1969), Australia (7th June 1971), New Zealand (29th May 1973), Mexico (18th May 1994), the Czech Republic (21st December 1995), Hungary (7th May 1996), Poland (22nd November 1996) and the Republic of Korea (12th December 1996). The Commission of the European Communities takes part in the work of the OECD (Article 13 of the OECD Convention).

Publié en français sous le titre :

QUESTIONS ET ÉVOLUTIONS DANS LA GESTION PUBLIQUE
Examen 1996-1997

© OECD 1997
Applications for permission to reproduce or translate all or part
of this publication should be made to:

Head of Publications Service, OECD
2. rue André-Pascal. 75775 PARIS CEDEX 16. France.

FOREWORD

This new *Survey of Issues and Developments in Public Management* is the successor to the series of surveys undertaken from 1990 to 1995. In addition to reporting on significant developments in OECD countries, it highlights and analyses key issues by drawing on the full range of activities carried out under the guidance and direction of the Public Management Committee (PUMA).

Part I advances "Perspectives" on three selected issues that are expected to be in the forefront of public management debate over the coming years. Part II analyses the current and ongoing issue of "Governing within Limits". Part III is made up of reports on important developments in each OECD Member country, provided by national authorities on their responsibility. The reports' common framework facilitates comparisons. A "Summary of Developments" based on the country reports precedes them. These analyses and reports are supplemented in Part IV by statistical and other reference information. An Executive Summary leads off the Survey. Detailed tables of contents begin main sections to assist those who wish to focus on their particular interests quickly.

Work on the Survey was completed in 1996. Special thanks are due to the national authorities who provided the country reports. The Survey is a collective effort which was planned and co-ordinated by Andy Johnson; other members of the Secretariat who made primary contributions to drafting sections of the Survey included David Shand, Jon Blondal, Ho Young Ryu (II.2); Maria Maguire, Chris Lidbury (II.3); Scott Jacobs (II.4); Rita Raizis (III.1). Further information about the work of the Public Management Service is in Part IV. The Survey is published on the responsibility of the Secretary-General of the OECD.

The Public Management Service will review experience with this first new Survey in order to improve it. Reaction and comments are invited, to:

Public Management Service (PUMA), OECD
2, rue André Pascal – 75775 PARIS CEDEX 16 – FRANCE
Fax: (33-1) 45 24 87 96 – E-mail: pum.contact@oecd.org – World Wide Web: http://www.oecd.org/puma

CONTENTS

FOREWORD: A user's guide to this survey   3

EXECUTIVE SUMMARY   7

I. PERSPECTIVES

Premises for perspectives   15
Re-examining roles   16
Clarifying accountability of devolved institutions   19
Building coherence strategically   22

II. GOVERNING WITHIN LIMITS

1. **The challenge**   31
2. **Budgeting and performance management strategies for governing within limits**   32
   Fiscal consolidation   33
   Budgeting for results   37
   Structural changes to government expenditure   43
3. **Managing human resources to govern within limits**   45
   Boosting productivity and efficiency   45
   Managing growth in public service employment levels   50
   Future directions   52
   Principles for successful human resource management strategies   53
4. **Managing government regulation within limits**   55
   Is there too much regulation?   56
   What are the implications for managing regulation within limits?   63
   What are the implications for the "limits to government" debate?   66

III. PUBLIC MANAGEMENT INITIATIVES IN OECD MEMBER COUNTRIES

1. **Summary of developments**   77

2. **Country reports:**

AUSTRALIA	85	
AUSTRIA	93	
BELGIUM	99	
CANADA	105	
CZECH REPUBLIC	115	
DENMARK	123	
FINLAND	129	
FRANCE	137	
GERMANY	147	
GREECE	155	
HUNGARY	161	
ICELAND	169	
IRELAND	177	
ITALY	189	

JAPAN	195
LUXEMBOURG	203
MEXICO	209
NETHERLANDS	217
NEW ZEALAND	225
NORWAY	233
PORTUGAL	241
SPAIN	247
SWEDEN	257
SWITZERLAND	265
TURKEY	273
UNITED KINGDOM	277
UNITED STATES	287

Common framework

- Main tendencies and overall priorities
- Context affecting public management
- Strategies and processes for planning and carrying out public management reform
- Policy-management capacities
- Human resources management
- Budget process and management of financial resources
- Performance management
- Changing structures of the public sector
- Regulatory management and reform
- Other

IV. REFERENCE

A statistical window on OECD Member countries' government sectors   299
The Public Management Service (PUMA) of the OECD   320
Glossary of selected terms   322

EXECUTIVE SUMMARY

Central to public management is the question of how governance can be strengthened in support of countries' economic and social goals. In facing this challenge, public managers and their ministers across the OECD find they have much in common, and much to be learned from each other's experiences. At the same time, while OECD countries face an increasingly common agenda of public management issues, and share a repertoire of responses, there is no single model for effective public management, nor any easy solution. Public management improvements require ongoing efforts suited to each country's circumstances.

In support of these efforts, this new *Survey of Issues and Developments in Public Management*:

- analyses selected key issues affecting public management and governance;
- reports on significant developments in OECD Member countries;
- communicates issues and developments that practitioners see as important.

Part I, PERSPECTIVES, poses three key issues with which countries will be concerned over the coming years.

Re-examining roles: Governments are and should be re-examining what they do and how they do it

A period of change in government, its economic and social context, and its functioning engages governments in re-thinking the role and operation of the public sector.

- Various approaches are at hand for re-examining roles. They include: special policy reviews; more comprehensive processes to review roles; and public management initiatives that may have the effect of encouraging re-examination of roles, explicitly or not (such as budgetary or service quality initiatives or regulatory reform). It is important to combine budgetary with policy or programme perspectives.

- Lasting effect can most likely be achieved through cumulative efforts, over time. This suggests the desirability of ongoing processes to call roles into question, or promote review – such as a "challenge function" at the centre, advisory councils or institutionalisation of a review process. Substantial re-examinations require a central focal point, linked to political leadership, with professional support.

- There will be different opportunities or "triggers" that move governments from re-examining roles to actually making changes. Each country should assess how best to re-examine roles without devaluing the exercise by making it mechanical or repetitious, and while taking account of opportunities and obstacles. The extent to which re-examining roles gains political credit for elected leaders is an important pre-requisite for success.

Clarifying accountability of devolved institutions: Governments confront the issue of clarifying accountability while devolving responsibilities

Many governments seek greater efficiency and flexibility in providing services through greater devolution of decision-making responsibilities and resources. The essential counterpart to greater devolution is clarifying accountability. The challenge is to clarify accountability while enhancing flexibility: an issue which applies to the public sector generally but is highlighted with the greater use in many countries of more devolved institutions such as agencies.

– The preferred strategy focuses on objectives and accountability for results, as opposed to compliance with rules – while maintaining basic reporting and professional requirements.

– Institutions' governing objectives must be clear: through a combination of governments' clarifying their high-level objectives and institutions' establishing corresponding operational goals, matched by measurement of results as far as possible. Information on objectives, services, resources and results should be provided and diffused widely.

– This approach is not limited to purely formal contracts or purely measurable results. Tensions or dilemmas are inevitable. Thus, while good performance measurement is difficult but essential, it is recognised that performance measures have their limitations, and should be treated as assistance in decision-making. Measurement does not replace judgement.

Building coherence strategically: Governments should seek policy coherence not only through "command and control" co-ordination but also through strategic approaches

Promoting a necessary degree of coherence in government policies and programmes is essential, and central to the OECD's advisory work. At the same time, seeking coherence largely through formal decisions risks immobilising creative responses to changing situations. And promoting coherence is long-term, not a quick fix.

– More strategic approaches to building coherence still require a strong centre of government. Indeed, "lean" governments need to maintain their capacities to develop and co-ordinate important policies, as well as to implement public services. But central capacities are not sufficient on their own.

– It is also vital to build bases for achieving coherence that depend less on central co-ordination and more on continuous, flexible interaction among institutions and people. These include policy capacities across the government, outside the centre; a sustained focus on public service values and people working together, cutting across traditional boundaries; and the careful management of information across government organisations and programmes.

– Strategically, offices at the centre of government can encourage these approaches. They should seek also to focus attention on major issues through "big levers", such as budgets and statements of government-wide priorities. These levers can help bring together political and governmental considerations, since administrative co-ordination cannot be a substitute for a broadly coherent framework of politically determined priorities.

Part II, GOVERNING WITHIN LIMITS, examines this current, ongoing issue from several points of view.

The challenge of governing within limits is not only to establish and meet limits, but also to design and apply them creatively, as a tool for achieving wider public policy and public management goals. While budgetary positions are now improving in many OECD countries, the careful application of limits and working through of their consequences for public services remains a constant preoccupation. The fundamental goal remains better government, whether or not that is also thought to require smaller government. The measures taken by governments should reinforce each other, in the fields of budgeting and performance management, human resources management, and regulatory management.

Budgeting and performance management strategies for governing within limits

While there are differences among OECD countries in the magnitude of budgetary problems and the comprehensiveness of responses, there is considerable convergence in their approaches.

- The most comprehensive budgetary reforms have emphasized achieving macro fiscal objectives – fiscal consolidation – while improving micro performance, including efficiency, effectiveness and quality of services. Budgeting systems with short-term, detailed control of inputs have generally been a disabling environment for public sector micro performance.

- Global targets appear to be a useful tool for moving budgets toward balance by setting overall fiscal policy objectives, making explicit how the government will meet them over a number of years, and translating these into operational terms, thus establishing a ceiling for expenditures. Once specific global targets have been set, ongoing political commitment is crucial to maintaining credibility. Fiscal consolidation is assisted by using cautious economic assumptions, and by expressing global targets and ceilings in nominal rather than real terms.

- A focus on budgeting for results has led to significant changes in budget processes and systems: multi-year budget planning, devolution and increased flexibility for managers, accountability for performance, and market-type mechanisms. These changes clearly aim both at budget savings and at improving public sector performance.

- Structural changes to government expenditure seem to be more effective in tackling budget deficits than one-off measures. They may be supplemented by organisational changes, redistribution of responsibilities, and improved public debt and assets management.

Managing human resources to govern within limits

Human resource management (HRM) reforms are used to support public service managers in accomplishing government goals and meeting work demands with fewer resources. Those reforms have focused on strategies both to boost productivity and efficiency, and manage growth in public service employment levels. Over the longer term, strategic use of HRM is crucial for maintaining quality public services through the capacity to attract (and retain) motivated, well-qualified public servants, as well as for ensuring workers' commitment to reforms. Principles highlighted by country experiences include:

- The larger the reduction in resources, the greater the need for flexibility in allocating and managing those resources. Devolution of HRM tools from central management agencies to line ministries and service agencies has been a common public management reform strategy.

- Successfully linking HRM reforms to productivity and efficiency goals requires integrating HRM into core activities such as strategic planning, budgeting and performance management.

- Strategies for structural changes (*e.g.* staff reductions, reorganisations) should be implemented in tandem with strategies for addressing how the workers will be affected and can best be brought along the reform path. Thus, managers need to be skilled in the people-side of managing change.

- Maintain a long-term perspective in implementing, investing in, and sustaining changes in the structure of the workplace and the workforce.

Managing government regulation within limits

The concern with limits applies just as well to government regulation. Governments in the OECD area believe they face a regulatory problem with serious economic and social consequences. Increasingly, it is recognised that there are limits to regulation, just as for other policy instruments, that regulatory costs are real and they matter.

- Just as governing within limits does not mean dismantling government, managing regulation within limits does not mean deregulation. Well-written rules based on effective policies that produce net benefits should be encouraged. There is potential for reducing the cost of regulation without sacrificing important policy objectives, through a regulatory reform strategy that focuses on improving the quality of regulations, finding cost-effective alternatives to regulation, and deregulating in certain sectors.

- Improving regulatory disciplines can also improve government effectiveness. Well-designed, cost-effective regulatory instruments should make governments' economic, social or environmental objectives more attainable.

- It may be counter-productive to cut the costs of government without also limiting regulation, in light of risks that regulations could be used to shift government costs to the private sector. As a step towards managing these risks, regulatory costs should be made visible.

- In the longer term, techniques for assessing regulatory costs and impacts on economic and social performance are needed. They do not exist now: managing regulation within limits will continue to be difficult without a better sense of the real impacts of regulation.

Part III, PUBLIC MANAGEMENT INITIATIVES IN OECD MEMBER COUNTRIES, presents reports on significant developments across the OECD country by country. They are accompanied by a "Summary of Developments" based on the country reports.

Country reports

Reports are provided by the national authority of each country. They cover recent and ongoing initiatives and, if possible, emerging issues. The reports generally follow a common framework including priorities and strategies as well as specific initiatives encompassing human resources management, budgeting, performance management, changing public sector structures and regulatory reform.

Summary of developments

The effort to achieve sustained fiscal consolidation emerges as one of the driving forces behind current initiatives, together with citizen demands for effective services and a push for improving government performance while containing its size – within the contexts of countries' own policy priorities. A wide range of approaches and specific initiatives has been adopted by governments, although the general directions for reform emerging from the reports share certain similarities. They include:

- a continuation of the trend towards devolving managerial authority to provide greater flexibility in achieving public policy goals, supported by improved resource management;

- a closer focus on results to complement the devolved environment, while enhancing accountability;

- a stronger service quality orientation that involves public consultation and leads to public services that are more relevant to needs and more responsive to demands;

- adapting organisational structures to improve service, performance, accountability and efficiency;

- a heightened focus on the importance of an effective public sector workforce and leadership, to facilitate the stronger performance orientation and service-oriented public service culture;

– regulatory reform as a tool to improve the capacity of governments to achieve policy objectives efficiently and effectively;

– a strengthening of steering functions to drive reforms strategically and promote policy coherence on cross-cutting issues.

Part IV, REFERENCE, provides background information in the form of a "statistical window" on OECD Member countries' government sectors as well as information on the Public Management Service and a short glossary of terms.

Part I

PERSPECTIVES

● Premises for perspectives 15

● Re-examining roles 16

● Clarifying accountability of devolved institutions 19

● Building coherence strategically 22

Notes 27

References 28

I. PERSPECTIVES

"Perspectives" advances key issues that are expected to be in the forefront of public management debate over the coming years. The issues reflect the work of the Public Management Service of the OECD, under the guidance of the Public Management Committee of OECD Member countries.[1]

Premises for perspectives

The Chair of the first Symposium of OECD Ministers concerned with public management said that the fundamental challenge for the future is "how governance can be strengthened in support of economic and social goals in Member countries" (OECD, 1997a). That challenge is reflected in a first premise underlying PUMA perspectives on public management: policy relevance. Improvements must continuously support public policy goals, encompassing economic growth and expanding trade together with social cohesion and political stability; all are necessary, and necessary to each other. As an IMF Executive Director noted, "The IMF, and other international bodies, now recognise the importance of each country's institutional structures – both private and public – to its long-term growth prospects" (Clark, 1996).

In facing this challenge, public managers and their Ministers increasingly find they have much in common, and much to be learned from each other's experiences. As the Chair of the Ministerial Symposium also concluded, "We are not alone! Despite all of the differences, ...we share...similar pressures, extraordinarily similar responses, and many similar dilemmas".

At the same time, OECD countries face their own policy challenges, and are marked by their unique history, constitutional and political systems, culture and economic and social circumstances. The *Czech Republic*, *Hungary* and *Poland*, for instance, are undertaking momentous transformations of their entire legal, economic and political systems. Others are modernising established systems of governance, whether to reduce the role and size of government or to enhance the public sector. Another premise is that, while OECD Member countries face an increasingly common agenda of public management issues, and share a repertoire of responses, there is no single model for effective public management, nor any "quick fix". Public management improvements require ongoing efforts suited to each country's own circumstances.

Yet we are concerned at the same time with looking ahead, to highlight key issues in the forefront of public management debate in the medium term. It is commonly recognised that the pressures OECD countries face are constantly evolving, as domestic and common international challenges also evolve. High budget deficits and public debt are being seriously addressed in many countries, yet they remain key problems and will evolve as longer-term issues come into play, of ageing societies, for instance, environmental issues, and renewing infrastructure. Globalisation of economies and communications, a product of the interaction between trade and technological progress, presents opportunities to individuals, enterprises, and countries; but taking advantage of these opportunities, as the annual OECD Council at Ministerial Level pointed out, requires rapid adjustment and continuous innovation (OECD, 1996d; 1996c; 1994b). And governments face a challenge of public confidence, with ever rising citizens' expectations.

From these premises, "Perspectives" poses three key issues with which countries are, or should be, concerned over the coming years:

- **re-examining roles;**
- **clarifying accountability of devolved institutions;**
- **building coherence strategically.**

These issues may be cast somewhat differently from country to country and will need to be addressed according to varying national conditions; they may emerge in the context of particular initiatives rather than as general issues; they will surely be accompanied by other, equally important issues. Nonetheless, how countries deal with these three issues will be central to public management improvements.

Re-examining roles

Governments are and should be re-examining what they do and how they do it. As the *German* Lean State (*Schlanker Staat*) Advisory Council reported, "there can be no stable list of functions…valid over many years; the key points of the activity of ministers are determined by changing policy goals" (Lean State Advisory Council, 1996). Another country reports, "This is a period of profound change in government and its functioning: like most countries throughout the western democratic world, *Canada* is engaged, at all levels, in re-thinking the role of government, the relationship between government and citizens and, in consequence, the role and operation of the public sector". Various **pressures** are involved:

- Globalisation enhances concerns for national economic competitiveness, including concerns that government activities should facilitate economic growth, consistent with national ideals. All countries would not agree on the roles of their governments, but globalisation encourages debate and re-examination in each country.

- As countries grapple with deficit and debt pressures, many for the second time in a decade or so, they appreciate the importance of structural change, to reduce government or make it work better.

- Technological change, including information technology, generates new possibilities, for governments to strengthen their performance or for the private sector to perform what may have been seen as a natural government responsibility. Examining "how" governments perform can lead to re-examining "what" they do.

- Political credit for change seems more common, even where re-examining roles raises controversial issues. Perhaps citizens in many countries are more convinced of the economic, financial and technological pressures for re-examining roles. Nonetheless, the brakes on change in each country should not be underestimated – from the desirability of reaching consensus among social partners or political coalitions, to the opposition of entrenched interests.

Levers for re-examining roles

Governments are re-examining their roles through **a variety of approaches, using different levers** ranging from the review of particular policies and programmes to the application of public management reforms.

Governments' roles in particular public programme areas – health, environmental or trade policies – are reshaped by special **policy reviews**. The processes and results reflect national circumstances.

However, more **comprehensive processes to review roles** may be pursued. A well-known case is *New Zealand* which, over a decade or more, has rigorously applied market economics to the management of public policy. The result has been fundamental transformation in government's roles. Yet that country's circumstances – its starting point for reforms, rooted in economic crisis and an extensively regulated but small economy and society – are not entirely replicated in other countries, few of whom are likely to apply the same approach wholesale. Other paths exist.

- A comprehensive process may be cumulative, over years. A striking instance is the *United Kingdom*, which – as flagged in its report – "has been subjecting all its activities to searching scrutiny" for several years, by posing what are called "prior options" questions, which require over time a comprehensive re-examination of roles. These questions ask: "Does the work need to be done at all?"; "If the work is necessary, does the government need to be responsible for it?"; "If the government does need to be responsible, does the work have to be performed by civil servants, or could it be delivered more efficiently and effectively by the private sector?"; "Where the job must be carried out within government, is the organisation properly structured and focused on the task?" In another instance, the Vice-President of the *United States* is leading the wide-ranging "National Performance Review", which promotes a multitude of initiatives for better service, consistent with less government, a market economy and individual responsibilities. The cumulative consequence may be that most organisations across the government re-examine their roles de facto, or can be expected to do so.

- On the other hand, searching questions may be asked of government roles through processes acting over a shorter period. The *German* Lean State Advisory Council recommended a regular review of the functions of the state, and to that end called on the federal government to review and report in 1997 on functions which could be privatised or transferred to subordinate public bodies or eliminated; *Canada* conducted a comprehensive "Programme Review" in 1994, and is following that up with a variety of initiatives most succinctly called "Getting Government Right", which together are redefining government roles and responsibilities. Re-examining roles is evidently part and parcel of the enormous changes to the state undertaken in the *Czech Republic, Hungary,* and *Poland.*

Other **key public management processes may have the effect of encouraging or levering substantial re-examination of government roles**, explicitly or not. The impact of these approaches should not be underestimated. They may be more feasible in circumstances where explicitly comprehensive approaches are considered unnecessary, undesirably rapid or politically unsuitable. Nevertheless, public management changes usually take place most effectively when they fit within a framework of political priorities.

- Re-examining the functions of government is inherent in **re-examining the respective roles of levels of government.** This has been a lever for fundamental change in the past – in *Spain* and *France* in the 1980s, or *Denmark* in the late 1960s and early 1970s, for instance, and in the *Czech Republic* recently – and may well be again in countries as diverse as *Switzerland* and Japan (see also OECD, 1997*b*).

- Stringent fiscal criteria may well prove to be a powerful lever for re-examining roles, and **budgetary processes** may be the route through which priorities are set which change government functions. *Hungary*, for instance, reports that deficit reduction "necessitates a fundamental reconsideration of the roles and responsibilities of the state", and much the same could probably be said of many other countries. Certainly budgetary pressures may be closely linked to other approaches, as in *Germany* where the government is following up on its Advisory Council's view that "slimming down the state implies above all the reduction and limitation of State responsibilities".

- OECD study suggests that a comprehensive focus on **service quality initiatives** can provide "an opportunity to re-examine the rationale for existing programmes", or "require public sector organisations…in some cases…to justify their role and existence" (OECD, 1996*e*). That has been the experience in *Portugal*, and may well be the case in *Italy*. *France* has improved service to citizens as a result of sustained action by successive governments, a priority which is reaffirmed by the current policy of *gestion de proximité*. The programme involves clarification of government roles in that light and in light of major policy priorities.

- **Regulatory reform** often involves profound re-examination of the roles of and interactions between the public and private sectors. Many reform efforts require regulators in different policy sectors to justify established, as well as new, regulations, and hence to re-examine the policy functions they are performing. In the OECD Recommendation on regulatory quality, Member countries agree that more attention should be given to justifying the need for government action (OECD, 1995). Alternatives to direct regulation, such as codes of conduct, can involve innovative public/private co-operation in which government acts as an enabler.

- Improvements in **administrative efficiency and management tools** are pursued in all governments, continuously or through special initiatives. They contribute to meeting fiscal objectives, improving programmes, and to better service. Sustained exercises in administrative improvements and programme evaluation also provide opportunities for reformulating government roles from the angle of "how" functions can be implemented. To cite only one instance, an objective of Austria's Administrative Management Project (concluded in 1994) was to tighten up management structures by asking whether some operational responsibilities could be cut back, transferred, or abolished.

Perspectives

These **various approaches, or levers, are at hand** for governments to meet pressures to re-examine their roles. For the most part they are not mutually exclusive and may well be mutually reinforcing. Governments should adapt these levers to their own circumstances, using the levers which show most promise at different times as well as in combination.

It is particularly important to **combine budgetary with policy or programme perspectives**: budgetary considerations on their own are likely to be too limited, but programme considerations need the discipline of budgetary realities. Together, they force attention to basic trade-offs and competing priorities. Offices at the centre of government (supporting prime ministers or presidents or councils of ministers) often play a key role in balancing budgetary and programme perspectives – or at least in bringing them together for political decision-making. Also, different approaches to re-examinating roles may highlight the policy or programme priorities to be taken into account in budgetary decision-making, as may some of the "big levers" for building coherence strategically (outlined below).

It seems likely also that the most lasting effect in re-examining roles is achieved through **cumulative efforts**, over time, which demonstrate successes and gradually build a culture of "continuous improvement". That seems to be the experience in the *United Kingdom* or *New Zealand* or with the *Netherlands* "reconsideration process" of the 1980s. Major changes take time to digest; a balance is often needed between too much or too little change; experience leads to adjustments; new pressures arise.

This suggests, too, the desirability of **ongoing processes to call roles into question**, or promote review. This might involve a "challenge function" at the centre of government, or institutionalisation of a review process. Or it might involve separate organisations ranging from think tanks within or entirely outside government, to advisory councils or special commissions or legislative reviews (such as *Finland's* current "futures" exercise). Ongoing reform processes may also provide this stimulus, in the course of putting priority upon regulatory reform, for instance, or managing relations among levels of government. Independent commissions may be another stimulus, whether permanent or short-term, as with the *German* Lean State Advisory Council, or the *Australian* National Commission of Audit, although they are unlikely to replace a central focal point within government.

Substantial re-examinations require a **central focal point**, linked to political leadership, with professional support. That may be a ministry of finance, acting through budgetary processes and fiscal targets, especially where fiscal consolidation has become a fairly widely accepted priority. It may be the prime minister or president, supported – as in *France* – by central offices concerned with modernisation and reform. It may be a government secretariat acting in close concert with the ministry of finance, as has been the case in *Canada*. Or it may be an expert advisory council with strong political engagement.

In each country, there will be different opportunities or "triggers" which move governments from re-examining roles to actually making changes. These may include a recognised economic or financial crisis (which played a part in *New Zealand*), or a crisis of political confidence (which some observors have pointed to in *Japan* or *Italy*), or a change of government (as in *Canada* or the *United Kingdom* in the past). Re-examinations of roles may also make their effects felt over time, through a series of policy, financial and public management decisions, without necessarily one radical or highly publicised turning point.

It will be important to assess in each country how best to re-examine roles over time without devaluing the process by making it mechanical or repetitious, and while taking account of both the opportunities and the obstacles. A critical point of interest is likely to be the extent to which re-examining roles gains **political credit** for elected leaders, and hence political support within government and outside it: that in itself is an important pre-requisite for success.

Clarifying accountability of devolved institutions

Many governments seek greater efficiency and flexibility in the provision of government services through greater devolution of decision-making responsibilities and resources to public service managers, or public institutions. This theme is often captured as "let the managers manage", or "make the managers manage".[2] The essential counterpart to greater devolution is clarifying accountability. The issue is how to clarify accountability while enhancing flexibility.

This issue is not new in itself; it applies to the public sector generally, especially with greater emphasis on performance management. But it is also highlighted with the greater use in many countries of more devolved institutions. *Iceland's* modernisation programme typically aims "to move increasingly towards giving individual agencies and their managers certain clearly defined targets and responsibilities, at the same time giving them increased freedom to manage". The *United Kingdom* has pursued its policy of "Next steps" agencies for some years. *Switzerland*, the *Netherlands*, the *United States*, *Germany* and others, are making greater use of agencies or their equivalents. The purposes include better service, greater efficiency, a focus on results, as well as clearer accountability relationships between the institution and the government.

- In practice, devolved institutions encompass a wide range of organisational forms where ministerial control is purposely put at greater arm's length than in the case of ministries or departments, within an agreed-upon policy and legal framework, yet where elected representatives remain ultimately responsible to taxpayers and voters for public funds, public policies, programmes and services, and public institutions. A distinction is often made between strategic or high-level objectives, which the minister or government (or the legislature) is responsible for setting; and operational goals or targets, responsibility for which is usually devolved to the institutions concerned.

- The precise organisational forms vary from country to country, and may or may not involve a legal status separate from the central administration. Often these institutions are called "agencies", although the meaning of that term is not necessarily the same in every country, as well as "subordinate bodies", "public enterprises" or "corporatised organisations", or alternatives extending to public/private partnerships. Generally they may be distinguished from privatised or contracted out activities performed by the private sector, from elected levels of government, and from departments and ministries traditionally under direct, detailed ministerial control (although in *New Zealand* core government ministries contract with the minister to provide policy advice, similar to agencies which contract with the minister to provide services). In practice, the issues and some of the levers for clarifying accountability may be similar for ministries and devolved institutions.

- Countries have their own traditions to draw on. *Nordic* countries, particularly *Sweden*, have relied upon agencies and public enterprises for many years to perform public functions; in other countries such as the *United Kingdom*, greater use of agencies may be seen as adapting private sector experience to the public sector aim of delivering better services. Some countries may choose to focus on one primary form for devolved institutions (as *Sweden* has done with its agency model, and in the *United Kingdom* where well over two-thirds of civil servants now work in agencies). Others follow a case-by-case approach (as *Canada* is doing with its exploration of "alternative service delivery", including the use of special operating agencies).

However, there are difficulties, and in particular political risks involved in devolution and managerial flexibility which give rise to **dilemmas**. The Chair of the OECD Ministerial Symposium noted "the tension between decentralising and delegating service delivery (with its greater acceptance of risk-taking) and pressures for accountability to the taxpayer"; and "a similar tension between the desirability for flexibility and experimentation on the one hand and the problems of avoiding politically embarrassing mistakes". These political dilemmas have been illustrated in recent controversies, for instance *New Zealand's* Cave Creek incident, where the collapse of a viewing platform, causing fatalities, led to a public dispute over whether the management agency alone was responsible, or the minister as well; while this controversy might have arisen regardless of devolution, devolution contributed an extra tension. There is a difficult balance to be struck between traditional democratic accountability to ministers and legislatures representing citizens as voters and taxpayers, and expressing the goals of devolved institutions in terms of services which respond to citizens' needs as users or customers, leaving the institution with greater flexibility to determine its own response.

Levers for clarifying accountability of devolved institutions

One potential lever in all countries is **adapting the framework of laws and rights governing the relations between citizens and public institutions**. In some traditions, notably in continental European countries, administrative law is traditionally the primary vehicle for expressing citizens' rights and administrative duties; legal redress is the citizen's normal recourse. Adjustments to the law have been important steps to clarify the duties of public institutions, while improving service for citizens. For instance, in *France* and *Spain* the law now states that in many cases a lack of administrative response to a citizen's application amounts to a positive answer, whereas until recently no answer meant "no".

A key lever is **clarifying institutions' governing mandates or objectives**, perhaps but not necessarily in law. This approach, in *Iceland* and *Norway* for example, would set strategic goals for government agencies without necessarily changing the legal framework, and would reduce the role of specific, direct instructions. *France* too intends a fundamental reform of its system of supervision (*tutelle*) over state enterprises, in order to better control them by focusing on their broad objectives. *Japan* launched in 1994 a review of the role and *raison d'être* of public corporations, which has or will culminate in changes to legal mandates.

Another dimension of clarifying accountability involves **improving the quality and accessibility of information on services provided and results achieved, including performance measurements and indicators**. Many countries are increasingly emphasizing performance measurement and indicators of standards and results to be sought, including benchmarking with comparable organisations. The most sustained effort has been made by countries such as *Australia*, the *United Kingdom* and *New Zealand*, and the *Nordic* countries. The *United States* requires all departments and agencies to establish performance standards and plans to achieve them. Experimentation is underway in *Mexico*, to require state agencies to define clear goals with measurable results thereby constituting a set of performance indicators, and in other countries.

Also important is the development of tools to bring together an institution's governing objectives (whether specified in law or not) with its operational goals and its results.

- A relatively recent development in this direction is **performance contracting** between governments and their devolved institutions. These contracts should bring together objectives with standards for measured results, as well as qualitative performance goals. *New Zealand's* government-wide "strategic result areas" are reflected in more specific "key result areas" for individual departments and agencies which are also incorporated in "performance agreements" between the minister and the "chief executive" of each department and agency; the performance agreements are in turn related to separate "purchase agreements" covering the goods and services to be supplied. Other countries are using or experimenting with contracts in their own ways, such as *Iceland, Denmark, Greece* and *France*. Of course contracts should not become a new occasion for multiplying rules.

– This approach is **by no means limited to purely formal contracts, and purely measurable results**. It should be part of a process which, in the words of *Sweden's* report, aims "to intensify and develop contacts between ministers and government agencies' heads through a regular dialogue concerning goals and results". In another instance, a review of reforms commissioned by *New Zealand* has expressed a concern that relying too much on the precise specification of accountabilities may unduly narrow the focus of executives, to the detriment of subjective judgement and public service values (Schick, 1996).

– This approach is increasingly expanded, in countries of varied traditions, by the use of **citizens' charters, or statements of service standards**, to express institutions' objectives in terms of the level of service quality to be provided to citizens. These express citizens' rights in terms of the results or standards of performance they can expect from public institutions, not only in terms of "due process". Charters may not have strictly legal force; redress may be primarily political rather than legal; but their force and usefulness is likely to be recognised more and more, and experimented with in diverse ways.

– **Budgetary reforms** can play an important part not only in setting broad fiscal objectives for devolved institutions but also, at the same time (as pointed out in the discussion on "governing within limits"), in improving performance through tools such as multi-year budget planning, increased financial flexibility for managers, and developing a closer linkage between performance issues and budgetary allocations.

– A fundamental tool for holding devolved institutions accountable remains **accurate, timely and accessible financial information on costs of programmes or services and overall financial results**: such information is basic to effective government and to accountability with devolution. As the *United States* reports, "An efficient, effective Government needs sound financial management, including management and reporting systems that produce reliable information. To develop these systems, the Administration is establishing Government-wide accounting standards, producing audited financial statements, streamlining management controls and reporting, and modernising debt collection". A number of countries are exploring accrual accounting as part of this process. Countries as diverse as *Finland, Mexico* and *Turkey* have recently launched government-wide reforms of financial reporting systems.

Perspectives

In addressing the issue of how to clarify accountability while enhancing flexibility, **the preferred strategy is to focus on objectives and accountability for results, as opposed to only compliance with rules** – while still maintaining basic reporting and professional requirements.

It is essential to **ensure that institutions' governing objectives are clear: through a combination of governments' clarifying the high-level objectives governing an institution, and institutions' establishing corresponding operational goals, matched by measurements of results** as far as possible. This may involve changes in institutions' legal mandates but also, often, management tools such as agreed statements of goals, targets and results, management or service contracts, or citizens' charters or statements of service standards. These tools can promote broad or strategic consistency between institutions' objectives and the government's overall priorities. They may well involve governments' strengthening strategic controls, while reducing detailed operational controls. Their exercise also requires judgement rooted in an understanding of the public sector context. Institutions need sufficient stability in their objectives, with sufficient flexibility in their operations, that they can get on with doing their jobs.

As part of clarifying accountability, **information on objectives, services, resources and results should be diffused widely** – for example through improved annual reports. **The aim is partly to inform decision-makers such as ministers and legislators, to whom devolved institutions are accountable, but also to improve the climate of discussion and debate affecting public institutions**, and to encourage institutions to provide responsive services within the legal and policy framework set for each. Pressures from the public can be perceived as a problem, but there are probably political as well as public management gains to be made from accepting and using those pressures as a lever for accountability that political leaders themselves can benefit from in their ongoing efforts to steer devolved institutions.

Nonetheless, **tensions are inevitable**. Some of those tensions are political: a key to managing them in each country is the degree to which citizens, the media, and political parties see ministers as directly responsible, whatever the formal accountability arrangements. There is also the tension between the desirability of measuring results and difficulties in practice: ongoing effort in performance measurement is essential, and so is an understanding of its limitations. There are continuing difficulties in fully defining each institution's goals or objectives (either in terms of outputs or outcomes) – which may encompass national unity or social cohesion, or other public policy goals, as well as service or commercial goals; in determining how far those goals are measurable and how far the institution's own work can affect goals, compared to the effects of larger economic or social factors; and in finding ways to measure results in practice, without biasing decisions toward only measurable goals. There is a general acceptance that good performance measurement is difficult but essential; at the same time it is recognised that all performance measures have their limitations and should be treated as guides or assistance to decision-making. Measurement does not replace judgement.

In these circumstances, movement by countries toward **more use of devolved institutions, as agencies for instance, is promising, but no definitive resolution of the issues involved should be expected**. No one form of devolved institution is best, nor one set of accountability arrangements. Different organisational forms may serve different policy purposes, depending on the degree of programme and managerial independence desired (for public broadcasting, or railways, or labour market training, etc.). Ongoing exploration of successes, of problems and their resolution, is desirable; governments will need to confront the issues of clarifying accountability while devolving responsibilities within a framework of agreed policy goals.

Building coherence strategically

Achieving coherence, or integrating multiple policy objectives, is a persisting major problem, central to all of the OECD's advisory work for governments. But **a growing issue is promoting key conditions which facilitate coherence strategically, over time, rather than relying only on co-ordination and prescriptions from the top down**. The pressures affecting coherence are varied.

- Major policy issues require concerted analysis and solutions which cut across ministerial and agency boundaries, perhaps across levels of government or international boundaries, and address longer term consequences: issues such as ageing societies, environmental policies, and budgetary actions to control deficits and debts while maintaining investment in top priorities. Multiple interests, with growing capacities to mobilise politically, must be integrated or dealt with in developing policies.

- The environment is ever more complex, especially with the pressures of globalisation. The international environment also requires greater coherence of policies across international boundaries. Yet rapid changes require flexibility to respond rapidly, which cannot always wait upon detailed prescriptions.

- Greater devolution of responsibilities risks fragmentation across programmes or less attention to politically determined priorities. The volume of information and citizen demands also may strain coherence.

- Co-ordination of all government activities into a coherent, prescribed plan has never truly been feasible and is even less so in this context. A search for too much coherence risks immobilising creative programme development and flexible responses, and may not be politically wanted.

Almost all governments have some established capacity at the centre of government to operate the processes by which decisions are reached for the government as a whole, collectively or by a chief executive – such as prime ministers' offices, presidencies, government or cabinet secretariats. This central co-ordination capacity remains basic to achieving coherence (see also OECD, 1996a). Nonetheless, there are limits everywhere to the co-ordinating capacities at the centre of government: limits of resources, of knowledge – especially compared to the expertise in operating ministries, of time, and – not least – political and constitutional limits.

Levers for building coherence strategically

One response to these pressures is to strengthen capacities at the centre of government to **focus attention on major issues through "big levers"**. *France's* reform of the state, for instance, aims to "improve decision-making and give central government a truly strategic function" (*L'État stratège*) (Pochard, 1996). To this end:

- Governments may explore new ways to enunciate **government-wide priorities and goals, especially focusing on the medium or longer term**. Traditionally this is done through electoral platforms, coalition agreements, or periodic Government or presidential or prime ministerial statements. A promising approach is being pursued in *Finland*, where a "Long Term Futures" report is being prepared for Parliamentary discussion over 1996-97. *New Zealand* has legislated fiscal responsibility requirements, leaving it up to the government of the day to enunciate and elaborate specifics, and has developed "strategic result areas" to translate political priorities into higher level government guidelines for actions; others may find this insufficiently rigorous or, on the other hand, too constricting for their real worlds of politics.

- **Budgets** are a powerful lever for the expression of government priorities. Even where other statements express strategic priorities qualitatively, if they are not translated into budgetary priorities they are unlikely to be taken seriously. Equally, budgetary decisions should reflect policy priorities. Budgetary reform often focuses most successfully on "big levers" in the form of major aggregates such as deficit and debt or borrowing targets, as well as aggregate spending levels for sectors of government activity, rather than on the detailed programme level.

- Another lever is the **re-examination of government roles**, through the approaches outlined earlier. *Canada*, for instance, concludes that its Programme Review has focused the national government on five core roles.

- Similarly, coherence can be promoted by **clarifying the strategic objectives of devolved institutions** consistent with the government's fundamental roles and priorities (although there may well be some tension between principles of institutional autonomy and coherence).

- **Public management reform programmes** can also serve as a "big lever", as with the recent comprehensive reforms announced in *Mexico* or *Ireland*, and *Germany's* "lean state" exercise.

An increasingly important lever or basis for building coherence strategically is the **policy capacities to be found across the government, outside the centre.**

- **Building these capacities may be a question not of "more", but "better", that is mobilising existing resources more effectively**. *Denmark* reports experience "that it was preferable that analytical capacity have higher priority in individual ministries" than at the centre. In *France*, the counterpart of transferring management activity to deconcentrated services is the reorganisation of central departments to focus on their strategic functions, as part of the larger reform of the state; and a similar emphasis is seen in the *Netherlands*. *Canada* is emphasizing a concept called there "portfolio management" to improve coherence across a minister's responsibilities for various organisations, and across government, in a more complex and less centralised public service. In practice these approaches are often a matter of decentralised capacities working in concert with central goals or guidelines, as with regulatory impact analysis, where a central issue is integrating multiple policy objectives.

- Also, **networks** may collectively take on important cross-cutting issues, even without the lead of a central agency. *Sweden*, for instance, has established an agency "formed, directed and financed by the other government agencies" to take on substantially increased responsibility, collectively, for their employer's role, as in negotiations over terms of employment. *Ireland* envisages more use of "dedicated cross-ministry teams, co-ordinated at a political level" to address cross-cutting issues.

- **Methods may be developed for different levels of government to co-operate more creatively in services delivery**, where responsibilities may overlap, for instance through intergovernmental councils (as in *Australia* or *Germany*) or joint administrative bodies (as being developed in *Canada*).

- In addition, many countries have experience with using independent or semi-independent **advisory bodies**, to help develop more strategic coherence, by taking a step back from government in order to look a step or two ahead.

A third lever is **promoting coherence strategically through a sustained focus on public service culture and people**. The working culture within the public service, particularly in an environment of devolution, can facilitate consultation, co-operation, and common understandings, which promote coherence... or it can exaggerate fragmentation. In the words of the *Canadian* Secretary to the Cabinet, "To perform well, the public sector needs cohesion. Cohesion is achieved through shared values, a common sense of purpose and a culture that facilitates collaboration and partnership among us" (Bourgon, 1996). Several promising aspects can be emphasized.

- A sustained focus on the people who do the work of the public service is the essence of **strategic human resources management**. It involves an investment in building and maintaining a quality public service – particularly in times of downsizing – as an essential basis for service to citizens, for economic competitiveness, and for quality public policies. It involves sustaining or promoting a public service ethos; recruiting and developing competent, creative officials; and paying them well enough. Personnel development policies should promote exchange of knowledge and ideas across the public service to encourage common values, cut across traditional institutional barriers, and build networks. As one instance, *Ireland* explicitly aims to "address every significant aspect of HR management" as part of its new strategy for "Delivering Better Government".[3]

- In this vein, an emphasis on **mobility** across ministries is a human resources tool of increasing interest, in countries such as *France*, the *Netherlands*, and *Norway* (and flagged also as a human resources concern in the discussion of "governing within limits").

- Some countries are also increasing their focus on **developing a cadre of senior executives**. Among those now considering this approach are the *Netherlands* and the *United Kingdom*, where a Senior Civil Service was created in 1996 to have "a broader identity as part of a cohesive group at the top... covered by a common framework".

- Another growing concern is and should be with the ethics and values which focus and guide public service efforts across each government, particularly as authority for managing resources and delivering services flexibly is devolved (see also OECD, 1996c). Ethics initiatives are currently being undertaken in over half of OECD Member countries.

An essential basis for more decentralised co-ordination can also be laid through **careful management of information across government organisations and programmes**. Sharing the right information, at the right time, promotes greater possibilities for coherence, especially as top down co-ordination becomes less sufficient by itself in the modern policy and management environment. But there are serious risks of information overload. There may be many promising ways to focus information promoting coherence; a few can be suggested here.

- The most basic information is news of what's happening across the government, and of best practices, upon which many countries are placing increased emphasis. In *Belgium*, for instance, the *Bureau Conseil* ABC promotes this. Information technology provides opportunities to share more, more widely, across traditional boundaries, and with less central involvement than ever before. Information on institutions' objectives and results encourages different ministries to take each others' concerns into better account, to learn from each others' experience, and to take a broader outlook on policy development – though there can be no guarantees this will happen. Moreover, consistent with the thrust of many public management reform programmes, thick rule-books can be diminished in favour of thinner sets of guidelines supplemented by analyses of best practices.

- The use of certain programme tools may also generate key information, analogous to market information. Vouchers, for instance, or targeted cash transfers, or competitive tendering can expose government services to market signals and market criteria, according to how citizens respond, thereby making their preferences and choices explicit.

- Decentralised co-ordination at the service-to-the-citizen level can be promoted by linking services together, for instance through single entry points such as *Finland's* multiservice centres providing two or more services, or *Norway's* or *France's* similar initiatives.

- In addition, improving the quality and transparency of information and analysis on goals, activities and results should improve opportunities for bringing together different points of view and integrating policy objectives – as regulatory impact analysis, for instance, can do. On this basis, too, public information and public dialogue can be a pressure on public services to respond to citizens more coherently.

Perspectives

Maintaining reasonable coherence in government policies and programmes is essential. Governments aim to provide and be seen to provide satisfactory public policy results, which integrate multiple objectives, address interconnections among important problems, and respond to the broad public interest. At the same time, seeking to achieve coherence largely through formal decisions risks immobilising creative responses to changing situations. And promoting coherence is a long-haul process, not a quick fix. **More strategic approaches to promoting coherence are increasingly required to supplement – and in part replace – "top down" or "command and control" co-ordination. There is a new balance to be struck.**

This balance must still include **a strong centre**. Central capacities cannot be taken for granted, for setting government-wide objectives, and for co-ordination and management of decision-making systems for the government as a whole; most countries seek to improve them continuously. Indeed, "lean" governments need to be concerned with maintaining their capacities to develop and co-ordinate important policies, as well as to implement public services. But central capacities are not sufficient on their own.

It is also essential to **build bases for achieving coherence which depend less on central co-ordination and more on continuous, flexible interaction among institutions and people**. These bases include policy capacities across the government, outside the centre; a sustained focus on public service values and people who need to work together, cutting across traditional boundaries; and the careful management of information across government organisations and programmes.

Strategically, offices at the centre of governments can encourage these several levers. They should seek also to strengthen their capacities to build coherence through focusing attention on major issues through "big levers", such as budgets and statements of government-wide priorities and goals, especially focusing on the medium or longer term, and public management reform programmes. These levers can help bring together political and governmental considerations, since administrative co-ordination cannot substitute for a broadly coherent framework of politically determined priorities.

NOTES

1. For information on PUMA's work programme, see the Reference section of this *Survey*. See also OECD, 1995*a*. Certain other publications are cited in this "Perspectives" section. Where no specific source is cited for a quotation on a country's initiative, the source is that country's report in this *Survey*.

2. On devolution, flexibility and performance management, see OECD, 1995*a* and OECD, 1994*a*.

3. On human resources management, see also the Governing within Limits section of this *Survey*.

REFERENCES

BOURGON, Jocelyne (1996), Address to the APEX Forum, Ottawa, 4 June.

CLARK, Ian D. (1996), "Global Economic Trends and Pressures on Governments", Opening address to the Annual Conference of the Institute for Public Administration of Canada, 26 August 1996.

Lean State Advisory Council (1996), *Interim Report on the Work of the Council of Experts on Leaner Government*, Bonn.

OECD (1994a), *Performance Management in Government: Performance Measurement and Results-Oriented Management*, OECD, Paris.

OECD (1994b), *Regulatory Co-operation for an Interdependent World*, OECD, Paris.

OECD (1995a), *Governance in Transition: Public Management Reforms in OECD Countries*, OECD, Paris.

OECD (1995b), *Recommendation of the Council of the OECD on Improving the Quality of Government Regulation*, OECD, Paris, 9 March.

OECD (1996a), *Building Policy Coherence: Tools and Tensions*, OECD, Paris.

OECD (1996b), *Ethics in the Public Service: Current Issues and Practice*, OECD, Paris.

OECD (1996c), *Globalisation: What challenges and opportunities for governments?* OECD, Paris.

OECD (1996d), *Meeting of the Council at Ministerial Level*, News Release, OECD, Paris, 22 May.

OECD (1996e), *Responsive Government: Service Quality Initiatives*, OECD, 1996.

OECD (1997a), *Ministerial Symposium on the Future of Public Services*, OECD, Paris.

OECD (1997b), *Managing Across Levels of Government*, OECD, Paris (forthcoming).

POCHARD, Marcel (1996), intervention at the OECD Public Management Committee, Paris, 28-29 March.

SCHICK, Allen (1996), *The Spirit of Reform: Managing the New Zealand State Sector in a Time of Change* (a report prepared for the State Services Commission and the Treasury, New Zealand), August.

Part II

GOVERNING WITHIN LIMITS

1. **The challenge** 31

2. **Budgeting and performance management strategies for governing within limits** 32

   Fiscal consolidation 33

   Budgeting for results 37

   Structural changes to government expenditure 43

3. **Managing human resources to govern within limits** 45

   Boosting productivity and efficiency 45

   Challenges raised by decentralisation and devolution of human resource management 48

   Managing growth in public service employment levels 50

   Challenges raised by staffing limits and reductions 50

   Future directions 52

   Principles for successful human resource management strategies 53

4. **Managing government regulation within limits** 55

   Is there too much regulation? 56

   What are the implications for managing regulation within limits? 63

   What are the implications for the "limits to government" debate? 66

Notes 72

References 73

GOVERNING WITHIN LIMITS

1. THE CHALLENGE

Resources are limited; choices are constrained; public management and public policy are necessarily governed by limits. Limits on the amount and growth of spending, on specific activities, and on the use of resources such as personnel, are nothing new. However, the pressures imposed through such limits have been growing as most governments' fiscal situations deteriorated in the early 1990s, and as governments became more concerned with the impacts of their activities on competitive economic performance in the context of globalisation. While budgetary positions are now improving in many countries, limits and pressures persist. The careful application of limits and working through of their consequences for public services remains a constant preoccupation in OECD Member countries.

Governments have explored different ways to set and achieve limits effectively, to make the required hard policy choices and public management changes, and to manage the consequences – and the opportunities – for public services. They have sought to apply limits to make government and the economy work better, not only to control growth.

This issue of "governing within limits" is addressed here by discussing:

- **budgeting and performance management strategies**, including both fiscal consolidation (reducing budget deficits and restraining debt levels) and the performance of the public sector, as well as structural changes to government expenditure;
- **managing human resources**, including strategies both to boost productivity and efficiency and to manage growth in public service employment levels;
- **managing regulation within limits**, including the relationship between fiscal and regulatory costs, and the importance of forming a global view of government costs and impacts.

These discussions point to common issues and approaches, as well as to differences. Certainly there are differences among OECD Member countries in the limits they set themselves: the level of government spending, for instance, ranges from around 60 per cent of nominal GDP in Sweden and Denmark to under 35 per cent in the United States; and their fiscal consolidation targets do not involve Swedes or Danes aiming to approach American levels of government spending, nor Americans aiming for higher levels. There is no "right" size of government.

Yet, as the first discussion below points out, while there are differences among OECD countries in the magnitude of budgetary problems and the comprehensiveness of responses, there is considerable convergence in their approaches to achieving those objectives. Moreover, the most comprehensive budgetary reforms have been in those countries which have emphasised achieving macro fiscal objectives (fiscal consolidation) while at the same time improving micro-performance, including efficiency, effectiveness and quality of services. A key challenge is to achieve both "better macro-control and improved micro-performance", through tools such as multi-year budget planning, devolution and increased flexibility for managers, accountability for performance, and the use of market-type mechanisms. In addition, structural changes to government expenditure seem to be more effective in tackling budget deficits than one-off measures.

In a similar vein, the discussion of managing human resources to govern within limits recognises that the call to public service managers to be more productive, more efficient, and more effective, all within the confines of declining resources, is being heard in nearly all OECD Member countries. Moreover, lessons drawn from country experiences are offering new insights into the integral part played by human resource management (HRM) reforms in supporting public service managers in meeting the challenge of accomplishing more with fewer resources. Indeed, the larger the reduction in resources, the greater the need for flexibility in allocating and managing those resources. It is important to integrate HRM into core activities such as strategic planning, budgeting and performance management. It is recognised that over the longer term, the anchor provided by well-implemented, strategic HRM policies will be crucial for maintaining quality public services, attracting high quality public servants, and for ensuring the continued commitment of public service workers to meeting the productivity and efficiency goals sought by reforms.

Moreover, the concern with limits applies just as well to government regulation. The discussion which follows recognises that governments in the OECD area clearly believe that they face a regulatory problem with serious economic and social consequences. Increasingly, it is recognised that there are limits to regulation, just as for other government policy instruments, that regulatory costs are real and they matter. However, just as governing within limits does not mean dismantling government, managing regulation within limits does not mean deregulation: Well-written rules based on effective policies that produce net benefits should be encouraged – there is great potential for reducing the cost of regulation without sacrificing policy objectives, through a strategy that focuses on improving the quality of regulations, finding cost-effective alternatives to regulation, and deregulating in selected sectors. It may be counter-productive to limit the size of government without also limiting regulation, in light of risks that regulations could be used to shift government costs to the private sector. To manage these risks, regulatory costs should be made visible. In the longer term, it is concluded, techniques for assessing regulatory costs and impacts at the national level are needed which do not exist now: managing regulation within limits will continue to be difficult without a better sense of the real impacts of regulation.

The limits of concern to governments therefore go beyond the purely financial, as the consequences of limits go well beyond purely financial measurements and affect citizens and the private sector as well as public services and governments. The challenge of governing within limits is not only to establish and meet limits, but also to design and apply them creatively, as a tool for achieving wider public policy and public management goals. The measures taken by governments to meet limits and manage their consequences should reinforce each other, in the fields of budgeting and performance management, human resources management, and regulatory management. The fundamental goal remains better government, whether or not that is also thought to require smaller government.

2. BUDGETING AND PERFORMANCE MANAGEMENT STRATEGIES FOR GOVERNING WITHIN LIMITS

Budgetary developments in OECD Member countries can be broadly described under three related objectives:

- **Fiscal consolidation – reducing budget deficits and restraining debt levels.**
- **Budgeting for results and improving the performance of the public sector.**
- **Structural changes to government expenditure.**

While there are differences between OECD Member countries in the magnitude of budgetary problems and the comprehensiveness of responses, there is considerable convergence in their approaches to achieving those objectives. Fiscal difficulties – large deficits and high debt levels, have been experienced by nearly all OECD Member countries. The most comprehensive budgetary reforms have been in those countries which have emphasised the need to achieve fiscal consolidation while minimising the impact on performance; that is achieving macro fiscal objectives while improving micro-performance, including efficiency, effectiveness and quality of services.

These reforms have involved considerable changes in budgetary processes. Traditional budgeting systems with short term and detailed control of inputs have generally been a disabling environment for public sector micro-performance. Traditionally, budgetary targets have been achieved by arbitrary reductions in inputs. Macro-objectives have thus often been achieved at the cost of micro-performance. The budget process has encouraged bids for additional resources rather than reallocation of existing resources.

Overwhelmingly, this traditional budgeting approach is no longer considered appropriate in OECD Member countries. Budgets have thus needed to become micro-performance management instruments as well as instruments of macro-control. The challenge is to incorporate both objectives into the budgetary system – to achieve better macro-control and improved micro-performance.

Fiscal consolidation

Fiscal trends

Before the first oil crisis in 1973-74, the economic performance of OECD Member countries had been generally strong and general government expenditure had increased faster than economic output. There had also been a marked change in the composition of public expenditure, with a growing share taken by interest payments on rising public debt and by transfer payments to households and the business sector. In particular, governments had broadened their role in redistributing income and the welfare state responsibility for the financial risks associated with economic fluctuation, old age and sickness.

From the first oil crisis through the second oil crisis of 1979-80, the combined impact of a sharp deterioration in economic performance and the consequent upward push on government spending for transfer payment made governments greater net borrowers. In the 1960s, it was rare for governments to run budget deficits. By 1982, 14 countries had budget deficits, ranging from 0.5 per cent of GDP in *Finland* to 13.2 per cent in *Ireland* (It should be noted that Ireland has since reduced its budget deficit to below 3 per cent of GDP).[1] Though there were substantial variations among countries, all countries experienced significant, in some cases quite dramatic, increases in the size of government expenditures.

During the 1982-90 economic cycle, economic recovery was moderate and the expenditure to GDP ratio was stabilised in most OECD Member countries. In fact, total government outlays in countries were a lower percentage of GDP in 1989 than they had been 7 years earlier. Extensive budgeting reforms, such as imposing top-down expenditure limits in the early stages of the budget formulation process, had been launched earlier in the decade. Though it seems probable that in some countries economic improvement reduced the sense of urgency for effective control and management of public expenditure, spending restraint still was a central element in economic policy.

During the recession of the early 1990s, fiscal positions deteriorated again in nearly all OECD Member countries. In 1993, the OECD-wide general government deficit reached 4.5 per cent of GDP. Among the G-7 group of countries deficits reached 4.2 per cent of GDP, while in OECD-Europe deficits peaked at 6.5 per cent of GDP. As a result of government actions and global economic recovery, budget positions are now improving in many countries. The total general government budget deficit is projected to decline, but remains high at 3.4 per cent of GDP OECD-wide in 1995.

As well as economic recession, external economic shocks created by historically unique circumstances, strongly influenced fiscal positions. For example, *Finland's* fiscal position deteriorated sharply as a result of the collapse of the *Soviet Union*, which had been one of *Finland's* main trading partners. *Germany* was also exposed to the unique fiscal shock created by the costs of unification, which have generated lasting and tight constraints on the budget.

Structural factors also negatively influenced deficits in many countries including *Australia*, *Italy*, *Switzerland*, and *Belgium*. In *Australia*, it is estimated that approximately 50 per cent of the increase in the budget deficit during the period 1987/88 and 1992/93 was due to structural factors. The fiscal positions of *Italy*, *Belgium*, and *Greece* have been, and continue to be, significantly affected by growing debt interest payments. In most OECD Member countries the already high gross debt to GDP ratio has continued to grow in recent years, rising OECD-wide from 57.7 per cent of GDP at the onset of the recent recession in 1989 to 72.4 per cent of GDP in 1995. Estimates indicate an unbroken increase of the debt burden up to 75.4 per cent of GDP by 1997, associated with a rise in general government net interest payments as percentage of GDP to 3.1 per cent by 1997, up from 2.6 per cent in 1989.

Belgium, *France*, and *Switzerland* identify over optimistic economic assumptions as having adverse consequences for their fiscal position. Fiscal positions were worsened by discretionary spending during the electoral cycle in *Belgium*, the large underground economy in *Italy*, or an underestimated length of the recession in *Switzerland*. The *United States*' legislative framework for budget consolidation was also built on more optimistic economic forecasts that assumed high growth, low inflation, and low interest rates.

Need for fiscal consolidation

The growth of the public sector in the 1970s and early 1980s set the scene for subsequent pressures for reform. It became increasingly clear that economic and social objectives could not be achieved without changes in the public sector. In particular, the magnitude of economic issues facing countries spurred a critical appraisal of the public sector's performance. First, fundamental questions were raised about the affordability of the public sector and whether it provided value for money. Second, earlier expansion had set clear limits to further growth. More and more, demands for new services and other expenditure pressures would have to be satisfied by offsetting reductions elsewhere. Third, there emerged a concern that the very size of the public sector was an impediment to its good management and its flexibility to adapt to new challenges. The difficulties of many organisations in the private sector show that this is not just a public sector phenomenon. Fourth, there were also concerns about the crowding-out effects of the public sector on the private sector.

The control of public expenditures and budget deficits is thus considered essential for a stable domestic financial environment and for promoting a durable reduction in real interest rates, which will help private investment to expand and thus promote sustained economic growth. In countries where deficits are large and public debt is rising strongly – and this is still the case in many OECD Member countries – further deficit reduction is considered necessary. Deficit reductions should be pursued in ways consistent with the objective of improving growth. In general, governments consider this is best achieved through stronger control over public expenditure rather than by raising taxation, which would damage incentives. Where the trend of rising public debt in relation to GDP is being reversed, and budget deficits have been reduced sufficiently to restore fiscal flexibility, further reductions may be less urgent. In this case, continued progress in containing public expenditure creates room for tax cuts.

Furthermore, the fiscal imperatives underpinning budgetary consolidation are accentuated by large future spending commitments, particularly in entitlement programmes as a result of ageing populations. Cyclical recovery alone in public finances will not be sufficient to overcome current fiscal imbalances, nor will it provide enough flexibility to cope with large long term spending commitments. To achieve sound medium term fiscal positions, it is essential that countries tackle the structural components of budget deficits.

Global targets for aggregate expenditure control

Most countries have thus highlighted the necessity for fiscal consolidation to balance policy objectives against the financial capacity of government and the need for global budgeting targets, typically covering several years ahead, within which annual spending decisions would be accommodated. In virtually all OECD Member countries, current budgetary goals are expressed as specific quantitative targets, not as general qualitative statements of intent. To be readily grasped by politicians, civil servants and the general public, they are summed up in a few numbers representing future directions the government intends to follow. Such precision provides an unambiguous message on a government's financial objectives to participants in the budget process, and at the same time restricts the ability of the government to subsequently adjust its aggregate revenue and expenditure levels for reasons of expediency. This restriction is increased when the targets are specified for each of several years ahead, rather than as a level to be achieved by the end of a future period.

The budget targets used in OECD Member countries can be grouped into three categories. Some countries rely on more than one of the practices to influence budgetary development.

1. A ratio, usually expressed as a percentage of GDP or some other indicator of aggregate economic activity. The ratio may relate to the level of public debt, the budget balance or the level of government borrowing, revenue or expenditure, or a combination of these factors.

2. A rate of change for expenditure. A common guideline has been zero real growth over the stated period, although the target could also allow some rate of increase or call for a reduction in real expenditure. Alternatively, the target may be expressed in nominal terms, and may be published alongside target ratios for the budget balance or revenues.

3. An absolute value for the target variable in nominal or real terms. These targets can be expressed as either the future level of expenditure or the deficit, or as the amount of desired change from some baseline level.

It is noteworthy that virtually all OECD Member countries have an explicit target for the deficit as a ratio to GDP. These global targets have been given impetus among European Union countries by the provisions of the Maastricht treaty. The treaty established objectives for achieving a deficit to GDP ratio of no greater than 3 per cent and a gross debt to GDP ratio not exceeding 60 per cent as a condition for joining the European Monetary Union. Many EU *countries* with budget deficits above the Maastricht target refer to this as their primary global fiscal goals. In these countries, the gross debt to GDP criteria is contributing to both the pressures and the resolve for fiscal restraint, and provides a clear rationale for governments seeking broad political and public support for the implementation of restrictive fiscal policies.

In addition, *Germany* specifies an objective to bring down the ratio of government expenditure to GDP to the pre-unification levels in order to create the necessary conditions for lower taxes and contributions, smaller deficits, more investment and employment. A target for government expenditure to GDP ratio of 46 per cent by 2000 will allow the general government deficit to be brought down to around 1 per cent of GDP (1996 estimates: 3.5 per cent) and the debt ratio to under 59 per cent (currently some 60 per cent). Projections for the period 2000 to 2005 suggest further reduction in the government expenditure ratio to 44 per cent (lowest figure since 1973), deficit ratio to less than 1 per cent, and debt ratio to less than 53 per cent.

Australia, *New Zealand*, and *Canada* define their fiscal policies in precise terms as well. *Australia's* medium term strategy implies a reduction in the deficit to less than 1 per cent of GDP by 1996/97 and balancing the budget by 1997/98. By pursuing the objectives set out in its Fiscal Responsibility Act of 1994, *New Zealand*, which is running a budget surplus, intends to reduce net debt to below 20 per cent of GDP, to reduce general government expenditure to below 30 per cent of GDP, and to restore net worth as set out in a consolidated government balance sheet to significantly positive levels. *Canada* has set a target deficit of 3 per cent of GDP by fiscal year 1996/97, 2 per cent of GDP by 1997/98, and aims to eventually eliminate the deficit. The *United Kingdom* intends to balance the budget in the medium term. In support of this, overall spending in the *United Kingdom* is planned to stay broadly flat in real terms from 1995/96 to 1998/99. *Iceland* intends to bring its budget into surplus in 1997.

Legislative requirements for fiscal consolidation

In some countries specific legislative requirements mandate either the specific means of enforcing spending reductions, or levels for revenue, expenditure or the deficit, or enhanced reporting of government strategies and progress in achieving them.

Over the last ten years the *United States* has made several legislative attempts to reduce the deficit including the Gramm-Rudman Acts of 1985 and 1987. They proved unsuccessful because the reductions required to reach targets would have been too painful politically and were built on economic forecasts that assumed high growth, low inflation, and low interest rates. The key current legislative framework in the *United States* is the Budget Enforcement Act. The Act provides for caps on discretionary spending and pay-as-you-go limits to enforce expenditure reductions and to ensure that legislative action does not increase the deficit through the 1998 fiscal year. Under the Budget Enforcement Act, a budget agreement was reached in 1993 that targeted deficit reduction of $500 billion over 5 years. Though the budget deficit for 1996 was $107 billion, the lowest in 15 years, without further action this target still could not be achieved. The President and the Congress have periodically passed legislation effecting more specific reductions such as cuts in discretionary and non-discretionary spending, and increases in receipts. This year both the President and the Congress have adopted the new medium-term fiscal policy objective of balancing the federal budget by fiscal year 2002. Congress has also periodically discussed the introduction of a balanced budget amendment to the Constitution.

New Zealand has established a somewhat different legislative track. It has established a number of principles of responsible fiscal management within the Fiscal Responsibility Act of 1994. The Act does not set a specific numeric target for expenditure, revenue or the deficit, but requires debt to be at prudent levels and a level of net worth that provides a buffer against adverse future events. For this purpose, the Act requires the government to regularly provide information on its strategic and detailed budgetary plans and its subsequent performance.

Top-down spending ceilings

To link ministerial budgets with global fiscal targets, top-down spending controls are being applied in a significant number of countries. Their main objective is to place an upper limit on the spending of ministries. They mostly take the form of expenditure ceilings which ministries and agencies must comply. Coupled, as they usually are, with flexibility in spending within the cap, they encourage ministries and agencies to establish their own priorities and actively seek out productivity gains.

A number of countries are increasing emphasis on top-down ceilings for ministerial budgets as a means of integrating policy and program choices within the agreed global targets. In deciding the ministerial targets, the central budget office evaluates the budget with respect to technical aspects such as: expected expenditure levels as presented in the multi-year budget estimates, changed demographic conditions, actual spending in the preceding year, and the level of total expenditure consistent with the target of a growth in total expenditure below the growth in the economy. Top-down spending controls are sometimes employed in combination with across-the-board or targeted spending reductions. Targeted spending reductions are more commonly applied than across the board spending reductions in most countries because the latter, though administratively simple, may work against equity and efficiency.

Countries which most extensively apply top-down ceilings as a policy tool for expenditure restraint include the Nordic countries (*Denmark*, *Finland*, *Iceland*, *Norway* and *Sweden*) and the *United Kingdom*. *Denmark's* general framework for the budget process is the setting of ceilings for each spending ministry which are decided by the cabinet and are politically binding within the government. During the 1980s *Finland*, *Austria* and *Denmark* introduced general cuts in the appropriations during the fiscal year to influence the expenditure allocations in the different ministries as well as to tackle ongoing budget deficits. In *Iceland* and *Norway*, each ministry's budget targets are developed through a combination of across the board spending reductions and targeted spending reductions in specific programmes. In the *United Kingdom*, the Cabinet establishes early in the budget process a ceiling for aggregate spending within the control total (covering about 85 per cent of total government spending) and the totals for departmental programs. This facilitates a discussion of relative priorities, while restraining total spending.

Conclusion

In general, **global targets appear to be a useful tool for moving budgets towards balance** by setting overall fiscal policy objectives, making it explicit how the government will meet them over a number of years, and translating these into operational terms, thus establishing a ceiling for expenditures. Once specific global targets have been set, ongoing political commitment is crucial to maintaining the credibility of government's fiscal policies. These may be supported by other procedures based on specific legislation and top-down ceilings.

Budget targets are not self-executing nor is it always within the grasp of government to meet them, no matter how strong its determination. Pursuing the budget targets may be affected by the short-term performance of the economy. When recessions occur fiscal targets may yield to economic pressures. Japan saw a need to maintain public expenditures during its recent recession as a counter cyclical measure, even though this has led to a significant increase in the budget deficit. Other external shocks, such as the reunification of *Germany*, can force the government to retreat from carefully developed fiscal objectives. Much also depends on the short-term control exercised by the government over key variables such as interest rates, and the cost of demand-led expenditure programmes. Therefore, the use of realistic and cautious forecasts of economic assumptions will assist fiscal consolidation efforts. Moreover, global targets and top-down ceilings in nominal rather than real terms can reduce the possible pressure on public finances in inflationary conditions.

Budgeting for results

As mentioned earlier, budget targets are not self executing. Action is needed by governments to achieve them. These actions can be divided loosely into:

- changes to budgetary processes aimed not only at achieving better macro-controls but at improving the performance of public sector programs (systemic changes);
- policy decisions to reduce or eliminate particular expenditures or programs or to increase revenues (substantive changes).

Because of the great variety of specific policy decisions made in different OECD Member countries, the discussion below focuses on changes to the budgetary process.

Reforms aimed at improving the resource allocation process and the performance of the public sector have included the following:

- The introduction of **a framework of multi-year budget planning to strengthen aggregate expenditure control.** This framework aimed at increasing medium-term flexibility and reducing the impacts of year-on-year incrementalism inherent in a purely annual focus.
- Increasing **devolution of managerial authority and providing flexibility in operational decisions.** These managerial changes have been introduced to achieve budget targets by providing managers with incentives and opportunities to improve performance and to do more with less.
- Pursuing performance goals through **strengthening accountability requirements that focus on results**, through establishing new performance measurement, contracting and reporting arrangements.
- Adopting **a more commercial and competitive approach in certain public sector areas**, through the use of market-type mechanisms as instruments for raising productivity and responsiveness.

Multi-year budget planning

Budgets are enacted on an annual basis in OECD Member countries. This short-term horizon is often criticised for impeding effective expenditure management. Decisions on resource allocation are said to be made on an *ad hoc* or piecemeal basis with the implication of past and present decisions beyond the next year being neglected. Strict annuality also provides little incentive to managers to economise resources or plan expenditures in an orderly fashion with a focus on results Thus, techniques have been implemented to incorporate a multi-year perspective into the budget process. This has involved multi-year budget targets or plans as previously discussed. On the expenditure side this has involved multi-year indicative levels of funding for organisations and programmes. By providing a degree of certainty on the level of funding and government expenditures over time, multi-year expenditure plans assist in lifting the sights of both managers in spending ministries and central budget office to more strategic questions of the best resource allocation mix and the most appropriate timing of expenditure in pursuing programme objectives.

Most countries have employed medium-term budget forecasts, with a 3-year time horizon being common. The United Kingdom was a pioneer in the area of multi-year budget forecasts in the 1960s and 1970s. In those years, it was used as a planning device, a means of identifying programme initiatives and setting aside funds for them in future budgets. As the growth of the public sector became unsustainable it was reoriented from forecasts to plans and from instruments of programme expansion to constraints on future spending. Multi-year budget plans are not always used to give indicative funding levels to individual ministries and specific programmes for the forecast period so as to prevent ministries and programmes from claiming ownership over these funding levels in case downward revisions become necessary. Thus, it could show the budgetary implications such as revenue increases or programme cut-backs to achieve the stated targets. However, if articulated only at a macro-level, they do not assist in achieving the focus on performance and reallocation which is needed at the micro- or organisational level.

To increase discipline in government expenditure, the medium-term forecasts have been formulated at the macro level by an interplay of the following:

– By setting overall fiscal policy objectives and making explicit how the government will meet them over a number of years, and by translating these into operational terms thus establishing a ceiling for expenditures.

– By showing the minimum cost of continuing existing policies. In a number of countries (including the United States, Sweden, and the Netherlands), this base line projection became the starting point for working on the budget. In most cases, the base line projection conveyed to spending ministers a powerful message for self-discipline in proposing new expenditures.

– By illuminating the budget implications of decisions in the next year's budget whose expenditure may not be fully reflected in the budget. This is especially relevant in indicating whether the full costs of proposals by ministries would be incompatible with the medium-term fiscal policy objectives.

The use of long-term budget forecasts has not been as widespread nor as uniformly as medium-term budget forecasts. In some countries, such as the United States and Denmark, long-term budget forecasts covering both budget revenues and expenditures for 30-40 years into the future have been prepared to identify adverse expenditure trends at an early stage as a warning system. As the ageing population is by far the greatest expenditure trend facing governments, the principal impact of long-term budget forecasts has been to indicate the effect of changing demography on government finances

New Zealand and Iceland have adopted accrual-based accounting for their whole-of-government financial statements and budgets. This has several implications for the incorporation of longer-term issues. First, expenses are recognised when they are incurred rather than when they are paid. As a result, expenditure items which are building up over time but are not payable until later are nonetheless reported as expenses. Second, all assets, such as highways and other infrastructure, are valued and reported in the balance sheet to pay attention to the management of those assets and the maintenance of their values. Third, all liabilities are recorded in the balance sheet. For example, the unfunded civil service pension plans are recognised as liabilities in the balance sheet and correspondingly the full increase in this liability is recorded as an expense in the budget operating statement. The cost of asset usage may also be incorporated in the operating statement by a capital charge. The experience in both countries suggests that accrual accounting increases the focus on longer-term issues.

Another recent technique for dealing with long-term issues, still under development, is generational accounting. It was first employed in the 1993 budget in the *United States* and later in other countries, including *Germany, Italy, New Zealand, Norway,* and *Sweden*. It was developed to estimate what different generations would pay in taxes and receive in benefits over their lifetimes given existing policies, thus focusing on questions of inter-generational equity. The basic difference between generational accounting and the traditional manner of accounting can be described as follows. The traditional manner of accounting sums up all government revenues and expenses for a fiscal year irrespective of which generation these transactions relate to. Multi-year budget forecasts project these totals over a number of years. Generational accounting, on the other hand, presents total government revenues and expenses summed on the basis of which generation these transaction are linked to irrespective of what fiscal year the transaction takes place in. In spite of the great many assumptions underlying it and the very long-term horizon involved, it can provide very useful information on inter-generational implications of the government's budgetary policies.

Devolution and flexibility in administrative expenditure

Devolving managerial authority and providing flexibility are an important reform strategy adopted in many countries. The traditional control systems have been criticised as having become too detailed, rigid, and in many cases, counter productive to both macro-control and efficiency. Devolution and flexibility is seen in many countries as enabling managers to improve efficiency and thus as a tool in achieving the tight expenditure targets which they have been set. The reforms are directed at giving organisations and managers greater freedom in operational decisions and removing unnecessary constraints in resource management. In exchange, organisations and managers are more directly accountable for results. In particular, managers must manage within the financial limits set, with supplementation of funds being available only in exceptional circumstances. Control through detailed appropriation of inputs is replaced by a framework of performance targets, incentives and performance measurement. Common budgetary incentives are greater end-of-year flexibility in managing resources, the consolidation of detailed appropriation items, and net appropriations.

Under traditional budgeting, funds unspent at the end of the year had to be surrendered in full to the centre, regardless of the reason for underspending. Often allocations in subsequent years are also reduced to reflect this underspending. This results in the well-known end-of-year rush to spend, regardless of whether the expenditure was cost-effective. This is related to the issue of providing medium-term indicative funding levels to organisations mentioned above. Under the reforms, the future indicative funding levels are not reduced by the underexpenditure in a previous year. The reforms have provided flexibility to carry over a proportion of unspent funds to the following year, and in some countries even to borrow from the following year. For example, *Australia* has increased the percentage of budget that can be carried over from 3 per cent to 6 per cent. End-of-year flexibility is now widely seen as a success.

The consolidation of detailed appropriation items and the consequent devolution of resource allocation decisions have been common elements of the devolution strategies. Such arrangements aim to give greater flexibility in the use of funds by eliminating over-detailed categorisation of budget allocations and making transfers among budget categories easier. An increasingly common approach is to consolidate all administrative expenditures, often including salary, into a single running costs appropriation subject to strict overall cash limits. A single budget line for administrative expenditure makes it possible to use different combinations of staff, information technology, and other resources to produce results in accordance with program targets. But restrictions remain on transfers between programmes and administrative expenditures so as to focus on administrative expenditure efficiency.

In *Australia, Denmark, Ireland,* and *Sweden,* the consolidation of administrative expenditure into a single expenditure item has been accompanied by a required efficiency dividend so that programme managers are required to achieve a minimum target in terms of improved productivity, based on the assumption that the greater budgetary flexibility facilitates productivity improvements. The annual budget allocation was reduced by up to 2-3 per cent in real terms. For the same reasons the *United Kingdom's* cash limits for running costs in recent years have not been adjusted upwards for changes in inflation but held constant.

Another arrangement providing greater flexibility is the introduction of net appropriations which allow ministries to retain all or some revenue raised from user charges. Expenditures can be increased to the extent of the additional revenue retained, even in tight budgetary situations. Net appropriations provide positive incentives to generate revenue that would not otherwise be generated and ensure greater responsiveness to customer needs. But these have raised concerns about a weakening of parliamentary control. In some countries, this serves as an incentive for the identification and sale of surplus assets. Agencies may be credited with a portion of the sale proceeds, rather than this going entirely to the central budget.

Accountability for performance

Budget offices have increasingly divested their detailed *ex ante* control of administrative expenditures and are now fostering a more performance oriented managerial climate. These changes are based on the view that concentrating on more strategic issues and performance are most useful in determining how to make best use of available resources. The new roles of the budget office are reflected in devising a more effective budget system to control the budget totals and to establish priorities among programmes, integrating budgeting with other management processes, requiring spending ministries to measure performance and evaluate results, developing new guidelines and methods for holding managers accountable, and promoting new information and reporting systems.

Performance management includes mechanisms, such as corporate planning, under which organisation and programme objectives are determined. Many OECD Member countries have had experience with some form of Planning, Programming and Budgeting System (PPBS) or similar systems that tried to link budgets and performance. One of the principal lessons from these experiences is that care must be taken to instil managerial responsibility and results at all levels of management rather than simply impose performance measurement from the top. In *Australia,* programme management and budgeting (PMB) has linked the aggregate control framework to the achievement of value for money by individual organisations and managers. PMB has focused attention on planning objectives, budgeting, implementing strategies, and assessing programme outcomes.

In some cases, performance objectives are made through formal contractual arrangements specifying the output or results that an organisation or a manager is committed to produce with agreed resources. The range of contractual arrangements developed in countries encompasses the following:

- Budgetary agreements between the central budget office and spending ministries that financial allocations are provided in return for an agreed level of performance. The *Australian* system of resource agreements illustrate this approach. PMB is the instrument for identifying objectives and placing them into an agreed framework that make it possible to set performance targets for managers at all levels.

- Legislative appropriations being made on the basis of the agency producing an agreed level of outputs as in *New Zealand*.

- Performance agreements within ministries on the services to be delivered and the level of performance to be achieved. The *United Kingdom's* annual performance agreements for executive agencies between a minister and an agency reflect this approach; they include specific performance targets against which the agency's performance is assessed.

But such a contractual approach has raised several problems. There are methodological and practical limitations on performance measurement It may also be difficult to establish a direct link between the level of performance and the budget, because decisions on resourcing take into account a number of factors other than performance. Thus in other countries, the drive for performance is less closely linked to budgeting but has a broader scope to strengthen the capacity of managers to take initiatives and accept responsibility for providing public services in an efficient and effective manner. Performance issues are seen as informing the budget process but the link is indirect rather than direct. These countries aim to establish performance measurement more firmly in the budget process by focusing the budget dialogue on past and planned performance.

To measure performance, most governments have put considerable emphasis on requiring agencies to develop performance indicators, and many of their published budget documents, annual reports, and other documents contain an extensive range of indicators. There has been a tendency in some countries to develop excessive numbers of indicators, without an adequate understanding of their interrelationships or of how the information might be used. It is important to choose key relevant indicators and keep the process simple.

Many countries have also taken steps to formalise requirements for program evaluation usually as part of reforms to the budgetary process. While evaluation is perceived as primarily the responsibility of individual agencies, selective programme evaluations are undertaken by the central budget office or by external auditors. In some cases, such as in *Australia*, the results of internal evaluations must be reported externally and be accessible by external review agencies such as legislative committees.

The role of external review agencies such as auditors may be enhanced under performance management reforms. Apart from carrying out performance reviews, the *United Kingdom's* National Audit Office has a role in reviewing the quality of performance information. In *Australia* and *Canada*, the external auditor may also review and evaluate the general adequacy of internal performance measurement and monitoring mechanisms.

Commercial and competitive approach: market-type mechanisms

Market-type mechanisms are used in many OECD Member countries' efforts to increase public sector efficiency, better control public expenditures, improve accountability relationships, and increase flexibility and responsiveness. The most commonly used instruments include user charges, internal markets, contracting out, vouchers and their equivalents, intergovernmental contracts, joint public/private financing of infrastructure, and corporatisation and privatisation. This diversity in instruments reflects the different characteristics of market arrangements: competition, private ownership, profit objectives, market entry, monetary incentives, pricing, decentralised decision making or organisational structure.

The strategies being applied vary among Member countries. Some countries such as the *United Kingdom* and *New Zealand* are using market-type mechanisms within the context of an overall readjustment of the respective roles of government and the private sector. In other countries, they are being used as techniques for improving efficiency and flexibility in a less changed balance between the public and private sector.

Vouchers are used as a means of empowering consumers of publicly funded services and stimulating supply-side improvements of these services, including lower administrative costs. The *United States* housing voucher programme is regarded as a success by providing greater real income benefits to the targeted population at lower administrative costs. The *United Kingdom* quasi-voucher scheme for residential care and nursing homes raised the problem of controlling total costs and distortions in meeting both the preferences and needs of recipients

A number of countries have created internal markets in the provision of internal government services such as printing, fleet and real estate management, consulting and legal services. This involves budgetary appropriations being given to the consumer agencies, who thus determine the type and amount of services they require rather than the decisions being left in the hands of the supplier. The supply may also be opened up to competition. Suppliers are required to achieve financial and other performance targets. By allowing agencies choice and providing competition, internal markets are able to bring about productivity increases as well as changes in the amount and composition of services purchased. These internal markets can be seen as an extension of the general trend towards the devolution of authority within administrations.

The creation of internal markets is also being pursued as an instrument of sectoral policies. The outstanding example is the internal market in the *United Kingdom's* National Health Service where the roles of purchaser and provider of services have been split.

User charging is a relatively straightforward instrument which aims to recover, either partially or fully, the cost of providing a government service from the user of that service. The objective is not only to raise revenue, but to eliminate excess demand and improve services through market signals. Novel examples of where user charging is being applied includes areas as diverse as weather forecasting and central statistical information.

Many countries have given increased emphasis to contracting out public sector activities as a means of reducing costs and increasing efficiency. Contracting out may also be used to meet service demands which exceed the capability of in-house staff, or to provide flexibility to meet temporary requirements. Services contracted out in OECD Member countries are diverse, ranging from simple activities like cleaning, printing and maintenance to more complex and strategic ones like information technology, auditing (*New Zealand*) and air force flight training (*Australia*). Since 1992, the *United Kingdom* has been implementing a comprehensive programme of market testing of government services against alternative private suppliers. In the *United Kingdom*, few activities cannot be subject to market testing and therefore managers are required to justify their decision not to market test activities. The evidence is fairly clear that contracting out can lead to substantial savings (typically 15-25 per cent), while maintaining or improving service levels.

In some countries, partnership arrangements with the private sector are increasingly being used to accelerate capital investment programmes. This private sector involvement often extends throughout the entire life of the capital projects: identification of need, design, financing, construction and operation. Examples range from highways in *France, Germany, Iceland* and *Mexico* to prisons in the *United Kingdom* and *United States*.

Proposals to extend conventional methods for provision of infrastructure were prompted by two main motives. First, to find ways to accommodate emerging infrastructure needs within tight fiscal constraints. In *Germany*, the magnitude of the costs involved in rejuvenating infrastructure in the east following reunification could not be met through the public budget. Similarly in the *United States*, debt and tax limitations at the state and local government level have seriously restricted the ability of governments to undertake infrastructure expansions for prisons and additional highway capacities. The other motives is to improve efficiency in determining and meeting infrastructure needs and improving the cost effectiveness of resulting service provision.

Reforms aimed at improving performance have also involved increased use of corporatisation and privatisation of state-owned enterprises.

New Zealand has corporatised numerous government departments producing goods and services, including electricity generation, forestry and postal services. They operate in a more businesslike way with substantial operating autonomy but are required to achieve clear financial and other targets while remaining under government ownership. In many cases, improved returns to the budget, by way of dividends have resulted, or losses previously subsidised by the budget have been eliminated. Corporatisation is often an interim step towards privatisation.

Countries such as the *United Kingdom* have implemented extensive programmes of privatisation in order to promote efficiency and to widen individual share ownership. The experience in the *United Kingdom* during the 1970s showed that nationalised industries, even fast-growing ones, experienced productivity declines and increases in unit costs. These enterprises were a huge drain on public resources. The *United Kingdom* has privatised most nationalised industries, including the electricity sector, the water sector and British Telecom. Another successful example of privatisation is the reform of the *Japan* National Railways in 1987. By breaking it up into 7 private companies, *Japan's* railways have experienced remarkable increases in performance and improved management.

Conclusion

The move to **a focus on budgeting for results has led to significant changes** to the budget processes and systems in OECD Member countries. All these changes – multi-year budget planning, devolution and increased flexibility for managers, accountability for performance and market-type mechanisms – clearly aim at budget savings to provide resources to meet expanding demands in some areas, as well as improving public sector performance. The budget process can, however, only act as an enabler or disabler for substantive policy actions. These decisions are discussed in the next section.

Structural changes to government expenditure

Up to 1990 fiscal consolidation in the OECD Member countries was largely through the curtailment of subsidies and reducing government consumption and investment expenditure, rather than social security and other transfer payments. During the 1979-1990 period the shift from consumption expenditure to transfer payments – social security and related income maintenance programs – was significant. In all countries except *Belgium*, social security and other transfer payments increased their share of GDP. In some countries social transfers now account for upward of 60 per cent of central government expenditure. Another long-term shift in the structure of government expenditure is the increase in debt interest payments, which have increased both as a share of GDP and of total government expenditure reflecting significant increases in debt levels.

The increasing share of these expenditures increased the structural rigidity of the budget. The entitlement programs for income maintenance were often tied to economic and demographic trends and therefore highly sensitive to changes in the consumer price index, the age structure of population, and the level of economic activity. Debt interest payments were also predetermined by the size of accumulated debt and the contracted interest rates. Both factors impaired the capacity of governments to adjust spending levels in response to changing circumstances or policy priorities.

Thus many countries have tried to reduce the structural components of deficits by concentrating on reductions in the transfer payments and entitlement programmes. These areas include social security expenditure, contribution to pension schemes, contribution to medical insurance schemes, and contribution to educational schemes. Reductions in other large spending areas such as defence and public service wage payments have also supported these consolidation efforts. These reductions seem to be more effective in tackling the budget deficits than one-off measures, such as sale of government assets.

Reducing expenditures in social security and other large spending areas

Reduction of transfer payments has been the most important instrument for achieving fiscal balance. In some cases, it was coupled with an increase of contributions in the revenue side. So far, this policy seems to be working to reduce the budget deficits in the OECD Member countries. But some equity problems have been encountered because most transfers are aimed at low income groups or rural areas with low average incomes.

France took remedial action in both revenue and expenditure sides of the general social security system and has achieved a marked slowdown in the growth of expenditure on health insurance. *Germany* froze subsidies to research and development expenditure, and programmes to support unemployed and a range of other social policies. *Japan* reduced contributions to medical insurance, health and medical service for the aged, and public pensions, and cut back subsidies to agriculture. *Canada* has made substantial cuts in subsidies to industry and regional development programs. *Belgium* froze in nominal terms subsidies to public enterprises and the social security system. Special measures to ensure greater control over health and unemployment payments were also made. *Austria* followed a similar path, including freezes in subsidies to industries and agriculture as well as targeted cuts in various welfare programmes such as family aid, unemployment insurance, pensions for public employees, and health. In the *United States* current budget discussion focuses on reductions in "mandatory" programs such as health care and social security.

Reflecting the improved global security environment, a number of countries including *Belgium*, the *United Kingdom*, *Germany*, and *France*, have frozen defence spending in nominal terms. Under the Budget Enforcement Act limits, *United States* defence spending was also projected to remain fairly constant over 1996-2000. As well, the majority of reductions in executive branch civilian employment, which was set by the Federal Workforce Restructuring Act of 1994, will be come from the defence sector. However a number of other agencies are taking the same or a greater percentage of cuts.

In some countries, expenditure reductions have been pursued by reductions in employees rather than in the number of agencies or programs. *Italy* and *Spain* have implemented either total recruitment freezes or reductions in the workforce, while *Germany* and *Canada* implemented real cuts in public sector salaries. In the *United States*, both the discretionary funding constraints and annually decreasing ceilings on employment are forcing agencies to reduce employees in the public sector.

Organisational changes

In *Iceland* and *Japan*, various government organisations and public corporations have been reorganised through mergers and abolitions. This has reduced the number of employees and operating costs as well as overlapping and duplication of functions between organisations, without affecting the level of service provided.

Reform of grants to sub-national governments has occurred in several member countries. One strategy has been cutting transfers to sub-national governments, often associated with eliminating specific purpose grants to local governments and replacing them by block grants. Another strategy has involved transferring functions to sub-national governments without a corresponding transfer of funds. For example, *Finland* has eliminated a number of specific grants to local governments and incorporated them into the general grants process where grants are determined on the basis of population and other statistical indicators. As a result transfers to local governments have been significantly reduced in recent years. *Switzerland* and *Canada* have also used this method by eliminating specific grants for health, education, and social assistance and replacing them by block grants.

A few countries have explicitly shifted national responsibilities and expenditure burdens to lower levels of government. Italy has recently proposed transferring a number of powers to local governments and reducing fiscal transfers. A*ustralia* is considering the redistribution of responsibilities for outlays in areas such as education and health. *Japan* has transferred expenditure for compulsory education to local governments and has reduced assistance to private schools. *Germany* has especially initiated a reorganisation of fiscal equalisation arrangements between the national government and the L*änder*. As a result, the economically stronger western L*änder* will have to bear a higher share of the current costs of reunification in the form of transfers to the East, thus creating some relief for the Federal budget in the medium term.

Effective public debt and assets management

Several countries have undertaken some innovations to better manage the public debt and reduce interest payments, with the development of their capital markets. *Greece* has auctioned, instead of issuing fixed rate bonds, floating rate bonds with medium and long term maturities in a competitive market, which has reduced the costs of borrowing. In the past three years *Iceland* has also sold most treasury bonds, particularly short term, through tender offers and now nearly all of its domestic debt is to be marketed on an offer basis. This will provide the lowest interest terms for government bonds. In the aftermath of the currency crisis, *Mexico* has lengthened the average maturity of the public debt to lower their funding costs. Part of short-term domestic debt was replaced by medium- and long-term borrowing from abroad on improving terms.

Improved assets management is one of the areas in which further development of the existing reforms is expected. Sales of idle assets can actually reduce operating costs by eliminting the unnecessary administrative burden. The revenue from those sales can be used to reduce public debt.

3. MANAGING HUMAN RESOURCES TO GOVERN WITHIN LIMITS

The call to public service managers to be more productive, more efficient, and more effective, all within the confines of declining resources, is being heard in nearly all OECD Member countries. For policy-makers and managers, the human resource management piece of this challenge to govern within limits is concerned with ensuring that the people who make up the public service and the resources used to pay and manage them are targeted in ways that contribute directly to carrying out organisational priorities and, moreover, anticipate *future* priorities. In this regard, the policies and practices being used in the central governments of many OECD countries to manage the public service workforce have been in an ongoing state of change and reform for more than a decade. Lessons drawn from country experiences are offering new insights into the integral part played by human resource management reforms in supporting public service managers in meeting the challenge of accomplishing more with fewer resources. The sections that follow explore the variety of approaches being used by Member countries in the context of governing within limits, and highlight the tensions, challenges and lessons that follow from them.

Boosting productivity and efficiency

The pressure to "govern within limits" is driving public service organisations to find ways for managers and workers to make more efficient use of resources. Indeed, the larger reduction in resources, the greater the need for flexibility in allocating and managing those resources. In this regard, **decentralisation and devolution of huuman resource management tools** from central management agencies to line departments and agencies (or even to line managers) has come to the fore as the most commonly adopted human resource management reform strategy. In the number of OECD countries, these reforms are being linked with new flexibilities in devolved pay bargaining, global budgeting, and performance management. As is discussed below, this trend toward decentralisation is raising new opportunities, as well as challenges, for improved human resource management.

MAIN HUMAN RESOURCE MANAGEMENT APPROACHES
TO GOVERNING WITHIN LIMITS

- **Boost productivity and efficiency of the public service workforce:**
  - give managers the tools and flexibility to manage more effectively;
  - link financial and pay delegations to better people management;
  - increase efficiency through targeted performance management.

- **Manage growth in public service employment levels:**
  - control growth over the long term through attrition and hiring freezes;
  - active reductions to rapidly streamline departments and agencies;
  - identify possibilities to shift central functions into public entreprise; or
  - transfer them to other levels of government or the private sector.

In the Public Management Service study of human resource management reforms in OECD countries during the 1980s and 1990s, countries that had sought significant decentralisation and devolution of human resource management functions reported that such reforms were instrumental in shifting from a rule-bound management culture to a performance-based management culture (OECD, 1996*b*) – a key priority in making the public service more effective and efficient. Moreover, managers in these countries were generally positive about devolution and decentralisation of human resource management functions, reporting that it had been instrumental in supporting broader organisational reforms such as devolved budgeting practices and increased local accountability for programmatic outcomes.

To promote more effective, as well as efficient, use of people and staffing resources, human resource management devolution has been aimed at giving line **managers staffing flexibilities for selection, hiring, deployment and performance management** – tools for ensuring managers have the means to get the right people in the right places in the organisation and afterward to manage their performance. The actual amount of human resource management devolution in Member countries falls across a broad spectrum. For example, it is most extensive in *New Zealand* and *Sweden* where central management agencies have only a minimal role in human resource management activities.[2] Significant devolution has also taken place in *Australia*, *Denmark*, *Iceland*, *the Netherlands*, and *the United Kingdom*, although the approach has tended to be more cautious and limited in these countries. A number of other OECD countries have made efforts toward devolution of staffing tools and report a commitment to increasing human resource management flexibilities to line departments and agencies.

While managerial devolution has been an essential element in creating more productive organisations, the need to offer tools and incentives for greater operational efficiency has been just as important a consideration. **Devolved budgets** and, particularly, **delegated pay strategies**, are being used to encourage departments and agencies to think in broad cost-benefit terms about managing resources to best achieve performance goals. Devolved "running cost" budgets are currently in place in Member countries including *Australia*, *Canada*, *Denmark*, *Finland*, *Iceland*, *Ireland*, *the Netherlands*, *New Zealand*, *Sweden* and *the United Kingdom*. Such systems remove central oversight and control over how money within a department's or agency's budget is allocated for personnel (including how many personnel are employed) administration, and other operating costs. In some cases, these systems allow for some carry-over of expenses from one fiscal year to the next and for borrowing against future-year appropriations. In countries that have adopted devolved budgets, giving line managers increased control over their financial resources is generally viewed as a powerful incentive for more effective management of people.

While many countries are including devolved budgeting schemes in their strategies to govern within limits, it is important to recognise that more than half of the Member countries continue to favour **centralised budget and pay systems**. *France*, *Germany*, *Japan* and *the United States*, for example, retain central, detailed control over the amount of resources dedicated to personnel (including staff numbers) and other administrative

---

LINKS BETWEEN HUMAN RESOURCE MANAGEMENT DEVOLUTION
AND GREATER PRODUCTIVITY (SEE OECD, 1996B)

- Promotes greater diversity of human resource management practices between departments and agencies, and provides the capability to better tailor those practices to specific programmatic needs.

- Enables departments and agencies to recruit and retain needed staff more easily and manage their people more efficiently in order to meet performance goals.

- Increases the responsibility and accountability of managers and enables them to manage in a more pro-active manner.

- Contributes to a sharper focus on efficiency and effectiveness, with positive effects on service delivery and responsiveness.

- Improves the links between policy and implementation.

- Tensions arising from devolution include the potential for loss of service-wide "unity", need for new tools for risk management and accountability for managers, and loss of career mobility and deployment flexibility across the public service.

---

expenses. Central controls in these areas are seen by policy-makers in these countries as a critical tool to manage within limits, control spending and allocate priorities across government. However, such a perspective may prove increasing difficult to sustain in countries such as *France* and *the United States* which also have stated a desire to pursue managerial devolution. The experience of countries well on the path to devolution indicates that devolved budgeting is a key underpinning of effective managerial devolution.

Several Member countries are also promoting local flexibility over resource allocation by giving department and agencies **authority to bargain individually on pay levels**. In *New Zealand* and *the United Kingdom* central pay bargaining has been abolished in favour of decentralised practices. In *Australia*, *Finland* and *Sweden* have also delegated pay bargaining, although the authority is more limited and supplemented by central bargaining. Indeed, in assessing the benefits of delegated pay as a resource management tool, a key point is to identify the degree of financial constraint that continues to be imposed by central government over the salary budget. Setting a general pay increase (as in *Australia*) or a minimum rate of increase (as had been the case until recently in *Sweden*) can be a tight constraint on the local budget flexibility in allocating financial resources according to internal priorities.

Use of **performance-related pay schemes** also appears as a common public service management tool aimed at giving managers more flexibility over allocating resources, in this case as an incentive to motivate staff to achieve higher levels of performance. A recent study by the Public Management Service found, however, that despite widespread use of performance-related pay programs across OECD countries, there is little evidence to show that such programs fulfil their goal (OECD, 1997a) It was generally believed that performance pay awards were not linked to performance and, therefore, undermined the perceived effectiveness of the scheme as a motivator for increased performance. However, where performance pay schemes have been done well, managers have cited the benefits of clear and regular feedback on performance (via the appraisal system) as a valuable addition to the overall performance management framework.

Classification is a difficult personnel tool to fit into decentralisation frameworks gaining hold in many OECD countries. While classification systems are often a large part of the problem of gaining flexibility in staffing and deploying the workforce – important issues in helping managers meet the challenge of governing with limits – such systems are also a significant part of the glue that holds the civil service together as a single employer. The common language of a classification system across a public service facilitates movement of people between and within agencies. On the one hand, there is a desire in some countries to make classification more flexible and better tailored to the staffing requirements of individual agencies to ensure that managers can place the right people in the right jobs, at the right level of pay. On the other hand, looser classification structures (such as "broad banding") often mean better pay progression, but raise concerns about comparability across, and even within public service agencies. Despite potential problems, however, many Member countries have removed or reduced central controls on classification, including *Australia, Canada, Denmark, Finland, Ireland, the Netherlands, New Zealand, Sweden, the United Kingdom,* and *the United States.*

Challenges raised by decentralisation and devolution of human resource management

A key challenge to successful devolution of managerial authority involves appropriate **training and development of public service managers** into the ethics and values of a devolved-management culture, thus ensuring they have the skills to carry out new responsibilities. It appears, however, that the rhetoric of the need for training is at odds with the reality of little time or resources being devoted to formal preparation for devolution. As a result, there are increasing concerns over accountability issues where managers have more discretion in applying staffing and budgetary policies. In this regard, some countries appear to be struggling with establishing accountability mechanisms that do not involve excessive oversight and control, yet protect public service-wide principles such as ethics, merit, fairness in the workplace, as well as broader issues of fiduciary responsibility in carrying out public service activities.

Despite increased devolution of staffing practices, managers continue to voice strong concerns that **delegations of authority are often incomplete**, particularly regarding the inability to remove or discipline chronic poor performers. Many managers identify this issue as an increasingly serious problem as organisations strive for greater efficiency and as streamlining the workplace means there are fewer workers to compensate for chronically unproductive workers. However, in most OECD countries the structures are in place for discipline and dismissal, but are seen as unsupported by top management or ineffective because of the "tenure" afforded public servants. The key issue may not be in finding new ways to sanction workers, but in shifting to a more proactive approach focused on motivation, job profiling (*i.e.* creating explicit job profiles and matching workers accordingly) performance feedback and appraisal and career planning. *Austria* is seeking to make changes in the direction of creating positive incentives for motivation and job satisfaction by linking individuals to jobs based on skill and competency evaluations. *Belgium* has also moved in this direction, but has taken a more limited approach, focusing on appraisal and incentives, without the next step of assessing the match between people and jobs as a motivating factor.

Issues of **incomplete delegations of authority are also raised by managers with respect to budgeting and pay bargaining**. Where local bargaining is supplemented by central bargaining, agencies only have partial control of their resources. Moreover, devolution is not always uniform. The efficiency of delegated pay authorities also may rest, in part, on ensuring that the incentives from central government are properly placed to encourage increased accountability, productivity and effective management of the pay bill at the decentralised level. In the near-term, attention from the central level must also be given to ensuring line departments and agencies have the capacity to negotiate pay properly, including a long-term framework for maintaining a pay strategy and a view toward issues of equity and fairness.

From a broad public management perspective, one of the largest casualties of devolution of human resource management policies is **public service "unity"**. Having moved to decentralise pay, classification and other staffing tools to individual departments and agencies, however, some governments are now looking back with concern and asking whether the public service is still a single employer, or whether the trend toward delegated authorities implies that it is now many employers, with multiple policies and practices. In most OECD countries, public servants take it for granted that there is a common thread running through the public service despite different departmental distinctions. In *Iceland* and *Sweden*, however, this is no longer the case. In both countries, managerial decentralisation has become a key public service priority, while employer-unity is no longer a concern or a desire. On the other hand, in countries such as *Germany*, *Hungary*, *Italy* and *Spain* the cultural emphasis on maintaining unified values across the public service has precluded active decentralisation. In most OECD countries, however, the situation is less well defined and there remain significant policy questions to be answered about balancing the potentially competing priorities for devolution and the status of government as a single employer.

One key policy for linking employment across the public service may be the through fostering **mobility**. This linkage becomes increasingly tenuous under delegated pay and classification structures, creating different managerial languages that may ultimately prohibit mobility even within large departments. The risk of loss of mobility should not be minimised. While the gain may be operational efficiency on one level, one cost may be in the loss of regular opportunities to share experiences, ideas and skills within the workforce. The loss of mobility may result in *less* flexibility in the long run for staffing practices regarding motivation, career development, and training, as well as in broader terms for deploying people across the public service. The solution to the problem is not be found in casting aside devolution, but in ensuring that important activities exercised from the centre, such as mobility, are preserved in the overall context of devolution. While the idea of mobility is not new to personnel policy, it is gaining new-found attention as a useful and cost effective management tool in countries representing a wide range of human resource management systems, including, *Belgium*, *Finland*, *France*, *Ireland*, *Japan* and *Norway*.

Linked closely to the issue of loss of unity, is the loss of a big-picture perspective of the goals of government as a whole. Incentives for senior managers to be preoccupied with looking inwards into their own programs and agencies may damage the capacity of the public service to coordinate policies and programs. Some countries (for example, *Australia* and *the United Kingdom*) are looking at the **incentives and structures used to manage the most senior public servants** as a way to address issues of public sector unity and mobility. Indeed, the way senior public servants are recruited and the extent to which they are mobile between ministries has a strong impact in terms of promoting coherence and a whole of government perspective. (OECD, 1997b) To this end, reforms affecting the composition and management of the senior executive group have been an important part of recent public sector reforms in some Member countries, particularly, *Australia*, *the Netherlands*, *New Zealand* and *the United Kingdom*. For similar reasons, in *Japan*, the issue of increasing occupational mobility at senior levels is also a matter of concern.

The trend toward decentralisation also has the potential for significant negative impact on **labour-management relations**. The changing role of the unions may well further diminish their power by changing their role relative to a new decentralised structure. Different people, conditions of work, competencies, and career patterns in each organisation, create a considerable challenge for public service unions that have built their information-bases and expertise on a unified and centralised personnel system. In order to ensure that trade unions maintain their status and power in a changing system it is necessary to increase the skills in negotiating and management for local representatives. This appears to be a growing issue in *the United Kingdom* and has been most evident with respect to local pay bargaining. In *Sweden*, interestingly, extensive decentralisation has not raised these problems. It may be that decades of co-operative labour relations ensure that unions continue to have the information and contacts to interact effectively, and thus mitigate the negative effects surfacing in other countries. While little information is currently available from Member countries on the effects of decentralisation on the relative power of trade unions, it bears consideration on the part of government to ensure that the local unions have access to the means to participate effectively in a decentralised environment.

Managing growth in public service employment levels

In many OECD countries, identifying opportunities for gains in productivity, efficiency and effectiveness has included **assessing the appropriate roles and functions of the public service and the appropriate size of its workforce**. For example, policy-makers may question whether existing functions could be carried out more efficiently in another sector of the economy, or through contractors or other more market-based operating systems. They may also question whether there are opportunities to do away with redundant functions and streamline the public service. In a few countries, addressing these questions has resulted in active redundancy programs, as well as efforts to transfer functions and workers to other sectors of government or the private sector. In several other OECD countries concerned with these issues, however, the direction taken has been much more passive, relying on a combination of natural attrition and hiring freezes to simply reduce overall workforce levels. While each type of workforce reduction programme is put in place with stated goals of reducing costs and enhancing public service efficiency, each also presents its own significant human resource management challenges. Left unaddressed, these challenges may undermine broader public service restructuring activities and, in the most serious cases, impair the capacity of the public service to deliver high quality services.

Several OECD countries have taken a **pro-active approach to staff reductions** through specific reduction targets and use of voluntary and involuntary redundancy programs. Large-scale reductions have been undertaken in *Australia, Canada, New Zealand, Sweden, the United Kingdom* and *the United States*. *Austria, the Czech Republic*, and *Mexico* also report the desire to reduce the public sector workforce making some use of redundancy programs. Active redundancy programs have included financial incentives to resign or retire voluntarily, layoffs, privatisation, commercialisation, or relocating activities to other levels of government. In *the United States* efforts are currently reducing the size of the national public service by 272 900 employees (12.5 per cent reduction), including cutting top management positions by 10 per cent. In *Canada*, a programme to reduce the budget deficit includes cutting 45 000 central government positions (14 per cent reduction). In *the United Kingdom*, the size of the national public service has been reduced by 248 000 (34 per cent) since 1979. The great majority of the reductions have been achieved through a combination of natural attrition and, increasingly since 1992, the use of financial incentives to encourage resignations and early retirement. *Sweden* also continues to engage in large-scale structural changes in its central government and has reduced its workforce by half, a cut of nearly 200 000 jobs, since 1990. In *Sweden* reductions have been most commonly due to transferring functions and workers to public enterprises, private or joint-stock companies, or by transferring functions to lower levels of government.

Several other OECD countries seeking to reduce or freeze public service employment levels, however, are relying on passive means such as **natural attrition combined with recruitment freezes**. In *Belgium*, a general hiring freeze has been in place for more than 10 years and public service organisations continue to rely on natural attrition and some provisions for early retirement. In *Greece*, a freeze on recruitment began in 1989 and is still underway. The freeze is maintained by keeping strict limits on the number of permanent contracts and making extensive use of fixed-term temporary contracts to meet changes in workload demand and to fill skill gaps. Limiting the size of the public service was a major concern in *Finland* where budget and staffing ceilings and restrictions on recruitment resulted in almost no new recruits during the period 1991 through 1994. To avoid layoffs during the reduction period, an internal mobility programme co-ordinated by the *Finnish* Ministry of Finance facilitated contacts between departments and agencies to redeploy excess staff. Curbing growth in staff numbers has been a long-standing policy also in *Japan*, which uses a "total staff number law" to limit new positions.

Challenges raised by staffing limits and reductions

Whether programs to limit or reduce the size of the workforce involve involuntary job loss or simply transfers of jobs to other sectors, such programs are generally controversial within the public service. The amount of political and media attention given to reducing public employment has generated a widespread perception that the jobs of public service workers are at risk and that they are losing the high level of job security that they have enjoyed relative to private sector counterparts. The negative effects of such perceptions on morale, productivity and worker acceptance of public service reform initiatives should not be underestimated. Perceptions regarding loss of job security must be dealt with openly and honestly as a key process issue in any plans to transfer or reduce functions in the public service. Indeed, each approach to staff restructuring (*e.g.* downsizing, privatisation, transfer of function, commercialisation) presents its own significant human resource management challenges regarding method of reorganisation, communication, morale and other process issues which, if not addressed, may seriously hamper the success of reform initiatives.

The need to **invest in training** as part of any programme to limit or reduce staff comes across very clearly from country experiences with such reforms. In the majority of Member countries training is reported as an important cross-cutting strategy in realigning the public service workforce in order to manage with fewer overall resources. Moreover, it is cited as particularly important during staff reductions periods where hiring freezes and voluntary redundancy programs slowly bleed a civil service of new talent and ideas, and where departures are not targeted or controlled resulting in mismatches between the workers on hand and the needs of workplace. Although, as noted earlier, despite the rhetoric training receives little priority and, where it is provided, is often not timely or sufficient to serve a valuable function. In this regard, it is encouraging to note that *Austria, Hungary, Ireland, Norway, Spain* and the *United Kingdom* have reiterated a central commitment to training and skill building in the public service, and in the cases of *Austria, Norway* and the *United Kingdom*, to taking a broad perspective on training by linking training and development to the goals and challenges facing departments and agencies.

Mobility programmes are also being highlighted in the context of programmes to reduce or limit staffing levels as an important tool for mitigating organisational side-effects of reduction programs on staff. *The Netherlands*, for example, is developing a mobility programme in order to combat workforce stagnation, as well as to reward high performers and keep them motivated and interested in maintaining public service careers. *France* reports initiatives underway to merge the complicated system of career structures in the public service to facilitate greater mobility as a tool for multi-skilling and more effective career management. In *Japan*, personnel exchanges are centrally co-ordinated in the public service, and government officials are required to have at least two work experiences at other ministries and agencies, international organisations, etc., before they are promoted to division directors. Particularly where countries are working under the constraints of hiring freezes, mobility programs as means to motivate, train and deploy staff are critical to ensuring that departments and agencies continue to be able to meet productivity and effectiveness goals, despite the lack of new talent (and loss of old talent) in the organisation. Moreover, as with training, mobility exchanges can be a cost-effective means of facilitating exchange of knowledge and skills, as well as a vehicle for building common values and culture.

In general, countries actively pursuing staff reductions are seeking out creative solutions to limiting the cost of redundancy and minimising negative effects on redundant workers. In many of these countries, devoting resources to active assistance to re-employment is an investment based on the fact that workers continue to receive their full salary during the notice period and each month that can be saved by finding new employment for individuals represents real savings for the agency. For example, intensive training programs, partnerships with local unemployment offices, and internal priority re-hiring or placement programs, are just a few of the tools countries are using to help redundant workers find re-employment as quickly as possible. Some countries are also developing partnerships with private sector companies to take on redundant workers and in exchange they receive money to retrain individuals or to pay salaries during the probationary period. *Australia, Canada, Norway, Sweden* and *the United States* offer central resources or programs to assist public service workers in securing new employment before the end of the redundancy notice period. *Sweden's* re-employment activities for workers in the central government appear to be the most pro-active across OECD countries.

Future directions

There is a broad spectrum of human resource management practices across OECD countries, ranging from the more centralised systems of countries such as *France* and *Japan*, to the almost complete devolution of management principles in *New Zealand* and *Sweden*. In general, however, countries faced with the need for major change in response to the challenges posed for managing within limits are migrating away from the command and control management toward a **greater focus on devolution and change management**. In addition to those countries well on the way to devolution, discussed earlier (*i.e. Australia, Denmark, Iceland, the Netherlands, the United Kingdom*), *Canada, Finland, France, Ireland, Norway* and *the United States* have all made some efforts toward devolution of staffing tools and report they are committed to continued efforts in this area. *Italy, Portugal,* and *Spain* have also reported a desire to increasing management flexibilities, especially in staffing and deployment. This shift is taking place largely because command and control management is neither fast enough nor flexible enough to keep pace with the changing environment of the public services in most Member countries. There is a growing recognition that success in implementing change requires creativity and innovation in finding new ways to motivate staff and re-align the workplace at the operational level and, moreover, that such change depends more on values and leadership than on compliance with rules and regulations.

Successfully linking human resource management strategies such as devolution or downsizing to achieving greater productivity and efficiency, however, depends on the ability of organisations to **integrate human resource management strategies into core business planning activities**. Yet, despite the importance of ensuring that workers are skilled and motivated to achieve organisational outcomes, actual strategies to link principles of human resource management into performance targets, resource allocations, or agency "vision" statements are still not common. Managerial devolution implies a much closer integration of human resource management with organisational goals and strategies than has been typical of public service organisations in recent decades. This is particularly important with regard to public service goals to gain higher levels of performance and efficiency with fewer resources, where there is much pressure to ensure that people resources are targeted in the best ways to contribute directly to organisational priorities. The **strategic management of workers** is a key, though currently insufficiently recognised, issue for successfully governing within limits.

Institutional problems with successfully linking human resource management to strategic planning is symptomatic of a larger problem facing many public service organisations – the need for managers to be skilled in the people-side of managing change. One of the more insidious side effects to efforts to push for efficiency in terms of leaner and more effective public services is the negative effects these changes are having on **motivation and morale** of the public workers – a problem common to many Member countries. Comments in this area appear to distil down to a few factors contributing to a level of morale and motivation described often as "low" or "worrying". These factors include change fatigue, demeaning public service workers by the media and politicians, and insecurity on the part of workers toward in the new work environment. As pressures increase for reform and measurable gains in effectiveness and efficiency, political leaders and top civil servants will continue to face the challenge of ensuring that the public service does not tear down its workforce, which is indeed its single greatest resource.

Programmes to limit the size of the public sector workforce will also continue to present both organisational and people management challenges to public service organisations. Issues of **career planning and motivation** in workforces which are stagnant rather than dynamic, and offering only limited career potential, will test managers to find creative uses for existing systems in order to motivate workers and ensure the public service performs to its potential. In addition, the **financial implications of redundancy** are significant in terms of severance costs and the organisational costs of supporting redundant workers in finding new employment. Some countries report that the combination of resource and morale problems are forcing them to consider easing workforce reduction efforts. Easing reductions, however, is at odds with internal and external pressures to continue to pursue efficiency reforms in the public service. Indeed, the future direction of organisational reform priorities may hinge on the decisions made with regard to the **policy and financial trade-offs** between slowing reform efforts aimed at efficiency and effectiveness, versus continuing pressure for ever greater efficiency gains but reducing the associated costs, such as those currently provided to support redundant workers. In the near-term, such questions can be expected to appear on the public management agenda in many OECD countries.

Principles for successful human resource management strategies

The variety of approaches to linking human resource management to the challenge of governing within limits discussed in the previous sections reinforce several cross-cutting principles for successfully linking human resource management reforms to broader public service reforms.

- Implement strategies for structural change in tandem with strategies for addressing how public service workers will be affected by changes in the workplace and how workers can best be brought along the reform path.

- Maintain a long-term perspective in implementing, investing in, and sustaining changes in the structure of the workplace and the workforce.

- Protect the capacity of the public service to recruit and retain the highest quality workers by ensuring that the needs of organisations and the broader public service are balanced with the needs of the workers.

The experiences of Members engaged in human resource management reform, indicate that simply rearranging the internal structures of the public service workplace – rules, regulations and organisational hierarchies or structures – is not sufficient to ensure the sustained changes in behaviour required to achieve the gains sought through the reforms. Strategies for structural change must occur in tandem with strategies for addressing how the people who carry out the business of government will be affected by changes in the workplace and what policies and programs must be put forward so that each group can best be brought along to achieve the desired outcomes. Strategic use of staffing tools is an important element in helping organisations maximise internal gains in efficiency and effectiveness. Key principles include:

- **Devolved budgeting** for agency resources, including human resources, within a tight accountability and resource framework, is an essential part of meaningful devolution of authority to line managers. It also offers a strong incentive to improve overall resource management, including managing people, to achieve performance goals.

- Link **performance appraisal** to better career management for staff at all levels. Where staff are required to adapt to new jobs and roles by necessity rather than choice, the result may be reduced motivation and productivity. Career development, mobility, training, and performance management may help managers and workers find a mutually beneficial path toward greater productivity.

- Ensure departments and agencies have the resources and the incentives to invest in **training and development** to support all forms of organisational change. Moreover, training should be viewed as an investment in promoting change and new organisational culture, rather than simply an expense to fix basic skill problems.

- **Mobility** should be viewed, like training, as an important management tool for promoting change, exchanging ideas and experiences, and providing opportunities in stagnant workforce environments. It is recognised, however, that the desire for mobility may vary significantly by country based on the organisational structure and culture of the public service.

– **Career management** should promote skill building in line with those cultivated in the private sector. Employers can assist workers in "self managing" careers by helping them measure and expand their job competencies, and by offering mobility paths for lateral and vertical career opportunities. The public service benefits through better qualified workers and by ensuring its workforce is more flexible in the overall labour market – an important factor where public services are moving away from a life-long career model.

Effective implementation strategies require a long-term perspective. In the public service, however, the desire on the parts of political leaders, media and general public for short-term financial and service gains, instead, tend to support reforms implemented in a "revolutionary" rather than an "evolutionary" way. Where this is the case, workers must adopt a siege mentality to find the momentum to keep up with a rapidly and radically changing environment. While the workplace may support such activity for a short-time, the most likely result is a return to original patterns once the intense pressure is off. In several OECD countries, decades of destructive reform cycles, with promising human resource management strategies ending in few real changes, can often be linked to revolutionary reform measures which failed to focus sufficiently on implementation or mechanisms to sustain the changes over the long-term. Key principles for promote and sustaining changes in behaviour sought by reforms, including strategies to:

– Maintain a **long-term perspective** in building human resource management reform into the overall priorities of the public service. Capacity to sustain change depends, in part, on ensuring that reforms do not change or cut too much too fast, and allow time and space for workers to "catch up" psychologically and in their skills with changes occurring in the work.

– Integrate human resource management policies and reforms into **core business planning activities** in departments and agencies. Recognising human resource management as a strategic tool for planning and carrying out organisational performance goals is one sure way to send a message to managers about the importance of mastering resource management skills to be an effective manager and a contributor to the output of the agency.

– Cultivating **leadership** and an ethos of change within the management. There is a tendency to think that having selected and recruited managers, the difficult part is done. In fact, the key task lies in instilling culture and values through development. Where managers are successfully integrated into the culture, authorities can be devolved secure in the knowledge that managers will make decisions within the shared value framework.

Thinking in the long term, a crucial element in the success of public sector reforms rests on the capacity of governments to continue to attract and retain the high quality workers needed to achieve productivity and efficiency goals sought by reforms. In this regard, policy-makers and managers alike must ensure that the needs of the organisation and the broader public service are balanced with the needs of the workers. This balance may require, for example, new strategies aimed at ensuring workers have rewarding career and advancement opportunities despite streamlined staffing structures; preserving morale and motivation in times of rapid change and job insecurity; communicating and working effectively with workers and their union representatives in ensuring worker "ownership" of a change agenda; and, where there is a need to make the workplace smaller, finding ways to support individuals in finding new employment while preserving the need of the organisation to achieve real savings and staff reductions. Several countries that have engaged in large-scale restructuring and staff reductions emphasise the need for protecting the commitment and loyalty of the workforce by treating all workers fairly, openly and honestly during periods of change and restructuring, including:

– In addition to **programs to assist redundant workers, strategies must support and train the *remaining* workforce**, including for example, deployment, mobility, training, development, or even recruitment, where needed. Moreover, priority should be given, where possible, to changing or enhancing the skills of the existing workforce to maximise flexibility and minimise redundancies.

– Setting a good example during downsizing and restructuring for **dealing fairly and openly with all staff** is crucial in staff motivation and morale over the longer-term. Country experiences in this regard also highlight the principle that how a department or agency deals with redundant staff sends a strong message to staff who remain about the organisation's true commitment to its people.

– **Effective communication** between management, workers and their union representatives is a key element in change management for preserving motivation and morale, for securing worker support and participation in reforms over the long-term, and in minimising the loss of productivity and efficiency that inevitably follows major reforms and organisational upsets.

The changes in human resource management policies and practices designed to help public service managers meet the challenge of "governing within limits" are also changing the nature of the public service workplace and content of public service careers. Many of these changes bode well for public servants, increasing opportunities for creativity, flexibility and participation in the way the work of the public service is carried out. However, widespread concerns about falling morale indicate these changes are not without their darker sides. Shifts in the tenure of public service employment, the balance of labour-management relations, limited career mobility, and overall uncertainty, are a few of the difficult issues in managing the public service workforce. Combating the downsides of changing career structures may require, for example, shifting the career focus from one of lifetime tenure and seniority-based career growth, to a focus on performance, career development, mobility and opportunities in exchange for more interesting work and challenges. Perhaps most importantly, however, the public service from the highest levels must cultivate the leadership and people-management skills discussed above as the foundation of a new workplace culture. These factors, in combination, amount to a **new psychological "contract" for public service workers** providing a much needed anchor in the otherwise turbulent environment of the public service workplace. Such an anchor is, in the current environment of change, reform and continuous improvement, perhaps the most important factor in ensuring the commitment and success of the public service's most important resource – its people – in meeting the challenges of governing within limits.

4. MANAGING GOVERNMENT REGULATION WITHIN LIMITS

Governments are today thinking in terms of "limits" to their activities, a concept with broad implications for the definition, prioritisation, and resolution of problems. Discussions of "limits" usually concern direct government expenditures, measured in terms of taxes, expenditures, and public employment. However, the concepts and concerns apply just as well to government regulation, which has expanded continuously in almost all OECD countries since the 1930s without any "limits", or indeed any (except rudimentary) capacities in governments to count costs, to manage limits, or even to decide what the limits should be.

Today, regulatory costs are the least controlled and least accountable among government costs. Most governments have no idea how much of their national wealth they are spending through regulation. Yet there is widespread agreement among businesses, citizens, and administrations from almost every OECD country that the volume and complexity of new regulations from all levels of government reached unprecedented levels in the 1980s, and that they continue to increase. At political and public levels, debates centre around the vivid themes of "regulatory inflation", and "the legal explosion". As the director of regulatory reform in *Canada* noted, "there seems to be no natural limit to the potential demand for regulatory intervention" (Martin, 1992). A *United States* economist wrote in 1995, "We are in the midst of a major escalation in the cost of regulation, a trend that in some ways represents the exercise of power without accountability" (Hopkins, 1995*a*).

These concerns about regulation suggest that it is appropriate to consider how the governing within limits debate is important for regulation. In doing that, this section attempts to answer three key questions:

i) **Is there too much regulation?** It is impossible to say in the abstract if there is "too much" regulation, because it is possible that any particular amount of regulation could be justified by benefits. However, substantial empirical evidence suggests that much regulation is not justified by its costs in terms of economic performance, that regulatory costs are high and undisciplined, and that the volume of regulation is causing problems for governments and businesses alike – therefore, it is reasonable to conclude that there *is* too much poor-quality regulation in OECD countries.

ii) **What are the implications for managing regulation within limits?** There is great potential for cost-savings through regulatory management programs. Regulatory costs should be contained through a multi-part strategy that focuses on improving the quality of regulations where they are justified by benefits, finding cost-effective alternatives to regulation, and deregulating in sectors where the evidence shows that markets work better.

iii) **What are the implications for the "limits to government" debate?** Strategies for governing within limits should always consider the global costs of government, including regulatory costs, within the "limits" being controlled. This will require as a first step that regulatory costs be made visible.

Is *there too much regulation?*

A great deal of the contentiousness of the political debate centres around this intriguing question. Governments from across the political spectrum have repeatedly expressed concern that the answer is "almost certainly".

– "The total volume of our legal rules and regulations is continuously increasing; this tendency, whose adverse effects are well known, must be curbed… " warned the *French* Prime Minister in 1987, a situation that by 1992 had turned into a "regulatory hemorrhage" according to the *French Conseil d'État*.

– In the *United Kingdom*, the Thatcher Government declared, "there is no doubt that we suffer from the sheer weight of legislation and controls. We want less – and better – regulation" (Government of the United Kingdom, 1985, p. 2).

– In *Sweden*, the government noted in 1985 that simpler and fewer rules were necessary for the regulatory system to operate as intended.

– The *Portuguese* government stated in 1990 that reform was needed to stem an "excessive production of rules".

– In 1988, the *Japanese* government identified reduction of regulation and government instructions as a top priority of administrative reform. In 1990, the Japanese Council, the second PCPAR (the Provisional Councils for the Promotion of Administrative Reform) proposed a goal of reducing regulations "to essentially half their present level".

– "At what point does regulation break the back of economic competitiveness?" the *Canadian* President of the Treasury Board asked in 1992, just before a critical Parliamentary inquiry reported "a vast expansion" in *Canadian* regulation.

– "Small business feels *besieged* by Government demands, and the psychological impact of the burden cannot be over-estimated, " a Small Business Deregulation Task Force in *Australia* reported in 1996, responding to a government request for measures to reduce burdens on small businesses by 50 per cent (Commonwealth of Australia, 1996).

– In 1996, the Irish Government stated that a "country which regulates badly puts itself at a serious economic disadvantage *vis-à-vis* its competitors" (Government of Ireland, 1996, p. 12).

To explore this question meaningfully, however, we need a clearer understanding of what is meant by "too much". Is there a metric we can use to judge how much regulation there is? Almost always, when people discuss this issue, they mean either the volume of regulation or the costs of regulation, both of which are partial measures, but the second less so than the first.

Volume of regulation

A popular approach in political discourse to discussing regulatory expansion is the use of graphic images of quantity. This metric is usually quantified in terms of pages of regulation, either in total or average length of individual regulations, or even in linear meters of rules. Can we use these kinds of measures to understand the question of regulatory volume more precisely? Some tentative measures are available:

- In the *United Kingdom*, the basic legal reference to company law increased from under 500 pages in 1980 to over 3 500 pages in 1991, a seven-fold increase. In the tax area, the average length of the annual Finance Act increased from 145 pages in 1975-1979 to 336 pages in 1988-1992, a 230 per cent increase (Government of the United Kingdom, 1975-1992).

- In *France*, the size of the *Official Gazette*, where regulations are published, more than doubled from 1976 to 1990. The annual production of new laws increased by 35 per cent from 1960 to 1990, and of decrees by 20 to 25 per cent. The average length of French laws increased from 93 lines in 1950 to over 220 in 1991 (*Conseil d'État*, 1992).

- In the *United States*, the comprehensive Code of Federal Regulations swelled from 54 834 pages in 1970 to over 138 000 pages by 1995.[3]

- The number of *Finnish* laws and decrees rose from 1 843 in 1980 to 2 915 in 1993, an increase of over 50 per cent, while the number of pages of laws and decrees increased by more than 100 per cent in the same period, revealing increases in both number and even more in length of rules.

- *Australia* experienced a doubling in subordinate legislation in the eight years from 1982 to 1990.

- A computer metric is cited in *Canada*, where, from 1978 to 1996, the volume of federal regulations doubled to 185 megabytes of computer storage (Martin and Iwankow, 1996).

These kinds of measures of numbers of laws and page lengths indicate, broadly, the direction and magnitude of regulatory expansion, though they can certainly be criticised on many grounds. The number of new regulations issued per year, for example, does not reveal whether those new rules are genuinely new or are revisions to existing regulations, or whether they add new requirements or eliminate old requirements. Most important, these figures reveal nothing about the quality of regulation: its costs or benefits, efficiency, cost-effectiveness, and so forth. New regulations can improve efficiency – in the United Kingdom, for example, privatisation of state-owned monopolies required large quantities of new regulations to foster competition in the new markets and meet social concerns. This is an example of "desirable inflation". Regulatory policy experts from OECD countries agreed at an OECD meeting in 1995 that, while they are politically popular, volume measures are not the real point of interest. and could be misused to divert attention from more important issues such as the need for regulation and the effectiveness of regulation.

Yet, although they are crude and insufficient as the basis for a programme to limit regulation, such measures in Member countries suggest that **regulatory expansion is genuine, widespread, and rapid**, and has three aspects: increases can be found in (*i*) the number of regulatory instruments issued by all levels of government; (*ii*) the average length of regulatory instruments; and (*iii*) an increasing rate of revision of regulations. (The OECD has previously used the term "regulatory inflation" to describe the steady expansion of regulation.) A report issued by the *French Conseil d'État* drew attention to these three aspects:

> "…inflationary growth of requirements and rules […] are a reality […] Above all, the figures for *France* […] do not tell the whole story, since they omit the mass of Ministerial, Prefectoral and Municipal Orders, decisions by "independent administrative authorities", central and local government circulars and instruments – not to mention the spate of regulations and circulars from European institutions […] what is more, length as well as numbers must be considered […] citizens today are worried not only because there are so many regulations, but also because those regulations change so quickly […] laws have a shorter and shorter lifetime…"

> *(Conseil d'État, 1992)*

Cost of regulation

The fiscal and economic costs of regulation are considerably closer to the issues of real interest in the "limits" debate. Governments have not traditionally considered regulatory costs as worth much attention. As recently as 1993, a government official in one OECD country responded, when asked about the cost of an environmental law: "It's a legal requirement, so the costs are not important".[4] But attitudes have changed enormously. Awareness of the effects of regulation on economic performance began to grow in the late 1970s, entered political debates in the 1980s, and by the 1990s most OECD countries had launched programs to control regulatory costs.

Emphasis on regulatory costs does not suggest that benefits are not important. Rather, the emphasis on regulatory costs follows the same logic used in budgeting: the amount of resources that can be used to satisfy regulatory requirements is inherently limited, but there is no reason to limit benefits (on the contrary, benefits should be maximised). Therefore, it is important to restrain costs and not benefits. Of course, many regulations produce more benefits than costs, and we would want to maximise those regulations.

Regulatory cost control programs in different countries are different in approach and objective, in part because governments have chosen to be concerned about different kinds of costs. Regulatory costs have four main components:

– Fiscal costs to government – the cost of administering the regulatory system itself, including development, compliance, and adjudication. This is the smallest but most visible cost of regulation, and the cost of great concern in most programs to control costs. In 1992, the minister responsible for the federal budget in *Canada* found "the cost of implementing regulation to be high… the money is simply not there anymore" (Canada House of Commons, 1992). Most countries have not produced measures of their expenditures on developing and administering regulations. In the *United States*, where a private sector body produces annual figures, on-budget regulatory costs increased substantially after 1970. Administrative on-budget costs of federal regulatory activities rose from $3.4 billion in 1970 to over $15.6 billion by 1995. Staffing of these agencies rose from 71 000 in 1970 to 133 000 in 1995 (see Table 1).

– Administrative and paperwork costs for businesses and citizens (operating costs). For most people, the scale of these costs comes as a surprise. If these studies can be extrapolated, for example, the amount that businesses and citizens spend on government paperwork every year is twice as much as the total wealth produced by the entire farming sector in OECD countries (1.7 per cent of GDP).

– Capital costs of compliance – Capital investment costs for businesses and citizens, that is, the costs of buying new equipment, reconfiguring production processes, relocating, and so forth. These are sometimes added to administrative costs of regulations to produce an estimate of total regulatory compliance costs. Total compliance costs are large, and may be climbing. Time-series data are available from only country: in the *United States*, total regulatory compli-ance costs are projected to climb to more than $700 billion annually by the year 2000 (see Figure 1), or about 10 per cent of GDP (Hopkins, 1996). Less complete estimates of regulatory compliance costs from *Canada* and *Australia* are also in the range of 10 per cent of GDP. Interpretation of these numbers must be done cautiously, since some fraction of the total cost is transfer costs, and only part represent dead-weight losses. But much of this cost represents investments diverted from production to government programmes, which may indeed be a wise investment, but one that is rarely assessed against benefits or opportunity costs by regulators.

– Indirect costs in the economy as a result of reduced competition and innovation, and hence slowed investment, output, structural adjustment and productivity growth. A growing body of evidence suggests that the greatest costs of regulation are found not in static effects on resource allocation, but in these dynamic effects. Table 1 shows a number of methods by which such effects have been assessed, both in terms of efficiency losses under current regulatory regimes and gains after reform.

Table 1 summarises the results of a number of selected studies of the four components of regulatory costs. There are three clear messages from this table. The clearest message is that **regulatory costs matter**. They are large, and increase as one progresses through the four categories. It is difficult to avoid concluding that a country that regulates poorly can do substantial and lasting damage to its economic performance and quality of life.

This leads us to the second message: the sheer magnitude of costs suggests that **there is potential for significant cost-savings from regulatory reform**.

The third message is that **most regulatory costs are not well studied in most countries**. Most governments have little understanding of the magnitude and scope of the costs of their regulations, which amplifies the difficulties of designing effective reform programmes.

Weaknesses of cost estimates

Among the many weaknesses of these data and indicators is that they are partial – they do not represent the full picture of regulatory activity at all levels of government. As regulatory competences are shifted among national, international, and subnational institutions, the relative importance of different levels changes. A decline at the national level, for example, can be offset by increases at other levels, and vice-versa. In general, the costs of regulations depend on many variables that are constantly changing – technology, trade opportunities, consumer demand. No static picture can be accurate. Hence, it is very difficult to generate a complete picture of the volume or cost of regulation in any country, much less data that are comparable between countries or over time.

However, the importance of the data reported in Table 1 is not that it is precise, but that an expanding body of evidence shows that regulatory costs are a significant component of the total cost of government, are growing steadily in many areas, and that reform can have important benefits.

Quality of regulation

We now know that **there is a great deal of regulation, that it costs a great deal, and that in some areas it is growing rapidly**. But these measures of the cost and volume of regulation, while suggestive of problems, do not tell us whether there is "too much" regulation, just as it is impossible

◆ Graph 1. **Annual US regulatory compliance costs**

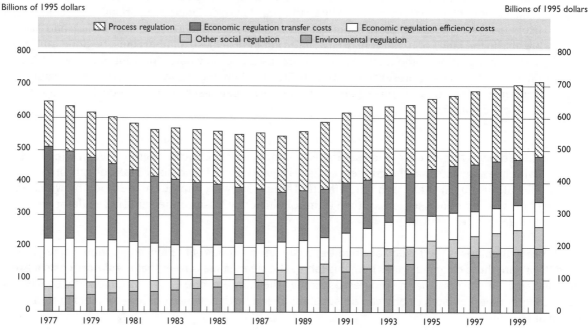

Billions of 1995 dollars

Billions of 1995 dollars

Source: Hopkins, 1995b.

to say in the abstract if there is "too much" taxation. The key tests, rather, are: **Are regulatory costs justified by benefits? Does regulatory intervention produce more social and economic benefits than would alternatives? Are regulations designed to achieve policy objectives at lowest cost?** In other words, the key issues center around broader concepts of the *quality* of regulation, rather than partial measures of quantity and cost. These questions are neutral: they can as easily identify where there is too little regulation as too much.

Now we can rephrase the central question more precisely: Do existing regulations meet these quality tests? If not, there is "too much" regulation. We can get a sense of how well regulation meets these tests by looking at its effects in three areas: effects on economic performance; effects on government administration; and effects on the legal system and rule of law.

Effects on economic performance

An efficient and well-functioning regulatory system supports national economic performance in many ways – defining property rights in socially efficient ways, protecting competition, correcting market failures, and providing legitimacy for market systems that must be seen as fair and equitable.

But there is strong evidence that governments often regulate economic activities badly, reducing national wealth. Consider, for example, the success of some countries reported in Table 1 in improving economic performance through regulatory reform. Reform that improves market competition has generally resulted in lower costs and prices for consumers and for user industries. Work currently under way in the OECD suggests that more efficient regulatory regimes in key infrastructure sectors could boost GDP by up to several percentage points, depending on current productivity levels. The nature of some needed reforms – enhancing competition in some sectors, for example – is suggested in Table 1. However, specific policy prescriptions for reform would have to be developed from case to case, because the nature of the regulatory costs, benefits, and implications for economic performance differ. A point that deserves considerable attention is that the costs of non-action are increasing – delayed reform means more costly reform.

Where monopolies or other market failures persist, governments have a strong case for regulation. But privatisation of public monopolies within regulatory frameworks providing incentives for innovation and productivity improvements have produced impressive gains. A variety of improved regulatory techniques can also boost efficiency when competition is not present. Compared to traditional rate-of-return regulation, price cap regulation appears to substantially increase productive efficiency and lead to more rapid diffusion of new technology.

With respect to regulatory distortion of international competition in goods and services, a growing body of evidence suggests that here, too, reforms – not only deregulation, but also co-operative regulatory approaches across national borders, including through multilateral trading regimes – can reduce costs.

There is also evidence that governments may unnecessarily harm economic activity when they use regulations to produce important social benefits in such areas as environmental and consumer protection, health and safety, and labour protections. The economic effects of these regulations are often incidental or even unanticipated, but they are nonetheless real and can be substantial. As Table 1 suggests, direct compliance costs are high, with negative effects on business formation and expansion. SMEs seem to be harder hit. Compliance costs also may increase product prices, and therefore reduce demand, job creation, and expansion. Indirect costs can be even more important. Product standards that differ even slightly among countries can protect domestic markets for single suppliers. Permits and licences intended to protect the public can delay investment decisions and increase uncertainty, reducing investment levels.

This is doubly tragic, because by squandering the scarce resources available for public goods, governments also reduce their ability to protect the environment, worker safety, and other social concerns. In many cases, social objectives can be achieved at lower cost by changing regulatory approaches, that is, by **using more efficient means to intervene in markets**. A variety of tools are available, such as flexible "performance regulation" that sets goals for enterprises, rather than detailing how enterprises are to achieve those goals. Regulators can also rely less on rules and more on other kinds of incentives. Emission trading and effluent fees can simultaneously increase environmental protection and reduce its costs. Many governments are also simplifying regulatory processes to cut costs to businesses and to themselves.

The direct and indirect effects of regulation on international competitiveness have concerned many governments. Direct evidence linking regulatory costs and competitiveness is weak, but it is logical that regulation that increases production costs for domestic producers could affect the international competitiveness of individual enterprises. Regulation that reduces competition or otherwise discourages innovation can weaken entire industries as rivals become leaner and more efficient. This point was made recently by representatives of European businesses:

> "The United States and Japan are leaving Europe behind in new high growth industries. Product market restrictions and regulations and labour market rigidity are the key reasons why the United States and Japan are stealing the lead on Europe and why job creation in Europe is lagging behind."
>
> (*Anglo-German Deregulation Group*, 1995)

The success of regulatory reform in some countries has fanned competitiveness anxieties: "The relative position of European companies will decline as *other* OECD countries lighten their regulatory burdens," a business federation warned in 1995 (UNICE, 1995, p. ii). Alarmingly, the government solution to regulation that reduces national competitiveness may not be *less* regulation, but *more*: regulatory barriers to trade may be erected to protect declining national industries. This could lead to a vicious circle in which bad regulation produces more bad regulation.

Effects on government administration and regulatory quality

There is very little information on how regulatory administrations are coping with regulatory inflation on a day-to-day basis. But it is odd that while the volume of regulations has doubled or tripled in many countries, the number of regulatory development and enforcement staff have not increased as much, or in some areas have decreased. In the *United States*, for example, staffing in regulatory agencies rose by 72 per cent from 1970 to 1992, but regulatory volume rose by 120 per cent. There are two possibilities: either regulatory administrators are more productive, or they are increasingly overloaded and producing regulatory outputs of lower quality.

What is the connection between regulatory expansion and the quality of regulation? Do increases in the rate of revision of laws mean that regulators are making more mistakes? If so, why? Or do more revisions indicate that regulators are more responsive to technological change? Are regulators so burdened with regulatory production that they spend too little time on quality control, evaluation, and impact analysis? Are longer laws so complex and so full of ambiguous legal criteria and, at the same time, minor details, that they are hard to implement? A prominent *German* jurist famously complained in 1987 that the *German* competition law was "no longer a law, but a novel" and impossible to put into effect (Teubner, 1987, p. 22).

There is evidence both for and against a decline in the quality of regulation. On the one hand, as the *French Conseil d'État* suggested, more mistakes are being produced by hasty and ill-considered regulation, and constant corrections are burdening the system even more. Too, regulators in all OECD countries spend very little time evaluating or reviewing or updating existing regulations. The lack of effort in this area is typically blamed on lack of resources, but that seems to be simply a priority issue that places production of new regulations above improvement of existing regulations. On the other hand, economic regulations in many sectors have been reformed over the past 15 years. Many OECD countries have developed systems of regulatory analysis and public consultation for new regulations, and the empirical basis for new regulations is probably improving in these countries. It is interesting that these systems have also seemed to slow the rate of growth of new regulations in some countries, suggesting that a resource trade-off is indeed occurring. Given these opposing factors and the lack of information, it is difficult to reach a global conclusion about whether the quality of regulatory outputs is increasing or decreasing. But it is an important question. Today's economic and social environment demands higher quality regulations than ever before, and it is worrisome that we have so few measures of regulatory quality to support reforms.

It is also possible that regulatory expansion would have the effect of making enforcement more inconsistent and unpredictable. Despite the myth that all laws are equal, regulators would be forced to select "regulatory priorities" that would change over time. The regulated public would be faced with seemingly capricious demands that varied from inspector to inspector and from week to week. Is there a trend in this direction? Again, we have little information on whether enforcement is getting better or worse.

Effects of regulatory inflation on the legal system and rule of law

The word "inflation" is interesting because it suggests that more frequent use of regulation progressively devalues its effectiveness. This point was made explicitly by the *French Conseil d'État*: "Inflation equals devaluation: when the law is long-winded, citizens listen with only half an ear." Concerns have been explicit that governments may be approaching the practical limits of the regulatory state. "Has juridification today already reached its 'limits of growth'?" asked a German legal philosopher in 1987 (Teubner, 1987, p. 19).

One problem is that new regulations might reduce attention to, or compliance with, other regulations. There is some empirical evidence to support this fear. A study of nursing home regulation in *Australia* and the *United States* found that the quality of care was higher with flexible outcome-oriented *Australian* regulations (numbering 31) than with detailed input-oriented *American* regulations (numbering over 500). The

U*nited States* system, concluded the analysts, "ended up with a complex set of standards which no one, inspectors included, can keep in their heads or consistently monitor" (Braithwaite, 1993) One reason for this is that those regulated, particularly small businesses, may find it simply impossible to keep track of all regulatory obligations. All too often, governments do not respect the practical limitations of the private sector in understanding and responding to rules.

Implicit here is the idea that society has a "saturation" point for regulations, that is, a threshold of quantity or burden beyond which the benefits of new regulations are exceeded by the damage they cause to the effectiveness and compliance level of the regulatory system as a whole. Passing the "saturation" point will result in falling respect for laws and regulations, in lower compliance rates generally, and in a reduced ability of the State to carry out policy. Clearly, different societies are prepared to live with different quantities of regulation. But changing external pressures, such as globalisation, and internal pressures, such as changing values of self-reliance, can change the capacity of societies to tolerate regulation. And even the most regulation-tolerant societies appear today to be stretching the limits, if one uses as an indicator the frequency of business and government complaints about the volume and complexity of regulations.

Carried far enough, these concerns lead to the conclusion that nothing less than the rule of law might be at stake. Widespread noncompliance induces contempt for the law and social equality. The present rate of growth of rules will lead to over-regulated societies in which complete compliance with the law is impossible, and citizens and governments will choose which rules to obey and to enforce. The *French Conseil d'Etat* has warned that citizens might be divided into classes: "the few who can afford expert advice on how to exploit to the full the subtleties of the law, and everyone else, hopelessly lost in the legislative maze, with no recourse to law" (*Conseil d'État*, 1992, p. 21).

Conclusions

Many regulations in OECD countries do not meet the quality tests suggested above. There is ample evidence that governments can do better in regulating economic activities. Continued regulatory expansion without adequate controls threatens to erode the relationship between citizens and the law, and the effectiveness and capacity of governments to carry out policy. **We can conclude that much regulation is of poor quality, that aggregate effects of regulatory inflation are negative, and hence that there is too much regulation. Efforts to manage regulatory limits are justified.** This is hardly a surprising conclusion for many enterprises in the private sector, who have long felt overwhelmed by the growing volume and complexity of rules with which they are faced.

What are the implications for managing regulation within limits?

Regulatory reform has already incorporated a good deal of the logic of limits. Since the 1980s, attempts have been under way in most OECD countries to bring regulatory activities within a framework of disciplines and controls. Most reform efforts are today directed at creating more efficient, flexible, and effective regulations. This emphasis on regulatory quality led in March 1995 to the adoption by the Council of the OECD of a **Recommendation on Improving the Quality of Government Regulation**, the first international standard on regulatory quality.[5]

This brings us to an important point in the debate about regulation: just as managing government within limits does not mean dismantling government, managing regulation within limits does not mean deregulation. All countries with major reform programs emphasize the balance between regulation and deregulation, as suggested by the political slogans that guide the programmes:

– *Australia*: "Minimum effective regulation".
– *Canada*: "Regulating smarter".

- *Japan*: "Freedom in principle, regulation as an exception".
- *United States*: "The American people deserve a regulatory system that works for them, not against them".
- *European Union*: "Less action, but better action".

At its best, managing within limits means an emphasis on quality, on maximum effectiveness with minimum cost, on regulation that balances multiple goals such as environmental protection and international competitiveness. This must be achieved in an environment where the pressures for more regulation are strong, and public appetite for new protections has not abated. The only response, as OECD governments have realised, is development of **a new management framework to discipline and control regulation**. What are the elements of such a framework?

Strengthening central management of regulatory development. Regulatory reform cannot be left entirely to regulators, just as budget decisions are not left to programme offices. Instead, reform must be a shared responsibility between central regulatory managers, who protect global values of regulatory quality, and regulators pursuing specific policy goals. There is increasing appeal to linking regulatory reform to government-wide principles of competition, job creation, and trade. Whatever institutional approach is used, experiences in OECD countries show no exceptions to the general rule that reform will fail if it is left entirely to regulators, but will also fail if it is too centralised.

In many OECD countries, specialised regulatory reform units have become a permanent part of public sector management. Although their functions and authorities continue to evolve as reformers seek more effective approaches, these units have developed a set of skills and experiences of great value to modern government. Further, the systematic processes of regulatory monitoring, tracking, and oversight established since 1980 enable governments to detect regulatory problems earlier, and to move more quickly in response. These bodies have produced regulatory systems that are more co-ordinated and coherent, and also – this is a crucial point – more manageable and responsive in helping OECD countries meet evolving challenges.

Regulatory impact analysis (RIA) is probably the single most effective process reform for reducing the cost of new regulations. Few countries have comprehensive programs of regulatory cost assessment, and no OECD country has a programme in place to monitor and assess aggregate regulatory costs. This means that in most cases there is no better way than regulation to hide the true costs of policies, which has obvious implications for budget-cutters seeking new ways to fund programs. Improving the empirical basis for regulatory decisions through impact analysis of new regulatory proposals is a popular reform strategy. By 1996, more than half of OECD countries had adopted RIA programs of one sort or another, up from one or two in 1980, and an increasing proportion of laws and other regulations affecting citizens are being shaped in part by various forms of RIA. In 1995, governments in all OECD countries agreed to use techniques such as RIA to improve the quality of new regulations (OECD, 1995).

RIA comes in many forms that reflect the varying concerns of governments with various components of regulatory cost. Some countries assess direct business impacts; others, administrative and paperwork burdens. Others use full-fledged benefit-cost analysis based on social welfare theories. In all cases, however, the purpose is to improve understanding of real-world impacts of government action, including both benefits and costs of action. This signals a growing concern about efficiency, both with respect to the private sector and to the operation of governments themselves. High-quality regulation is increasingly seen as that which pursues efficient policies as cost-effectively as possible. Depending on how it is used, RIA can inform the decision process about the efficiency of the policy, and about the cost-effectiveness of the instruments.

Has RIA been effective in reducing regulatory costs? There is nearly universal agreement among regulatory reform offices that RIA, when it is done well, improves the cost-effectiveness of regulatory decisions (see OECD, 1997c). In 1987, for example, the *United States* Environmental Protection Agency evaluated 15 RIAs, and found that they cost $10 million to conduct but resulted in revisions to regulations with estimated net benefits of about $10 billion, or a benefit-cost ratio of about 1 000 to 1 (United States

Environmental Protection Agency, 1987). RIA contributes to a "cultural shift" whereby regulators become more aware of the costs of action, and more ready to adapt decisions to reduce costs. RIA also improves the transparency of decisions, and enhances consultation and participation of affected groups, thereby adding an empirical dimension to consensus and political decision methods.

Yet positive views are balanced by evidence of massive non-compliance and quality problems in RIA, and it is clear that governments have not invested resources in building skills and management frameworks necessary for high-quality analysis. Governments met at the OECD in May 1996 to examine best practices for improving the effectiveness of RIA programs (OECD, 1997*c*).

Continual review and upgrading of existing regulations is essential to eliminate unneeded regulations that accumulate over time, and to reduce the drag of outdated regulations on economic and social adjustment. *Sweden*'s famous guillotine rule of 1986 eliminated at one stroke hundreds of outdated regulations. In particular, systematic review and evaluation of rules is needed to identify those with undesirable effects on trade and competition. Such reviews should support targeted deregulation programs, particularly for economic regulations in the telecommunications, transport, and energy sectors, where technological change is quickening and product cycles are shortening. Staged repeals, review clauses and sunsetting might be other strategies that deserve a fresh look.

Australia launched in 1996 a national programme of review based on competition policy principles that is perhaps the most ambitious in OECD countries, but many countries have carried out *ad hoc* reviews of business regulations. In most cases, reformers have claimed substantial savings from identifying and revising inefficient regulations (in *Australia*, annual gains of 5.5 per cent of GDP, and A$ 1 500 per household) (Commonwealth of Australia, 1995).

Increasing transparency in the regulatory process is another important strategy to offset the tendency to pass invisible costs to the private sector. Transparency is also useful in controlling vested interests. A strong trend toward renewal and expansion of public consultation in regulatory development is under way in OECD countries. Much has been invested in efforts to make more information available to the public, to listen to a wider range of interests, to obtain more and better information from affected parties, and to be more responsive to what is heard. A well-designed and implemented consultation programme can contribute to higher-quality regulations, the identification of more effective alternatives, lower costs to businesses and administration, better compliance, and faster regulatory responses to changing conditions. Yet effective consultation is difficult to carry out, and can be costly in terms of time and resources.

Using alternatives to regulation. Many alternative policy instruments have been developed in OECD countries. In most cases, they are justified as being more cost-effective than traditional government rules. They include:

- **Economic instruments**. There are many theoretical reasons to believe that economic instruments, such as taxes and tradable permits, offer the potential for static and dynamic efficiency gains, compared to traditional command and control regulation. And in fact there is a rising trend in OECD countries in the use of economic instruments. But a recent study has found that little empirical evidence is available on the scale of efficiency gains from economic instruments, though the implicit evidence suggests that such gains exist. Part of the problem in generating data is that a considerable period of time is needed before the benefits of economic instruments are fully realised (OECD, 1997*d*).

- **Cost recovery**. The evidence on how cost recovery affects net regulatory costs is ambiguous. Of course, charging for regulatory services such as inspections can be a convenient way to shift costs to the private sector and give the illusion of down-sizing to budget inspectors. But the question here is: Does this method increase or reduce net costs? An Efficiency Scrutiny in the United Kingdom expressed concern that "EC directives which allow recovery of the full costs of inspection do not impose sufficient disciplines on enforcers or test houses to recognise quality of service and efficiency, and may result in high costs to businesses. " Evidence of problems was cited (United Kingdom Department of Trade and Industry, 1993, p. 17). In some cases, however, cost recovery can be advantageous to both government and businesses. In Queensland, *Australia*, the licencing system for retail food premises, which involved 17 different licences administered by four different authorities, was unable to maintain hygiene standards, did not provide authorities with the power to deal promptly with problems, and was administratively costly. It was replaced in 1990 by a new scheme in which licencing powers were replaced by powers to inspect and issue orders, inspection fees are charged based on the cost of the service, and businesses with good hygiene records are inspected less often. This user-pays principle established an economic incentive for businesses to self-regulate to reduce their costs of inspection. The innovation was judged to be a success. "The introduction of fee for service inspections has delivered a regulatory system which is considerably more efficient and effective in achieving the policy objective…" (Australian Department of Business, Industry and Regional Development).

– **Self-regulation**. Properly done, and there are pitfalls, the efficiencies of self-regulation can be substantial. The *Australian* Industry Commission estimated that replacement of a detailed system of meat processing inspections by a self-regulated quality assurance scheme will, in the longer term, result in savings of one per cent of total production costs (Commonwealth of Australia, 1995, p. 139). In *Canada*, a series of Codes of Practice developed by the chemical industry went far beyond the capacity of the government to monitor, given current levels of resources available, and hence meant that more environmental quality could be delivered.

International co-operation. Harmonization and mutual recognition of standards and data can greatly reduce the cost of product development and marketing, and reduce entry barriers, thereby enhancing competitive pressures. These measures can also reduce government costs. In *Iceland*, a programme of harmonized product standards and mutual recognition of tests and certifications for imported products, combined with contracting-out of inspections, reduced total on-budget costs in the public agency for electrical safety by about 75 per cent in two years.[6]

To manage the aggregate costs of regulation, **regulatory budgeting**, an idea first suggested in the 1970s, would involve developing a budget for regulatory costs similar to that used for fiscal expenditures. Here, a government would establish an annual ceiling on the total amount of new costs that it would impose on the private sector through regulation. This total would be allocated among regulatory bodies, which would then allocate the budget among the possible regulatory options. No country has a regulatory budget in place, although proposals for establishing one in the *United States* were debated in the United States Congress in 1996. The main problem is that accounting techniques dealing with issues such as the indirect costs of regulation are not yet available. These practical problems are not, however, insurmountable, and regulatory budgeting may some day become a reality (Morrall, 1992).

Conclusions on a new management framework. More work is needed on the effectiveness of various regulatory cost control strategies. But it is clear that none of these strategies is, by itself, a sufficient condition for improvement. If such strategies are to produce genuine benefits in the quality of regulations, or to have any hope of reducing costs, governments must develop systematically organised procedures, with **sustained political support at the highest levels**, for the implementation of quality principles. That is to say, changing a phenomenon with such deep and tangled roots as growing regulatory costs requires broad institutional and cultural reform within governments. Isolated and quickly abandoned "reform" programs will produce only failure and cynicism.

What are the implications for the "limits to government" debate?

As an instrument of governance, regulations will continue to be used to meet a wide variety of legitimate social and economic needs. But governments in the OECD area clearly believe that they face a regulatory problem with serious economic and social consequences. Increasingly, it is recognised that there are limits to regulation just as for other government policy instruments, and managing within limits, conceived as a programme of cost-effectiveness and quality improvement, should be incorporated into regulatory reform. Regulatory costs are real and they matter. Well-written rules based on effective policies that produce net benefits should be encouraged – there is great potential for reducing the cost of regulation without sacrificing important policy objectives.

Less often recognised is the fact that improving regulatory disciplines can also improve government effectiveness. If governments are to maximise economic wealth or pursue social objectives such as environmental quality and social cohesion, they must be capable of choosing the right policies, designing cost-effective regulatory instruments, and responding more quickly to change. As the *Swedish* government has pointed out, such reforms do not contradict the use of regulation to achieve public objectives; rather, improvements to policy instruments make the goals more attainable.

What is important for the "limits to government" debate is the message that it may be counter-productive to cut the costs of government without including regulation. Budget-cutting is usually justified on grounds that reducing government costs will free up resources for more efficient uses in the private sector, that is, it is an economic growth policy. But the practice of cost-cutting is vulnerable to the accounting mechanisms that describe the size of government, and to reliance on misleading indicators of fiscal expenditures and number of employees. Setting limits on government activities based on partial accounting of costs could have three damaging effects on the efficiency of national regulatory systems, and hence on economic performance:

i) A programme to manage limits based solely on these indicators could damage economic growth by inducing governments to use regulatory mechanisms to simply shift costs to the private sector, in effect making them "disappear. " This illusion, however, produces no benefits for the economy. Indeed, governments under pressures in fiscal budgets are actively seeking ways to shift costs to the private sector. **Pressures to spend through regulation will increase as governments cut budget deficits and seek other, less transparent avenues for satisfying constituency groups or passing costs to the private sector.**

ii) Governments can use regulations as a non-tax revenue-generating mechanism. Raising funds this way can be enormously damaging to private sector efficiency. This approach produces incentives to *increase* regulatory barriers to competition, for example in privatisation programs, and to maximise the quantity of obligatory "regulatory services" for which fees can be charged. Licenses and permits are common revenue-raisers. In some countries, revenues from the sales of business licences and permits are substantial, and budget pressures tend to directly stimulate new regulations to raise more funds. Regulations can be used as an indirect form of taxation by blocking competition, and siphoning off some of the excess profits into the treasury. A very serious concern is that governments are using privatisation primarily to raise funds. Since monopolies fetch a higher price on the market, governments have powerful incentives to maintain anti-competitive regulatory controls that create private rather than public monopolies. A minor example can be seen in New York, which has fixed the number of cabs at 11 787 since 1937. In 1996, it increased the number by 400 and auctioned them off for $200 000 each, raising $80 million for city coffers, but certainly not doing very much for the taxi passengers, who paid for the licences through increased fares (*The Economist*, 1996, p. 43).

iii) Governments over-focussed on cutting budgets may neglect important investments in regulatory quality, such as in capacities for regulatory impact analysis and quality control, that will have far greater benefits in economic performance. We have already seen how governments under-invest in the procedures needed to produce high-quality regulations – analysis, consultation, review, evaluation. This is another example of a classic problem: the costs of investments in regulatory quality are seen in the short term and on-budget, while the benefits emerge over the longer term, and off-budget.

The point is that narrowly conceived programs of fiscal consolidation could damage the quality of national regulatory systems, and hence damage national economic performance. To manage this risk, policies to manage limits to government should take a global view of the cost of government. Such programs should set priorities among possible reforms, and should properly value investments in governmental quality improvements that support economic performance.

The single most important step is that **regulatory costs must be made visible.** If governments are finding it difficult to control fiscal costs, which are highly visible, how much more difficult is it to control the invisible costs of regulation? More complete accounting will increase the transparency of cost-cutting activities, support the proper trade-offs between public and private-sector costs, and reduce the temptation to simply shift costs from public to private sectors, as well as support the efforts under way in most OECD countries to produce higher-quality regulations.

But is this feasible? Accounting capacities for regulation, even if rudimentary, are needed. Yet it is a mistake to believe that governments must have accounting systems for regulatory costs as finely developed as those for budget expenditures – current budget techniques have taken many decades to develop. In fact, governments can begin by ensuring that all regulatory decisions are preceded by a simple assessment of the cost impact on businesses, and by expanding consultation mechanisms and making them routine, to ensure that affected parties have an opportunity to comment on the cost assessments.

In the longer term, as a recent meeting of regulatory policy officials at the OECD concluded, techniques for assessing aggregate regulatory costs and impacts on national economic and social performance are needed. These techniques do not exist now, and managing regulation within limits will continue to be difficult without a better sense of the real impacts of regulation.

Table 1.   **Summary of selected evidence of costs of regulation**

What is measured	Cost estimates	Source
Administrative costs to government		
Costs for staffing and operating federal regulatory agencies in the *United States*	$15.6 billion in 1995 (133 000 civil servants)	Center for the Study of *American* Business, *Reforming the Federal Regulatory Process: Rhetoric or Reality?* (Occasional Paper 138, June 1994), St. Louis, Missouri, United States
Administrative costs of regulatory bodies at the federal level in *Canada*	Operating costs of regulatory programmes (not including tax regimes) in 1995-96 C$1.8 billion; 20 000 people employed in inspection and regulation fields	Treasury Board of Canada data, cited in Martin, James and Cassaundra Iwankow (1996) *The Canadian Government Perspective on Cost-Effective Regulation.* Prepared for the Canadian Nuclear Association and Canadian Nuclear Society Annual Conference, New Brunswick
Administrative costs to firms and citizens		
Cost of EU and national administrative burdens on European firms	540 billion ECU/yr (3-4% of GDP)	Third Annual Report, The European Observatory for SMEs, EIM, the Netherlands, 1995
"Tax operating costs" for firms (administrative and compliance costs of taxation) in the *United Kingdom*	More than 5 billion pounds sterling/yr (1986-87), or 4% of total tax revenue (1.5% of GDP). 58 pounds/employee for firms with 1-5 employees, 11 pounds/employee for firms with over 500 employees	Sandford, Cedrick (1989) *Administrative and Compliance Costs of Taxation*, Bath Centre for Fiscal Studies, Fiscal Publications, UK
Administrative compliance costs of taxation, social insurance, and subsidy applications in *the Netherlands*	Gld. 7.2 billion (1989), or 1.5% of GDP	Allers, Martin (1994) *Administrative and Compliance Costs of Taxation and Public Transfers in the Netherlands*, Woters-Noordhoof, Groningen, 1994
Costs of paperwork and operational requirements of regulation (excluding capital costs) Clerical cost and time, in firms, due to regulatory requirements	Two-thirds of firms in US spend an average of $17 000 per employee on regulatory compliance US firms with 1-4 workers spend $2 080 per employee, firms with 500-999 spend $120 per employee	Hopkins, Thomas (1995) A *Survey of Regulatory Burdens*, Report to the US Small Business Administration, June, Washington, DC
Hours of time per year spent by businesses, state governments and citizens in the *United States* on federal paperwork, data collection, and information retention requirements	In 1996, 6.85 billion hours were spent complying with federal paperwork requirements	*United States* office of Information and Regulatory Affairs, Washington, DC
Measure of recurrent direct costs of federal government information requirements to small and medium enterprises in *Canada*	Businesses with fewer than five employees spend 8% of revenues on federal information requirements; with 5-19 employees, 3.8%; with 20-49 employees, 2.4%; with 50-99, under 2%	"Federal Information Costs for a Panel of Small and Medium Enterprises", Final Report by Information Management and Economics, Inc., Toronto, Ontario, December 1995
Direct compliance costs		
Total compliance costs in the *United States* (including administrative costs) to firms and citizens of federal regulations, plus efficiency losses of regulations in some sectors	$617 billion in 1996 ($5 700 per household)	Hopkins, Thomas (1995) "Federal Regulatory Burdens: An Overview," in *The Hidden Costs of Regulation in Europe*, European Policy Forum, London, UK

Table 1. **Summary of selected evidence of costs of regulation** (*continued*)

What is measured	Cost estimates	Source
Compliance costs of federal regulations in *Canada*	C$ 30 billion/year (20% of federal budget expenditures)	Martin, James and Cassaundra Iwankow (1996) *The Canadian Government Perspective on Cost-Effective Regulation.* Prepared for the Canadian Nuclear Association and Canadian Nuclear Society Annual Conference, New Brunswick
Total costs of pollution abatement and control expenditures in various countries	1-2% of GDP in OECD countries; $135 billion in 1992 in the *United States*	OECD US Environmental Protection Agency (1990) *Environmental Investments: The Cost of a Clean Environment*, Washington, DC
Direct compliance costs to small businesses (less than 20 people), including paperwork, fees, and new equipment purchases, of compliance with five sectors of regulation in Queensland, *Australia*	Annualised average compliance cost per small business is A$ 17 094. Road freight transport showed the highest costs	Australia, State of Queensland (1996) *Final Report: Impact of the Cost of Compliance with Government Regulations, Licences, Taxes, and Chargers on Small Businesses in Queensland*, prepared for the Department of Tourism, Small Business, and Industry (19 August)

Indirect economic costs

Annual efficiency costs of economic regulations in the *United States*	$43.3-$46.5 billion/yr (1988 dollars)	Hahn, R. and Hird, J. (1991) "The Costs and Benefits of Regulation: Review and Synthesis," *Yale Journal of Regulation*, Vol. 8, No. 1
Annual welfare changed (1990 dollars) due to deregulation in four major sectors (transport, communications, energy, financial services) in the *United States*	$36-46 billion/yr (7-9% gain in the output of affected industries)	Winston, Clifford (1993) "Economic Deregulation: Days of Reckoning for Microeconomists", *Journal of Economic Literature*, September
Measures of productivity and "competitive intensity" in four regulated service sectors (airlines, banking, telecommunications, retailing) in *United States*, *Japan*, and Europe	Substantial differences in productivity in all four sectors (for example, output per employee for European airlines was 72% of US level in 1989) suggest that inefficiencies in *Japan* and Europe are due to regulation and weak competition, state-ownership, and monopolies	Baily, Martin Neil (1993) "Competition, Regulation, and Efficiency in Service Industries", Brookings Papers, *Microeconomics* 2, pp. 71-159
Telecommunications – relative prices of baskets of services in regulated and deregulated national markets	From 1990-1994, business prices fell by 8.6% in competitive markets, compared with 3.1% in non-competitive markets. Residential charges fell by 3.1% in competitive markets, but increased by 8.7% in non-competitive markets. Since the deregulation of the tele-communication market in *Japan* in 1985, relative telephone charges have fallen by more than 40%. The abolition of entry regulations in the *United Kingdom* in 1991 prompted an increase in labour productivity of up to 100 per cent in the dominant telecommunication company	OECD (1995) *Communications Outlook* 1995, OECD, Paris

Table 1. **Summary of selected evidence of costs of regulation** (*continued*)

What is measured	Cost estimates	Source
Surface freight – welfare gains to society after deregulation in various countries	Annual benefits from rate and service changes estimated at $20 billion (1988 dollars) in the United States. Road transportation deregulation in most countries typically led to rapid price reductions. The liberalisation of road freight transport in France in 1986 showed up in a 6% fall in prices in 1987. However, a sharp reduction in prices in long-distance coaching after deregulation in the UK in 1980 was subsequently reversed, largely because the dominant firm was not prevented from maintaining some degree of monopoly power	Winston, C., T. Corsi, C. Grimm, C. Evans (1990) *The Economic Effects of Surface Freight Deregulation*, Washington, DC., The Brookings Institution
Efficiency gains from a national reform programme in 1996-2000 for structural reform of government monopolies and review and reform of a wide range of regulations impeding the functioning of markets	Annual gains in real GDP of 5.5%, or A$ 23 billion per year. Consumers would gain by A$ 9 billion, or A$ 1 500 per household	Government of Australia (1995) *The Growth and Revenue Implications of Hilmer and Related Reforms*, A Report by the Industry Commission to the Council of Australia Governments, March
Airlines – various measures of price and quality of service effects of deregulation	Industry-wide studies all indicate substantial positive effects from deregulation. Annual economic benefits in United States estimated at $6 billion in 1988 prices Average costs of airlines in US reduces 10-20 by deregulation, output increased 30% Average fares in Australia reduced by 15-41% Dublin-London route economy fares dropped 50% after liberalisation Loss of consumer surplus in Europe of $4 billion due to lower efficiency	Morrison, S. and C. Winston (1989), "Enhancing the Performance of the Deregulated Air Transportation System", *Yale Journal on Regulation*, Vol. 4, pp. 393-494 Baltagi, B.H., J.M. Griffin, and D.P. Rich (1995) "Airline Deregulation: The Cost Pieces of the Puzzle", *International Economic Review*, Vol. 36, No. 1 Sinha D. and T. Sinha (1994) "The Effects of Airline Deregulation – the Case of Australia", *World Competition, Law and Economics Review*, Vol. 17; June, pp. 81-95 Button, K. (1995) OECD *International Futures Programme: Functioning of Competition*, OECD, Paris Good, D.H., L-H Röller, R.C. Sickles (1993) "US Airline Deregulation: Implications for European Transport", *The Economic Journal*, Vol. 103, pp. 1028-1041
Effect on national economic growth rates in Japan of "vigorous" deregulation in key infrastructure sectors	Deregulation would almost double national growth rates in Japan – to 3% – in the years 1996-2000	Government of Japan, Economic Planning Agency, Economic Plan of December 1995, Tokyo
Effects on EU long-term growth rate of the European Single Market Programme to remove barriers to competition among European firms	Increase of between 0.2 and 0.9 percentage points in long-term growth rate	Baldwin, Richard *The Growth Effects of* 1992
Effect of environmental and worker safety regulations on economic productivity	0.44%, or one-third of the total, of the decline in US manufacturing productivity in the 1970s was due to these kinds of regulation Using general equilibrium analysis, the dynamic consequences of environmental regulation are estimated to increase consumer prices by over 6% in 1990, and reduce GNP by 5.85%	Gray, W. (1987) The Cost of Regulation: OSHA, EPA and the Productivity Slowdown, *American Economic Review*, December, 77, pp. 998-1006 Hazilla, M. and R. Kopp (1990) "Social Cost of Environmental Quality Regulations", *Journal of Political Economy*, 98, pp. 853-873

Table 1. **Summary of selected evidence of costs of regulation** (*continued*)

What is measured	Cost estimates	Source
Effect of deregulation on price of electricity	Electricity market deregulation in *Norway* (1990) prompted a reduction in spot prices of 20% (partly reflecting overcapacity in the industry), and privatisation and regulatory reform of the *British* electricity industry was accompanied by sharp cost compression (*e.g.* labour productivity up by 50% and an improvement in capital productivity)	
Effects of liberalisation in the retail sector in *Japan*	Liberalisation of the Large Scale Retail Store Law in *Japan* over the past 5 years has contributed to falling prices. The implicit price deflator for distribution fell by 2% in 1992 and 1993	OECD (1995) *Economic Survey of Japan*, 1995, OECD, Paris

NOTES

1. See OECD 1996*a*, figures refer to general government; figures not available for all Member countries.

2. In 1994, the Government created the Swedish Agency for Government Employers as a central independent agency financed by "dues" from participating agencies (rather than from the budget). Unlike a traditional central management agency, the SAGE is directed and financed by a consortium of departments and agencies to conduct central negotiations on minimum wage increases and other minimum conditions of work – thus balancing a desire to maintain some central negotiations with unions with the policy for near total decentralisation of human resource management policy to departments and agencies.

3. Information from the Regulatory Information Service Center, Washington, DC.

4. Remark by a German official about a national recycling programme, quoted in The Economist, 29 May 1993, "Survey: Environment", p. 18.

5. The Recommendation noted that high-quality regulation is crucial to government effectiveness and to economic growth, and urged Member countries to take steps to improve the quality and transparency of regulations issued by all levels of government.

6. Information taken from case studies carried out for the OECD Public Management Service.

REFERENCES

Anglo-German Deregulation Group (1995), "Deregulation Now", March.

Australian Department of Business, Industry and Regional Development (1991), *Fee for Service Health Inspection of the Retail Food Industry in New South Wales*, No. 3, Occasional Paper Series, Business Regulation Review Unit, Queensland, August.

BRAITHWAITE, John (1993), *Improving Regulatory Compliance: Strategies and Practical Applications in OECD Countries*, OECD Public Management Occasional Papers, Regulatory Management and Reform Series No. 3, OCDE/GD(93)63, OECD, Paris.

Canada House of Commons (1992) "Notes for a Statement on Regulation and Competitiveness" by the President of the Treasury Board and Minister Responsible for Regulatory Affairs to the Sub-committee on Regulation and Competitiveness of the Standing Committee on Finance (May 12).

Commonwealth of Australia (1995), *The Growth and Revenue Implications of Hilmer and Related Reforms,* A Report by the Industry Commission to the Council of Australian Governments, March.

Commonwealth of Australia (1996), "Media Release of the Small Business Deregulation Task Force", 4 September, Canberra.

Conseil d'État (1992), *Rapport Public 1991*, La Documentation française, Paris.

The Economist, 3 February 1996, "New York's cabs: A revolution!", p. 43.

Government of Ireland (1996), *Delivering Better Government*, Second Report to Government of the Co-ordinating Group of Secretaries, Dublin.

Government of the UK (1985), "Lifting the Burden", White Paper presented to Parliament by the Minister Without Portfolio, Her Majesty's Stationery Office, London.

Government of the UK (1975-1992), Finance Acts, HMSO London.

HOPKINS, Thomas (1995*a*), "Federal Regulatory Burdens: An Overview", in *The Hidden Costs of Regulation in Europe*, European Policy Forum, London.

HOPKINS, Thomas (1995*b*), "Profiles of Regulatory Costs", report to the Small Business Administration, Washington, DC, November.

HOPKINS, Thomas D. (1996) "Regulatory Costs in Profile", Center for the Study of American Business, Policy Study Number 132, August, St. Louis, Missouri, USA.

MARTIN, James (1992), "Implementing Regulatory Policy: Similarity of Canadian and American Issues", a presentation to the Conference on the Cost of Regulation and Red Tape (mimeo), Rochester Institute of Technology, New York.

MARTIN, James and Cassaundra IWANKOW (1996), "The Canadian Government Perspective on Cost-Effective Regulation", Prepared for the Canadian Nuclear Assocation and Canadian Nuclear Society Annual Conference, New Brunswick.

MORRALL, John (1992), *Controlling Regulatory Costs: The Use of Regulatory Budgeting*, Public Management Occasional Papers, Regulatory Management and Reform Series No. 2, OCDE/GD(92)176, OECD, Paris.

OECD (1995), Recommendation of the Council of the OECD on Improving the Quality of Government Regulation, 9 March, Paris.

OECD (1996*a*), *Economic Outlook No. 59*, OECD, Paris.

OECD (1996*b*), Integrating People Management in Public Service Reform, OECD, Paris.

OECD (1997*a*), *Performance Pay Schemes for Public Sector Managers: An evaluation of the impacts*, Public Management Occasional Papers No. 15, OECD, Paris.

OECD (1997*b*), *Management of the Senior Public Service*, OECD, Paris (forthcoming).

OECD (1997*c*), *Regulatory Impact Analysis: Best Practices in OECD Countries*, OECD, Paris (forthcoming).

OECD (1997*d*), *Evaluating Economic Instruments for Environmental Policy*, OECD, Paris.

TEUBNER, Gunther (1987), "Juridification: Concepts, Aspects, Solutions", *in* Teubner, Gunther (ed.), *Juridification of Social Spheres*, Walter de Gruyter, Berlin.

UK Department of Trade and Industry (1993), *Review of the Implementation and Enforcement of EC Law in the UK*, an Efficiency Scrutiny Report, London.

UNICE (1995), "Releasing Europe's Potential Through Targeted Regulatory Reform", Brussels.

US Environmental Protection Agency (1987), *EPA's Use of Benefit Cost Analysis: 1981-1986,* EPA-230-05-87-028, EPA, Washington, DC.

Part III

PUBLIC MANAGEMENT INITIATIVES IN OECD MEMBER COUNTRIES

1. **Summary of developments** 77

    User's guide to country reports 77

    Approaches to reform 77

2. **Country reports:**

    Australia 85
    Austria 93
    Belgium 99
    Canada 105
    Czech Republic 115
    Denmark 123
    Finland 129
    France 137
    Germany 147
    Greece 155
    Hungary 161
    Iceland 169
    Ireland 177
    Italy 189
    Japan 195
    Luxembourg 203
    Mexico 209
    Netherlands 217
    New Zealand 225
    Norway 233
    Portugal 241
    Spain 247
    Sweden 257
    Switzerland 265
    Turkey 273
    United Kingdom 277
    United States 287

Common framework for country reports

A. Main tendencies and overall priorities
B. Context affecting public management
C. Strategies and processes for planning and carrying out public management reforms
D. Policy-management capacities
E. Human resources management
F. Budget process and management of financial resources
G. Performance management
H. Changing structures of the public sector
I. Regulatory management and reform
J. Other

Annexes

A   Principal recent public management developments
B   Institutional responsibility for public management improvement
C   Key public documents on public management issues and developments

PUBLIC MANAGEMENT INITIATIVES IN OECD MEMBER COUNTRIES

1. Summary of developments

User's guide to country reports

This part of the Survey presents the most important initiatives related to public management in OECD countries as identified in the reports provided by the Member countries.

The reports present developments of an ongoing nature which have become an integral part of public services, initiatives put into place since publication of the previous PUMA Survey and, wherever possible, emerging issues of concern.

Country reports follow a common framework which includes context, major priorities and strategies and more specific public management initiatives in a broad range of areas. While the framework facilitates comparison, countries were encouraged to use it selectively to report on areas relevant to their circumstances. Reports were generally reviewed by the countries concerned during September 1996. A contact appears on the final page of each report as the source for the country contribution and as a contact point for further information on the reforms in place. Finally, a glossary annexed to this Survey is provided to assist with terminology, although countries naturally follow their accustomed use of terms.

Approaches to reform

Governments continue to report both a call by citizens for responsive and efficient services, and significant pressures to reduce deficits and control public expenditure. These pressures are reinforced by the requirements of prospective adoption of a single European currency, increased competition arising from globalisation, and the longer term budgetary impacts of ageing societies. The effort to achieve sustained fiscal consolidation emerges as one of the key driving forces behind the current reforms, together with citizen demands for effective services, in the contexts of countries' own policy priorities.

Although a range of policy responses has been adopted by governments to meet these key challenges, the general directions for reform share many similarities. They have as their common focus attempts to contain, or in some cases reduce, the size of government while improving its performance – or to do more with less – an objective now pervading all areas of public management.

Budgetary pressures combined with an increasing orientation towards performance and accountability has forced an increasing number of countries to re-examine the role of government – the fundamentals of what government is now doing and what it should be doing. For other countries the preoccupation is more with strengthening "how" government is fulfilling its role, and less with issues of the core role of government. One thing is certain – no government can ignore issues of public management reform.

Governments engaged in ongoing, high-profile and comprehensive reform plans include (amongst others) *Mexico* with the launch of its "Program to Modernise the Public Administration 1995-2000" (announced in 1996); *Denmark* with its "New Views of the Public Sector" (1993) followed by "Welfare for Citizens" (1995);

the United Kingdom with its "Continuity and Change" (1994) and with later initiatives; the United States with its National Performance Review (begun in 1993); Canada with its "Getting Government Right" (1996); France with its current plans to modernise the State (begun in 1995); Ireland with its "Delivering Better Government" (1996); and Germany with its "Lean State" reforms (1995-1997).

These reform plans encompass a wide range of issues and approaches to integrate initiatives into overall programmes of change, sometimes involving extensive consultative and participative structures. Ireland's initiative, for example, involves high-level working groups and front-line groups drawn from across the civil service and overseen by a co-ordinating group (illustrated in the diagram following that country's report).

Reform plans sometimes focus on one or more key themes. Ireland's "Delivering Better Government" (DBG), for example, has as its central theme the delivery of quality services, including policy advice to the government and the public. Canada's "Getting Government Right", on the other hand, identifies four objectives: to clarify federal roles and responsibilities; to devote resources to the highest priorities; to respond to the public demand for better and more accessible government; and to achieve more affordable government by reducing the deficit and debt pressures. The United States aims to create a government that "works better and costs less", building on four National Performance Review Principles: putting customers first; empowering employees to get results; cutting red tape; and cutting back to basics.

Some governments are entering a phase of consolidation and reflection. New Zealand, having undergone a radical restructuring of its public sector over the last decade, is a notable example: with the foundation for the public and state sector management framework set in place, the focus is now reported to be turning to such issues as accountability with the aim of minimising compliance costs and disincentive effects on agencies while maximising effectiveness.

There is a large group of countries reporting approaches to reform with their particular emphases (e.g. Austria, Belgium, Japan, the Netherlands, Portugal and Switzerland). When reforms have been under way for some time, the cumulative effects may be very substantial – as, for instance, the United Kingdom and Nordic countries' reports suggest.

There is also the select group of countries meeting the significant challenge of transforming their overall systems of governance and public management (notably Hungary and the Czech Republic, and in Germany with the transformation of the administrative systems of the Länder formerly in East Germany).

A number of reform strands emerge from the country reports, reflecting this range of approaches:

- a continuation of the trend towards **devolving managerial authority** to provide greater flexibility in achieving public policy goals, supported by improved resource management;
- a closer **focus on results** to complement the devolved environment, by improving performance and enhancing accountability;
- a stronger **service quality orientation**, which involves public consultation and leads to public services that are more relevant to needs and more responsive to demands;
- a focus on **adapting organisational structures**, to improve service, performance, accountability and efficiency;
- a heightened focus on the importance of an effective **public sector workforce and leadership**, to facilitate the stronger performance orientation and service-oriented public service culture;
- **regulatory reform** as a tool to improve the capacity of governments to achieve policy objectives efficiently and cost-effectively;
- a **strengthening of steering functions** at the centre to drive reforms strategically and promote policy coherence on cross-cutting issues, in the face of complex policy problems and a more devolved public sector environment.

Each of these themes is outlined below with selected illustrations from the country reports.

Devolving authority

Reforms to further devolve managerial authority and provide flexibility are the most consistent thread running through the country reports, as countries recognise that providing greater freedom in operational decisions is important to improving public sector performance. The reforms involve replacing detailed traditional input controls for the management of financial and human resources by a framework of incentives and more global controls, in exchange for holding managers more directly accountable for results. *Sweden* and *New Zealand* have probably gone furthest in this regard, with devolution of varying degrees found in many other countries, among them *Australia*, *Canada*, *Finland*, the *Netherlands*, and *Portugal*. Recently, countries such as *France*, *Ireland*, *Mexico* and *Switzerland* report managerial devolution as a reform priority.

Countries view improved **financial management systems** as a necessary basis for supporting a more devolved management environment. Many countries have already significantly devolved financial management responsibilities, with an instance of recent developments being *France's* piloting of service contracts which aim to provide local administrators with greater budgetary responsibility.

Where increased devolution has been in place for some years, activity is focusing on strengthening accountability through fine-tuning incentive structures, improving measures of performance and strengthening requirements for performance reporting (discussed further below). For example *Denmark*, among other countries, has a very decentralised budget system since reforms in the 1980s, and has recently introduced a requirement for state institutions to prepare annual reports.

An important aspect of devolution involves setting in place **incentive structures for improving financial management**, for example allowing a limited carryover of funds into the next fiscal year (as in *Iceland*, amongst others). Further development of **medium-term resource planning** is also found in the reports (*e.g.* in the *Netherlands'* new budgetary system which establishes stricter spending limits over a three-year period).

In respect of most of these reforms, there is a continuing concern with ensuring appropriate accountability, while still promoting flexibility and innovation (including in the management of human resources, noted below). There is also a concern that devolution should not erode the coherence of government action (also noted below).

Strengthening performance and accountability

Devolution is generally seen as a necessary but insufficient condition for improving performance. The counterpart to providing flexibility is to introduce **mechanisms which focus on results and enhance accountability**, by making managers responsible for meeting performance goals within specified resources.

These mechanisms can take a variety of forms. In the *United States*, "performance-based intergovernmental partnerships" between the Federal and other levels of government provide more administrative flexibility in exchange for commitments to specific performance levels. Other countries, too, are using or experimenting with performance or service contracts, such as *Denmark*, *France*, *Greece*, *Iceland* and *New Zealand*.

Putting in place methods to **assess performance against objectives and ensure transparency through effective reporting** are viewed by many countries as vital elements of accountability. The way in which objectives are framed, and the extent to which they focus on efficiency, service quality or effectiveness aspects, will invariably influence program performance.* Initiatives in setting performance targets are

---

* The type of measure used differs among countries, with some preferring to rely on measures of output, which are easier to specify and frame within service contracts, and others attempting the more challenging task of specifying programme outcomes.

reported by countries such as *Belgium*, where departments are beginning to develop management control and performance monitoring functions, assisted by audit or internal evaluation units; *Austria*, where a system of performance indicators is being planned as a tool for improving resource allocation decisions and providing basic information for the benchmarking of programs; and *Iceland*, which expects to move increasingly towards setting agencies clearly defined targets and more use of activity indicators.

There is an increasing realisation of the need to **select performance targets carefully**, to ensure they are consistent with program objectives and continue to be relevant. The development of appropriate techniques for measuring performance is often complex in practice. *Sweden* observes that while formulating program objectives is relatively easy, breaking them down into specific, quantifiable targets that are able to be monitored poses a greater challenge, and may require a closer specification of activities.

Providing responsive service

Countries increasingly identify **the improvement of service delivery** as a priority issue, frequently emphasising service quality aspects although in a few cases focusing on efficiency through means such as streamlining of structures and procedures. Many countries report progress in providing more responsive service to their citizens: in *Portugal*, for instance, where service quality is a primary theme of several years standing, or in *Mexico* where one fundamental priority in its new modernisation programme is to implant a deeply rooted service ethic.

Ireland's "Delivering Better Government" is an example of a comprehensive program centred on delivery of quality services to the public as customers, clients and citizens. It covers various facets of service improvement, including consultation with and participation by customers, specification of the quality of service to be provided, and "reasonable choice" of service delivery methods for customers.

The use of **service charters** is found increasingly as a tool for creating more transparent and responsive client services. The *United Kingdom's* "Citizen's Charter" recently completed the first half of its ten-year programme; in the *Netherlands* government departments are being encouraged to develop quality charters which include "qualitative agreements"; *Belgium's* Public Service Users' Charter now includes the piloting of customer satisfaction measures and service quality standards, as a basis for an "unwritten agreement with users"; departments in *France* are to be asked to draw up service charters emphasising service quality aspects in consultation with citizens; and *Hungary* is examining the possibility of introducing standards in certain social services on the basis of prior experience with its Citizens' Charter.

The **integration of services delivery** is reported as a strategy for increasing access to public services for citizens and businesses. *Canada's* Business Service Centres for example provide a single access point for federal, provincial and municipal programmes and services for business, accompanied by the adoption of quality principles and practices; *Norway* is piloting co-ordination of local and central government services from a variety of sectors into a single joint office; and *Finland* has in place a large number of "multiservice" *centres* with many offering an enhanced range of services as part of a pilot project.

There is a growing emphasis on **citizen consultation and participation** on service provision by improving access to information and exploring methods of obtaining client feedback. *Norway* for example has put in place a comprehensive information policy, which provides information on all aspects of public services and seeks to inform residents of their "rights, obligations and opportunities". *Denmark* is strengthening avenues for consumer influence through legislation establishing consumer councils and requiring local authorities to inform citizens annually about local services. One of *Spain's* priorities is to "improve the quality of public services by means of an open, informative, participatory assessment and public report"; among various initiatives is a "negotiating table with citizens" to discuss and assess the quality of public services. The *Netherlands* is piloting "integrated government information centres" on, for example, citizens' rights, and plans to experiment with the use of information technology to stimulate public participation in political decisions.

Governments face a number of challenges in developing a service quality strategy, such as defining the relevant client groups and finding effective consultation mechanisms. Specific issues include the need to ensure that charters include measurable standards of service, at levels achievable within limited resources; that the means for complaint and redress for citizens are clearly articulated; and that strategies are developed to obtain and use client feedback, to ensure services which are responsive to client needs.

Adapting organisational structures

Many countries are **adapting their organisational structures**, sometimes in radical and controversial ways. Countries report changing their structures to enhance their capacity to provide more responsive services; improve performance; strengthen accountability (whether through devolution, or through a clarification of roles); and create efficiencies, through market-type mechanisms or by reducing government activity to a set of core functions – or, as is frequently the case, some combination of these objectives. As *New Zealand* observes, "Little is static… and changes and refinements are being made or considered continuously" in the structures of the state.

Organisational changes in some countries such as the *United Kingdom* and *New Zealand* have separated organisations providing services from the provision of policy advice. These countries rely on having a wide range of government services provided through agencies or other devolved institutions. Another distinction raised by *Norway* is the need to address the role of the state as provider of services on the one hand, involving the state in the market, and the role of the state as regulator of the market; it is suggested the two roles should be separated as far as possible to prevent a conflict of interest developing.

Most countries, however, rather than relying on a single approach to organising their public services, are seeking to **adopt different models, to tailor organisations to meet the needs of the citizens** they serve. *Canada*, for example, reports that key elements of its transportation infrastructure are being transferred to community-based groups, municipal authorities and the private sector; and many revenue collection services which are currently undertaken by federal and provincial governments separately may be integrated into a new partnership body, a National Revenue Collection Agency.

Countries report a wide range of issues and initiatives: to rationalise organisational structures (*e.g. Australia, Austria, Hungary, Japan, Mexico,* and the *United States*); separate service functions into organisational units with greater autonomy, as agencies or devolved institutions (*e.g. Germany* is increasingly transferring tasks to "subordinate authorities", or agencies, of the federal government); corporatisation and/or privatisation strategies (*e.g. Sweden, Iceland*); or use of a variety of market-type mechanisms such as contracting out (*e.g. Denmark, Finland*).

Developing effective human resources leadership

Many countries are facing the challenge of **reforming human resources management** while managing staff reductions in response to fiscal constraints. The dominant response running through the reports is one of strengthening leadership capacity and equipping staff to meet the challenges of the new public sector, with an emerging focus on ways to enhance staff flexibility.

A number of countries report initiatives including **mobility** policies to broaden experience and prepare for the challenges of ongoing restructuring (*e.g. Austria, Finland, Japan, Norway, Sweden,* and *France* where the emphasis is on creating conditions conducive to "harmonising career structures"). In some countries the approach emphasises development of human resources leadership through structures such as *New Zealand's* Management Development Centre designed to "increase the size and quality of the senior management pool across the Public Service", or the *United Kingdom's* new Senior Civil Service framework.

Measures are in place in most countries to strengthen **the focus on performance and to enhance accountability** within the new devolved environment, as countries recognise the need to forge closer linkages between human resources management and organisational goals and strategies. In *Ireland* a reward system is envisaged to promote effective performance, particularly by teams, and more effective mechanisms for dealing with underperformance; and in *Belgium* a staff appraisal system is being phased in which recognises the importance of prior training in this area.

An important dimension of performance is promoting and ensuring **ethical behaviour** in public administration, a theme in many countries. Recently, *Mexico* reports a code of conduct for public servants, updated legislation on accountability, and sanctions for infringements; in *Norway* an emphasis is on agencies developing their own strategies for addressing potential ethical dilemmas encountered by public servants; and *Finland* is considering the desirability of disclosure of financial and other commitments of senior civil servants prior to their appointment.

Other issues include a search, reported by certain countries, for ways to manage **the ageing of the public sector workforce**, in the context of ageing populations and also public sector downsizing. The *Netherlands* is currently developing policies in this area, driven by concerns that ageing will increase staffing costs and reduce public service mobility in the future. Ageing is also a significant issue for *Finland*, where the emphasis is on improving opportunities for older staff to continue in their positions; and for *Japan*, where a new re-employment system for officials in their early sixties is being examined.

Although the extent of reform to human resources management differs markedly between countries, many have to some extent relied on the devolution of authority to improve performance, particularly in operational aspects of human resources management. Current issues include the extent to which it is beneficial to pursue devolution in human resources management, and the need to ensure that line managers are sufficiently skilled and supported to carry out their responsibilities within the new devolved environment.

Improving regulatory management

Measures to **improve the quality of regulation and to make it more results-oriented** are being pursued in a number of OECD countries. There is a growing sense that regulations have been allowed to proliferate unabated, have too often been cumbersome and costly, and that regulatory systems have often been out of step with other areas of public management reform. For example in *France* the Council of State has been critical of the proliferation of rules and regulations which is seen as weakening the law and creating instability. In many countries alternatives or complements to regulatory solutions are being pursued, ranging from enhanced provision of consumer information to deregulation to allowing market forces to operate more effectively.

Ireland is proposing to develop a comprehensive regulatory reform program governed by principles of improving the quality of regulations; eliminating inefficient or unnecessary regulations; simplifying necessary regulations; reducing the cost of regulatory compliance; and increasing the transparency of regulations.

An important focus of regulatory reform is to curb **regulatory inflation**, on the basis that allowing regulations to continue to proliferate makes it difficult to ensure compliance and leads to a disproportionate increase in costs. The costs associated with regulation however are frequently indirect and so more difficult to measure (*e.g.* *Norway* is putting a strong focus on determining the costs of regulatory as well as other reforms). Countries which have initiated or strengthened programs to rationalise the number of regulations include *Austria, France, Germany, Hungary, Japan,* and *Mexico* which in 1995 put in place the most comprehensive deregulation initiative in its history.

Reforms in many countries are also aimed at improving the **quality of regulation**. *France's* programme, for example, includes regulatory impact studies and quality improvements; the programs of both *Sweden* and *Mexico* include the use of checklists to improve the quality of new regulations; the focus in the *Netherlands* is on assessing the likely effects of regulations and ensuring their transparency, consistency and ease of enforcement; and *Finland* launched a program in 1995 to improve the quality of legislation, which requires regulatory impact analysis of proposed legislation and improved co-ordination of legislative activity.

Countries identify a number of important issues in the area of regulatory reform. In *France*, Mr. Jean Picq's 1994 report on the French State ("L'*État en France*") emphasized the need for "legislation in moderation" to accommodate the need for compatibility between "national rules" and the "many other sources of law, be they international or local, professional or contractual". *Iceland* points to some of the newer pressures for regulatory control such as environmental concerns which may lead to a proliferation of regulations, requiring careful regulatory management.

Ensuring coherence

Countries are recognising the need to **strengthen the coherence of government action within the new devolved environment** and with the greater complexity of issues which demand a strategic, whole-of-government response. Devolution focuses managers on performance at the organisational level which can lead to fragmentation and an undermining of collective interest. There is some concern with adapting central bodies or other co-ordination mechanisms to improve policy-making capacity and to focus on longer-term perspectives.

Amongst various initiatives designed to strengthen the coherence of government action, *Switzerland* has launched a wide-ranging project to strengthen the role of the Federal Council as the supreme executive authority and as a "collegiate governing body"; the *Netherlands* is reorganising its system of advisory bodies so they are more strategically focused; the *United States* has several bodies in place (the President's Management Council, the Chief Financial Officers' Council, and the President's Council on Integrity and Efficiency) to encourage the cross-agency dissemination of ideas; *Canada* has underway initiatives to improve longer term planning and strategic policy making, including "portfolio management (an overall direction and co-ordination of policy, legislation and activity) to provide more integrated advice" to individual ministers; and *New Zealand* has launched a co-ordinated study of long-term, cross-portfolio applied social science research and evaluation needed to support policy advice, planning and co-ordination.

Implications include the need for both central and line agencies to further adapt their roles to the devolved management environment. They have a valuable role to play together in developing and promoting public policy and public management reforms, yielding the most benefits through a partnership approach.

AUSTRALIA

A. Main tendencies and overall priorities

Review of the Public Service Act

In 1994 the previous government commissioned a review of the Public Service Act (the McLeod Review). This recommended that the lengthy, complex and prescriptive current Act be replaced with a streamlined, principles-based Act which offers a more flexible employment framework in keeping with the operating environment in the 1990s and beyond.

In June 1996, a National Commission of Audit set up by the new government recommended that the Public Service Act be simplified to promote improved performance.

The Minister for Industrial Relations and Minister Assisting the Prime Minister for the Public Service announced on 20 June 1996 that he would embark on a consultation process to develop a reform package for the Australian Public Service. Issues to be covered include the response to the McLeod review of the Public Service Act, the impact on public service enterprise bargaining arrangements, reforms to the Australian industrial relations system and options for improving management processes.

B. Context affecting public management

In March 1996 there was a Federal election, as a result of which a new government formed by the Liberal/ National Party Coalition under the leadership of the Hon. John Howard MP took office. The party came to government on a platform of fiscal consolidation and industrial relations reform. A deficit reduction strategy has been put in place, to be achieved mainly through cuts to expenditure rather than increasing revenue.

One of the major priorities of the new government elected in March 1996 is reform of the national industrial relations system. In May 1996 it introduced into the Parliament the Workplace Relations and Other Legislation Amendment Bill 1996. This seeks to bring about more decentralised arrangements in order to foster greater flexibility and productivity in the workplace. These new provisions will apply to the federal public sector on the same basis as for the rest of the workforce. This legislation is still before the Parliament.

Up-to-date information on the new legislation and industrial relations issues in the Australian Public Service is available on the Department of Industrial Relations Home Page on http://www.nla.gov.au/dir/.

National Commission of Audit

The National Commission of Audit was established by the Commonwealth Government in March 1996 in accordance with its pre-election undertaking. The National Commission of Audit was asked to report on aspects of the management and financial activities of the Commonwealth Government and how they are recorded. The Commission operated as an independent entity. The Chair, Executive Officer, and remaining three Commissioners were drawn from academia and the private sector.

The Commission's examinations proceeded from the following basic premises:

- that governments do need to operate efficiently;
- that the community would prefer action to make delivery of services more efficient rather than cutting assistance to those in genuine need; and
- that well-managed government contributes to a more competitive Australia.

The Commission's report was framed against the following questions:

- Are particular activities best handled by government? If so, by which level of government?
- Are Commonwealth Government services being provided in the best way?
- Will changes in the population structure put pressure on Commonwealth finances?
- Is there enough government investment in infrastructure: that is, transport, communications and the like?
- Is there a better way to record Commonwealth Government activities?
- What is the financial position of the Commonwealth Government as a whole on the basis of the latest complete set of financial statements?
- Can present arrangements for the setting and reporting of fiscal policy (that is, government spending and revenue decisions and their effect on the economy) be improved?

The Commission adopted a frame work of principles, cognisant of the broad economic and social goals of government, to guide its analysis and recommendations for improvements. The framework included the following decision sequence:

- assess whether or not there is a role for government;
- where there is, decide which level of government should be responsible, and assess whether or not government objectives are clearly specified and effectively promoted;
- assess whether or not effective activities are being conducted on a "best practice" basis.

The Commission presented its report to the government on 19 June 1996. Copies of the Commission's report are available on the Internet (http://www.finance.gov.au/pubs).

C. Strategies and processes for planning and carrying out public management

Public sector reform

The government is embarking on a process to develop a reform package for the Australian Public Service (APS). An Issues Paper will provide the framework for meetings with public servants at all levels, relevant unions, management consultants and other interested parties. Some of the issues that will be discussed include a response to the McLeod Review of the Public Service Act, the interaction of the new Workplace Relations Bill with public service enterprise bargaining arrangements and options for improving management processes in the APS. When announcing this consultation process, the Minister Assisting the Prime Minister for the Public Service stated that he wants to ensure "that workplace structures, systems and culture in the APS emphasise innovation and recognise creativity and commitment".

Downsizing

In response to planned reductions in departmental running costs, the Public Service and Merit Protection Commission developed and obtained government endorsement of a broad framework for managing the resulting reductions in staffing in the Australian Public Service. In addition to issuing guidelines and providing briefing sessions to assist agencies in developing a strategic plan for managing their staff reductions, the PSMPC also put in place a system for screening APS vacancies for possible matches with excess APS officers before those vacancies are published. A Committee of senior officials, chaired by the Public Service Commissioner, is overseeing the downsizing process.

E.   Human resources management

Industrial relations

The current Industrial Relations Act enables the reaching of enterprise agreements.

At present a single enterprise agreement between the previous government and public sector unions, "The Continuous Improvement in the Australian Public Service Enterprise Agreement 1995-96", applies throughout the core public service. This provides for common salary adjustments in recognition of the contribution of staff, through a Continuous Improvement Strategy, to ongoing improvements in productivity, efficiency and overall performance as well as union commitment to progress genuine workplace reform and best practice at the agency level. The Agreement also enables the reaching of agreements on workplace reform at the agency level. Agency agreements can provide employment conditions which are more tailored to the individual workplaces or vary the application of essential standards, but cannot vary pay.

Agency agreements currently apply in 64 agencies, covering nearly 88 per cent of core APS staff.

Many agencies have taken advantage of agency bargaining to tailor conditions of employment to their own needs and those of their staff. In 1996 the Department of Industrial Relations has published examples of such innovative conditions in APS *Agency Agreements and Innovative Employment Conditions, a Resource Guide* (ISBN 642 24529 0). This sets out examples of initiatives in areas such as leave (including family, bereavement and carer's leave), hours of work including flexitime, more flexible forms of employment including part-time and home-based work, other conditions of service such as overtime, shifts and shift penalties, and human resource management issues such as anti-discrimination and competency-based training. The Department of Industrial Relations has published details of some of the most innovative initiatives.

Outside the core public service, over 99 per cent of staff of Government Business Enterprises are covered by enterprise agreements. There are also a number of statutory authorities which are not staffed under the Public Service Act. While a number of very small agencies employ staff on a contract basis, overall most such agencies have had workplace agreements certified, covering about 95 per cent of staff employed in these authorities.

Like the APS, Government Business Enterprises and statutory authorities have emphasized using workplace bargaining to achieve workplace reform and introduce productivity initiatives. Examples include productivity improvements built around co-operation, quality service programs, simplification of leave provisions, and flexible attendance and absence arrangements to assist staff in balancing their work and personal responsibilities.

A major current issue is what form of bargaining and pay arrangements should be adopted after the current APS Enterprise Agreement expires and the new Workplace Reform legislation comes into effect.

There have been several other major recent reforms to the industrial relations framework applying to the Australian Public Service.

These include significant rationalisation and modernisation of industrial awards. On 14 December 1995, the Australian Industrial Relations Commission ratified an integrated set of nine new Awards which apply to staff employed under the Public Service Act. These replaced over a hundred awards which provided an administratively complex variety of conditions of employment, some of which applied just to members of a single union. The new Awards are drafted in plain English and standardize previously varying conditions. They also build in significant flexibilities for agencies to vary award conditions to meet the needs of their organisation and allow staff to achieve a better balance between work and family responsibilities.

Another aspect of sound personnel management in a devolved environment is having high quality, up-to-date, easy to follow reference material for managers and staff. In 1996 the Department of Industrial Relations launched *Guide to APS Pay and Conditions of Employment*, along with a ready reference guide for managers and human resource staff titled *Questions and Answers: APS Pay and Conditions of Employment*. These have been written in plain English and have been well received by client agencies.

A particular emphasis of recent Government policy has been to promote family-friendly workplace practices. This has included the development of carer's leave that enables staff to take leave to care for sick members of their immediate household. In addition it has sought actively to promote examples of innovative work and family activities.

Guidelines on Official Conduct

To take account of changes in the public sector environment the 1987 Guidelines on Official Conduct were revised in 1995. The new version includes extended coverage on fraud prevention and a new section on whistleblowing. A national series of ethics awareness workshops were held to promote understanding of the Guidelines and the standard of conduct expected of APS staff. The Management Advisory Board published a booklet *Ethical Standards and Values in the Australian Public Service* which examined approaches to complex ethical situations.

Achieving Cost Effective Personnel Services (ACEPS)

Due to a concern about the cost and effectiveness of personnel services in the APS, the Management Advisory Board set up a project team to gather and analyse information on personnel/HR services in the APS and to compare performance between the APS and "good practice" private sector organisation. One of the overall findings that emerged from this project is that there is a need for fundamental change in the way personnel services are designed and delivered. A group of ten agencies (representing 50 per cent of APS staff) which had participated in the ACEPS study have gone on to conduct a detailed business process re-engineering review of their people management processes and practices. The findings of this review indicate that with changes to agency practices and "whole of government" approaches it will be possible to redesign people management practices in the APS and achieve significant cost savings. Working groups are undertaking review of a range of issues related to performance management, the employment framework, selection and recruitment activities and the administration of pay and conditions to make recommendations for HRM reforms.

F.   Budget process and management of financial resources

Accrual accounting

From 1994-95 all public entities, including government departments have been required to prepare and submit audited accrual financial statements (operating statement, statement of assets and liabilities, program statement and cash flow statement).

A trial set of consolidated financial statements for the whole of government was prepared for the financial year ended 30 June 1995 on an accrual basis. The statements also show the financial results for each sector that comprises the whole of government (general government, public trading enterprises (PTEs) and public finance enterprises (PFEs) sectors).

The government has agreed, subject to a scoping study which will examine costs, coverage and transitional arrangements, to implement an integrated budgeting, resource management and financial reporting framework by the year 2000. The first phase of the implementation will require audited consolidated financial statements of the Commonwealth to be tabled in the Parliament for the 1996-97 financial year.

The objective is to build a consistent financial framework within which financial objectives/targets can be determined and performance against those objectives/targets can be measured and reported on a reliable and consistent basis. This will improve the transparency of government activities and facilitate structural change necessary to create a more contestable and businesslike public sector.

G.   Performance management

Competitive tendering and contracting – Industry Commission Report

The Industry Commission (IC) was commissioned in 1995 to report to Parliament on the nature, extent and scope of competitive tendering and contracting (CTC) by Commonwealth, State and Territory, and Local Governments and their agencies.

The report was released by the government on 18 June 1996.

Specifically, the report identifies some of the costs and benefits of contracting out and also develops a set of indicative principles for public sector managers to use in assessing the scope for the more cost effective use of contracting out.

The IC report suggests that CTC can increase the level of contestability and efficiency in the provision of public services. Where viable markets exist or can be developed for the provision of "public" goods and services, this brings into question the need for continued direct government involvement in the actual delivery of a good or service. Under CTC, these contestable public services are provided by the most competitive provider which may be either in-house government agencies, the private sector or other public agencies. CTC provides one avenue through which governments can increase the level of contestability and reduce the cost of the provision of Commonwealth, State and Local Government public services.

The government is considering each of the IC recommendations in detail and will respond to the IC report in the last quarter of 1996.

I.   Regulatory management and reform

Competition policy and systematic legislative review

In response to a wide-ranging report on a national competition policy for Australia, the Council of Australian Governments (comprising the heads of federal, state and territory governments) signed in April 1995 the Competition Principles Agreement. Part of this agreement obligates governments to review and reform by the year 2000 any legislation which restricts competition, unless it can be demonstrated to be in the public interest.

Governments have satisfied the first requirements to develop by mid-1996 schedules as to what legislation is to be reviewed. The Commonwealth Government has announced a program of 98 reviews including, for example, foreign investment policy and of intellectual property legislation.

Reflecting the substantial potential gains to the nation from such regulatory reform, the Commonwealth will make payments to the state and territory governments if they satisfactorily meet their obligations under the Competition Principles Agreement.

Small Business Deregulation Task Force

There has been an increasing appreciation that regulations impose a disproportionate burden on small business, yet that sector has the most potential to provide employment opportunities. Accordingly, the Commonwealth Government established a Small Business Deregulation Task Force which is to report in November 1996 on revenue-neutral measures to reduce the burden of paper work and compliance costs on small business by 50 per cent.

The Prime Minister, in announcing the establishment of the Task Force, said that as a downpayment on further initiatives, "the Australian Bureau of Statistics has guaranteed to reduce the cost to small business of completing statistical returns by 20 per cent".

Mr. W. J. Blick
First Assistant Secretary, Government Division
Department of the Prime Minister and Cabinet
3-5 National Circuit
Canberra A.C.T. 2600
Tel.: (61-6) 271 57 61
Fax: (61-6) 271 57 76

Annex A

PRINCIPAL RECENT PUBLIC MANAGEMENT DEVELOPMENTS

1993

- Mutual recognition of other State and Territory regulations on the sale of goods and practice of registered occupations
- Strategic Plan for Equal Employment Opportunity
- Guidelines on Official Conduct of Commonwealth Public Servants
- Establishment of Central Redeployment Unit to assist in the redeployment of excess staff in the APS

1994

- Report of the Public Service Act Review Group
- Public Service Commission and Merit Protection Review Agency merged to form the Public Service and Merit Protection Commission (PSMPC)
- Eastern Regional Organisation for Public Administration seminar held in Canberra

1995

- Competition Principles Agreement signed, obliging governments to review and reform legislation which restricts competition
- Continuous Improvement in the Australian Public Service Enterprise Agreement
- More than 80 per cent of APS employees covered by agency agreements by end of 1995
- First Annual Report of the Steering Committee for the Review of Commonwealth/State service provision
- Office of Government Information Technology released an Exposure Draft – Framework and Strategies for Information Technology in the Commonwealth of Australia
- Launch of *Productive Diversity in the Australian Public Service* to assist agencies in recruiting and utilising people with diverse cultural and linguistic skills

1996

- Establishment of Small Business Deregulation Task Force
- Management Advisory Board/Management Improvement Advisory Committee (MAB/MIAC) project "Achieving Cost Effective Personnel Services" reviewing the costs and effectiveness of personnel service across the APS against the private sector
- MAB/MIAC project "2 + 2 = 5: Innovative Ways of Organising People" to consider the value of teams in the APS and the issue of hierarchy
- MAB/MIAC project "Raising the Standard: Benchmarking for Better Government" – the practical skills and tools for the essential tasks of comparing performance with current best practice.(The web site for this report is http://www.innovations.gov.au/benchmar.htm)
- Government response to the Industry Commission Report on Competitive Tendering and Contracting Out by Public Sector Agencies
- A framework is developed for managing redundancies in the APS
- National Commission of Audit Report
- MAB/MIAC project "Guidelines for Managing Risk in the Australian Public Service" in response to the need for greater recognition of the place of risk management in maximising program effectiveness as an important issue in the ongoing APS reform program
- MAB/MIAC project "Ethical Standards and Values in the Australian Public Service". The purpose of the paper is to contribute to the maintenance and development of high ethical standards in the APS Service by increasing awareness and understanding of the issues involved.

Annex B

INSTITUTIONAL RESPONSIBILITY FOR PUBLIC MANAGEMENT IMPROVEMENT

ORGANISATION	TASK AND RESPONSIBILITIES	OTHER INFORMATION
Department of Finance (DOF)	• Financial Management Improvement Programme (FMIP): coordinator • Programme Management and Budgeting (PMB)	
Public Service and Merit Protection Commission (PSMPC)	• Statutory responsibility for the Senior Executive Service, EEO and grievances and appeals • Policy development, advice and guidelines on performance management, recruitment, ethics and training	A small independent statutory body. In December 1995 the Public Service Commission and Merit Protection Review Agency were amalgamated to form the PSMPC.
Department of Industrial Relations (DIR)	• Industrial relations issues	
Department of the Prime Minister and Cabinet (PM&C)	• Advice to Prime Minister and Minister Assisting for the Public Service on public service issues • Responsibility for some aspects of administering Public Service Act 1922 • General responsibility for machinery of government • Support to Secretary of the Department as chairperson of Management Advisory Board • Secretariat support to MAB	The heads of the DoF, the PSMPC and DIR are members of the MAB.

AUSTRIA

A.   Main tendencies and overall priorities

B.   Context affecting public management, and

C.   Strategies and processes for planning and carrying out public management reforms

The last few years have led to a significant increase of the budget deficit from 56.7 billion schillings in 1992 (2.8 per cent of the GDP) to 116 billion schillings in 1995 (4.9 per cent of the GDP).

This growing budgetary pressure made it necessary to define a strategic savings plan at the political level. Some of its key elements are:

- 4 per cent saving within two years at the federal level, which represents a reduction of 11 000 posts in the public service;
- to keep the overall personnel costs for the public service during 1996 and 1997 at the level of 1995;
- no salary increases within the public sector during 1996 and 1997; and
- upward adjustment of the *de facto* retirement age (from 56 now to at least 60 years).

To support this downsizing programme an administrative management development plan was established, based on the comprehensive Administrative Management Project (AMP) carried through in the beginning of the 1990s.

The Division for Public Administration Development was also subject to budget cuts, and with fewer resources it became necessary to set priorities for the reform work.

The overall objectives of the AMP were:

- to tighten up operational and management structures so they are focused on core business, and identify responsibilities which could be cut back, transferred or abolished;
- to increase the administrations' productivity by 20 per cent over the next four years, and develop strategies including specific cost and performance data;
- to reduce administrative costs by introducing cost accounting systems and other measures with the aim of making the public administration more cost-conscious;
- to concentrate on management issues such as staff motivation and personnel development as well as strategic performance targets;
- to create a balanced division of labour for staff in public administration; and
- to create a more citizen-oriented public administration.

The AMP was concluded in 1994 with a Project Report which covered both interministerial (*e.g.* 'leadership and personnel'; 'budgeting and controlling') and intraministerial subprojects (*e.g.* the successful privatisation of Schönbrunn). As public administration is a permanent process of development, the main objectives of the Administrative Reform Project were renewed in 1995 and the priorities for the coming years were set as follows:

- continuing efforts to implement cost accounting systems in the public administration;
- building up a performance measurement system for the federal administration;

– supporting the development of a results-oriented culture with special training and information initiatives;

– further work in defining the core activities of agencies and reducing activities which are no longer necessary; and

– organisational development as a result of newly defined tasks.

Some details of development plans and measures already implemented are referred to in the sections which follow.

E. Human resources management

The recruiting procedures are improved by introducing Assessment-Centre-Methods within the framework of the job announcement regulations (*Ausschreibungsgesetz*).

The Federal Chancellery offers a job information service (*Job-Börse*) to all federal civil servants with the aim of improving mobility within the service.

The 1994 *salary reform* is the first step in reshaping the legal framework for the federal civil service.

The next step will be the implementation of an instrument based on management by objectives. The so-called "*Mitarbeitergespräch*" (annual structured dialogue leading to agreements on core objectives and tools for personnel development) will be mandatory starting 1 January 1998.

The following subjects are in the drafting stage:

– Contractual Personnel Act: It will bring a shift in salary determination from the emphasis on age or length of service to the predominance of responsibility and performance and therefore especially encourage ambitious younger members of the service. For federal public service employees under this Act there will be no special pension scheme. They will be covered by the general old age insurance system like employees in the private sector.

– Reform of training: Training on the job will not be confined to the initial phase of the career but be transformed into a continuous process.

Since the administrative culture is very much input-oriented and job performance is primarily measured with reference to the precise execution of laws and regulations there is an urgent need for a broader perspective in training efforts.

Firstly, the new training on the job seeks to enhance the social competencies of civil service personnel. Secondly, elements of economics and business administration will be integrated. This will allow for economic aspects in the rendering of services to become part of the criteria for excellent public administration.

F. Budget process and management of financial resources

The government's strategic savings plan is outlined above. Certain specific financial management steps are also noted in Annex A.

G. Performance management

Consistent with the strengthening of a results-oriented culture and the focus on performance-oriented management, a project on a performance measurement system for the federal administration was launched.

With the support of OECD-PUMA a system of performance indicators should be established which enables public management to optimise decisions about resource allocation and which provides public administration with basic information for benchmarking programmes. As a first step performance indicators already existing should be analysed in four pilot ministries. The result should answer the question, which existing indicators could be used for an overall performance measurement system and which indicators are still to be developed to receive a clear view of the public administration's performance.

In order to strengthen competition within Public Administration, Austria is taking part in the third Quality Award SPEYER 1996. After half a year's preparation, seven Austrian public administrations at local level (four cities and three communities) also decided to present their modernisation concepts and implementations based on the ideas of New Public Management. For the first time this kind of international benchmarking includes administrations of all German speaking parts of Europe (Germany, Switzerland and Austria). The quality of the candidates' papers is rather high and three of the Austrian candidates get a Quality Award. The final presentation of the winners is in December 1996.

In order to support the efforts to introduce the idea of "controlling" in Austrian public administration, a Controlling Handbook was published and presented in June 1996. The main issues of this kind of manual for public servants are general remarks about the meaning and the functions of controlling, and the advantages of controlling for more efficiency within public administration. A big part of the book deals with promising practices in several areas of public administration, where controlling systems have already been established. At the moment a special training programme for public managers and future controllers is being developed to breath life into the controlling handbook. ("Controlling" must be understood as a method of *steering* public administration's performance towards fixed targets, as opposed to the meaning of the word "controlling" in the sense of supervision).

I. Regulatory management and reform

The Federal Chancellery is heading a project for the elimination of obsolete laws and for a general decrease in the number of laws (thereafter referred to as "The Consolidation Project"). The current first phase of the Consolidation Project encompasses all laws which were enacted before 1945 and are still in force (about 515), some 20 per cent of which are completely obsolete. A portion of the remaining laws will be abolished after adding the provisions which remain relevant to these laws. The Ministry of Justice (about 220 laws) and the Ministry of Health and Consumer Protection (about 60 laws) were the first ministries to embrace the Consolidation Project, with the rest expected to follow soon. No precise long-term schedule is available.

Mr. Emmerich Bachmayer
Head of Department II
Federal Chancellery
Ballhausplatz 2
A-1014 Wien
Tel.: (43-1) 531 15 22 60
Fax: (43-1) 531 15 24 61

Annex A

PRINCIPAL RECENT PUBLIC MANAGEMENT DEVELOPMENTS

1993
– Continuous implementation of reform measures (for example cost accounting and performance measurement system in the Austrian Federal Accounting Service, cost accounting systems in several agencies and in the federal ministry for economic affairs; a Facility Management System where spaceplans are digitised and space administration is ADP-based; privatisation initiatives).
– Project evaluation.

1994
– Presentation of the *Administrative Management Project-Report*.

1995
– On the basis of the project evaluation and in a climate of a permanent raising budgetary pressure new priorities and initiatives for administrative development were discussed.

1996
– Priorities and new initiatives were fixed as follows:
  • cost accounting systems within public administration;
  • a performance measurement system for the federal administration;
  • defining core activities; and
  • organisational development.

Annex B

INSTITUTIONAL RESPONSIBILITY FOR PUBLIC MANAGEMENT IMPROVEMENT

ORGANISATION	TASKS AND RESPONSIBILITIES	OTHER INFORMATION
Federal Chancellery	• personnel policy across the federal administration • constitutional and legislative services and data protection issues • administrative reform • economic co-ordination and structural policies • IT policy and co-ordination • privatisation issues • co-ordination of auditing and control practices	The Federal Academy for Administration operates under the Federal Chancellery and is responsible for public service training programmes
Ministry of Finance	• budget process • improvement of financial management	

Annex C

KEY PUBLIC DOCUMENTS ON PUBLIC MANAGEMENT ISSUES AND DEVELOPMENTS

Projektstudie "*Personalentwicklung in der österreichischen Bundesverwaltung*", 1990.

Handbuch "*Was kostet ein Gesetz?*" zur Berechnung der finanziellen Auswirkungen von Gesetzen, 1992.

Projektbericht "Verwaltungsmanagement", 1994.

Controlling-Handbuch für die öffentliche Verwaltung, 1996.

BELGIUM

A. Main tendencies and overall priorities

The policy of improving the efficiency of public administration has remained a government priority. This priority was emphasized when the new government was formed after the parliamentary elections in Spring 1995.

It is a policy that reflects the trend towards:

– better relations with the public;
– closer working contact between politicians and the administration;
– greater transparency in public service, thus enhancing democracy;
– continuity with the measures taken by the previous government.

The priorities that have emerged are:

– modernisation of information policy, as regards both intra-government information and information disseminated to citizens (databases and networks, particularly modernisation of statistical instruments, contact points, mediator services);
– application of the principles of the Public Service Users' Charter (published in December 1992) and regular evaluation of such application;
– development of objective and professional personnel management in the areas of recruitment, appraisal and training; development of mobility;
– flexibility in working hours, greater flexibility in public opening hours, development of homeworking and redistribution of working time;
– greater accountability of the administration and its management staff, particularly through protocols on relations between the political offices and the administrations;
– completion of the restructuring carried out following the in-depth study of the public sector (1991-1993), particularly in National Defence, Finance, the Buildings Office and the Auditing Committee (administrative police).

B. Context affecting public management

The process of analysing the context of administrative reforms involves identifying the sources of pressure behind change. One important source is the desire to consolidate the Budget, even though the aim of achieving short-term accounting goals can also be a barrier to more radical management reform and to spending on modernisation.

The international context plays an important role. Globalisation and the requirements of competitiveness push the private sector to lobby policy-makers for efficient public services. Inspection and control bodies also have a part to play in this respect since they ensure that economic operators are not able to break the rules of competition.

The single European market is also a driving force and the projects backed by the European Commission to help create an "information society" are a considerable spur.

There is also constant pressure from the electorate, and the extremist voting tendencies nurtured by feelings of insecurity, exclusion and poor public services make politicians aware of the need to reform the public sector. The tragic events of the summer of 1996, involving the kidnapping and murder of children and the arrest of the culprits, considerably increased this pressure from the public, who believed that such incidents could have been averted, had the justice system worked better.

The setting up of a separate Public Service Ministry, thus making one minister fully responsible for this issue, is a clear indication that politicians are taking the question seriously.

Finally, mention should be made of the authorities' perception of the role of the public sector as the vehicle for social change that could be an inspiration to society in general. Examples include flexible working hours, encouraging and protecting female participation, use of telematics, etc.

C. Strategies and processes for planning and carrying out public management reforms

Strategic approaches have been set out by the College of Secretaries-General and by the Public Service Ministry.

The College of Secretaries-General has produced a document entitled "*Le Collège des Secrétaires généraux, un acteur du renouveau administratif*", in which it traced the history of its role and described its future role in the administrative reform process, identifying priority projects.

The departments within the Public Service Ministry have written a legislation document "*Législature 1995-1999 – Eléments de politique générale du pôle Fonction publique*".

On the basis of these two documents, the Minister for the Public Service has produced a general policy paper on the civil service which, in the chapter on administrative reform, outlines the government's agreement and establishes a programme of work for the legislature. This paper was approved by the Government and used as a basis for parliamentary debate.

Other strategy documents or work programmes have also been submitted to the Government by ministers with more specific responsibilities such as, for instance, the Plan for scientific and technical support for the information society – "Scientific and technical support initiative for the provision of telematic facilities in federal services", proposed by the Minister for Science Policy, or the Prime Minister's document establishing plans to develop information highways.

Finally, departmental plans projecting several years ahead have been drawn up in some ministries, for instance in the Ministry of Finance, to establish the programme for the radical restructuring of the tax authorities.

In terms of resources, and complementing these strategy documents setting out goals and measures, it is important to mention the growing use of networking, whereby delegates from different ministries and bodies who are responsible for modernisation plans can meet, swap experiences, implement joint projects and develop a results-orientated culture of co-operation. This is the case of the College of Secretaries-General, civil servants responsible for training, communications, evaluation, computerisation and provision of telematic facilities, implementing the Public Service Users' Charter, etc.

D. Policy-management capacities

An initiative worth mentioning is the introduction by each minister of a general policy document as this has improved policy co-ordination and coherence and encouraged proactive policy formulation in the medium term. These documents give clear guidelines for administrative action.

The same documents also serve as a basis for the budget debate in Parliament.

E. Human resources management

One of the most important projects at the present time is the reform of the staff appraisal system. A major investment is being made, particularly in terms of communications, training of appraisers and the design of tools to analyse jobs in order to prepare appraisal criteria which, in tabular form, will constitute the reference document. The preparation of criteria according to jobs is planned for October 1997. The first evaluation will take place in 1998.

This project is being implemented in accordance with the new general terms of staff employment. The aim is to obtain a true assessment of the contribution of each staff member to the functioning of the service. Appraisal results will have practical consequences for the careers of staff.

In addition, departments are in the process of implementing reforms to simplify career structures. Other projects aim to develop flexible work time patterns, something which, as stated above, responds to a major employment policy concern. A project to explore the feasibility of home-based work has also been under way since September 1995, with phase one due to finish in September 1997.

G. Performance management

As part of implementation of the Public Service Users' Charter, pilot schemes are under way to enable services to measure customer satisfaction and to set publicised service quality standards which to some extent provide a basis for an unwritten agreement with users. Often, these standards relate to response times.

Results from the pilot are expected at the end of 1996, and if promising they may lead to the wider implementation of the measures once suitable training has been given.

A number of departments are starting to develop management control and performance monitoring functions. To aid them in their new task, some Secretaries-General are setting up audit or internal evaluation units to monitor the performance of the departments under their authority in the ministry. This arrangement should facilitate the assessment of a fair distribution of resources in relation to the targetted results to be achieved by each department. The Secretaries-General are given the initiative for this process.

There is another stimulus for this kind of development, namely the European Union requirement for quality audits in the implementation by national governments of policies subject to European directives.

A bill is under discussion to give social security bodies greater management autonomy under a management contract scheme.

Performance audits along functional lines have been carried out, particularly at interdepartmental level.

H. Changing structures of the public sector

A separate Public Service Ministry was established on 1 January 1995, containing the following departments:

- the General Administration Service responsible for personnel management and employment rules;
- the Training Institute;
- the Organisation and Management Consultancy Bureau (ABC Consultancy Bureau) which is an amalgamation of the former ABC Bureau and the Information Technology Consultancy Bureau;
- the Permanent Secretariat for Recruitment;
- the Federal Purchasing Bureau;

- the Buildings Office;
- the Auditing Committee (administrative police).

Other structures have been or are being developed, amongst other things as a result of the in-depth study. This applies in particular to the Ministry of Finance, where the tax authorities have undergone radical restructuring.

J.   Other

The Public Service Users' Charter forms the basis for a communications and information policy. Thus, a guide to the different ministries, aimed at the general public, has been published with the help of the network of information officers. In addition to the current pilot projects (Section G), the Charter is the subject of regular meetings to assess its effectiveness.

On the initiative of the Prime Minister's Office, a project to modernise the federal information network is under way. A complementary study of information needs is also being carried out, and will serve as the basis for an inter-administration data exchange network.

Mr. Jean-Marie Mottoul
Chef de Corps
Bureau Conseil ABC
Ministère fédéral de la Fonction publique
Résidence Palace
Rue de la loi, 155
B-BRUSSELS
Tel.: (32-2) 287 40 07
Fax: (32-2) 287 40 10

Annex A

PRINCIPAL RECENT PUBLIC MANAGEMENT DEVELOPMENTS

1994

– Reform of job schedules in departments with simplification of career structures and separation of remuneration from upgradings.
– Introduction of a plan of action to implement the Users' Charter. Creation of the post of information officer in each department.
– Auditform, a project to simplify administrative forms.

1995

– Completion of major restructuring such as the creation of the Ministry of the Public Service, the merger of the Ministry of Agriculture and the Ministry for the Middle Classes (the self-employed and small and medium-sized enterprises) and of the Ministry of Social Affairs and the Ministry of Public Health.
– Adoption of rules on the new appraisal system and pilot schemes to implement the system.
– Rules to introduce flexible working time.

Annex B

INSTITUTIONAL RESPONSIBILITY FOR PUBLIC MANAGEMENT IMPROVEMENT

ORGANISATION	TASKS AND RESPONSIBILITIES
Ministerial Management Committee – Prime Minister, Minister of the Public Service and Minister for the Budget	• informal committee which, on behalf of the government, meets with the College of Secretaries-General
College of Secretaries-General	• is consulted on management issues, particularly concerning staff
Ministry of the Public Service – Federal Administration Training Institute	• readability of official forms and documents, communication, training
– General Administration Service	• reform of staff employment rules, assessment of staffing requirements, pay
– ABC Consultancy Bureau	• organisation and management consultancy for the civil service and the government • information technology consultancy
Prime Minister's Office	• institutional reforms • modernisation of the federal information network
Ministry of Finance – Budget and Expenditure Control Division	• budgetary reform

Annex C

KEY PUBLIC DOCUMENTS ON PUBLIC MANAGEMENT ISSUES AND DEVELOPMENTS

Reports by the General Delegation for the Reform of State Accountancy, Ministry of Finance, 1985-1987

Stratégies d'actions prioritaires pour la modernisation des services publics, Secretary of State for modernisation of public services, 1986

Opération Logos – Le retour d'image, Ministry of the Public Service, 1990

Royal Decree on the general rules of staff employment, 1991

La radioscopie des besoins en personnel de la Fonction publique admninistrative, ABC Consultancy Bureau, 1992

Public Service Users' Charter, 1992

Les Agences dans la Fonction publique administrative fédérale, ABC Consultancy Bureau, 1993

Policy document issued by the Ministry of the Interior and Public Service, 1993

Report to the Government assessing the Users' Charter, ABC Consultancy Bureau, 1994

Le Collège des Secrétaires généraux – un acteur du renouveau administratif, College of Secretaries-General, 1995

General policy document produced by the Ministry of the Public Service for the financial year 1996, 1995

Un nouveau système d'évaluation des agents de la Fonction publique, Ministry of the Public Service (in publication)

Vade-mecum du gestionnaire de système d'évaluation, ABC Consultancy Bureau, 1996

CANADA

A. Main tendencies and overall priorities

Canada has made major progress in turning around the deterioration in the fiscal situation, while at the same time reducing waste and inefficiency, strengthening the public service to efficiently and effectively deliver programmes and services, and redefining and redesigning the government's programmes and activities.

In 1994, the federal government launched a Program Review, the comprehensive review of all government programmes to bring about the most effective and cost-efficient way of delivering programmes and services. It was part of the government's strategy to implement significant but orderly declines in programme spending. In addition to providing expenditure savings, Program Review has further reformed and renewed federal programming. The goal is programmes that are more focused, more efficient and more affordable, and that reflect changing priorities.

As a result of the work of Program Review, the role of the government of Canada is now centred around five core roles:

- to ensure that Canada speaks with one voice in the community of nations;
- to protect and promote the efficiency of the Canadian economic union;
- to protect and promote the Canadian social union – the sharing community;
- to manage the "pooling" of resources for the pursuit of collective goals in those cases where efficiency gains dictate;
- to be the guardian of Canadian rights, values and entitlements.

The Canadian government has put in motion a number of initiatives to follow up on Program Review. The most significant of these is actions in *Getting Government Right*. The objectives of *Getting Government Right*, announced on 7 March 1996, are to:

- clarify federal roles and responsibilities in order to make the federation work better and reduce costly overlap and duplication;
- ensure that resources are devoted to the highest priorities so that Canada is well positioned to face the economic and social challenges of the 21st century;
- respond to the public demand for better and more accessible government by involving clients more in decision making and using modern and practical service delivery tools; and
- achieve more affordable government by reducing the deficit and debt pressures, and allow the government to effectively address issues that are important to Canadians.

Under the banner of a range of "alternative service delivery" initiatives, the government is making significant progress in exploring ways to improve the delivery of services and reduce costs. This has already led to a major redefinition of the role of the federal government in several areas. Departments across government have been taking initiatives to provide services in new ways. The essence of these changes is to give service delivery organisations greater autonomy to provide their services in more cost-effective ways and in ways that are more responsive to the needs of their clients. This is being accomplished by departments adopting quality service principles and practices as part of their overall strategy for delivering services to Canadians. An example is the Canada Business Service Centres, a single access point for federal, provincial and municipal programmes and services of interest to businesses.

As part of *Getting Government Right*, the government has recognised the need to reform the public service. Accordingly, on 7 March 1996, the President of the Treasury Board announced that:

- beginning in February 1997, the wage freeze in the federal Public Service will be lifted and collective bargaining will resume;
- beginning June 1996, annual increments (which had been suspended for two years) will be reinstated and performance pay (suspended since 1991) will also be reintroduced;
- the *Public Service Superannuation Act* will be changed to improve the portability provisions of Public Service pensions, bringing them in line with most plans offered by other Canadian employers.

B. Context affecting public management

This is a period of profound change in government and its functioning: like most countries throughout the western democratic world, Canada is engaged, at all levels, in rethinking the role of government, the relationship between government and citizens and, in consequence, the role and operation of the public sector.

Canadian public management is currently affected by fiscal restraint and the government's commitment to reduce the federal deficit to 2 per cent of GDP in 1997-98. Canada's public management is also affected by the vastness of the country; its multicultural, bilingual population; and issues surrounding national unity and the threat of Quebec secession.

Trends within the public service include:

- a renewed focus on service to the public in the context of citizens, clients and taxpayers;
- public service downsizing;
- changing demographics;
- a critical public environment; and
- recent changes in the public service employment contract.

The Canadian federal government is ensuring that:

- clients perceive government as flexible and client-centred;
- overlap and duplication are eliminated;
- those who deliver service have the flexibility and autonomy they need; and
- those who develop policy are able to focus on strategic planning rather than crisis management.

C. Strategies and processes for planning and carrying out public management reforms

Public Service renewal, an element of the broader government renewal effort that has been underway over the past two years, has the goal of modernising the way government delivers its services, strengthening policy capacity within government and building a public service that is a vibrant national institution adapted to future needs.

Canada has begun to transform the relationship between the federal public sector and other organisations and stakeholders. The government has made significant progress in streamlining its operations, redefining its fundamental roles and responsibilities and *Getting Government Right* through:

- Program Review: determining what programmes and services the government is involved in and how these services are delivered;

- Efficiency of the Federation Initiative;
- review of boards and agencies; and
- several fundamental policy reviews (*e.g.* defence, foreign policy).

Getting Government Right has wide-ranging objectives. They include:

- reaffirming public confidence in government generally, and in the federal government in particular;
- finding a new equilibrium where the role of government is more sensibly and reasonably aligned with its competence and resources, and refashioning federal programmes so that government spends less but provides the best possible service to Canadians within the limits of available resources;
- clarifying the responsibilities of the federal government in relation to those of the other levels of government; and
- improving the climate of federal provincial relations while reaffirming in the minds of Canadians the value and importance of the federal government, and of the federation itself.

An examination of how Canadians are served – by federal departments and agencies, and by other governments – is also taking place, another part of *Getting Government Right*. Organising the business of government, particularly service delivery, from the citizen's point of view involves a major transition which will take some time to complete. It is essential that transition be guided by a clear set of principles, with a focus on service delivery, and the government has therefore adopted a Declaration of Quality Service Principles to guide the government's service delivery policy. Initiatives include:

- an examination of alternative service delivery mechanisms (including opportunities for partnering with other levels of government and the private sector; employee take-overs; commercialisation of services);
- improvements in accountability to make services convenient, flexible, efficient and relevant (bench marking; development of best practices and of service standards for business lines); and
- the use of modern information technology concepts and tools to improve services to Canadians, to streamline operations, and to reduce the cost of government.

In response to challenges confronting the public service identified by the Clerk of the Privy Council, seven Deputy Minister Task Forces were set up to examine issues related to the Future of the Public Service, Service Delivery Models, Federal Presence, Overhead Services, Values and Ethics; Policy Planning; and Horizontal Issues. The work of the Task Forces will contribute to future policy and management decisions and will feed into the work being done elsewhere in the federal government, such as Program Review. Each Task Force has a specific mandate and they are now completing their work and reporting back with results (the Task Forces are also discussed in sections D and E).

D. Policy-Management capacities

The federal government has recognised the need for greater long term planning and the need to improve strategic policy making. There are several ongoing initiatives to address this, including the Deputy Minister Task Forces which focus on policies and strategies for the future.

The purpose of portfolio management – an overall direction and co-ordination of policy, legislation and activities – is to provide more integrated advice to Ministers. It responds to the more complex and less centralised public service in which departments are devolving programmes to new alternate service delivery vehicles, and to the fiscal pressures for budget saving across entire portfolios that the government is facing.

A portfolio is simply all of the organisations reporting to a Minister – the department, service agencies, administrative tribunals and Crown corporations.

Portfolio management is designed to become part of the culture of each organisation in a portfolio. Portfolio management means above all a change in culture, and a change in approach. It means a more deliberate approach to co-ordination of organisations in a portfolio:

– to support Ministers in overseeing portfolios by giving them the best public service advice – co-ordinated and coherent;
– to improve coherence of government policy and decision-making; and
– to ensure policy coherence across government as new service delivery agencies are established.

Organisations within a Ministerial portfolio can co-operate, while respecting their individual mandates, so that together they can:

– contribute to policy formulation;
– provide advice on legislative reform;
– exchange information and learn from one another on best management practices; and
– work on horizontal issues.

E.   Human resources management

A current challenge facing the government is ensuring continuity in the leadership of the Public Service and building a culture where each and every public servant is dedicated to leaving behind a better institution than the one they inherited. The government has launched *"La Relève"* as a concerted effort to meet these objectives and to build a public service for the future that is competent, professional and respected.

To facilitate the moving of service functions away from the federal government, the government has introduced transition measures for employees affected by alternative service delivery and is working on changes to the portability provisions of public service pension plans.

The wage freeze will also be ended and the resumption of collective bargaining is planned (other initiatives relevant to this are discussed in Section A).

F.   Budget process and management of financial resources

The federal deficit, which amounted to about 6 per cent of GDP in 1993-94, will be down to 2 per cent of GDP in 1997-98. As a result, Canada's deficit as a share of GDP will have fallen from double the G-7 average in 1992 to well below the G-7 average in 1997. The government's fiscal strategy is consistent with the broader approach discussed earlier which aims to bring about a significant but orderly decline in public expenditure.

As well, a number of provinces have balanced their budgets, and some have started to repay their accumulated debt. Note the discussion in sections A and B on the context and priorities for budget management.

G.   Performance management

A three-point strategy for enhancing performance-based management within the federal government was announced by the President of the Treasury Board in November 1995:

– As part of the expenditure management system, federal departments and agencies will identify in planning documents clear and measurable results expected for their major programmes and business lines, so that Canadians will know what they can expect to receive for their tax dollar.

- The responsibility is placed on programme managers to measure their achievements in a way that clearly shows how government programmes have performed.

- Managers will make this information readily available to colleagues so that best practices can be followed more widely in the public service; and will make sure parliamentarians and the public are fully informed. In 1996, on a pilot basis, six departments submitted annual Departmental Performance Reports to Parliament.

Canada's strategy for performance-based management will:

- identify clear and measurable results for government programmes;
- measure achievements and inform Parliament; and
- make results public to establish best practices and improve performance.

A report on Strengthening Government Review is tabled annually in Parliament. The 1995 report focused on "Strengthening Government Review" as an important aspect of moving to a results-based management culture.

H. Changing structures of the public sector

A major priority of the current reform directions in Canada has involved exploring alternative service delivery mechanisms with the aim of improving the effectiveness and cost-efficiency of public services. Canada is moving towards a future where we will be able to use different models in the public service to meet different needs. Canada will not just rely on one approach of public service for serving Canadians. Instead, it will be possible to tailor the organisation to meet the needs of the citizens it serves. This has the potential to profoundly renew the public sector and to make an important contribution toward renewing the Canadian federation.

In the 21st century, there are areas where the federal government does not have to be involved. Components of Canada's transportation infrastructure are being transferred to community-based groups, municipal authorities and the private sector. The government is prepared to withdraw from its functions in such areas as labour market training, forestry, mining, and recreation that are more appropriately the responsibility of others, including provincial governments, local authorities or the private sector. For example, an agreement in principle has been reached to transfer Transport Canada's Air Navigation System to Nav Canada, a new private sector corporation controlled by stakeholders and operating on a cost recoverable, not-for-profit basis.

Several new organisations have been proposed:

- A single Food Inspection Service: an agency that will integrate interdepartmental services, bringing together a function that is currently spread over three departments, so that clients can be served better. As progress is achieved, the new food inspection service will serve as a vehicle to perform food inspection functions for the provinces, as well as the federal government.

- A Canadian Securities Commission: a national organisation that will provide common services and be mandated to serve both federal and provincial levels of government.

- A National Revenue Collection Agency: a new integrated approach to border services and to tax collection that will allow for the collection of all federal taxes (income, corporate and sales taxes) and permit tax collection on behalf or the provinces, providing more flexible, more timely and more efficient service than departments at the two levels of government are able to provide today.

- A Parks Canada Agency: a separate service agency to manage and preserve a system of national parks, national historic sites and canals and related protected areas for the use and enjoyment of Canadians. The agency will provide better services to Canadians and visitors through simplified human resource and administrative rules and more flexible financial authorities. A key to the agency's future success will be its expanded ability to enter into new partnership arrangements with Parks Canada employees, the private sector and voluntary organisations.

Employee take-overs are another alternative for commercialising government service delivery. An employee take-over policy was recently approved.

I.   Regulatory management and reform

The Government will ensure through regulatory reform that requirements are strong and clear, delays are minimised and activities are co-ordinated between departments and between levels of government. Canada's approach is multi-faceted with a range of incentives and disincentives for departments and is characterised by political leadership and partnerships.

In 1994 the federal government released *Building a More Innovative Economy*, which launched initiatives across the government to improve economic efficiency – an important component of regulatory reform. This initiative had a number of components, including the identification of priority sectors, reducing the paper burden, training, and community building and culture change.

By the end of 1996, major regulating departments will be required to implement regulatory process management standards.

Ms. Nicole Jauvin
Assistant Secretary to the Cabinet
Machinery of Government
Privy Council Office
80 Wellington Street
Ottawa, Ontario, K1A 0A3
Tel.: (1-613) 957 5492
Fax: (1-613) 957 5034

Annex A

PRINCIPAL RECENT PUBLIC MANAGEMENT DEVELOPMENTS

1993

- 25 June 1993 Reorganisation:
  - departments reduced from 32 to 23;
  - number of Cabinet Ministers reduced from 35 to 25;
  - Cabinet Committees reduced from 11 to 5;
  - full Cabinet restored as forum for decision-making;
  - fundamental re-design and re-organisation of departments.
- 4 November 1993 New Government:
  - departments increased from 23 to 24;
  - replacement of Public Security Portfolio with a re-created Solicitor General portfolio and the creation of the Department of Citizenship and Immigration;
  - number of Cabinet Ministers reduced from 25 to 23 with 8 Secretaries of State (who are not members of Cabinet) to assist Ministers;
  - Cabinet Committees reduced from 5 to 4.
- Federal Provincial Relations Office integrated into the Privy Council Office.
- Office of the Comptroller General integrated into the Treasury Board Secretariat.
- Temporary controls on most recruitment into the public service imposed to give priority to employees displaced by restructuring.
- Major initiative launched to make better use of information technology in streamlining the delivery of services to Canadians and reducing the cost of administration. Chief Informatics Officer established within the Treasury Board Secretariat.
- Improvements to service to the public to increase efficiency, effectiveness and accountability.

1994

- Major Government Reviews:
  - Program Review: a comprehensive review of all government programmes, produced decisions for long-term structural change in what the government does, as well as substantial reductions in the cost of government;
  - Agency Review: review of all federal boards, agencies, commissions and advisory bodies, resulted in decisions to eliminate outdated organisations and streamline others;
  - review of major sectors (social security, defence, foreign policy) and horizontal activities (science and technology, small business, efficiency, special interest group funding).
- Reform of the Decision-Making Process: strengthened ministerial accountability by allowing ministers to run their departments without resort to a complex Cabinet Committee system.
- Annual Strategic Planning Cycle, based on June, October and January special Cabinet meetings, introduced.
- Renewal of Expenditure Management System:
  - budget planning process now integrated with the Cabinet planning cycle;
  - new policy and programme proposals are considered in the context of the government's overall priorities and fiscal framework;
  - expenditure decisions on new priority initiatives are made in Cabinet;
  - ministers have greater individual responsibility and accountability.
- Efficiency of the Federation Initiative: a process of intergovernmental collaboration aimed at making governments work better (increase administrative efficiencies, improve client service, harmonise procedures and regulations, reduce both costs and unnecessary overlap and duplication).
- Greater use of intergovernmental and interdepartmental co-operation: *e.g.* establishment of Canada Business Service Centres in all provinces to provide single-window service and bring together the activities and services of 19 federal departments, often including provincial and private-sector participation.

– Federal Budget announced service standards to be developed for all departments and agencies.
– Second Annual Report to the Prime Minister on the Public Service of Canada.

1995

– Continuation of Program Review.
– Quality Services Initiative approved by Cabinet requiring all government departments and agencies to focus on serving their clients better.
– Deputy Ministers Task Forces (Future of the Public Service, Service Delivery Models, Federal Presence, Overhead Services, and Values and Ethics, Policy Planning and Horizontal Issues).
– Federal Budget requires departments to establish service standards for major business lines.
– Public service downsizing: 45 000 fewer public service jobs over the next three years (with special programmes to provide for early departure and early retirement).
– Third Annual Report to the Prime Minister on the Public Service of Canada.

To May 1996

– Jobs strategy, with particular emphasis on youth, science and technology, and trade.
– Strengthening the economic framework, *e.g.* legislative improvements in competition, bankruptcy and copyright, financial institutions, *Canada Labour Code*.
– Environmental security, *e.g.* changes to the *Canadian Environmental Protection Act*, new legislation to protect endangered species.
– Renewal of the federation: strengthened partnership with the provinces focusing on such priorities as food inspection, environmental management, social housing, tourism and freshwater fish habitat.
– Economic Union: *e.g.* working with provinces and the private sector to achieve a more open Internal Trade Agreement, improving labour mobility, developing single national agencies (*e.g.* food inspection, Canadian Securities Commission).
– Securing the social safety net: *e.g.* health care; child support; seniors' benefits; Canada Pension Plan reforms; new Employment Insurance System; agreements with provinces on labour market training.
– *Getting Government Right*: modernising federal programmes and services to meet the needs of Canadians, both as citizens and clients.

Annex B

INSTITUTIONAL RESPONSIBILITY FOR PUBLIC MANAGEMENT IMPROVEMENT

ORGANISATION	TASKS AND RESPONSIBILITIES
Privy Council Office (PCO)	• non-partisan support and advice to the Prime Minister and the Cabinet on issues facing the government and on organisational and legislative changes for the public service • support to the Clerk as head of the Public Service on the co-ordination of strategic management initiatives and priorities • (note that the Federal-Provincial Relations Office was re-integrated into the Privy Council Office in 1993)
Public Service Commission (PSC)	• independent agency, accountable to Parliament for the application of the *Public Service Employment Act* • staffing of the Executive Group and interpretation and application of merit in staffing public service positions • middle management, supervisory, speciality and language training
Treasury Board Secretariat (TBS)	• administrative arm of and support to the Treasury Board as employer and general manager of the public service • general management of financial, human and material resources, and information systems and management, concerning both policy and expenditure proposals
Canadian Centre for Management Development (CCMD)	• orientation, training and development of senior managers • management research and development of learning strategies to enhance and broaden range of management courses offered by federal government
Department of Finance	• advice on economic and financial affairs of Canada • manages government's fiscal framework and accounts and presents fiscal projections
Office of the Auditor General	• performs audits of departments, agencies and Crown corporations regarding efficiency, economy and cost-effectiveness; whether reliance can be placed on an organisation's financial statements; and, whether activities have been carried out in compliance with legislation, regulations and other authorities

Annex C

KEY PUBLIC DOCUMENTS ON PUBLIC MANAGEMENT ISSUES AND DEVELOPMENTS

General

Third Annual Report to the Prime Minister on the Public Service of Canada, Clerk of the Privy Council and Secretary to the Cabinet, Minister of Supply and Services, Ottawa, 1995.

Quality Services: An Overview, President of the Treasury Board, Minister of Supply and Services, Ottawa, 1995.

Framework for Alternative Program Delivery, Treasury Board of Canada, Secretariat (1995), Minister of Supply and Services, Ottawa.

Getting Government Right: A Progress Report, Privy Council Office (1996), Minister of Supply and Services, Ottawa.

Specialised

Make or Buy? Stretching the Tax Dollar Series, Treasury Board of Canada, Secretariat (1993), Ottawa.

Staffing in the Public Service, Public Service Commission (1993), Ottawa.

Blueprint for Renewing Government Services Using Information Technology, Treasury Board of Canada, Secretariat (1994), Ottawa.

Quality Services: Guides I-IX, President of the Treasury Board, (1995), Minister of Supply and Services, Ottawa.

Strengthening Government Review: Annual Report to Parliament by the President of the Treasury Board, President of the Treasury Board, (1995), Minister of Supply and Services, Ottawa.

Stretching the Tax Dollar: The Federal Government as "Partner": Six Steps to Successful Collaboration, Treasury Board Secretariat, (October 1995), Minister of Supply and Services, Ottawa.

Trust within the Organisation – Part 1 and 2, Public Service Commission (1995), Ottawa.

A Guide to Costing Service Delivery for Service Standards, Stretching the Tax Dollar Series, Treasury Board of Canada, Secretariat (1995), Ottawa.

Quality and Affordable Service for Canadians – Establishing Service Standards in the Federal Government, Treasury Board of Canada, Secretariat (1995), Ottawa.

Dispelling the Myths: Employment Equity/Managing Diversity, Public Service Commission (1996), Ottawa.

Downsizing: Its Effects on Survivors, Public Service Commission (1996), Ottawa.

The Governance Scenarios, Task Force on the Future of the Public Service – Excerpts (1996), Ottawa.

CZECH REPUBLIC

A. Main tendencies and overall priorities

This report covers the period beginning with November 1989, and ending with June 1996, defined by the following events: the overthrow of the totalitarian rule of a single communist party (17 November 1989), the beginning of a reconstruction of the State administration and centralist economic system (January 1990), the first democratic parliamentary elections to the Federal Assembly, Czech National Council and Slovak National Council (June 1990), the split of the Federal State into the Czech and Slovak Republics and the establishment of a public management system of the new State, the Czech Republic (1 January 1993). The distinct priority of the first phase was decentralisation, *i.e.* the restoration of communal territorial self-government together with the abolition of the previous system of the so-called National Committees (local, municipal, district and regional) with the first democratic elections to communal representative bodies (November 1990). The priority from 1992 was economic reform with a marked privatisation of State property and the aim of creating a market economy.

With the first parliamentary elections in the independent Czech Republic (31 May-1 June 1996) certain changes in governance can be expected.

The major public administration priority for several years was reform and decentralisation of the State administration as necessary prerequisites to the success of economic transformation to a free civic society. The municipality became the basis of local government, a public law corporation with its own property and financial resources. Experience with decentralisation so far has been satisfactory. There are difficulties however posed by the preponderance of communes (6 230 altogether), the majority with very small populations (almost 5 000 communes with a population below 1 000). The process of decentralisation of the State administration has not been completed, as the intermediate (regional) tier of self-government, provided by the Constitution of the Czech Republic of December 1992, has not yet been established. The Government drafts of Constitutional Acts on the establishment of Higher Territorial Self-Governing Units (HTSGU) and the competence of HTSGU were rejected by the Parliament where the required constitutional majority (three-fifths of all Deputies) was not achieved. In the near future, another change in central Government in connection with the further devolution of State administration to regional level will have to be made.

The process of decentralisation of State administration was paralleled by the process of deconcentration of State administration in the territory to be nearer to the clients. A number of deconcentrated State administration agencies have been created [*e.g.* Labour Offices, Financial (Inland Revenue) Offices, School Offices, Customs Offices, District Social Security Administrations, Inspectorates of the Czech Commercial Inspection, Inspectorates of the State Energy Inspection, District Veterinary Administrations, Cadastral Offices, and others], resulting in an increase in State administration and its costs. In September 1994, the government adopted a resolution providing for the checking of the effectiveness of deconcentrated State administration agencies and the abolition of some of them. However, the process is very slow. It has been confirmed that it is much quicker to establish an office than to abolish it.

With the establishment of the Czech Republic it was also necessary to make changes in central government. New ministries and other central State agencies, previously existing at a federal level only, had to be established, including for example the Ministry of Defence, Ministry of Foreign Affairs, Ministry of Transport, Office of Industrial Property, Administration of the State Material Commodities Reserves and the State Office for Nuclear Safety. The responsibilities of some Ministries shifted, as a consequence of privatisation and greater use of devolved public institutions, from production and delivery of goods and services to responsibility for policy-making.

B. Context affecting public management

The priority during the period 1992-1996 was the completion of economic reform, with the decentralisation of State administration having retreated into the background.

The public did not participate in the debate on public administration reform. The approach of the media was not expert enough, was subject to political pressures, and the public was somewhat apathetic to the issue.

Concerning socio-economic factors, in 1994 the government began conceptual work on reform of the social security system. The government approved a concept of social welfare policy based on three cornerstones: social insurance, State social support, and social assistance.

Education and public health are undergoing general reform which has not yet been completed. For instance, minor medical institutions, particularly local health centres (including dental surgeries) have been privatised, although the majority of major medical institutions have not. Restructuring of hygiene services is in progress in connection with the drafting of a new Public Health Protection Act, although further progress in restructuring public health is uncertain.

C. Strategies and processes for planning and carrying out public management reforms

In its resolution of 20 September 1995, the government adopted certain rationalisation measures including a "downsizing plan" incorporated into the 1996 Public Budget Act. The staff reductions concern ministries and other central fully or partly budget-financed organisations. The reduction rate in central and district authorities is 5 per cent, in subordinate organisations 2 per cent. The overall reduction represents 4 398 scheduled jobs, although actual staff reductions will be fewer as this figure is inclusive of current vacancies.

Paradoxically, the number of qualified officials is decreasing in spite of an increase in administrative staff as a whole. The mobility of this staff is considerable. The intention to reduce the number of civil servants is producing an entirely opposite effect which decreases the effectiveness of their work. The general impetus to encourage public servants to develop new attitudes and higher competencies should be provided by a new Civil Service Act under preparation. Qualified officials are likely to leave in view of the uncertainty surrounding prospects in the civil service, and (considering the low unemployment rate in the country) they really do not have any problems with finding more attractive employment. In October 1995 the Cabinet proclaimed several concrete measures focused on the development of a new attitude for civil servants and local government employees in their relations to citizens to encourage better service by officials and administrative staff (consumer orientation). Red tape should be restricted and institutional machinery should become more transparent.

Leadership for public administration reform has been focused since 1992 in the Office for Legislation and Public Administration, under the Vice Prime Minister. Since 1989 public administration has been undergoing marked technological modernisation. Individual units have been provided with computers and commensurate training computer networks and on-line systems are expanding, software products are providing faster access to information and rationalisation of processes are being introduced. Primarily the central State administration authorities and agencies have been connected to Internet.

D.   Policy-management capacities

Since the origin of the Czech Republic (1 January 1993) as an independent State, pressure has been exercised for speedy changes in central government. This has limited the creation of a longer-term perspective of policy-making in public management development. Experience is being evaluated, and it is expected that further progress will be difficult without a coherent long-term concept of public management reform.

Since 1 July 1993, the Supreme Audit Office has been operating in the Czech Republic as an independent agency which submits its reports to the Chamber of Deputies, the Senate and the government. It is responsible for management of State property and the fulfilment of the State Budget. The evaluation of experience of the Supreme Audit Office should be used also in further reform steps in public management.

E.   Human resources management

Employment in the public sector has been influenced by the transformation of the economy, a change in the development strategies of individual branches of the public sector and, importantly, by macro-economic policy. Although the size of the public sector has increased in overall terms, individual sectors within it have been differentially affected. (Refer also to Section C.)

Personnel policy is governed generally by the Labour Code; a special legislation for civil service has not been adopted yet. Preparation of all legislation concerning employment, wages and social security is discussed in tripartite committees by the government, trade unions and employers.

According to the Labour Code, training to improve the skills of employees skills is the duty of the employer. The training of employees takes place mostly in the training centres of employer organisations, but is offered also by schools or private training institutions, often with foreign aid. According to existing legislation employees improving their qualifications may be granted certain advantages, such as modification of working hours or time off with pay. There is as yet no training institution for civil servants. The need for administrative studies brought about an increase in University faculties or departments concerned with State or public administration in some way, although the further idea of establishing a specialised public administration school is under consideration.

The salaries of public sector employees are governed by an Act of 1992, under which the remuneration is based on:

- salary classes (according to the complexity, responsibility and exertion required by the work);
- granting of extras (for the management and control of employees or organisational units, the performance of work in aggravated and health endangering conditions, the results of work performed); and
- extraordinary bonuses for the performance of extraordinary and particularly significant tasks.

Lately the tendency to gradually equalise earnings of public sector and business sector employees is coming to the fore. In the public sector the earnings, in particular of employees performing more qualified, complex and responsible work, are being increased gradually.

The strengthening of ethical principles in the professional public service is an urgent challenge. Initiatives concerning public sector ethics found application in a Draft Civil Service Act of 1995, although this has yet to be discussed by the government.

F.   Budget process and management of financial resources

The government's goal is to achieve a sound fiscal position introduced and followed by a balanced budget performance, low indebtedness and a reduction in public expenditure as a percentage of GDP.

The major tasks in the coming period include improvement of the public expenditure control system. The Czech Republic has started to pilot and then practice budgeting methods based on efficiency analyses. For this purpose and to improve the transparency of government operations new budgetary classification will be introduced from 1997 onwards.

Basic budgetary legislation (called Budgetary Rules) is currently under preparation. Its major content can be characterised as a transformation of the present organisations in the public sector, and more comprehensive financial controls. The present budgetary rules are based on the fact that fully or partly budget-financed organisations of the State are separate legal entities. Under the new budgetary rules these organisations will be transformed; some will lose their separate legal status and will become integrated organisational components of the State, some will be put outside the State and will acquire the form of either public enterprises or private businesses and the remainder will be dissolved. The draft legislation also provides for more comprehensive financial controls.

Public Treasury guidelines as a comprehensive infrastructure for cash management, debt management, public expenditure and budget development monitoring are being prepared.

H. Changing structures of the public sector

Since January 1991, two types of privatisation have been undertaken. The so-called "small privatisation" was intended to create the necessary conditions for the establishment of small and medium enterprises. Its focus was primarily on the privatisation of retail trade services and minor production facilities, and it was conducted through public auctions.

The next step was the so-called "big privatisation" which used several privatisation methods, namely, public tender, public auction, direct sale, changing the property status of a privatised unit into a joint-stock company, privatisation of State joint-stock company's shares, and free transfer of property.

Apart from these standard privatisation methods a specific, very important position was occupied by the so-called "voucher privatisation". Its political significance is illustrated by the new arrangements put in place for investment vouchers for the purchase of shares in privatised enterprises, which enable citizens older then 18 years to be incorporated into the privatisation process.

Institutionally the lead in the process of "big privatisation" is taken by the Ministry for National Property Administration and Privatisation and the National Property Fund of the Czech Republic. Both of these institutions are responsible for the transformation of property relations to State property. The Ministry, which assures accurate and complete records of privatised property, is to hand over its responsibilities on 1 July 1996 to the Ministry of Finance together with one third of its staff (some 100 people).

New property relations arise from the free-market mechanism. In industry the juridical form of the new subjects is a joint-stock company in most cases. Non-state organisations have more than a 60 per cent share in industrial production (private sector – 48 per cent, enterprises with foreign participation – 12 per cent). The public sector is represented by state enterprises, state joint-stock companies, mixed joint-stock companies, international firms and municipal companies. Public sector employees represent 57 per cent of total employees in industry.

I. Regulatory management and reform

Transformation of the economy necessitated an extensive and fundamental change of the whole legal system. The new Constitutional order which came into force on 1 January 1993 emphasized the need for the re-emergence of public law as a guarantee for the rights and freedoms of human beings. The new provisions of the Constitution in this context as well as the Charter of Fundamental Rights and Freedoms were incorporated into the Constitutional order as a great challenge for the public law of the Czech Republic deformed by the communist past. The period of 1990-1992 was characterised by an enormous rise of legislative activity which rose again in 1993, after the split of the Czechoslovak Federation.

It is only now that a purposeful deregulation and clarification of the legal system can begin. This process proceeds in two directions: *a*) verification of the compliance of all legal regulations with the new Constitution of the Czech Republic and *b*) verification of the further need for regulations predating November 1989 as well as the post-November 1989 period of the Federation (1989-1992), still forming part of the legal order on the basis of the so-called reception law.

An important role in the pre-parliamentary legislative process is played by the Legislative Council, an expert advisory government body with a co-ordinating role. It has 21 members headed by the Vice Prime Minister and receives recommendations from expert groups. New legislative rules regulating in some detail the technical legislative requirements imposed on the drafting of laws, with the purpose of improving their quality, simplicity and understandability, are under preparation.

At present groups of experts are working on the recodification of the Civil Code, Commercial Code, Family Law and Penal Law. Also new Administrative Procedure and Administrative Judiciary Acts are being drafted, scheduled for completion in 1998. The individual ministries are working continuously on the harmonization of Czech law with European law under the co-ordination of the Office for Legislation and Public Administration.

Assoc. Prof. Olga Vidláková
Director
Department for Public Administration
Office for Legislation and Public Administration
of the Czech Republic
P.O. Box 596, Vladislavova 4
117 15 Praha 1
Czech Republic
Tel.: (42-2) 24 22 46 35 / 96 15 32 11
Fax: (42-2) 24 22 46 35

Annex A

PRINCIPAL RECENT PUBLIC MANAGEMENT DEVELOPMENTS

1990

- The government decided on the abolition of the whole system of national committees and on the drafting of a new law on municipalities, a law on the capital City of Prague, a law on municipal elections and a law on District Offices as State administration bodies, and the Parliament enacted all Governmental Draft laws. A governmental advisory Commission for *Länder* establishment was created. The Commission ended its work by proposing four possible alternatives of which none was realised.
- On 29 November the first free, democratic communal elections to newly established municipal local councils were held.
- A new system of state administration and self-government in education started in December.

1991

- In July the government entrusted the Minister of the Interior with preparing a structure of local government and administration. The concept of decentralisation was approved.
- In July a new Office on Economic Competition as a central State agency was established (later, in October l992, changed into a Ministry).
- In connection with the restitution of private ownership and property rights a new law on real estate regulation and establishment of *Länder* register Offices came into force in July.

1992

- After the June election the new government's Declaration made public administration reform a priority, the stress being put on further decentralisation.
- In Autumn, the split of the Federation became a necessity. All efforts were concentrated on preparation of the new independent State, the Czech Republic.
- In September, the government nominated a Governmental Committee for the preparation of a new Constitution of the Czech Republic, which ended its work in November. The Parliament enacted the Constitution on l6 December.
- In October, the Office for Legislation and Public Administration of the Czech Republic (OLPA) started its activities under the chairmanship of the Vice Prime Minister.

1993

- In February, the Vice Prime Minister entrusted with chairing the Office for Legislation and Public Administration established a working group for preparing the concept of local government reform. The resulting report was submitted to government in June.
- In August, the government approved basic principles of the Civil Service Law.

1994

- In June, the government decided on the Draft Law on the establishment of the Higher Territorial Self-governing Units (HTSGU) and passed it to Parliament.
- In July, the Government decided which legislative regulation in connection with the establishment of the HTSGU should be drafted and entrusted the Ministers of the Interior and of Finance with this task.
- In August, the government decided on the Draft Law on the Competences of the HTSGU.
- In September, the government approved a document prepared by OLPA called *The Intentions of the Government in the Field of Public Administration Reform* and passed it to Parliament.

1995

- In March, OLPA submitted to the government a document on the institutionalisation of state administration on the intermediate tier (HTSGU).

- In September, in connection with negotiation of the 1996 State budget, the government decided on a staff reduction in Ministries and other central State agencies and District offices by 5 per cent of the number approved for 1995 and in their subordinate fully or partly budget-financed organisations by 2 per cent.
- In October, the government decided on an Index of measures for simplification and improvement of state administration in relation to clients.

Annex B

INSTITUTIONAL RESPONSIBILITY FOR PUBLIC MANAGEMENT IMPROVEMENT

ORGANISATION	TASKS AND RESPONSIBILITIES
Office for Legislation and Public Administration (OLPA)	• general responsibility for conceptual work in the field of public administration reform (decentralisation, restructuring of central government and administration)
Ministry of the Interior	• issues related to district offices and co-ordination of other ministries activities in this sphere; the territorial-administrative division of the country
Ministry of Labour and Social Affairs	• civil service pay
Ministry of Finance	• budgetary reform, financial management improvement

DENMARK

A. Main tendencies and overall priorities

The conservative-liberal minority government under Prime Minister Poul Schluter was replaced in January 1992 by a coalition government under the leadership of Prime Minister Poul Nyrup Rasmussen (Social Democrat). The Modernisation Programme, which was started in 1983, and which had been the umbrella for administration policy guidelines in Denmark for ten years, was discontinued. It was replaced by new reform guidelines. There have been five central elements in recent years' administration policy guidelines:

- focus on the consumer;
- focus on employees as an important resource in the public sector;
- continuation of budget reforms with stress on decentralisation of authority;
- use of contracts in policy management of public institutions;
- extensive use of the limited company as an organisation form in public sector activities.

B. Context affecting public management

Several factors have affected recent reforms in the public sector. First, the public sector has become more commercial as a result of, amongst other things, European Union requirements and an increasingly international economy. This has meant that the range of public tenders has grown, and state-owned companies, which previously were controlled by traditional public bureaucracies, have more independence and a greater degree of freedom. This reorganisation has often meant that state-owned enterprises have been converted to limited companies that compete on the open market.

A second important trend has been the broad political agreement to increase consumer influence in the public sector. This has led to the establishment of consumer councils in legislation for primary and lower secondary schools, upper secondary schools, day-care centres and in care of the elderly. It has also led to a legal requirement from 1 January 1997, that all local authorities every second year inform citizens about local services.

Third, it should be noted that the requirement for efficient public sector operation is still a significant basis for many administrative reforms. This applies to continuing reforms of the State budget and appropriation system and to the experiments which have been conducted with contract management of public institutions.

C. Strategies and processes for planning and carrying out public management reforms

Since 1992, public administration policy has comprised a number of independent initiatives. Amongst these, the following publications are of particular note: New Views of the Public Sector from June 1993, and Welfare for Citizens from September 1995.

In New Views of the Public Sector, a policy for the public sector is presented as well as the role of the public sector in the social economy. This programme is characterised by considering development of the public sector as a strategic and necessary basis for Danish commerce and the Danish welfare society. New *Views of the Public Sector* was later followed by *Welfare for Citizens* which dealt with problems such as:

- the relationship between the minister and the work of civil servants;
- the overall management of ministerial areas;
- effective operation and restructuring of individual institutions;
- citizen and consumer satisfaction with public services;
- user influence;
- service labelling;
- quality.

As an appendix to the report, a number of specific tools are outlined.

In both *New Views of the Public Sector* and *Welfare for Citizens*, a management philosophy is introduced where focus is shifted from pure expenditure control to a form of management which considers both input and output. The management philosophy is based on frameworks, explicit result requirements, and local priorities and performance measurement.

In 1994, the tendency to combine expenditure policy and administration policy more tightly led to the merging of two departments at the Ministry of Finance – the Administration and Personnel Department and the Budget Department. The two departments were combined to form a new unit – the Finance Department.

D. Policy-management capacities

Since the 1970s, no attempt has been made to create a planning centre in the Danish central administration. Experience from the 70s showed clearly that it was preferable for analytical capacity to be given higher priority in individual ministries. A number of ministries therefore publish analyses within their respective areas. The Ministry of Finance, for example, publishes an annual *finance report*, which contains analyses of the Danish economy, and an annual *budget report* which contains analyses of public expenditure. Co-ordination of various policies is also delegated to individual ministries. The Ministry of Foreign Affairs, for example, co-ordinates all international co-operation.

E. Human resources management

In February 1994, the Ministry of Finance launched a collective personnel policy for State employees called *Human Resource Development in Danish Central Government*. The State personnel policy contains three minimum requirements:

- local personnel policy should be assessed at least every other year;
- annual interviews should be conducted between employees and their immediate superiors;
- the State Works Committees, which are committees where both staff and management are represented, should work systematically to combine the strategy of institutions with plans for competence development.

In June 1996, the Ministry of Finance published results of two major surveys on life at work and personnel policy in the public sector which described how minimum requirements are met in State institutions.

F. Budget process and management of financial resources

Through the 1980s, extensive decentralisation of the State budget and appropriation system was carried out. This decentralisation has subsequently been continued so that, compared internationally,

Denmark has a considerably decentralised budget system. At the same time as this process of decentralisation, there has also been increasing focus on the achievement of results. In several areas therefore, long-term contracts have been entered which state objectives and the time scale in which they are to be achieved. The latest development is that it has been decided that all State institutions should prepare annual reports.

Annual reports show the results of the organisation. The annual reports contain four elements:

- *Appropriations*: The annual reports shall provide information on appropriations for the year and relate these to the financial result.
- *Expenditure and sources of finance*: The annual reports shall provide a view of total expenses and how they are financed.
- *Results*: The annual reports shall provide a view of activities and results. This report balances the freedom State institutions have been given over the past ten years.
- *Costs*: The annual reports shall outline costs in State organisations. They shall outline where these operate in competition with the private sector so that any subsidies are clearly evident. They shall also show where costs are covered by income (financing from charges or directly attributable costs).

It is hoped that annual reports will contribute to a greater focus on results in State organisations.

G. Performance management

Initiatives consistent with strengthening performance management are noted throughout this report. Annual reports are one of the most recent examples of experiments with performance management in Denmark. Also noteworthy is contract management which has been applied to several areas. Two areas in particular can be mentioned. First, since 1992 experiments have been conducted where State institutions have entered a contract with their department and the Ministry of Finance. These contract management trials were assessed in 1995. The assessment showed that the contracts had resulted in a significantly greater awareness of results.

As a supplement to the contract management trials, in 1995 the Ministry of Finance started a trial with contracts for directors generals at large State institutions. The contracts set objectives and results for the directors general for the coming year. In 1996, twenty directors general will enter contracts.

H. Changing structures of the public sector

At the end of the 1960s and in the early 1970s, a reform of local government was carried out which has resulted in a very decentralised public sector in Denmark today. Since then, there have been no such fundamental changes in the structure of the public sector, *i.e.* changes in the relationship between central, regional, and local government. The most important structural changes in the public sector in recent years have been the conversion of state-owned enterprises to limited companies. Almost a third of State personnel today work for state-owned limited companies operating under free market conditions. In 1993, a report was published of experience with state-owned limited companies which has since become the foundation for policy in this field.

I. Regulatory management and reform

Work on regulatory management and reform is primarily the responsibility of the Danish Ministry of Business and Industry. The ministry conducts assessments of the financial consequences for business of legislation, in the same way as the Ministry of Finance assesses the administrative and economic consequences of proposed legislation, and the Ministry of Environment the environmental consequences. In addition, trials have been established for enterprise panels which will assess initiatives for legislation.

J.   Other

In 1997 administration policy initiatives will be combined in a report on administration policy which is expected to be published in October. Among other things the report will deal with contract management in the public sector. Of future important initiatives, a cross-ministry analysis of consumer influence under the leadership of the Ministry of the Interior could be mentioned. The increase in consumer influence in the public sector has been one of the most important innovations of administration policy in recent years and will be analysed in relation to actual experience, principal problems and future possible applications.

Mr. Peter Kjaersgaard Pedersen
Ministry of Finance
Christiansborg Slotsplads 1
DK 1218 Copenhagen K
Tel.: (45-33) 92 33 33
Fax: (45-33) 32 80 30

Annex A

PRINCIPAL RECENT PUBLIC MANAGEMENT DEVELOPMENTS

1983

– Modernisation Programme for the Public Sector introduced with the aims of increasing efficiency and improving service quality at all levels of administration and improving motivation and job satisfaction.

1983-85

– First Phase of Modernisation Programme offers incentives for modernisation including relaxed control on expenditure and number of posts in each ministry:
  • information and publicity campaign for Programme launched;
  • deregulation programme started.

1986-87

– Under the Second Phase of the Modernisation Programme, each ministry prepared implementation plans with sectoral goals according to Ministry of Finance guidelines.
– Scheme for compulsory rotation of professional staff introduced.

1988-89

– Third Phase of Modernisation Programme, with comprehensive "Review of the Public Sector 1988" produced by the Ministry of Finance increasing emphasis on reducing public expenditure.
– Similar review in 1989 included focus on reducing personnel and further decentralization.
– Debureaucratisation initiative launched with aim of reducing, simplifying and decentralising administrative functions and improving citizen orientation.

1990

– Government submitted evaluation of Modernisation Programme to Parliament.
– Major technical reform of central government budgeting and appropriation system (to take effect in 1991) included a more programme-oriented structure and modernisation of the computerised system.
– Government policy for management developments in the 1990s.

1991

– Government submitted "The Public Sector in the Year 2000" programme to Parliament.
– Market-type mechanisms introduced further and a committee recommended promoting contracting out.
– Projects on service and quality set up within all ministerial areas.
– New privatisations of banking, telecommunications and computer services bodies.
– Citizens' choice for hospital care introduced through agreements between some regional governments.

1992

– Office of Auditor-General published a report on the effects of the Modernisation Program in some State institutions and recommended further emphasis on evaluating economic results.
– Seven contract agencies set up, in some cases in association with multi-year budget agreements and contracts established for a further six.
– Introduction of market-testing for all State activities suitable for contracting out.
– Independent committee for complaint and control established.
– New rules gave State institutions greater freedom and more incentives to generate revenue.
– Citizens' choice for hospital care extended in general law passed by Parliament.
– Guides published on performance assessment of public leaders and on senior staff policy.
– Committee on Public Information Technology Policy published a White Paper and a co-ordination plan.

1993
  – Report on restructuring the public sector: *New views of the public sector*.
  – Report on experience with state-owned limited companies.

1994
  – Government published a collective policy for human resources management in the publication: *Human Resource Development in Danish Central Government*.
  – Ministry of Finance combined the Administration and Personnel Department with the Budget Department in order to ensure better integration of administration policy and expenditure policy.
  – First report on a simplification of the State appropriation system (supplementary appropriations).

1995
  – Assessment of contract agency trials.
  – First trials with contracts for Directors General.
  – Two final reports on a simplification of the State appropriation system which include proposals for trials with annual reports.
  – Trials with annual reports.
  – In September, the Ministry of Finance published *Welfare for Citizens*, which contains a number of specific guidelines on how government institutions can be made more efficient.

1996
  – Annual reports made permanent.
  – Two major surveys of government work on human resources management published in June.

Annex B

INSTITUTIONAL RESPONSIBILITY FOR PUBLIC MANAGEMENT IMPROVEMENT

ORGANISATION	TASKS AND RESPONSIBILITIES
Ministry of Finance	• personnel and administrative policy; co-ordination of renewal and management development in the public sector • budgeting and expenditure control
Prime Minister's Office	• change in the responsibilities between ministries
Ministry of the Interior	• renewal of local government

FINLAND

A. Main tendencies and overall priorities

The core of the public management reform policy in Finland has been a transition to a performance-oriented public sector entrusted with a special emphasis on accountability of decision-makers and an increased use of market-type mechanisms in public sector management and operations.

The present coalition government came into office in April 1995. One of the priorities of the government is public management development. The objective of the government according to its programme is to secure the basic services connected with the welfare society in the whole country. The government states that the administration will be made more efficient, functional and service-minded. On all levels of administration, the opportunity for citizens to exercise real influence will be improved, and the administration will be made more open to the public. The division of tasks between levels of government and their financing will be clarified.

The strengthening of municipal autonomy will continue, with municipalities remaining responsible for the availability and quality of basic services, and for deciding how services are to be delivered.

B. Context affecting public management

During the two previous governments a ministerial committee was set up to guide work on public management development. In September 1995 the current government established a ministerial working group with responsibility for preparing the necessary decisions-in-principle for the measures to be carried out. The ministerial working group handles assignments relating to important reform projects prior to their launch, and surveys legislation and other proposals for regulations that are of significance to public administration. A key role for the group is to communicate with interest groups, and monitor and steer public management developments, particularly from the perspective of the general development of public administration and its integrity. The group is currently monitoring for instance projects on evaluation (discussed in Section C) and strategy (discussed in Section D).

C. Strategies and processes for planning and carrying out public management reforms

The Ministry of Finance is conducting a large evaluation programme of the Finnish public management reforms of 1987-94. The last ten years have been an active phase in public management reform, but it was felt that reforms needed to be evaluated more thoroughly than they had been previously. The current evaluation programme will provide background and support in directing new reforms and in assessing the ongoing projects. Work on strengthening the evaluation culture in Finland is also in progress.

The Ministry has set up a cross-sectoral steering group to conduct twelve individual evaluation studies, including studies of State-owned enterprises, evaluating evaluation, results-oriented management, regional and provincial administration, citizens' views of public services, financial effects of the reforms, and international comparison of public management reforms. The final report, due for publication in 1997, will assemble the findings of other studies and present an overall evaluation of the success of the reform programme.

It is stated in the programme of the present government that it will give a *Long Term Futures* report to the Parliament. The government has appointed two working groups and one steering group to prepare the report, with the first working group to consider issues relating to the future of Europe (due to report to Parliament in September 1996) and the second concerned with issues relating to the future of Finland, such as future questions on economy, employment and welfare (due to report to Parliament in March 1997). The aim of the reports is to promote employment possibilities and strengthen the nation's economic growth. The *Long Term Futures* report will present the government's strategic goals and proposed courses of action on the subject.

D. Policy-Management capacities

The Finnish government is developing a strategy for improving the governance and management of the public sector, through a project due to conclude at the end of 1997. The purpose of the project is to develop a strategy for the development of the three parts of the Finnish public sector: first, the traditional public administration, or "core State", which is responsible for the general security and democratic order of society and the basic rights of citizens; second, the market-oriented public enterprises and companies; and third, the public services delivered to enterprises and citizens. For all these parts of the public sector different organisation, guidance, finance and owner strategies should be developed, corresponding to their purpose and functions within the State.

The project will have three outputs. First, it will prepare a governance strategy for the government; second, a report on public management development will be prepared for Parliament; and third, projects to implement the governance strategy of the government will be launched. The most important of these projects are:

- reform of decision-making in the Cabinet and Ministries according to principles of strategic planning;
- reform of the system of budgeting by results;
- owner control and owner policies of the market-oriented public enterprises and companies;
- co-ordination of matters related to the European Union (EU) in the Ministries;
- co-ordination of social security administration under the control of the Ministry of Social Affairs and Health; and
- development of relations between the government and municipalities.

E. Human resources management

A seniority policy for the State as employer is planned for publication in 1996. The government wants to emphasize the great value of experienced older employees. The effects of ageing on mental and physical performance and consequent special requirements should be taken into account in continuous staff development, in the actual duties of staff and in efforts to maintain working capacity. Every State agency should develop its own strategy on improving the opportunities of older staff members to continue in their jobs.

The Ministry of Finance is to launch in early 1997 a project for training office employees. The development programme will consist of work rotation in another State agency and some training courses. The programme is designed for clerical staff with lengthy experience but insufficient vocational qualifications. The aim of the project is to improve training opportunities for office staff, who are mainly women.

The Ministry of Finance plans to start a project to promote mentoring as a way of developing managers and managerial potential in the State agencies. It is envisaged that the agencies taking part in the project will be provided with expert support, information and networks. The impact of mentoring on the opportunities of the potential women managers will be particularly evaluated at the end of the project.

The Ministry of Finance has also appointed a working group with the task of developing criteria and methods for selecting top civil servants. The objective is to draw up a set of criteria including formal qualifications for positions, which will secure the continuity and independence of the civil service and reinforce a set of high ethical standards for civil servants.

The second task of the working group is to establish whether it is necessary to develop specific approaches to selection of top civil servants, and to define and improve existing management potential within the civil service. The working group will also consider the desirability of requiring senior civil servants to provide full disclosure, before their appointment to a post, of their financial liabilities and other commitments. Such disclosure is currently demanded only of Cabinet ministers. A government decision on the subject is planned before the end of 1996, when guidelines will also be published.

F. Budget process and management of financial resources

The Ministry of Finance has initiated a study to determine the impact of the EU financial management regulations on the internal control systems of the Finnish State agencies across different sectors. The workability of the EU regulations within the Finnish State agencies will also be examined. The work includes examining the feasibility of setting up an interministerial centralised internal control unit and determining other possible requirements for developing the internal control of state agencies and institutions.

Another study will be conducted on reform of the budget structure, with the aim of reflecting accrual budgeting and closer adherence to accepted budgetary principles. One of the starting points for this study is to bring the budget structure in line with accounting reforms. The timetable for the government-wide accounting reforms is to achieve a complete extension of accrual accounting across the State administration in 1998. A report on the budget reform principles was prepared in May 1996 and proposals for implementation are due to be finalised at the end of that year.

The Finnish State subsidy system scheme is to be reformed with the objective of equalising the burden to the municipal economy arising from organising basic services. The reform is to be carried out in two stages. The first stage (which has been in progress since early 1996) involves reform of the system of equalising financial differences between municipalities. The municipal State subsidies are being equalised on the basis of the tax revenue of the municipalities. The second stage (to begin in 1997) will consist of three elements: equalisation of the municipal State subsidies on the basis of the tax revenue of the municipalities; State subsidies for consumer economy-based indicators; and State subsidies for investments.

G. Performance management

A system of statutory annual reports for all ministries and agencies was introduced for all government organisations from the beginning of 1993. However, recently both the Parliamentary Auditors and the State Audit Office have paid attention to the need to improve the quality of performance information included in these reports. The Parliamentary Auditors have particularly emphasised the information needs of the Parliament, whereas the State Audit Office points out the inadequacies in the performance measures used by the ministries and agencies. A project set up by the Ministry of Finance in March 1996 will propose improvements to the system of monitoring performance and the quality and coverage of information produced to the Parliament and to the ministers. The project will base its work on pilot projects set up in the ministries, and will develop a model for the ministries on how to report on the performance of all their major policy areas within a single report. Performance information will also be included in the Government's report to the Parliament.

In a research and development project initiated by the Ministry of Finance and the Government Institute of Economic Research, market-type methods for producing and steering services were surveyed, as well as the possibilities of applying these methods. The possibilities of using the provider-purchaser model and the voucher model were evaluated particularly in child care services, educational services, health care services and services for the elderly. The project concluded that it is possible to employ market-type models (primarily voucher and provider-producer models) in the provision of welfare services, noting that experiment and assessment work in this area should be continued, and that laws on service production would have to be developed to enable versatile ways of producing and organising services. A new research and development project to carry through the ideas was launched in 1995, to support the evaluation and assessment work carried out on services produced or financed by public funds. The project will also carry forward development work aimed at reforming the regulations and steering mechanisms so that they better support more effective operation. The emphasis is on client-oriented services, quality and cost-effectiveness. Section H below also makes reference to performance issues.

H. Changing structures of the public sector

The proposal of the "regional administration 2000-project" provides for an Act on Provincial State Offices and Division of Provinces. The proposal suggests that the provincial governments be called Provincial State Offices. The Provincial State Offices would function as regional general administrative authorities with head offices, headed by governors. The proposal suggests confirmation of the position of Provincial State Offices as authorities responsible for administration and security. It also suggests that labour protection district offices be connected to the Provincial State Offices. The aim is to bring together matters related to the security of people and conditions to the best possible extent under the same authority in Provincial State Office. It is also proposed to adjust the Act on Division of Provinces so that the number of provinces be decreased from eleven to five.

The regional administration 2000-project also suggests that employment and economic development centres be established and assigned for regional promotion of economic activities and regional employment administration. These centres would comprise present services in this field. The new Provincial State Office would promote and support development within its own region and be responsible for allocating most of the regional development funds entered in the State budget.

The means and targets for reorganising State agencies and institutions into State-owned enterprises were put in place ten years ago, and the changes have been implemented as planned. Although the State-owned enterprises operate outside the State budget, the Parliament can set them service and other operational targets. In June 1995 a working group was set up to study the State-owned enterprise model, including its steering and development needs, based on the experience gained and the assessments made. The proposals made by the working group in May 1996 were aimed at making the State-owned enterprises more compatible with competition in open markets. One of the goals was to increase the flexibility of their operations in the future and to provide improved opportunities to respond to developments in the competitive environment. The working group suggested that only the most far-reaching and principal matters would be decided at government level. The ministry in question would be responsible for steering performance and service. The State-owned enterprises are in charge of managing their own operations.

There are roughly 110 multiservice centres (one-stop-shops) in Finland at present. The term "multiservice centre" refers to a single locale which offers the public services of two or more service providers either separately, or together, in which case general personnel carry out the service duties. A significant number of these multiservice centres are participating in what is called a welfare pilot project organised by KELA (the Social Insurance Institution), together with the local authorities. Additional client services provided by multiservice centres include the function of official registrar, taxation advisory services, tax form retrieval, police district payments (passports, identity cards, driver's licences, etc.), permits for lotteries, fund-drives and entertainment, dog tax, display of district plans, sale of public transport tickets and the distribution, and retrieval of the most commonly used forms used by the co-operating authorities, as well as the requisite advisory services.

The Ministry of the Interior has launched a new multiservice project to facilitate setting up of diversified multiservice centres by co-operating authorities which make extensive use of information technology, including the development of functional service centres which will guarantee quality and availability in local services.

I. Regulatory management and reform

The government adopted in May 1995 a programme for improving regulatory management. The focus is on drafting of legislation within the ministries. The main objective is to improve quality of government Bills and thus the quality of legislation. Another objective of the programme is to improve regulatory analysis and assessment of impacts of proposed legislation. The programme applies also to lower-level regulation.

The programme includes thirty-three principles on regulatory management. One specific objective is that legislative activities within ministries would be properly planned and different projects to prepare government Bills better co-ordinated. Ministries are required to develop and introduce by 1997 an overall schedule of their on-going and future regulatory activities.

The background for the programme was widespread concern about the quality of legislation. In particular, the Constitutional Committee of the Parliament criticised in its 1994 report the quality of present drafting of legislation. In accepting the report the Parliament stated that it expected the government to take all the measures needed to draw the ministries' attention to the drafting of legislation and to increase the quality of government Bills.

The low quality of government Bills has occurred for a number of reasons. The pressure to draft legislation quickly has increased during the past few years, mostly due to the rapid adoption of EU-legislation. Also, changes in management culture may have led to poor regulatory analysis and preparation of government Bills.

In response to the report of the Parliament, the Ministry of Justice and the Ministry of Finance launched in late 1994 a common initiative to improve regulatory management. This project produced a report which preceded the regulatory programme of May 1996 and provided background analysis for it. Also further studies have been carried out on drafting government Bills and how the impacts of proposed legislation are assessed in them.

The programme requires a number of cross-governmental measures to be taken. For instance the Ministry of Finance is required to prepare common guidelines for assessing economic impacts of legislation. A working party will be set up to study how the OECD recommendation on regulatory quality of March 1995 should be implemented in Finland.

J. Other

Information technology – IT

A system for preparing and distributing decision documents for weekly official Cabinet meetings was initiated in early 1996. The system has varying degrees of access limited to ministers, their assistants and the several hundred civil servants who prepare such documents, using the ministries' fibre ring covering the Helsinki area. Documents can be forwarded to the Parliament or to printing, as the case may be.

A database with information on job vacancies, including vacancies in other Nordic countries, and on labour market training, with an electronic mail facility, has proved to be a highly successful service.

Mrs. Katju Holkeri
Senior Adviser
Tel.: (358-9) 160 32 61
Public Management Department
Ministry of Finance
P.O. Box 275
SF-00121 Helsinki
Fax: (358-9) 16 03 234

Annex A

PRINCIPAL RECENT PUBLIC MANAGEMENT DEVELOPMENTS

1993

- Government decision-in-principle on measures to reform central and regional government
- Government decision-in-principle on developing data security
- Productivity and quality programmes
- Act and Government decision on joint service units

1994

- Comprehensive reform of the municipalities Act
- New State Civil Servants Act
- New permit decision on rationalisation of permit procedures
- Government decision on developing new information management
- The National Forestry Administration turned into a State-owned enterprise
- Post and Telecommunications and Map Centre reorganised into joint-stock companies
- Regional development Act (the regional development functions transferred from the provincial State offices to regional councils operating as joint municipal boards)

1995

- State Railways, the Government Purchasing Centre, the State Uniforms Factory, State Granary and public building services reorganised into joint-stock companies
- Administrative Development Agency reorganised into a State-owned enterprise and renamed The Finnish Institute of Public Management
- Regional Administration 2000 project
- Ministerial Working Group on Public Management
- The Evaluation Programme of Public Management Reforms
- A Programme for improving the regulatory management

Annex B

INSTITUTIONAL RESPONSIBILITY FOR PUBLIC MANAGEMENT IMPROVEMENT

ORGANISATION	TASKS AND RESPONSIBILITIES
Ministry of Finance – Public Management Department	• policy of governance, improving public sector performance and competitiveness of public services, evaluation of the reform policies, regulatory reform, information society and administration, development of public enterprises • provides assistance to the ministerial group, which guides and follows up public management improvement
– Budget Department	• budgetary reform, financial management improvement, improving public sector performance and competitiveness
Ministry of the Interior	• issues related to regional and local administration, decentralisation, ensuring high-standard State services for regional and local administration, co-ordinating regional development, strengthening municipal autonomy, use of IT between counties and municipalities
Prime Minister's Office	• development of Cabinet decision-making procedures
Finnish Institute of Public Management (a State-owned enterprise)	• consultancy support for managerial improvement and reforms and in-service training

Annex C

KEY PUBLIC DOCUMENTS ON PUBLIC MANAGEMENT ISSUES AND DEVELOPMENTS

Liikelaitosmallin kehittäminen (*Developing the State-owned Enterprise model*), Ministry of Finance (available only in Finnish).

Public Management Reform Policies, Ministry of Finance, 1994.

Finland's Way to the Information Society, The National Strategy, Ministry of Finance, 1995.

Hyvinvointipalvelut – kilpailua ja valinnanvapautta (Welfare Services – competition and freedom of choice), Government Institute of Economic Research, 1995 (available only in Finnish).

Kehittyvä julkinen hallinto (*Public Management in development*), Ministry of Finance, 1996 (forthcoming summary report in English).

Lainvalmistely ja vaikutusten ennakointi, (Preparation of legislation and assessing impacts), Ministry of Finance and National Research Institute of Legal Policy, 1996 (forthcoming summary report in English).

FRANCE

A. Main tendencies and overall priorities

The President of the Republic and the Prime Minister have placed reform of the State at the top of France's agenda for the next few years.

The policy is based on four main objectives which were mentioned for the first time in the Prime Minister's circular of 26 July 1995 on preparation and implementation of the policy to reform the State and public services, then set out in greater detail in a draft reform plan which was the subject of large-scale consultation and discussion. The four main objectives are to:

- provide a better service to citizens;
- modernise human resources management;
- delegate responsibilities;
- improve decision-making and management.

A *better service to citizens*

This is the reform's fundamental "raison d'être". The State is considered both too remote and too authoritarian, with rules and procedures which are overly complicated.

The State must therefore simplify its structures and procedures, ease the restrictions on freedom of initiative, and become more accessible.

The draft reform plan recommends the adoption of a series of practical measures for achieving these ends, notably simplification of several hundred administrative authorisation procedures, greater use of rules allowing firms to comply with various formalities by means of a single declaration, creation of special centres (*maisons de services publics*) providing a range of different public services in areas where access to such services is currently poor, allowing for the greater use of modern payment methods for public services, etc.

A further aim is to enhance the quality of the services provided. To this end, ministerial departments will be asked to draw up special service charters, giving greater priority to service quality in both their day-to-day functioning and in the policies they develop.

Modernise human resources management

Public servants are the State's prime asset. It is their skills and their commitment which determine the capacity of public services to meet the country's needs.

Consequently, modernisation of human resources management is crucial. The main aspects of such modernisation are developed under Section E of this report.

Delegate responsibilities

The policy of deconcentration embarked on by France several years ago will be resolutely carried through to the end.

The aim of deconcentration is to improve efficiency, both as regards the taking of major policy decisions – the responsibility of central government – and the way government policy is implemented by the deconcentrated services.

By way of example, the reform of the financial control of spending by the deconcentrated services will gradually be extended to the whole of France, having been the subject of pilot experiments in two regions in 1995. This will, in particular, lead to greater deconcentration of human resources management (*cf.* section E of this report).

Improve decision-making and management

The trend towards deconcentration will be accompanied by extensive structural reform.

Central government departments will be required to redefine their role by strengthening their capacity to draw up and assess public policy. Their structures will be streamlined and staffing levels reduced.

The deconcentrated services will be reinforced. Structural reform will help users understand better the way the State operates and enhance the effectiveness of measures carried out locally, particularly in cases where one policy calls for the involvement of several ministerial departments.

B. Context affecting public management

The principle of adopting a plan to reform the State was announced within weeks of the President's taking up office. Work on the plan is currently in its final stages.

In a circular dated 26 July 1995, the Prime Minister stressed that the reform's sole *raison d'être* was to take greater account of citizens' needs and expectations.

According to the circular, "the administration must help citizens cope with the challenges of modern society, [and] the location and organisation of public services must help to promote measures in favour of distressed urban areas and to combat rural exodus as well as exclusion".

In the present context of insecurity, unemployment and urbanisation, coupled with the greater complexity of society and the rules by which it is governed, management of public services at local level has become a necessity for meeting users' needs.

If, in this difficult context, the State wishes to carry out its function of creating social cohesion to the full, its dealings with its citizens must be as close and as responsible as possible.

In order to achieve such close contact and be able to adapt to public needs, and so provide a better service, the government decided to embark on a policy of deconcentration and reorganisation.

C. Strategies and processes for planning and carrying out public manageement reforms

The plan to reform the State was launched when the Prime Minister issued a circular setting forth the main objectives on which the government was to base its policy. These objectives were clarification of the role of the State and the scope of public services, greater account to be taken of citizens' needs and expectations, central government reform, delegation of responsibilities, and modernisation of public management.

The circular also included a section on government participation in the reforms. In particular, it envisaged the creation of a high-level interministerial body to be responsible for formulating operational proposals and co-ordinating the implementation of decisions.

A decree of 13 September 1995 set up an interministerial committee for State reform, including representatives from all the main ministries concerned by the reform, (replacing the CIATER), and the high-level interministerial commission for State reform, the body promised in the circular.

The draft reform plan, drawn up by the reform commission in liaison with all the ministries, was submitted to the interministerial reform committee for examination. During the first quarter of 1996 it was the subject of very broad consultation and discussion. The last proposals were submitted in May 1996, and at a meeting of the interministerial committee on 29 May, the plan was finally approved.

D.   Policy-management capacities

Section A above lays out the goals of the plan to improve decision-making and management.

The plan for the reform of the State aims to strengthen the capacity to draw up and assess public policy. The re-organisation of central departments should allow the setting up or consolidation of structures covering strategy, future planning and evaluation in each ministerial department.

In addition, the role of audit bodies and general inspectorates will be reinforced, and their work better co-ordinated.

The General Planning Commission will be restructured, as well as the mechanisms for assessing public policy.

E.   Human resources management

Recent initiatives in the field of personnel management concern:

- Deconcentration of careers management: implementation of this policy is still very uneven depending on the particular government department and occupational groups (*corps*) of civil servants concerned. A number of measures focus on efforts to overcome the legal and practical impediments to deconcentration, by:
  - removing legal obstacles;
  - developing social dialogue at local level;
  - modifying the way the administration is organised, with a view to increasing the deconcentration of personnel management;
  - increasing the number of deconcentrated procedures.

- Rationalisation and deconcentration of recruitment procedures:
  Government departments are encouraged to organise their competitive recruitment examinations at deconcentrated levels whenever the number of available places allows. This procedure has already been extensively adopted by the Education and Interior Ministries.

Deconcentrated competitive examinations common to more than one government department are still fairly difficult to organise.

– Reduction in the number of civil servant occupational groups (*corps*):
There are still some 1 700 civil servant occupational groups: They can be broken down into 900 "active" occupational groups (600 at the level of the ministries and 300 sharing the same service regulations), 300 specific job categories, 300 occupational groups for the State-owned industrial and commercial establishments and offices and, finally, 190 occupational groups which are currently being phased out. This fragmented structure is not only very costly to manage, it also restricts staff mobility and versatility. It was for these reasons that the government decided to adopt a new approach, initiated with a protocol agreement in 1990 and then stepped up with vigour in 1995. There are two aspects involved:
  • the merger of ministerial occupational groups to produce larger units thus facilitating management;
  • the introduction of interministerial service regulations in order to harmonise career structures and increase mobility. The adoption of identical career structures will also facilitate possible mergers in the future.

– Three agreements have been signed with six of the seven labour organisations that represent the Public Service:
  • A 3rd **framework agreement on continuing training**, applicable over a three-year period (1996/1997/1998) and mainly aimed at ensuring continuity, in particular by consolidating past achievements in the area of personalised training management and by establishing social dialogue, but also comprising a number of new initiatives which build on existing measure;
  • A **protocol agreement aimed at reducing insecure employment** reflects the determination to end the uncertainty surrounding the position of a large number of staff; the agreement covers a four-year period and will address the situation in all three sectors of public service, with due account taken of their respective special features. The agreement has three parts:
    a) the first is aimed at securing a reduction in the existing level of insecure employment;
    b) the second aims to ensure there is no return to insecure employment in the future, by means of an analysis that examines the reasons for resorting to it in the past;
    c) the third part is aimed at improving the welfare protection system for non-permanent staff.
  The position of staff recruited on a contractual basis under the employment-solidarity scheme is being dealt with separately.
  • An **agreement in favour of early retirement as a way of promoting the employment of young people** in the Public Service. This agreement establishes the possibility of granting "special leave" to staff nearing retirement age. It will apply from 1 January to 31 December 1997 and should allow for the recruitment of 15 000 young people, who will replace public servants aged between 58 and 60 who meet certain conditions with respect to length of service.
  The agreement applies to staff working in all three public service sectors (central government, hospitals, and local government). Public servants benefiting from the scheme will receive replacement income equal to 75 per cent of their gross salary over the past six months, exclusive of all allowances, even those subject to pension contributions.

F.   Budget process and management of financial resources

France has decided to effect far-reaching changes to its budget procedure in order to tighten its control of the public deficit and increase spending efficiency. In addition, the reform includes two measures which should improve the conditions for government decision-making on budget policy:

Clarification of the budgetary remit and priorities

The first aspect of the reform is clarification of the medium-term financial outlook as a result of the *five-year law* on the control of public finance which establishes the overall framework for the budget procedure.

The second aspect is to ensure that a continuation budget *analysis* that has the agreement of the Budget Ministry and the other ministries is available at the beginning of the year, so that all the technical aspects can be resolved, the situation with regard to the outrun of the previous year's budget – known earlier thanks to the shortening of the extra budget implementation period – assessed, and a more informed decision taken on a continuation budget for the following year.

The third aspect is a greater *collective element in budget decisions* and a procedure for determining necessary savings. In April a full government meeting takes place to fix firm budget lines on the basis of the continuation budget. At the meeting, the margin for manoeuvre based on the continuation budget is identified so that the total savings effort needed can be determined.

The fourth aspect is *parliamentary involvement* in the procedure to prepare the Finance Bill. This takes the form of a budget debate held in the spring. The debate means that the members of parliament are able to take part in the main budget decisions, which will be incorporated in the Finance Bill presented to parliament in the autumn.

The development of transparent accounting and greater accountability of administrators

As *more account is taken of the need to improve public finances*, ministers must be made more accountable for how they use the funds allocated to them.

Greater budget transparency is an essential part of the reform. The intention is to achieve this aim through publication of the State budget situation, henceforth on a monthly basis, clearer presentation of budget documents, and giving parliament access to a *budget databank*.

Definition of related aggregates and indicators should produce a better understanding of the control of public spending in relation to program expenditure public policy evaluation.

Clarification of the rules governing management of budgetary restraint in the course of the year. If the twofold objective of limiting public spending and improving management of resources is to be achieved, administrators need to be bound by a contingency reserve of funds and posts set up at the beginning of the financial year.

G. Performance management

Progress to date

On the basis of recent experience acquired thanks to a number of measures taken over the past few years which have increased the accountability of local administrators and improved the quality of their services, it is now possible to take further steps towards greater delegation of responsibility. These measures include:

a) Grouping together running cost appropriations in a single overall budget.
b) Developing a new system for managing these appropriations within the framework of "responsibility centres". The new system has already been taken up by the majority of ministries and will be extended to all government departments by the end of 1996.
c) Pilot experiments carried out in several government departments to define the role of the different services and assess their results.

Service contracts

Better delegation of responsibilities is one of five main objectives identified by the Prime Minister in his circular of 26 July 1995 on reform of the State and public services. Within the framework of this objective, it was decided to experiment with service contracts.

Recourse to service contracts, initially on an experimental basis, should give local administrators greater budgetary responsibility, provide a more efficient service to users, and involve staff in helping to improve management. Sophisticated management tools will be developed to support this approach, which consists in:

a) defining tasks and assessing results. Results will be assessed, analysed, and, wherever possible, compared with results obtained by other services performing the same tasks, and, where appropriate, those of comparable enterprises in the competitive sector;

b) improving service quality;

c) giving greater budgetary responsibility to administrators. Within the framework of existing budgetary and accounting rules, services will be granted a wider margin for manoeuvre, essentially when preparing their annual budget. Global operating budgets that include human resources will be discussed between local services and their central government departments;

d) encouraging staff to become involved and take an interest in management improvements;

e) developing sophisticated management tools.

The increase in the amount of freedom granted to services must be accompanied by the development of tools for facilitating budgetary management, identifying costs, and measuring services' relative efficiency. The new responsibilities of local public services in the human resources field will involve the use of forward planning to manage posts and staffing levels.

I.   Regulatory management and reform

In its annual reports over the past ten years or so, but particularly in the reports for 1991, 1992, and 1993, the Council of State has criticised the proliferation of rules and regulations which is seen as weakening the law and making for instability.

Mr. Jean Picq's 1994 report on the French State (*L'État en France*) emphasised the need for "legislation in moderation", particularly since national rules must henceforth be compatible with the many other sources of law, be they international or local, professional or contractual.

It is estimated that nearly 8 000 decrees are currently in force in France. Such proliferation generates a sense of legal uncertainty and the maxim "ignorance of the law is no excuse" becomes untenable.

The French government has therefore decided to carry out an extensive simplification of the law and administrative formalities, to target efficiency on a systematic basis by means of impact studies, and, in so doing, to limit regulatory inflation. It has also decided to facilitate access to legal rules and regulations and to improve their readability by speeding up the codification process.

Considerable efforts to simplify the administrative formalities applicable to enterprises have been carried out within the framework of COSIFORM (*Commission pour la simplification des formalités*). The government has concentrated on reducing the number of formalities (*i.e.* forms) firms have to comply with and, consequently, the number of administrative bodies they have to deal with. For example, as of 1 January 1996, the 11 notifications that had to be submitted by a firm whenever it recruited someone have been replaced, following a pilot experiment, by one standard form. The first steps towards introduction of a single declaration of social security contributions were also taken on 1 January 1996.

Mr Marcel Pochard (Mrs. Martine Leroy-Bouveyron)
Directeur général
Ministère de la Fonction publique,
  de la Réforme de l'État et de la Décentralisation
32, rue de Babylone
75700 Paris
Tel.: (33-1) 42 75 80 00
Fax: (33-1) 42 75 88 62

Annex A

PRINCIPAL RECENT PUBLIC MANAGEMENT DEVELOPMENTS

1993

- Creation of an ethics committee to supervise the departure of public servants to the private sector.
- 23 July 1993: Adoption of 315 deconcentration measures by the CIATER (interministerial committee on territorial administration).
- Drafting of 4-year ministerial plans for reorganisation and deconcentration.
- Report by the mission led by Mr. Picq on measures to improve the efficiency of the State.

1994

- Adjustments to judicial boundaries.
- On 16 June 1994, a joint declaration was signed by central government, local authorities, public establishments and welfare agencies on the quality of customer service in the public sector.
- Organisation of 11 interregional fora on the quality of customer service. Each forum was attended by 400 to 600 participants: front-line staff dealing directly with public service users, managers, elected representatives, user representatives. The fora provided an opportunity for presenting model examples.
- On 30 June 1994, the interministerial committee for rural planning and development (CIDAR) decided to set up special centres for people in rural areas to ensure that all citizens have equal access to high quality services. A budget of FF 15 million a year for three years (1995-1997) has been earmarked for this scheme.
- Circular of 13 July 1994 on the control of financial management.
- Act of 28 June 1994 laying down conditions governing the appointment of civil servants and the access of certain civil servants to jobs in the private sector, strengthened the procedure for supervising departures to the private sector.
- Act of 25 July 1994 on the organisation of work time, recruitment, and transfers in the public sector reinforced the latter's contribution to urban policy by making it possible for motivated public servants to be posted to urban areas suffering from severe social problems and high levels of insecurity.
- Circular of 26 August 1994 on adaptation of the rules governing the management of State employees to deconcentrated services.
- 20 September 1994: the CIATER studied the ministerial plans, placing special emphasis on central government structures and staff redeployment to deconcentrated services in line with the transfer of responsibilities.

1995

- In accordance with the Act of 4 February 1995 on regional planning and development, which sets out a plan to reorganise State services, all decisions concerning the reorganisation or abolition of a public service must be preceded by an impact study that considers the opportunities presented by distance working.

- On 24 February 1995, a national "synthesis" forum chaired by the Prime Minister on customer services in the public sector led to the announcement of short-term recommendations for improving relations between service users and the administration.
- A pilot experiment was carried out in two regions concerning the deconcentration of financial control of deconcentrated spending.
- Responsibilities for real estate were grouped together in the context of pilot experiments in six departments.
- Circular of 23 February 1995, in which the Prime Minister asked ministers and prefects definitively to adopt the measures introduced and to prioritise customer service improvements as a permanent strategic objective of public policy.
- Circular by the Prime Minister on 26 July 1995 on implementation of the reform of the State and public services.
- 13 September 1995: creation of the interministerial committee for State reform and of the State reform commission.
- 14 September 1995: Government seminar on State reform.
- Start of preparatory work on a three-year plan for reforming the State.

1996

- 22 February 1996: 3rd three-year framework agreement on continuing training
- Extension of the reform of financial control of deconcentrated spending.
- Preparation of the draft reform plan which addressed four main concerns:
  - putting users' needs first;
  - modernisation of human resources management;
  - delegation of responsibilities;
  - better decision-making and management.

Annex B

INSTITUTIONAL RESPONSIBILITY FOR PUBLIC MANAGEMENT IMPROVEMENT

ORGANISATION	TASKS AND RESPONSIBILITIES	OTHER INFORMATION
Ministry for the Public Service, State Reform and Decentralisation		
– General Directorate for Administration and Public Service	• directs modernisation programmes • co-ordinates policies concerned with personnel management, and the organisation and functioning	
– State reform commission	• proposes reforms • co-ordinates the preparation of government decisions • serves as secretariat for the interministerial committee for State reform and the standing committee (budget, interior, territorial development, public service)	Set up for 3 years

ORGANISATION	TASKS AND RESPONSIBILITIES	OTHER INFORMATION
Council of State	• advises the government on legal and administrative matters • proposes reforms • supreme court for administrative matters	
Government general secretariat	• organises the work of the government • gives legal advice to the government on drawing up legislation	Directly attached to the Prime Minister
Interministerial committee on the use of information and office technology in the administration (CIIBA)		Abolished by decision of 14 September 1995
Budget Ministry – Budget Division	• manages and adjusts budgetary, accounting and financial procedures at interministerial level	
General planning commission	• draws up medium and long-term national plans and supervises their execution	Under the authority of the Prime Minister
Court of Auditors and regional accounting chambers	• supervises the appropriate use of funds and the application of Finance Acts • supervises the financial management of government departments and public establishments • in annual reports, brings anomalies and cases of mismanagement to the notice of the authorities and the general public	A Central Investigation Committee examines the cost of the public sector
National Mediator	• proposes reforms on the basis of his observations of the way public services and territorial authorities operate	Independent status, appointed for 6 years

ORGANISATION	TASKS AND RESPONSIBILITIES	OTHER INFORMATION
COSIFORM – Committee for the simplification of administrative formalities	• supports government policy to promote the simplification of administrative formalities and procedures and exchanges of information with enterprises and the public • its tasks include: – monitoring enterprise formality centres and the directory of firms – managing the transfer of social security data – it performs its work in co-ordination with international bodies	Chaired by the Prime Minister 7 representatives from the Ministries 10 members appointed for a 3-year period

GERMANY

A. Main tendencies and overall priorities

Public management reforms in Germany aim at an overall increase of effectiveness, efficiency and quality within the administration. In light of Germany's federal structure, it is not possible to give an overall review of problems and developments in public sector management in all of Germany. Various significant initiatives are being pursued at the *Länder* (state or province) level. So this report can only indicate some general directions of *Länder* initiatives, with a few illustrative examples. (Information on public management reforms in the individual *Länder* has been provided by the German authorities and is available from the Public Management Service.)

The federal public management reform concept is guided by the idea of streamlining government functions and institutionalised by the creation of the Lean State ("*Schlanker Staat*") Advisory Council in July 1995. The Council has called for a re-examination of federal government functions, and in particular concentrates on recommendations for the reduction of ministerial tasks, their transfer to subordinate authorities (or agencies) of the federal government (*nachgeordnete Bundesbehörden*), privatisation and regulatory reform. The work of the Lean State Advisory Council draws upon a variety of initiatives developed within federal ministries or commissions. In centralising and supporting these initiatives, the Council acts as a catalyst for reform. In addition it makes suggestions for changes and issues interim reports with recommendations. The recommendations on modernising the federal administration reflect the way the streamlined and reformed ministries are to look like by the time the ministries move to Berlin, but also as soon as possible in Bonn. The council is scheduled to complete work in 1997, culminating with a high-level conference in February 1997.

At the *Länder* level, recent reforms focus on three central areas: human resource management, organisational changes reflecting the review of tasks, and decentralisation of resource management responsibilities requiring the development of new budgetary instruments that allow more flexibility. Furthermore, privatisation and regulatory reform are important elements of public management in some of the *Länder* and are becoming increasingly important issues in the light of economic and financial pressures.

B. Context affecting public management

First of all it should be mentioned that there is a great interest in reform activities all over Germany. On the federal level, government statements and the coalition agreement for the 13th period of the German *Bundestag* declared administrative reform to be one of their main objectives. In addition, the parliaments and governments of the *Länder* are particularly interested in promoting modernisation and reorganisation of their administration. On the other hand, pressures for public management reforms come from a worsening budget situation, partly reflecting the costs of German reunification, and the overall economic conditions characterised by persisting high or increasing unemployment and small increases in growth rates. It is felt that state action in the normative, administrative and judicial fields are to be restricted to what is necessary to streamline bureaucracy in respect of strengthening Germany as an internationally competitive location for business.

Similar pressures also concern the *Länder* and local level governments in Germany, which are not excluded from a generally strained financial situation. The five new *Länder* that joined western Germany in October 1990 faced special conditions for reform. While the first step of administrative reform in the new *Länder* has been functional reforms aiming at an optimal allocation of administrative responsibilities among institutions, the discussion has now turned to how to increase effectiveness of the administrative organisation, and how far to introduce business practices into the administration. Experience in Saxonia-Anhalt suggests, for example, that the modernisation of the public sector is facilitated in the new *Länder*, even though they must address significant differences of approach and training among staff from different parts of Germany. Since the organisational structures of the new *Länder* are more flexible compared to the Western *Länder* or the federation, as they are newly installed, changes are easier to get implemented and the general climate is favourable for innovation.

C.   Strategies and processes for planning and carrying out public management reforms

Corresponding to the Advisory Council activities, the main reform strategies at the federal level are:

– critical review of tasks, including cost and results accounting;
– organisational and structural adaptation of the federal administration on the basis of organisational studies, partly based on external studies;
– delegation of tasks to subordinate authorities and elimination of some tasks;
– privatisation of tax-related areas and of service and technical sectors;
– relocation and reduction of staff in socially acceptable steps;
– waiving and reduction of government instruction and regulation;
– acceleration and streamlining of administrative procedures;
– transfer and promotion of individual responsibility and competence, to subordinate federal authorities.

As concerns the subnational level, elements of a "new steering model" (NSM), developed in 1991 by an association of municipalities, is being implemented in many German cities. Also *Länder* reform initiatives generally reflect this management approach beginning in the mid-1990s, and different institutions within each *Land* administration or within the *Land* parliament have been created to support implementation of reforms. The building blocks of the NSM are:

– strategic management: "steering at arm's length" instead of by detailed rules;
– output and customer orientation: transparency of output, costs and impacts;
– steering instruments: replace control through rules by performance contracts;
– decentralised structures: increasing managerial freedom and bringing administrative action closer to citizens;
– personnel management: training as a basic requirement to put the NSM into practice.

E.   Human resources management

Personnel planning is closely linked with organisational changes and the critical review of tasks, and organisational studies have been carried out for parts of the federal administration. Human resources management activities concentrate, among others, on discussions with staff regarding consultation, promotion and management of staff, on needs-oriented training, and on the development of strategies that guide the reform process by describing the characteristics of the "ideal" administration ("*Leitbild*").

An important step providing the legal basis for a more efficient personnel management – at the federal and at the subnational level – is amendment of the federal civil servant Law, decided in June 1996 by the *Bundestag*. (The legislation has still to be approved by the second chamber, representing the interests of the *Länder*.) The cornerstones of the reform are:

- introduction of a test period for leading positions;
- optimisation of personnel resources;
- extension of part-time employment in the public service;
- improvement of evaluation schemes;
- more flexible career paths;
- modernisation of remuneration regulations;
- cost reduction in the area of service provisions.

At the *Länder* and municipalities level, consistent with the concept of the new steering models, personnel management and training are regarded as basic requirements for implementing reforms. Most of the *Länder* have, for example, developed personnel management concepts that focus on training and education (mostly to enhance knowledge of business administration), on the development of managerial skills for senior officials, and on the delegation of tasks so that lower administrative levels can assume more responsibility, allowing greater flexibility within internal administrative procedures. As on the federal level, staff are engaged in defining "*Leitbilder*" describing the quality of administrative services and a generally co-operative and customer-oriented environment.

F. Budget process and management of financial resources

Since 1995, pilot schemes have been introduced to test flexible budget instruments within several subordinated authorities of the federal government, while remaining consistent with the constraints of the basic requirements laid down in the federal budget law ("*Haushaltsgrundsätzegesetz*"). A basic element, for example, is the new possibility to carry over unspent resources beyond the budget period. In addition, a cost-accounting system within the federal and the *Länder* administrations has been developed in co-operation with the *Länder*; implementation started in 1996 in certain specific areas, and the conference of the ministers of Finance (a co-operation forum between the federation and the *Länder*) will present a progress report by autumn 1996.

In the *Länder*, an important element of the new steering model is the introduction of a decentralised resource management responsibility; many *Länder* have tested its implementation within pilot schemes (*e.g.* Hesse, Bavaria), while others implemented it globally (Lower Saxony, Baden-Württemberg, North-Rhine/Westphalia). Other projects aim at the introduction of more flexibility into the budget process and the building up of a cost accounting system. In one *Land* (Berlin), reforms went relatively far by introducing a cost accounting system for all parts of the state administration since 1994. Instead of such a global approach, most of the *Länder* rely on pilot schemes; for example, cost accounting systems are often introduced in the field of universities. To allow more budget flexibility, some *Länder* implemented specific legal provisions for experiments. Another example is the recently developed "Thuringian model" of budgeting which aims to present a new style of budget which is project-oriented and to create a tool for policy-making and budgeting covering all activities and their financial impacts.

G. Performance management

The employees of the administration, as those who actually perform the tasks, have to be involved in the elaboration of the guiding principle for reform ("*Leitbild*"), which is an orientation framework for modern administrative activity that defines the purpose of administration – that of a service organisation geared to the needs of the citizen – as well as its essential mission and the core functions of government. It is felt that it is of major importance in this process to reform the organisational structure of the central management areas of ministries by creating bigger, more flexible work units, co-operative leadership responsibility, and teams working on their own responsibility, as well as efficient steering in accordance with clearly formulated aims. This includes the development of work indicators and bench marks. Quality management is the method of choice to trigger off a continuous process and to prevent this from being a one-off measure.

The *Länder* have started to search for possibilities of more effective steering at all administrative levels. Partly, for this purpose, computer assisted project catalogues are developed for administrative services. Many new forms of organisation and steering in a variety of projects are being tested, aiming to strengthen management in the public sector and the delivery of services. In addition, the quality management aspects described for the federal level are being closely considered for the *Länder* and local levels as well.

H. Changing structures of the public sector

In accordance with the government's main strategies for reform, service delivery functions generally are to be transferred to subordinate federal authorities. The streamlining of the federal administration aims at the creation of small, policy-oriented ministries by minimising service activities within the ministries, their delegation to subordinate federal authorities, or to subordinate authorities of the *Länder*. At the same time, the lean state programme foresees a reduction and merging of subordinate federal authorities. The ongoing federal privatisation policy affects big infrastructural areas such as the federal railways and the postal service. Discussion of how to implement the subsidiarity principle is also ongoing as part of the discussions about a "leaner state".

At the *Länder* level, the decentralisation of administrative services and the reduction of hierarchies are important issues of public management reforms. The new administrations in the eastern *Länder* have generally fewer intermediary levels than their counterparts in western Germany (two instead of three). The general trend is to give more managerial freedom to the municipal communities (communalisation of tasks). Among the tasks that are transferred are air, water and nature protection and work security protection. A critical review of tasks and basic discussion of the role of the state have also been important issues at the *Land* level, but privatisation is generally not a priority in most *Land*. However, there are some states (*i.e.* Bavaria, Baden-Württemberg, Saxonia) which have announced privatisation and the reduction of public tasks as major goals of their government reform programmes.

I. Regulatory management and reform

Since the early 1980s, regulatory reform has been part of the government's programme and the elimination, amendment or streamlining of regulations has been undertaken. As regards the improvement of new regulations, the Lean State Advisory Council draws upon previously undertaken federal initiatives and in particular on the work of the Independent Commission for Simplification of Administration and Law operating since the early 1980s. The Council has made recommendations for new reform steps, that have so far been partly implemented. These concentrate on a strengthening of the requirement for justification before preparing a new regulation and a more rigorous assessment of the follow-up costs of these regulations – for business as well for the lower level administration responsible for implementation. Therefore, a new checklist for the review of new regulations, replacing the so-called "Blue Checklist", is currently under preparation within the Ministry of Interior.

Another important initiative, also supported by the Lean State Advisory Council, aims at an acceleration of administrative procedures (*e.g.* licensing procedures in construction and environment legislation). An amendment of the administrative procedure Act was decided in July 1996 providing for more flexibility in the permitting procedure, although some of the related legal proposals affecting for example environmental regulations are still under discussion (elements of which have already been experimented with in the eastern *Länder* where special legislation allowed faster permitting procedures). The success of the measures will depend on the *Länder* since they are responsible for implementing the reform.

As the German *Länder* have legislative responsibilities of their own, issues of regulatory management and reform are also important concerns at the *Länder* level. The importance of avoiding overregulation and prevent rising regulatory burdens for citizens and business are increasingly recognised; some of the *Länder* have developed criteria for reviewing regulations and created an institutional structure that allows, despite general ministerial autonomy, a possibility for central and independent review. To some extent, these initiatives are cited as possible models in discussion of reforms at the federal level.

Mrs. Petra Wuttke-Götz
Assistant Secretary
Subdivision of Administrative Machinery
Ministry of the Interior
Graurheindorfer Str. 198
D-53117 Bonn
Tel.: (49-228) 681-4182
Fax: (49-228) 681-4199

Annex A

PRINCIPAL RECENT PUBLIC MANAGEMENT DEVELOPMENTS

1983
- Government resolution to promote debureaucratisation and simplification of law and administration and to set up an independent Commission within the Federal Ministry of the Interior.

1984
- Cabinet Decision initiated by Federal Ministry of the Interior to install the "Blue Checklist" for improving federal legislation.

1983-6
- Improved flexibility in working time, especially concerning part-time jobs.

1986-9
- Amendment to Federal Budget Code to create a uniform accounting system in three steps involving organisational simplification and better use of IT.

1988
- Federal Cabinet defines "Guidelines for the use of IT in the Federal Administration".

1989
- Federal Ministers of Interior and Justice promote a Cabinet Decision on improving legislation.

1990
- Unification Treaty ends division of the two German States and makes provision for transitional arrangements for administrative institutions, legal status of personnel and financial management in eastern Germany.
- Federal Academy of Public Administration embarks on major in-service training programme for the new *Länder*.

1991
- Federal Parliament (*Bundestag*) decides that the seat of Parliament and the Federal Government will be Berlin; that the removal from Bonn to Berlin will take place over the next ten years; and that a number of federal ministries and authorities will remain in Bonn.

- Large scale secondments of civil servants from all levels of government to the eastern *Länder* along with major training efforts.

1992

- Basic Law amended to give *Länder* more powers to influence decision-making on matters of the European Union.
- All federal ministries establish organisation units to examine European legislation issues, co-ordination and implementation requirements.

1994

- Minister of the Interior presents a report on perspectives of the public service law, draft of a Public Service Reform Act already presented to Parliament.

1995

- Federal Cabinet establishes an Lean State Advisory Council to facilitate the public management reform process.

1996

- Federal Ministry of Finance initiates a Cabinet Decision on improving the organisational structure of the Federal Administration especially in respect of the government removal from Bonn to Berlin.

Annex B

INSTITUTIONAL RESPONSIBILITY FOR PUBLIC MANAGEMENT IMPROVEMENT

ORGANISATION	TASKS AND RESPONSIBILITIES	OTHER INFORMATION
Federal Chancellery	• general co-ordination and setting of guidelines	
Federal Ministry of the Interior		Improvement of public management is decentralised to the federal states. Every Minister has independent competence for this sector within guidelines set by the Chancellor.
– General Directorate "D" (public service law)	• general responsibility limited to matters relating to the public service and to public service law	
– General Directorate "O" (organisation)	• general responsibility for promoting the exchange of information between the heads of sections of Administrative Machinery of the Federal Ministries, preparation of interministerial Guidelines on organisational matters	
Federal Academy of Public Administration	• in-service training; research on public administration and public management reform	Under the authority of the Federal Ministry of the Interior.

ORGANISATION	TASKS AND RESPONSIBILITIES	OTHER INFORMATION
Federal Ministry of Finance	• budget process	
Länder		Many inputs to management development originate at the level of the *Länder* and communities.
Independent Federal Commission to Simplify Law and Administration	• promotion of debureaucratisation and deregulation • streamlining of administrative procedures	Appointed by Cabinet; within the Federal Ministry of the Interior.
Lean State Advisory Council	• streamlining bureaucracy in respect of a lean state, *i.e.* working out restrictions for state actions in the normative, administrative and judicial fields	Established by Cabinet Decision, Secretariat in the Federal Ministry of the Interior.

GREECE

A. Main tendencies and overall priorities

The main tendencies and overall priorities are to:

- strengthen deconcentration and decentralisation;
- combat waste in the public sector;
- cut public spending;
- effect a general reorganisation of public services, based on the elimination or consolidation of public services and agencies (under a long-term plan drawing on current international trends in this area, and European Union requirements for the convergence of national economies);
- reduce the number of public-sector employees (by instituting the principle that only one civil servant is to be recruited for every three who retire);
- speed the pace of privatisation;
- absorb EU resources more rapidly.

B. Context affecting public management

The context affecting public management is characterised by:

- budgetary restrictions;
- efforts to combat tax evasion and broaden the tax base.

C. Strategies and processes for planning and carrying out public management reforms

A programme (the *Klisthenis* Programme) to modernise the Greek public administration was approved as part of the second Community Support Framework (CSF). Its primary goal is to upgrade information technologies and computer systems within the administration, improve human resources management (and especially the training of civil servants), reorganise public administration and simplify and rationalise procedures.

A plan for administrative reform was approved by the European Commission in July 1996, within the framework of the *Klisthenis* Programme.

The main aspects involved:

- legislative simplification and consolidation;
- simplification of complex administrative procedures and adoption of quality criteria for administrative activity;
- organisation and implementation of the administration's social protection scheme;
- development of the administration's human resources;
- improvement of the decision-making process;

– functional organisation of departments;
– functional modernisation at regional level;
– support for and upgrading of initiatives by "second-level territorial authorities";
– analysis of administrative activities, assisted by Geographical Information Systems (GIS).

A study on the introduction of e-mail in the Greek administration was conducted (during the first four months of 1996), with assistance from the European Commission under the Interchange of Data between Administrations (IDA) Programme.

D. Policy-management capacities

The following initiatives have been taken in the realm of policy management:

– Creation of the National Public Administration Commission, representing all political parties (Law 2333/1995, Act of the Council of Ministers 87/4-41996). The Commission is chaired by the Minister of the Interior, Public Administration and Decentralisation and is composed of:
  • MPs designated by each political party represented in the national or European Parliament;
  • the chairman of the parliamentary committee on public administration.

When discussing a subject, the National Commission may request the participation of the relevant minister and hear any civil servant or expert. It expresses opinions and formulates general policy proposals, for the purpose of establishing common positions and/or a strategy in respect of national policy for public administration.

– Merger of the Ministry to the Presidency of government and the Ministry of the Interior (September 1995) and creation of the Ministry of the Interior, Public Administration and Decentralisation (Presidential Decree 373/1995).
– Transfer of the Secretariat General for Social Security to the Ministry of Labour (September 1995, PD 372/1995).
– Merger of the Ministry of Tourism, the Ministry of Industry, Energy and Technology and the Ministry of Commerce (January 1996) and creation of the Ministry of Development (PD 27/1996).
– Reorganisation of the Secretariat of the Council of Ministers to co-ordinate government policy(PD 86/1996).

The Secretariat of the Council of Ministers is now known as the Secretariat General of the Council of Ministers. The Secretariat General is an autonomous public service responsible directly to the Prime Minister. It is a strategic public service which assists the Prime Minister and the government in the exercise of their responsibilities and provides secretariat services for the Council of Ministers and the government's collegiate bodies and committees, unless provision of those services is assigned to other bodies. The Secretariat General implements the decisions of the aforementioned bodies and, in general, exercises all of the powers provided for by law, as well as those conferred on it by Presidential Decree 86/1996.

The Secretariat General of the Council of Ministers comprises:

– the private office of the Secretary-General of the Council of Ministers;
– the office of administrative and financial support;
– the office of legislative affairs;
– the office of support for the co-ordination of government measures;
– the Central Commission for the Drafting of Legislation (KENE);
– the telecommunications office.

The Secretary-General is appointed by the government. He is the direct assistant to the Prime Minister.

E. Human resources management

Recent initiatives involving human resources management include:

- (in 1995) the first recruitment competition to be carried out in accordance with the system set up by Law 2190/1994; recruitment of specialised staff based on priority lists established by that same law;
- ratification of International Conventions 151 and 154 on the introduction of collective bargaining in the public sector (Laws 2403/1996 and 2405/1996, respectively);
- new staff regulations for civil servants (under preparation by a committee of experts);
- preparation of a draft Code of Administrative Procedure;
- a new performance appraisal system (under preparation);
- study of a new public-sector pay system.

F. Budget process and management of financial resources

Budgetary and financial reform is proceeding, with:

- further efforts to combat tax evasion and broaden the tax base;
- institution of a task force to counter tax fraud (Law 2343/1995); this task force has broader powers of investigation and prosecution than the police, the tax administration or any other law enforcement agency, and is equipped with ultra-modern technology;
- creation of the Treasury Department, within the Ministry for Finance (Law 2343/1995);
- establishment of institutions to bolster the process of economic development (Law 2372/1996).

G. Performance management

Performance management involves a reorganisation of the institutional framework for public enterprises, in order to assess their results according to criteria used by the private sector (Law 2414/1996). This Law seeks to modify the institutional framework that governs public enterprises, in order to redefine the role of those enterprises within the State, modernise their organisation and operations, bolster their management independence and enhance their profitability.

Accordingly, public enterprises:

- are now public limited liability companies.
- all establish a Strategic Plan, which maps out long-term objectives consistent with government policy, and an Operating Plan, which sets medium-term goals for the implementation of Strategic Plan objectives.

On the basis of the Operating Plan, a management contract is concluded between the Chairman and Executive Counsel, for the public enterprise, and the government. The contract is filed with the relevant parliamentary committee.

The Management Contract sets out the results expected and the management objectives that corporate executives must aim for in the medium term (3-5 years). The objectives agreed upon by both parties are equally binding for the management of the public enterprise and the State. The operational effectiveness of public enterprises is measured against realisation of these agreed objectives.

The Strategic and Operating Plans, as well as execution of the management contract, are overseen by the ministry responsible for public enterprise, the Ministry of National Economy, and the relevant parliamentary committee. Public enterprises are managed by:

– a Board of Directors, which formulates corporate strategy and development policy;
– an Executive Counsel;
– a Management Board, which provides the necessary operational co-ordination and cohesion and attends to routine management.

Public enterprises are required to establish a Charter of Obligations vis-à-vis consumers. These Charters set forth the responsibilities of public enterprises towards consumers, and require that firms make amends for any failure to meet those responsibilities.

Employees of public enterprises are entitled to bonuses, and provisions have been made for productivity-linked pay in cases where output can be measured.

Public enterprises are going to adopt new organisation charts and staff rules, as well as staff training programmes.

H. Changing structurs of the public sector

The primary change in the structure of the public sector is a reorganisation of Greece's regions as administrative units of the State. This reorganisation is being undertaken to meet the needs of planning, scheduling and co-ordinating regional development, in order to facilitate more effective implementation of the transfer of powers from the central government to the regions, and to provide a link between the centre of government and local authorities.

Under draft legislation to enhance the regional organisation of the State, each region would become a decentralised administrative entity having a unified structure and its own staff. Regions would also be equipped to create new services and consolidate existing ones, inasmuch as the interdepartmental and regional services of the ministries would be abolished and their powers exercised by the relevant regional services.

The same legislation provides for a further transfer of power from the central government to local authorities.

I. Regulatory management and reform

See the action to be undertaken under the plan for administrative reform discussed in Section C.

J. Other

Draft legislation to create an Ombudsman's post.

Mr. Vassilis Andronopoulos
Director-General
Ministry of the Interior, Public Administration and Decentralisation
Secretariat General for the Public Administration
15 Vasilissis Sophias Boulevard
10674 Athens, Greece
Tel.: (30-1) 33 93 337
Fax: (30-1) 33 93 300

Mrs. Kanellio Sakellariadou
Ministry of the Interior, Public Administration and Decentralisation
Secretariat General for the Public Administration
15 Vasilissis Sophias Boulevard
10674 Athens, Greece
Tel.: (30-1) 33 93 337
Fax: (30-1) 33 93 300

Annex A

PRINCIPAL RECENT PUBLIC MANAGEMENT DEVELOPMENTS

1993

– Achievement of a certain degree of decentralisation through a transfer of executive responsibility from the central government to prefects.
– Efforts to limit the size of the public sector (a continued freeze on appointments and recruiting; privatisation).
– Introduction of an objective system for job transfers.
– Measures to improve relations with citizens (creation of a standardised form to be sent to all administrative services, extension of a government computer system to cover the entire country).

1994

– Continued freeze on public-sector appointments and recruiting.
– Restrictions on public spending.
– Creation of "second-level territorial authorities", each headed by a prefect and a prefectoral council, both locally elected.
– Introduction of a new system of public-sector recruiting, based on competitions for administrators and on priority lists for specialised staff and auxiliaries.
– Creation of an autonomous "Commission for Personnel Recruitment" to administer the system of public-sector recruiting.
– Introduction of a new administrative hierarchy.
– Creation of the Economic and Social Committee, an advisory body responsible for promoting social dialogue on the main aspects of socio-economic policy.
– Approval of the *Klisthenis* programme to modernise the Greek public administration, under the second Community Support Framework.

1995

– Creation of the National Public Administration Commission, representing all political parties.

1996

– Drafting of an administrative reform plan as part of the *Klisthenis* Programme, which is funded under the second Community Support Framework programme.
– Reorganisation of the institutional framework for public enterprises.

Annex B

INSTITUTIONAL RESPONSIBILITY FOR PUBLIC MANAGEMENT IMPROVEMENT

ORGANISATION	TASKS AND RESPONSIBILITIES
Ministry of the Interior, Public Administration and Decentralisation	
– Secretariat General for the Public Administration	• overall co-ordination of the improvement of public management • organisation • public-sector personnel policy • relations between citizens and the administration • information technologies
– Secretariat General for Local Authorities	• decentralisation and deconcentration • enhancing the autonomy of local authorities
Ministry for Economic Affairs	• management of public enterprises • regulatory policy for the private sector
Ministry for Finance	• civil service pay • budgeting • financial management

HUNGARY

A. Main tendencies and overall priorities

In the course of the political transition emphasis was placed on development of a **democratic** institutional system, including establishment of external controls of public management by various institutions (State Audit Office, Constitutional Court, Ombudsman, and extension of the scope of court revision of decisions) and within the system of public management, the controlling function of bodies elected directly by the citizens (the representative body of local government) has increased.

The institutional and legislative transformation has also been concluded on the basis of principles of democracy, within the areas of defence and police management as well. The changes that have occurred in public management have been fundamentally influenced by the endeavour aimed at Hungary's Euro-Atlantic integration, as a result of which Hungary became a member of the Council of Europe in 1990 and then entered into an Agreement of Association with the European Community.

In 1990, as a result of a substantial **decentralisation** process, a new, up-to-date system of municipal governments developed, which exercises public power on an autonomous basis, decides in public affairs of local interest and as a basic task, organises and/or provides local public services.

Following the establishment of the democratic institutional system the improvement of **efficiency**, economy and effectiveness became the highest priority, and the aim is to develop a model for the state as service provider. This is served by the reform of the public finance system and the programme of modernisation of public administration. At the same time, preparations have commenced for the implementation of the tasks associated with the accession to the European Union.

B. Context affecting public management

A fundamental burden for the economy of Hungary is that besides the inherited external debt, a substantial volume of internal state debt has accumulated over the past several years. Measures are being taken to improve the balance of public finances and to eliminate the causes of the decline of the balance. The intended reduction of the deficit of the central budget necessitates a fundamental re-consideration of the roles and responsibilities of the state and development of a public sector in line with the capacities of the economy of Hungary.

The required reduction of the roles and responsibilities of the state should be achieved through rationalisation of the operation of areas, responsibilities and institutions that were formerly financed by the state, and through transfer of certain tasks currently performed by the state, to non-governmental organisations and/or to the business sphere.

The Euro-Atlantic integration, and generally convergence towards the community of developed countries, promotes the process of the modernisation of Hungary. Accession to the European Union plays an important role in this process, in the preparation of which, the public administration fulfils key functions in several areas, including:

 – creation of a favourable environment for restructuring and development of the economy;
 – legal harmonization: gradual convergence of the laws that remain in national competency, to the legislative system of the Community;
 – provision for the adoption and application of the mechanisms of operation (*"acquis communautaire"*) of the Community, through development and operation of an adequate institution system.

C. Strategies and processes for planning and carrying out public management reforms

In order to ensure concerted foundation and implementation of the comprehensive measures for reform of the central and local public administration and the governmental tasks relating to the ongoing modernisation of public administration, the Government appointed a Government Commissioner for the Modernisation of Public Administration in August 1994.

On the basis of over half a decade's experiences relating to the development and then operation of the new type of local and central public administration, the Government Commissioner prepared a strategy for the Public Administration Reform Programme, which the Government approved on September 1996, including action plans.

Within the organisation of the Prime Minister's Office a programme office has been set up to prepare the strategy of modernisation. In May, 1996 the Government approved the political concept of its modernisation programme ("Hungary in the new Europe") along with the plan of actions, the aim of which is to prepare Hungary for the Euro-Atlantic integration.

In order to prepare the transformation of the public sector the Government set up a Committee for Public Financing Reform in December, 1994 and then in April 1996 they defined the major objectives and system of requirements for reform of the public finance system, in respect of the areas concerned (*e.g.* pension scheme, health, the social/welfare benefits system, public education, higher education, municipal governments, the system of central budgetary institutions, tax and contribution policy, financial reform) and the plan of actions for the elaboration of the concrete reform proposals.

D. Policy-management capacities

Since 1990 the meetings of the permanent heads of the ministries and of the permanent state secretaries have been the technical forum for the preparation of decision making by the Government, where all proposals and reports to be submitted to the sessions of government are previously discussed from technical/professional aspects; where opinions differ, the participants record their positions, prior to submission of the materials to the Government.

The political preparation of the decisions to be made by the Government and their implementation is co-ordinated by the Government through its "cabinets" (*i.e.* committees of ministers). The Ministers participate in the work of those of the four cabinets (Government Cabinet, European Integration Cabinet, Economic Cabinet, National Security Cabinet) which deal with issues pertaining to their respective departments.

Besides preparation of decision making, controlling implementation is growing in importance:

 – in October, 1994 a separate Government Control Office was set up as a central state organisation with a nation-wide competency, with the purpose of exercising budgetary control of organisations of the executive power, and for the assessment of the implementation and enforcement of the decisions made by the Government;

– in May, 1995 a Co-ordination Council for the Protection of the Economy was set up to plan the institutional and legal requirements of the "fight against the black economy" and to monitor the process of implementation;

– in April, 1996 the Evaluation and Controlling Secretariat was established within the Prime Minister's Office.

In 1996 further development of the system of public administration with an orientation towards integration was assigned special importance. As part of this effort, the Government set up a European Integration Cabinet in February 1996, to discuss strategic issues relating to the accession to the European Union, to prepare proposals relating to the definition of the national strategies and institution system, to direct the preparation of the political decisions that need to be made in connection with the integration and to co-ordinate the implementation of such decisions.

The activities of the European Integration Cabinet – which is headed by the Prime Minister – are supported by the Integration Strategy Working Group comprised of acknowledged experts. The task of the Working Group is to organise and implement co-ordinated strategic research for the benefit of the European Integration Cabinet.

Since May 1996 public administration co-ordination relating to the integration with Europe has been performed by the Integration State Secretariat set up within the organisation of the Ministry of Foreign Affairs. This central organ performs the inter-departmental administrative co-ordination tasks over the whole of the process of integration, such as preparation of the answers to be given to the EU Questionnaires.

The technical co-ordination of the governmental responsibilities relating to the implementation of the Europe Agreement and to the preparation for the accession to the European Union and the harmonization of the activities of the various Ministries relating to the process of integration is carried out by the Inter-Governmental Committee for the European Integration.

E. Human resources management

A specific feature of the Hungarian system of public service is that the legal status of employees of public services is not defined by a single comprehensive law, but the various areas of public services have their own specific legal regulations. As a first step of the development of an up-to-date and uniform civil service system, the Parliament adopted in 1992 the Act on the Legal Status of Civil Servants. This introduced a system of promotions based on performance – in contrast to the negative traditions of the preceding era; provided for predictability of the professional careers of the civil servants; and laid down the legal bases for the development of a civil service sector that is independent from changes in the political composition of the Government, and is stable and loyal to the government in office, in line with the European standards. The new statutory regulations regards as a common basic value civil service that is highly qualified and neutral from the aspect of party politics. As a first step to facilitate the evolution of such an organisation the Government introduced a system of examinations based on uniform requirements of technical/professional qualifications. The introduction of the examination is also highly important in that it is almost unprecedented in the history of Hungarian public management that within a relatively short period of time general technical assessment of the whole staff was concluded.

Also since 1992 a regulation similar in nature has governed the legal status of public servants (*e.g.* teachers, doctors) employed by the budgetary institutions of the state and of local governments; while the legal status of the professional staff of the armed organisations was regulated in a different Act by Parliament in 1996.

In 1995, as part of the efforts aimed at economic stabilization, the number of civil servant jobs was reduced by over 16 per cent. In the implementation of the downsizing a differentiation according to the changed responsibilities of the Ministries, was applied to the portion over the minimum staff cut of ten per cent that was mandatory for all of the Ministries. The funds saved as a result of the redundancy scheme were left within the system of public service, and in order to improve quality, the civil servants performing substantive tasks received improved remuneration in the 1996 budget year.

F.   Budget process and management of financial resources

The macroeconomic criteria of the state are defined in a medium range programme of economic policy, to define the major targets, tasks of the given time period and the macroeconomic framework.

Planning and financial management are performed on the basis of the annual budget. Upon approval of the budget law, the Parliament decides on the appropriations and the Government is responsible for implementation of the budget.

Prior to the preparation of the proposed annual budget the Government approves of the budgetary guidelines for the given year, where, on the basis of the macroeconomic projections the leeway of the central budget is defined along with the priorities.

The budget is not prepared in a branch structure, but by chapter (for the Ministries and organisations of nation-wide authority, that constitute chapters in the budget). The budgets of the chapters contain the appropriations for the tasks to be performed by the budgetary organisations established by the Parliament, the Government and the Ministries, as well as for other centrally handled tasks, including the subsidies granted to the local governments. The central budget, therefore, includes the budgets of the organs of central powers and public administration, those of higher education, research, defence, public law and order and the judicatory organisations. The operation of these organisations at acceptable standards is a responsibility of the state as the organisation in charge of the maintenance thereof.

In respect of the central budget, from 1997 a scheme of rolling planning shall be introduced, where in 1997 forecasts shall be included in the budget concerning macroeconomic trends for 1998 and 1999. This, however, shall not constitute a commitment, since over-year commitments shall be limited, as far as possible, on the basis of the Act on the Public Finance System.

The implementation of the budget and the economic events are recorded in a cash-flow based system, using double entry book keeping. Budgetary organisations do not perform accounting of profits and losses (as had been the practice until 1993), but there is an intention to return to such a system. No accounting for due dates is performed.

G.   Performance management

One of the objectives of the reform of public administration is to have the existing hierarchic system of public administration be replaced by a system of public management operating for the benefit of and as required by the taxpayer citizen. To prepare this – following earlier assessments of efficiency and the analysis and evaluation of foreign experiences – a project was launched in 1996 to assess possible introduction of norms of public management services in central budgetary institutions. In the course of the assessment, service activities performed by the central budgetary institutions are analysed and the services for which normative standards can be established are assessed and then the criteria for introducing such standards are examined.

Besides the central public administration, increased importance was attached to local government management, since it is this sphere which provides the majority of the services that directly affect citizens. In this area assessment of the feasibility of introducing service standards began in relation to four areas (public education, health, social/welfare and communal services) on the basis of experience with the Citizens' Charter.

H.   Changing structures of the public sector

As a result of a process of substantial decentralisation, the system of local governments was developed in 1990, the regulation of which was fully in line with the provisions of the European Charter of Local Self-Governments. In accordance with the universal values of modern self-governance the local communities have a right of autonomous decision-making in respect of public issues of local importance and they have also been granted the required economic – budgetary and property – criteria. On the basis of the principle of subsidiarity, the multitude of municipal governments have been given extensive scope for responsibilities and competencies and they can formulate local politics as the local pillars of democracy.

Over the first governmental cycle the municipal governmental system quickly solved the difficulties that necessarily arose from the transition and it not only preserved its operability but it also successfully achieved substantive improvements. On the basis of the experiences gained form the operation, the Act on Local Governments was amended in 1994, the adjustments (including direct election of Mayors and the members of county representative bodies, precise definition of the scope of competency of the Budapest General Assembly, elimination of the institution of the republic's regional commissioner) all serve to improve the system of municipal governments.

In the second cycle the municipal governments commenced operating under less favourable economic conditions which called for an exploration of local resources and rationalisation of the available budgets. The municipal governments were forced to revise their institution systems, their own apparatuses and look for forms and areas of co-operation. On the whole, the system of municipal government remained stable and despite the difficulties it provides the required basis for public services to the citizens, but as a result of the bankruptcies that were perceived as a warning sign, the Act on Local Governmental Bankruptcy was adopted.

Following revision of the responsibilities of the fragmented regional organs of public administration, a proposal was prepared that called for elimination of certain state responsibilities and/or decentralisation thereof to local governments, as well as for the establishment of a government office (county and Budapest public administration offices) to assist co-ordinated action by Government. The objective of the measure was to develop a more co-ordinated and smaller system of public administration at the county level.

I.   Regulatory management and reform

In January 1995, the Government launched a programme to revise statutes of law from the aspect of the requirements of deregulation. One of the fundamental goals of deregulation is to eliminated over-regulation and over-complicated regulation, to reduce state intervention and the relating administrative burdens, to increase the freedom of action of citizens and organisations and to increase their autonomy in self organisation. The general deregulation revision covers legislation by decrees (both those in force and those submitted for adoption) while in defined cases statutes of law may also be made subject to partial deregulation.

Legal regulations will be revised in two stages:

– by the end of June 1996 regulations adopted prior to 30th June 1990 have been revised;
– by the end of December 1996 regulations adopted between 30 June 1990 and 31 March 1995 will have been revised.

The phased deregulation is directed and co-ordinated by the Government Commissioner for the Modernisation of Public Administration, who has issued a deregulation guide in co-operation with the Minister of Justice, in the preparation of which they took into account the relevant OECD recommendations. In October 1995, the Government abolished almost 400 pieces of regulations.

A key issue for the integration of Hungary with the European Union is incorporation of the Community rules in Hungary's legislative system: the Government adopted a legal harmonization plan of actions to ensure that this is properly carried out. According to the plan of actions complete legal harmonization shall be implemented in two five year cycles following the entry into force of the Accession Agreement, progressing from the harmonization of laws of higher levels towards those at lower levels.

Dr. Imre Verebélyi
Government Commissioner for the Modernisation of Public Administration
Prime Minister's Office
4 Kossuth tèr Budapest 1357, POB. 2.
Tel.: (36-1) 268 32 00
Fax: (36-1) 268 32 18

Annex A

PRINCIPAL RECENT PUBLIC MANAGEMENT DEVELOPMENTS

1990
- Free Parliamentary elections.
- Adoption of the Act on Local Governments.
- Operation of decentralised system of local governments following the local general elections.

1991
- Evolution into general practice of court revision of decisions made by the public administration.

1992
- Act on Civil Servants regulates the legal status of the staff of the public administration.
- Adoption of the Act on Public Servants.
- Adoption of the Act on the Public Finance System.

1993
- Legal regulation of the parliamentary commissioner of citizens' rights.

1994
- The government submitted its application for accession to the European Union which started a new phase in the preparation for the EU integration.
- The government appointed a Government Commissioner to harmonise reform measures that have comprehensive effects on the central and the local public administration.
- The government set up a Public Finance System Reform Committee to prepare the reform of the public finance system.

1995
- Plan of Action for legal harmonization.
- Programme concerning revision of the legal statutes from the aspect of the requirements of deregulation.
- Stabilisatory measures to improve the position of the balance of the public finance system.
- 16 per cent redundancy programme in the system of central public administration.
- Introduction of public procurement scheme.
- The government decided the directions of the reform of the territorial state administration.

1996
- Introduction of Treasury financing.
- The government adopted of the political concept of its modernisation programme.
- The government defined the basic principles of the reform of the public finance system, its major goals and requirements in respect of the areas concerned and the plan of action that supports implementation.
- Debate over the concept of a new Constitution in Parliament.
- The government approved the strategy of Reform of Governance and Public Administration.

Annex B

INSTITUTIONAL RESPONSIBILITY FOR PUBLIC MANAGEMENT IMPROVEMENT

ORGANISATION	TASKS AND RESPONSIBILITIES
Prime Minister's Office – Government Commissioner for the Modernisation of Public Administration	• policy co-ordination • control of implementation • IT policy co-ordination • administrative modernisation • deregulation • top civil service training
Ministry of the Interior	• central-local government relations • civil service regulation and training • immigration • law enforcement
Ministry of Finance	• public finance reform • budget process • treasury system

Annex C

KEY PUBLIC DOCUMENTS ON PUBLIC MANAGEMENT ISSUES AND DEVELOPMENTS

Act on Municipal Governments, No. LXV Act of 1990.

No. XXIII Act of 1992 on the Legal Status of Public Servants.

The draft programme of the reform of governance and of public administration 1996.

Hungary in the new Europe, Political Concept of the Government's Modernisation Programme, May 1996.

ICELAND

A. Main tendencies and overall priorities

Iceland's present government took office in the middle of 1995. It is a coalition government, consisting of the Independence and Progressive Parties, under the premiership of Mr. Davíd Oddsson, Chairman of the Independence Party. He was also Prime Minister of the previous government, a coalition of the Independence and Social Democratic Parties, which took office in 1991. The present government's policy platform includes objectives of working towards a balanced fiscal budget, a balance on current account, a reduction in external debt, continued price stability and a reduction in unemployment. It also aims at the privatisation of public enterprises with the establishment of a plan of concerted action. It intends to corporatise and/or privatise a number of public enterprises and state-owned financial institutions. Government operations will be restructured through such initiatives as increased tender purchases, outsourcing and merging of government agencies.

More than a year has passed since the government took office. During this period it has pursued a policy of growth revival, paying careful attention not to rekindle inflation which was endemic in Iceland for many years. Growth is now reviving, after a period of stagnation for several years.

The government has also set itself the goal of eliminating the fiscal deficit over a period of two years, 1996 and 1997. For 1996, it passed a fiscal budget with a deficit of 4 billion krónur (out of a total expenditure of some 120 billion, less than one per cent of GDP), and for 1997 it aims at a surplus of about 1 billion krónur.

B. Context affecting public management

In recent decades, limited attention has been paid to the growth and development of central and local government. Until 1987, rapid growth of the economy ensured a rise in public revenue to finance the expansion of government activity. Government functions and tasks have increased in number through evolution, often to meet the demands of the day. Serious questions about the size and scope of government were not raised until the economy began to grow more slowly after 1988. No concerted review of the need for government agencies or the streamlining of their functions has taken place. The government's role of serving the citizen, particularly in health and welfare coverage, has increased sharply in the past three decades.

This has led to an overlap in the duties of many government agencies and some have not moved in step with changing needs over time. The effort to bring fiscal finances into balance has served to focus government attention on the need for and usefulness of many government services.

Moreover, the central government has paid increasing attention to the longer-term outlook for fiscal finances and expects that public expenditure will increase after the turn of the century as large generations reach retirement age at the same time as the working age population will shrink in relative terms. The goal of the government is to keep the public sector within manageable proportions so as to be able to meet the challenges of growing public service tasks in the next century without placing undue burdens upon the taxpayer.

The government takes the view that the public sector is already at its limit. It should preferably be reduced or, at best, its growth should be arrested. Substantial new taxes to finance continued government expansion will be difficult to pass. The culture in the public sector does not support radical changes in government services. Government agencies are not in a position to take the initiative for change nor are civil servants encouraged to do so.

C.   Strategies and processes for planning and carrying out public management reforms

To reach its goal of a balanced budget in 1997, the government has undertaken a review of government functions and operations. The central government must cut current operations expenditure and moderate the increase in entitlement transfers. For this purpose it is considering plans to merge and redefine a number of government agencies so as to provide more effective service to the citizen at a lower cost.

The government is also in the process of preparing the corporatisation of several large government agencies, including its two commercial banks. The Postal and Telegraph Administration has been turned into a public limited company and will commence operations as such at the beginning of 1997. The state is the sole owner of the company's stock which cannot be sold without the express consent of the A*lthing* (legislature). The corporatisation and privatisation of agencies in the power sector must come under active consideration in the near future (see also Section H).

D.   Policy-management capacities

The centralisation of the government management process is one of the key issues in the discussion of government reform. Given Iceland's small population and the hands-on involvement of the government authorities in most facets of economic life, the central government became gradually and perhaps unintentionally centralised in nature. Many lower-level decisions are taken at the ministerial level which, as is now realised, could better be left to middle government management or to market forces. In recent years the tendency has increased to shift operational decisions to the middle management level and let ministries concentrate increasingly on policy. The government takes the view that the state should withdraw from activities and services that the market could handle, although it may pay for a part or all of the service.

E.   Human resources management

One of the key elements in government reforms is to review the Civil Service Act of 1954. The Act guarantees lifetime employment to a very large number of government employees. The pay and promotion structure of the government system was largely based on seniority. The 1996 Act, passed this past spring, abolishes the lifetime employment guarantee for most government employees (exceptions include judges, policemen and ministers of the church). Senior civil servants of the central government will be on five-year fixed-term contracts. All others will be hired on an open-ended basis and can be terminated (with severance pay according to time of service) as the need arises.

This change is considered necessary as an element in the decentralisation process of the government, where individual managers will be given defined tasks and clear goals along with increased flexibility to do their job as they see fit. This frees them to shift personnel to achieve a more goal-oriented staff.

The government also intends to decentralise its pay structure so as to give increased flexibility to managers to pay their staff. The age and seniority-based pay structure would gradually be done away with and replaced by a performance structure, where staff would be remunerated according to product and ability.

The move towards decentralisation will also mean that line managers will be given increased responsibility for managing their areas at the same time as they will have increased control over their own staff. This will mean that the human resource environment in the public sector will gradually be aligned to conditions prevailing in the private sector.

F. Budget process and management of financial resources

The Ministry of Finance has in recent years placed increasing emphasis on the longer-term projection of fiscal trends. It has projected current fiscal trends to the end of the decade and thereby developed indicators for fiscal targets in the shorter term. This method has helped the government realise that a medium-term outlook is a necessary tool for fiscal strategy and it has helped influence fiscal policy in the short term. The Ministry of Finance publishes its medium-term fiscal projections with the budget Bill every year in order to bring the message home to the legislature and the public that longer-term fiscal dynamics do matter.

Two major changes have been made in budget processes since 1991. First, the 1992 budget was the first budget drawn up under the frame method. This method consists of a working process whereby the government commences by setting a fiscal target for such key parameters as the budget balance, the borrowing requirement, taxation and the budget frame for each ministry. It is then left to each minister to allocate funds to each project and agency under his auspices. Second, as of 1992 the Ministry of Finance has developed rules on the treatment of year-end surpluses and deficits for each item (project or agency) of the fiscal budget, and how they are carried over into the new fiscal year. The new rules replaced older rules whereby the spending authorisation of each year expired at the end of the year and could not be carried over. Under the new rules, each agency is in a position to plan its finances on a longer-term basis and carry over surpluses from year to year instead of being compelled to spend funds under a sunset deadline.

This winter, the government introduced a Bill in the *Althing* for a Government Financial Management Act. The main elements of the Bill deal with a reorganisation of the budget, whereby individual agencies and functions of the central government are regrouped according to international government accounting standards. The budget will be presented on an accrual basis as well as a cash basis for better comparison with the government accounts. The credit budget (covering central government borrowing and repayment, a separate legislation) will be merged with the fiscal budget. The accounts of government agencies will be prepared in accordance with private sector accounting principles with the exception that assets are in most cases written off in the first year.

G. Performance management

The government has begun a modernisation programme of government operations whereby it expects to move increasingly towards giving individual agencies and their managers certain clearly defined targets and responsibilities at the same time giving them increased freedom to manage. The government has already concluded five experimental management contracts with agencies and expects such contracts to increase in number over the next several years.

The Ministry of Finance has begun work on a systematic collection of data for activity indicators from all government agencies and has already published its first annual edition of such data. The idea of activity indicators has not caught on as a useful tool of government management and for some it has been seen as another piece of unnecessary paperwork. The goal of these indicators is to develop a set of standards by which one can in due course measure what the government is getting for its money. This ties in with the notion that the government is moving away from being a provider of services to the public as owner-operator of government service functions towards being a buyer of public services on behalf of citizens/taxpayers.

The Minister of Finance has instituted awards for those government agencies that have shown excellence in management. Such awards were bestowed for the first time this year when five agencies received the awards on the basis of criteria relating to the setting of goals, the quality of service, financial management, the search for progress amongst others.

The Ministry of Finance has established a working group to develop proposals for introducing performance management in the public sector. The working group is developing a framework for contracts and a systematic follow-up between ministries and agencies whereby the latter would receive standards and goals in return for management flexibility.

H.   Changing structures of the public sector

One of the priorities of the government that took office in 1991 was to privatise state enterprises engaged in commercial activity. The present government is continuing this endeavour. In the years 1992 to 1994 twelve public enterprises were privatised for a total of 2.1 billion krónur in sales proceeds. Amongst the privatised companies were the State Herring Oil and Meal Factories, the Gutenberg State Printing Works, the State Shipping Company and the State Pharmaceuticals Import Company. The privatisation effort is continuing under the present government, whereby it intends to sell its shares in several corporatised enterprises, such as the State Cement Works, the State Fertilizer Factory, the Government Data Centre, the Motor Vehicles Inspection Company and others.

The second stage of this effort is to corporatise a number of wholly state-owned companies. The Postal and Telegraph Administration is now a public limited company where the government will be the sole owner. The same is intended for the state-owned commercial banks and investment credit funds.

Another part of the government's effort to change the role and structure of the public sector is to gradually convert the activity of government from that of being a producer of services towards being a purchaser of services on behalf of the taxpayer. To this end, it is gradually developing its use of outsourcing and tenders to purchase services for the public. So far, the public sector uses bidding and tenders for most of its construction activity. It is now extending such use to a number of other activities and intends to broaden this area further in the near future. The present effort is directed at the outsourcing of ancillary services, such as catering procurement, maintenance, etc.

All primary schools were transferred to municipalities as of the beginning of August of this year. This will mean some net expenditure. The municipal share of the personal income tax will be increased to compensate for the cost transfer with the central government share being reduced commensurably. In addition the central government will participate in the expansion of the primary school system to eliminate double-shifting in several crowded primary schools.

The municipalities have operated the premises of all primary schools from the beginning. The state, in turn has paid teachers' salaries and the salary cost of supplemental services (remedial teaching, school psychologists) and it has directed educational policy. The municipalities have assumed responsibility for the construction of primary schools since 1990.

The division of tasks between the central government and the municipalities is another issue for review in the effort to modernise the role of the public sector. The central government and the municipalities have reviewed and changed their division of labour from time to time. The latest such review took place in 1989. The general trend of such reviews has been to shift tasks to the central government to ease the service burden of financially strapped municipalities. In recent years the government has begun the process of reversing this trend on the theory that some functions of public service are better run and financed at the local level, such as primary schools. The government is studying the possibility of transferring all of its services to the old and handicapped to the municipalities.

The central government has concluded a number of four-year pilot contracts with municipalities on the transfer of services from the state to the municipalities. As a general rule, the municipalities receive grants from the state to finance such tasks. The contracts call for a fixed annual appropriation from the state to finance the contracts. The services provided are in the area of health, services to the old, infirm and handicapped, and contributions to cultural activities. At the end of the contract period, the experience from these contracts will be assessed to decide whether such tasks should be fully transferred to municipalities.

The government intends to conclude formal service contracts with all larger non-governmental institutions that currently perform services on behalf of the state. This would apply to a number of nursing homes, drug rehabilitation centres, retraining centres for the handicapped and similar institutions.

I. Regulatory management and reform

The government has placed emphasis on reviewing regulatory activities in order to simplify the current regime and do away with unnecessary regulations. To this end, the Prime Minister set up a committee on public regulatory activities in 1993. The committee's report, submitted late in 1993, was approved by the government and was followed by a draft Bill on Regulatory Activities that has been submitted to the *Althing*. The Bill is still under consideration. Some of the main elements of deregulation and liberalisation in recent years include:

- price controls have been abolished and replaced by the Competition Act and the Competition Surveillance Agency;
- motor vehicle inspections have been privatised;
- quality controls in the food and fish-processing industries have been restructured;
- electrical safety controls have been simplified;
- consumer product safety legislation has been passed and a consumer products safety scheme has been initiated.

These efforts notwithstanding, it is exceedingly difficult to prevent the growth in government regulations. Two areas of government, environmental control and the EU/EEA (European Union/European Economic Area) legal regime, demand a proliferation of regulations not previously in existence.

Mr. Halldór Árnason
Director
Bureau of the Budget
Ministry of Finance
Arnarhvoll
IS-150 Reykjavík
Tel.: (354-5) 60 92 00
Fax: (354-5) 62 82 80

Annex A

PRINCIPAL RECENT PUBLIC MANAGEMENT DEVELOPMENTS

1991
- Accrual accounting standards adopted as the basis for financial reporting by government and the first accrual financial statements published for the year 1989.
- A special commission appointed by the Prime Minister to illuminate the Treasury's hidden liabilities.

1992
- A comprehensive programme of privatisation of state-owned companies launched with seven enterprises privatised and several identified for privatisation.
- A decision in principle that the budget should be presented to Parliament on both accrual and cash basis.
- Major campaign launched to make managers of government agencies more financially aware, using training courses to help them draft the detailed financial plans now required of them at the beginning of each year.
- A significant increase in the reliance on user fees for financing government operations.
- A project launched to introduce "yardstick competition" into agencies by comparing and analysing trends in unit costs across several groups of homogeneous government agencies.
- The 1992 budget drawn up under the so-called frame method.
- Rules adopted about how surpluses and deficits are carried into the new fiscal year.

1993
- Government competitive tendering policy was published. The main aim is contracting-out of goods and services.

1994
- Medium-term projection of fiscal finances for the years 1995-1998 with two projection scenarios.
- Five management contracts between ministries and agencies were conducted.

1995
- Systematic collection of activity indicators from all government agencies for publication.

1996
- Number of four-year experiment contracts conducted with municipalities on the transfer of service from the state.
- Management and financing of primary schools transferred from the state to the municipalities.
- Institution of awards for those government agencies that have shown excellence in management.
- New Civil Service Act passed by the *Althing*.
- The government has introduced a Bill in the *Althing* for a Government Financial Management Act. The budget will be presented on an accrual basis as well as on a cash basis.

Annex B

INSTITUTIONAL RESPONSIBILITY FOR PUBLIC MANAGEMENT IMPROVEMENT

ORGANISATION	TASKS AND RESPONSIBILITIES
Ministry of Finance	• overall responsibility for public management reforms • financial management

IRELAND

A. Main tendencies and overall priorities

"Delivering Better Government"

Notwithstanding a number of initiatives to improve the system of public management in recent years, the view has been taken that significant improvements would only be brought about through the introduction of an integrated programme of change. Known as *Delivering Better Government* (DBG), such a programme was formally launched by the Government on 2 May 1996. DBG is an outgrowth of, and is situated within, the Strategic Management Initiative (SMI), a programme for improving the management of the civil service which was introduced in February 1994 (see Annex A).

The central thrust and primary objective of SMI/DBG is the delivery of quality services, including policy advice, to the government and the public as customers, clients and citizens of the State. To this end, DBG sets down, within an overall vision for the civil service, a framework for change embracing a series of interacting, interdependent initiatives which collectively are aimed at improving the management and performance of the civil (and public) service with a view to meeting the needs of government and the public more efficiently, effectively and economically.

Key initiatives include:

– delivery of quality services;
– regulatory reform;
– open and transparent service delivery;
– effective management of cross-cutting issues;
– devolving authority and accountability;
– new approaches to human resource management;
– more effective financial management; and
– improved use of information technology to meet business and organisational needs.

Widening the SMI process to include the wider public service and deepening it within the civil service, so that it informs the day-to-day work of management and staff at all levels, are central to advancing and implementing the programme of change. Effective leadership and dialogue to involve staff at every level in developing the key initiatives are crucial to the successful implementation of the programme. Accordingly, consultative and participative structures are being put in place in individual ministries and offices and a number of Working Groups and Frontline Groups drawn from across the civil service to develop the key initiatives have been established (see C below and attached diagram).

B. Context affecting public management

DBG arose out of the SMI which was a response to growing internal and external pressures for more effective management of the civil service. In essence, events in the latter half of the 1980s, when economic and budgetary pressures led to cuts in public expenditure and reductions in staffing levels, gave rise to concerns about the overall efficiency and effectiveness of the civil (and public) service. Such pressures and concerns were being repeated in other countries where varying responses by way of reform programmes were being applied. In addition, it became widely accepted that long-standing barriers to better management of the civil service needed to be addressed. Practically all of these had been targeted by a reform initiative in the mid 1980s – Serving the Country Better – which met with little success. The subsequent events in Ireland and elsewhere reopened the debate on the need for change, significantly within the senior and top management levels of the civil service. This manifested itself in the development of a strategic planning/management process in the early 1990s which was put on a formal footing in 1994 by the then Prime Minister under the Strategic Management Initiative. SMI has had the commitment of successive governments and attracts cross-party support.

C. Strategies and processes for planning and carrying out public management reforms

Structures

Delivering Better Government sets out structures for advancing the programme of change. These include:

- an overall Co-ordinating Group comprising civil service, business and trade union representatives to oversee and direct the change programme and report regularly to government on the progress being achieved;
- working groups, comprising senior civil servants and non-civil servants to develop further the key initiatives in each of the following areas:
  - service delivery;
  - openness and transparency;
  - regulatory reform;
  - human resource management;
  - financial management; and
  - information technology;
- a working group to advise on the changes in legislation required to underpin the change process;
- frontline working groups to advise on issues relating to the frontline delivery of services, training and development, and the use of information technology;
- central support and advice provided by a cross-departmental team, located in the Department of the Taoiseach (Prime Minister), and the recently established Centre for Management and Organisation Development (CMOD) in the Department (Ministry) of Finance;
- establishment of consultative/participative structures in each ministry and office.

The structure is illustrated in the attached diagram.

Consultancy

Consultancy input is also being availed of, especially in relation to communication, human resource management (including performance systems) and the management of change.

Strategic Results Areas

Other features of the overall strategy are a vision for the civil service and the development of "Strategic Results Areas". The latter, in particular, are seen as a means of articulating more clearly cross-cutting issues, the resolution of which requires input from several ministries. The use of dedicated cross-ministry teams, co-ordinated at a political level, is envisaged to address the most pressing such issues.

A *new authority and accountability framework*

The growing complexity of government business requires a more flexible framework for devolving authority and accountability. Increased delegation/devolution, as well as an effective system of performance management, would be difficult to achieve without significant amendments to the principal statute underpinning the Irish system of governance, the Ministers & Secretaries Act, 1924.

> *It has long been recognised that the existing structures and reporting systems promote a risk-averse environment where taking personal responsibility is not encouraged and, equally, where innovative approaches to service delivery have not been developed.*

> (*Delivering Better Government*, p. 22)

Current long-standing practice has tended to concentrate too much responsibility in ministers for matters in which they may have no direct or immediate involvement. As a result, the lines of accountability are often ill-defined. The role of civil servants under the law, including that of the permanent heads of departments, is inadequately addressed at present. This gave rise over time to a tendency for decisions to be taken at too high a level and for authority to become unduly centralised. Vagueness regarding the allocation of authority and responsibility, and the lack in many instances of clear lines of accountability, led to structures which were often ill designed to ensure the optimum degrees of efficiency and effectiveness.

As a consequence of DBG, the 1924 Act will be amended to define the respective roles of ministers and permanent heads of departments, as well as civil servants at lower levels. The roles of junior ministers and special advisers to ministers will also be more clearly specified. However, the changes will not affect the essential requirement of ministerial accountability, under the Constitution, to the Irish Parliament.

Delivery of quality services

A key aim of SMI/DBG is to bring about a clearer focus on objectives, particularly the needs of the consumer of public services. With a few exceptions, the culture of the civil service has not been conspicuously customer-oriented leading to insufficient emphasis on service delivery.

> *There are those who say, if it's not broken, don't fix it. But I feel one should pursue excellence wherever possible. In other words, if it's working, why not explore ways of making it work even better? This is what the delivery of quality services is all about.*

> (Minister for Finance, speech to the IBEC Conference in Dublin, 10 May 1996)

DBG proposes a new approach to quality service delivery based on the following principles:

- specification of the quality of service to be provided;
- consultation with and participation by customers;
- the provision of quality information and advice to customers;
- reasonable choice for customers in relation to the methods of delivery of services;
- the integration of services at local, regional and national levels;
- a comprehensive system of measuring and assessing customer satisfaction;
- complaints and redress mechanisms, which operate close to the point of delivery.

A quality service initiative will be introduced as part of the overall implementation of SMI.

Quality service delivery also embraces the provision of policy advice by civil servants to ministers. This, together with the revised accountability framework and SMI generally, is aimed at improving policy advice and strengthening the decision-making processes.

Openness and transparency

A further important element of the overall strategy is greater openness and transparency, particularly in relation to service delivery. This will be underpinned and driven by freedom of information legislation which will be discussed by Parliament in late 1996. There will also be new legislation, to be discussed in Parliament in late 1996, addressing the appearance of civil servants, among others, before parliamentary committees. The Ombudsman's Act will be amended to extend the areas under his remit.

Information technology

Effective use of information technology (IT) to support business needs and objectives and to facilitate structural and organisational change is seen as essential to the overall strategy for advancing the change process. In this regard, the use of IT to improve, and enable innovative approaches to, service delivery will be pursued.

D. Policy-management capacities

DBG includes a number of initiatives to improve both policy advice and the capacity to manage better cross-cutting issues; see C above – Strategic Results Areas – for principal measures.

E. Human resources management

Traditionally, sufficient priority has not been given to the HR function. Before the advent of SMI, Departments did not normally set formal long-term objectives. As a result performance management systems, which require such a framework, did not evolve. It is recognised that an improved system of accountability, as well as a more customer-oriented environment for service delivery, will require a corresponding improvement in staff management and greater attention to the needs of staff.

> Delivering Better Government *is designed to strengthen the strategic management process so that staff can be readily redeployed to areas of greatest need, where our best resource can be used to best effect, where staff have the opportunity to use their skills and potential in the most creative and satisfying ways, and where the most productive individuals receive rewards commensurate with their performance.*
>
> (Minister for Finance, *op.cit.*,1996)

There will be an increased emphasis on skills acquisition, training and development, with each Department increasing its training budget to 3 per cent of payroll (compared to an average of 0.75 per cent at present). DBG envisages the introduction of a reward system which promotes good performance, particularly by teams, as well as more effective mechanisms for dealing with under-performance.

In all, DBG will address every significant aspect of HR management: recruitment (including atypical recruitment), development, performance appraisal, performance management, probation, promotion, multiple grade structures, and gender-related issues, and terms of employment. In relation to the latter, at present civil servants are appointed by ministers and hold office "at the will and pleasure" of the government. It is envisaged that, subject to appropriate safeguards and to natural justice, the power of dismissal, as well as powers in relation to appointment and discipline, would vest in the permanent heads of the departments.

F.   Budget process and management of financial resources

The introduction of an effective accountability framework, involving greater delegation and increased emphasis on the measurement of results, necessitates the development of better financial management systems and the adoption of a more devolved approach to expenditure management generally.

> [Departments] *claim that they are neither given sufficient flexibility in the management of resources allocated to them nor incentives to achieve greater efficiency and effectiveness in the management of these resources.*

> (*Delivering Better Government*, p. 54)

The system of multi-annual budgeting, announced by the Minister for Finance in his 1996 budget, will operate to a fixed annual cycle to produce a rolling three-year budgetary process. This will facilitate changing circumstances, both budgetary and economic, while accommodating existing and emerging priorities in public expenditure. It is envisaged that the process would include the creation of a contingency reserve. Moreover, each programme of expenditure will be subject to a thorough review at least once every three years.

The budgets covering administrative costs were delegated in 1991 in most cases. While this initiative has been broadly successful, DBG identifies a number of areas where further improvements are necessary.

It is accepted that current financial management systems are not capable of fully supporting SMI, with its focus on outputs, devolved control, the clear assignment of responsibilities, and a better match between resource allocations on the one hand and outputs and strategic priorities on the other. Also, being cash-based, they provide limited information on the emerging budgetary position. Thus enhanced financial management systems will be introduced to address these deficiencies, with the capability, in certain areas and to the extent required, of providing accruals-based accounting.

G.   Performance management

Central to DBG is the putting in place of an effective performance management system. Principal features of the proposed approach are outlined in E above. The performance management system will both reinforce, and be reinforced by, the new framework for devolving authority and accountability, the setting of objectives and related performance measures/indicators inherent in the SMI process, greater openness and transparency, improved financial management systems, and the customer-oriented approach to service delivery. It will also be underpinned by the greater emphasis to be given to training and development and the acquisition of skills generally.

H.   Changing structures of the public sector

The continuing process of "decentralising" parts of central government ministries and offices to provincial centres, the setting up of executive type agencies where deemed appropriate, and privatisation will not be changed under the new programme. In particular, DBG recommends that provision be included in the general legislative changes to permit the delegation of certain tasks to executive agencies, or other appropriate bodies, where there is merit in so doing.

A recent notable development has been a strategic alliance between a private telecommunications company and the state-owned Telecom Éireann (see Annex A).

At present there is a Commission examining the devolution of greater authority and powers to local authorities.

I.   Regulatory management and reform

It is proposed to pursue a proactive programme of managing and reforming government regulations and the regulatory process. Principles governing regulatory reform include:

- improving the quality of regulations;
- eliminating inefficient or unnecessary regulations (including legislation);
- simplifying necessary regulation and related procedures as much as possible;
- lowering the cost of regulatory compliance;
- making regulations more transparent and intelligible.

Measures are proposed also to review regulations every five years, to undertake an employment impact analysis of new regulations, and to consolidate and codify existing legislation. Regulatory management and reform are seen as essential elements of the SMI process.

Mr. Eric Embleton
Centre for Management & Organisation Development
Department of Finance
Lansdowne House
Lansdowne Road
DUBLIN 4
Tel.: (353-1) 67 675 71 (ext. 3566)
Fax: (353-1) 66 821 96
E-mail address: embleton@cmod.finance.irlgov.ie

◆ *Delivering Better Government*
Institutional Framework[1]

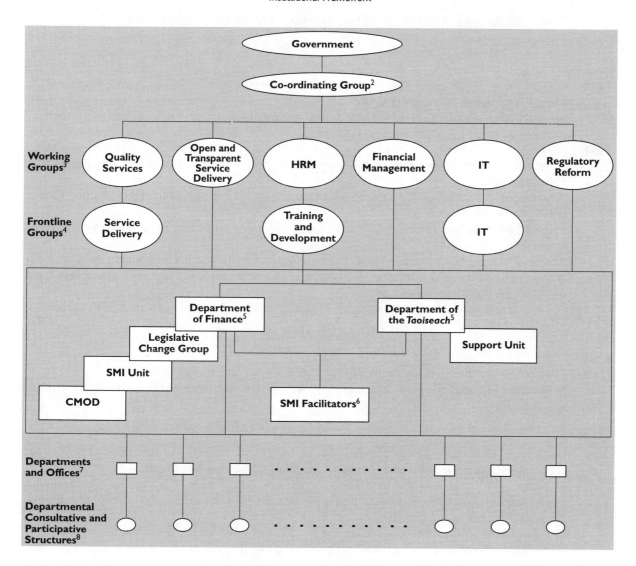

Notes:

1. All flows are two-way.
2. The Co-ordinating Group comprises senior civil/public servants, trade union officials, senior private sector people and an academic (21 members), and is chaired by the Secretary of the Department of the *Taoiseach*.
3. Working Groups comprise civil servants drawn from the top three grades across the civil service, together with non-civil servants from the public and private sectors (12-15 members each). The chairpersons are from various Departments.
4. The Frontline Groups are essentially focus groups comprised of civil service middle managers and clerical, etc., grades (12-18 members). Each group is chaired by the chairperson of the higher-level Working Group.
5. The Central Departments of Finance and the *Taoiseach* (Prime Minister) provide support to the Co-ordinating Group, Working Groups, Frontline Groups, SMI Facilitators and Departments/Offices.

   A dedicated Support Unit is being established within the Department of the *Taoiseach* to assist with those activities – it will also monitor progress on behalf of the Co-ordinating Group and disseminate best practices.

   The Legislative Working Group comprises senior civil servants and ministerial advisors drawn mainly from the central Departments and including a representative from the Office of the Attorney General and advises the Minister for Finance on the drafting of legislative proposals. CMOD: Centre for Management and Organisation Development.
6. The SMI Facilitators are civil servants assigned in each Department/Office to support and co-ordinate local SMI activities and actions arising out of *Delivering Better Government*.
7. Each Department/Office is responsible for the internal development and deepening of the SMI process and its widening to public service agencies under its aegis. Each will also be responsible for implementing initiatives arising out of *Delivering Better Government* locally and their roll-out to its agencies.
8. Each Department/Office is expected to put in place structures to facilitate consultation with, and participation by, staff at all levels in relation to the SMI and the implementation of change initiatives and programmes arising out of SMI/*Delivering Better Government*. Such consultation and participation includes also management-union dialogue.

Source: Government of Ireland.

Annex A

PRINCIPAL RECENT PUBLIC MANAGEMENT DEVELOPMENTS

1985
- White Paper *"Serving the Country Better"* published.
- Decentralised, planning-driven approach to IT established.

1987
- Budget goals defined to contain public expenditure in real terms at or below 1986 levels as a percentage of GNP.
- Department of Public Service merged with Department of Finance which takes leading role in public management reform.
- Embargo on recruitment introduced across public service and programme of enhanced early retirement announced.
- Government accepts in principle a report by an independent Review Body on Higher Remuneration in the Public Sector which recommends that the pay of a senior management grade (assistant secretary) be performance-related.
- Government announces programme to relocate some 3 000 civil servants from Dublin to 12 regional centres.

1988
- Comprehensive three-year agreement with public service unions negotiated.
- Programme initiated to review statutory and information requirements which affect business and industry.

1989
- Department of Finance survey of public offices to identify if adequate standards of privacy for client interviews being used and if suitably qualified staff being employed.
- In budget statement, Minister for Finance announces new system of budgetary allocations for administrative or running costs based on a three-year period and on delegated spending authority.
- Review of the role of the Comptroller and Auditor General by Department of Finance.
- Efficiency Audit Group created to examine practices of government departments and to make recommendations for reducing costs and enhancing efficiency.

1990
- Filling of essential posts authorised but no general resumption in public service recruitment.
- Performance-related pay scheme introduced for assistant secretary grade.
- Country-wide Government Telecommunications Network launched to improve communications and support decentralisation.
- Government announces that a further 1 200-1 500 civil servants to be moved from Dublin to five regional centres.

1991
- A "Programme for Economic and Social Progress" signed by the government and the social partners to provide a strategic framework for development over the next decade and specific proposals to 1993.
- Three-year administrative budgets for 1991-93 introduced in most (23) departments aim to reduce running costs by 2per cent in 1992 and to improve efficiency and effectiveness by delegating more expenditure authority to line departments and line managers.
- A financial management software package begins to be introduced to support the three-year administrative budgets.

- A strategic initiative is launched to base staff development on needs analysis and guidelines of best practice.
- Two commercial State enterprises privatised.

1992

- White Paper "*The Role of the Comptroller and Auditor General*" is published with proposals to extend his remit to examining economy, efficiency and management effectiveness in departments and a range of other bodies and boards.
- A monitoring committee including representatives of the Department of Finance set up in each department covered by the administrative budget programme to review progress.
- Steady privatisation of commercial State enterprises continues.
- Joint working group of the Department of Finance and Comptroller and Auditor General's Office examines accounting procedures with view to improving accountability and transparency in use of resources.

1993

- Comptroller & Auditor General (Amendment) Act, 1993 enacted to give effect to proposals in White Paper (*cf.* 1992).

1994

- Introduction of the Strategic Management Initiative announced by the *Taoiseach* (Prime Minister) in February, 1994.
- Publication in July 1994 of revised Guidelines for the Appraisal and Management of Capital Expenditure Proposals in the Public Sector.
- A "Programme for Competitiveness and Work" signed by the government and the social partners to provide a strategic framework for development over the years ahead, with specific proposals to 1996.
- Government announces in its programme, A Government of Renewal, proposals for reform of public institutions at national and local level to provide an improved quality of service and greater accountability, transparency and freedom of information (including Freedom of Information legislation).

1995

- Restructuring of PSEU (lower middle management) grades to provide for greater flexibility in the performance of duties.
- Publication of Committees of the Houses of the *Oireachtas* (Compellability, Privileges and Immunities of Witnesses) Bill, 1995.
- Ethics in Public Office Act, 1995.
- Government established a Devolution Commission to make recommendations for the renewal of local government.

1996

- Government announces and initiates a system of multi-annual budgeting.
- Government establishes a Commission to review public service pensions.
- Telecom *Eireann* agrees to enter into a strategic alliance with another provider (20 per cent stake with an option to purchase an additional 15 per cent within 3 years).
- Cost and Competitiveness Review of the Electricity Supply Board completed in preparation for the opening of the electricity market to competition.
- Department of Finance sets up the Centre for Management and organisation Development (CMOD) to provide unified and better targeted advisory and support services to other departments/offices in relation to IT, HR development, organisation development and management services generally.

- Government launches (2 May) Delivering Better Government, a comprehensive change programme for the civil (and public) service as part of the Strategic Management Initiative, comprising proposals for:
  - an improved framework of accountability and delegation/devolution;
  - greater openness and transparency;
  - quality delivery of customer services;
  - improved human resource management;
  - improved financial management systems and procedures;
  - an improved public expenditure management framework;
  - regulatory reform;
  - better use of information technology;
  - better co-ordination between departments, including the identification of Strategic Result Areas.
- A high-level Co-ordinating Group, representative of civil service, business and union interests, established to guide the programme, supported by a number of working groups. The programme will comprise a number of legislative changes.
- Government formally connects to the Internet and sets up a publishing site (http://www.irlgov.ie).

Annex B

INSTITUTIONAL RESPONSIBILITY FOR PUBLIC MANAGEMENT IMPROVEMENT

ORGANISATION	TASKS AND RESPONSIBILITIES	OTHER INFORMATION
Department of Finance	• overall responsibility for public management reforms • monitoring performance of departments	– In 1987, the Department of the Public Service was merged with the Department of Finance. – An Efficiency Audit Group was established in 1989. It includes representatives from the Department of Finance and the Department of the *Taoiseach* (Prime Minister), and prominent businessmen from the private sector (one of whom is the Group Chairman). Its task is to examine the operations of government departments. Responsibility for the Group was transferred to the Department of the *Taoiseach* (Prime Minister) in 1994 (see below). – In 1996, following a review of the organisation of the Department, the Centre for Management and Organisation Development (CMOD) was set up to provide a unified and better

ORGANISATION	TASKS AND RESPONSIBILITIES	OTHER INFORMATION
		focused advisory and support service to other ministries and offices, particularly in relation to SMI/DBG developments. CMOD incorporates the former Central IT Services, Civil Service Training Centre, Management Services Unit and Operations & Research Section of the Department.
Department of the *Taoiseach* (Prime Minister)	• co-ordinating, facilitating and monitoring the Strategic Management Initiative/ *Delivering Better Government* (SMI/DBG) • supporting and providing the secretariat for the Co-ordinating Group overseeing the SMI/DBG • overseeing the conduct of efficiency audits	– A Cross-Departmental Team set up within the Department to facilitate and support SMI/DBG. – Responsibility for the Efficiency Audit Group was transferred to the Department in 1994 from the Department of Finance; the work of the Group is now carried out, in response to Government decisions or requests, by *ad hoc* Groups representative of the Departments of the *Taoiseach*, Finance, the Department/ Office involved in the efficiency audit and selected members of the Co-ordinating Group.

Annex C

KEY PUBLIC DOCUMENTS ON PUBLIC MANAGEMENT ISSUES AND DEVELOPMENTS

Serving the Country Better, 1985. A wide-ranging public management reform white paper.

Report of the Commission on Health Funding, 1989.

The Role of the Comptroller and Auditor General, 1992. White paper discussing changes which led to the Comptroller and Auditor General (Amendment) Act, 1993.

Shaping a Healthier Future: A Strategy for Effective Healthcare in the 1990s, Department of Health, 1994. Strategy and targets in the health sector.

Charting Our Education Future: White Paper on Education, 1995. Wide-ranging white paper on education.

Report of the Courts Commission, 1996. Report on the structure and management of the courts system.

Delivering Better Government, 1996. Comprehensive public management change programme.

The Financing of Local Government in Ireland, 1996.

Towards Cohesive Local Government – Town and County, 1996. Report of Reorganisation Committee.

ITALY

A. Main tendencies and overall priorities

Italy's main priorities relate to continuing the process of reforming the civil service by:

- delegating tasks and functions that are currently the responsibility of central government to the regional and local authorities;
- redefining the objectives of central government administration by merging some ministries;
- initiating a regulatory reform process and simplifying administrative formalities for the public and for enterprises.

B. Context affecting public management

The new government elected in April 1996 approved the priorities outlined above and also showed its intention to improve relations between the administration and the general public, which sees the need to reform central government.

C. Strategies and processes for planning and carrying out public management reforms

Pending the reform of the Italian Constitution, the government and parliament are pressing ahead with the devolution of central government functions and tasks to the regional and local authorities, as this can be done without revising the Constitution.

The process of devolution to local level will give more power to local authorities, whose activities affect the public more directly, and will make them more accountable.

The government's strategy has the support of the public.

D. Policy-management capacities

As part of the regulatory reform process and the simplification of administrative procedures, the government plans to reform the central government budget in order to turn it into a more rational instrument that will better match its policy management capacities.

Separating the legislative and directive powers of the policy-makers from the executive powers of the civil service will allow the government to meet its targets more quickly. These targets will be reviewed by an inspectorate that is to be set up under each administration's internal audit service and the Court of Auditors.

E. Human resources management

The first point to note is that almost all civil servants are now employed under private law contracts governed by the civil code.

Currently, the employment contracts and wages of "privatised" civil servants are negotiated by the most representative trade unions and the Agency for Relations with the Unions (*Agenzia per la Rappresentanza Negoziale delle Pubbliche Amministrazioni*) which follows the directives issued by the Minister for the Civil Service on the government's behalf. The terms negotiated for employment contracts and wages apply for four years and two years, respectively.

F. Budget process and management of financial resources

The government's commitment to keep as tight a rein as possible on spending over the next three years means that it will not be possible to recruit more civil servants in 1997, while in 1998 and 1999, the intention is to replace only 10 per cent of those retiring.

This decision will mean a L 250 billion savings for the government.

G. Performance management

The measures that have been implemented over the last few years and those currently being adopted by the newly elected government are aimed at improving relations with the general public and with enterprises as well as raising the standard of service provided by civil servants.

Executives have extended their responsibilities, "Codes of conduct" for civil servants have been drafted and "Service Charters" covering required standards of service have been introduced in each sector of the administration.

A Directive issued by the President of the Council of Ministers provides for the introduction of a computer network linking up all government departments in addition to local networks within each administrative unit.

H. Changing structures of the public sector

A bill now passing through parliament provides for continuing the devolution of central government tasks and functions to regional and local authorities (municipal and provincial). As part of this process some of central government's local offices will be transferred to those authorities.

The policy of privatising the autonomous state-owned companies and administrations (*Aziende* and *Amministrazioni Autonome dello Stato*) is proceeding. Recently the central Post and Telecommunications administration was split into public companies. Order No. 29/93 has confirmed the managerial responsibilities of executives (heads of division) and chief executives and has assigned independent powers to them.

I. Regulatory management and reform

The ongoing regulatory reform process is based on "de-legislation" and deregulation, often leaving the public and enterprises free to take the initiative (in some cases they simply have to notify the administration of their plans). The administration generally has thirty days in which to reject plans that do not comply with the regulations. The result has been a substantial reduction in costs to the public.

A bill now passing through parliament will simplify administrative procedures still further and will considerably reduce the formalities that the public and enterprises had to comply with. This is in keeping with the government's objective of improving relations between the public administration and the users of its services.

Dr. Antonino Vinci
Director-General
Civil Service Department
Office of the President of the Council of Ministers
Palazzo Vidoni
Corso Vittorio Emanuele, 116
I-00186 Rome
Tel.: (39-6) 687 50 01
Fax: (39-6) 680 03 321

Annex A

PRINCIPAL RECENT PUBLIC MANAGEMENT DEVELOPMENTS

Main regulatory measures implemented over the period 1993-1996

1993
- Order No. 39 of 12 February 1993 "Rules governing computerised information systems in public administrations pursuant to Section 2.1 of Act 421 of 23 October 1992".
- Act no 537 of 24 December 1993 – "Public finance corrective measures".

1994
- Presidential Order No. 144 of 25 January 1994 – "Regulation concerning the rules for the organisation and operation of the Agency for Relations with the Civil Service (ARAN).
- Order No. 174 of 7 February 1994 issued by the President of the Council of Ministers – "Regulation concerning the rules of access to civil service jobs for nationals of European Union member states".
- Cabinet order of 31 March 1994 – "Code of conduct for civil servants".
- Order No. 609 of 14 April 1994 by the – "Regulation on the rules for the organisation and operation of the Civil Service information Technology Authority (AIPA)".
- Prime Ministerial Order No. 439 of 21 April 1994 – "Regulation on access to executive posts".
- Presidential Order No. 487 of 9 May 1994 – "Regulation on the rules of access to jobs in the civil service and on procedures for competitive examinations, entrance examinations and other forms of recruitment for jobs in the public sector".
- Presidential Order No. 716 of 16 September 1994 – "Regulation on the rules of procedure governing the mobility of Civil Service employees".
- Presidential Order No. 692 of 18 October 1994 – "Regulation on the rules for determining the criteria for appointing experts as Chief Executives and for the assigning Chief Executive functions by means of private law contracts".
- Prime Ministerial Order No. 770 of 27 October 1994 – "Regulation on the rules of procedure governing secondment, leave of absence and time off during working hours for trade union activities in public administrations".
- Act No. 724 of 23 December 1994 – "Measures to rationalise government finances".

1995
- Executive order No. 112 of 27 February 1995 – "Regulation on the rules of procedure for the declaration of supernumerary staff and leave of absence for public sector employees".

- Prime Ministerial Order No. 207 of 24 March 1995 – "Regulations concerning provisions for the organisation and operation of a Higher School for Public Administration".
- Prime Ministerial Order of 19 May 1995 – "Initial identification of public sector service providers with a view to publication of general guidelines for Public Service Charters".
- Act No. 481 of 14 November 1995 – "Rules for competition and regulation of public utility services, institution of the public utility services authority".
- Prime Ministerial Directive of 5 September 1995 – "Principles and methods for the installation of a standardised information network for the Civil Service".
- Executive order No. 497 of 25 November 1995 – "Privatisation of the autonomous general air traffic assistance company".
- Executive order No. 541 of 23 Dec. 1995 – "Urgent provisions for the organisation of the Audit Office".
- Act No. 549 of 28 December 1995 – "Measures for the rationalisation of government finances".

1996

- Executive order No. 29 of 24 January 1996 – "Privatisation of the autonomous general air traffic assistance company".
- Circular No. 8/96 of 29 December 1995 issued by the Minister for the Civil Service – "Training of civil servants. Information and training initiatives for civil servants in public administrations responsible for structural funds in the *Mezzogiorno*".

Annex B

INSTITUTIONAL RESPONSIBILITY FOR PUBLIC MANAGEMENT IMPROVEMENT

ORGANISATION	TASKS AND RESPONSIBILITIES
Presidency of the Council of Ministers	• general guidelines and co-ordination • general and sectoral policy formulation
Department of the Public Service	• co-ordination of public management initiatives • recruitment planning • administration of civil service entrance exams • ARAN directives for collective bargaining with trade unions • control of efficiency and evaluation of work performance
Treasury Ministry **Government Accounting Office** (*Ragioneria Generale dello Stato*)	• spending policy and control • co-ordination of legislative initiatives (financial and economic) • legal measures relating to income and expenditure • collection and updating of public sector accounts • review of reforms of the accounting system and of the preparation of the budget • auditing and inspection of public bodies

ORGANISATION	TASKS AND RESPONSIBILITIES
Ministry of Finance	• setting guidelines and updating fiscal policy in line with budget revenue • systematic control and updating of fiscal procedures • measures to support budget policy • structure of the fiscal system; evaluating actual fiscal yields (fraud and evasion prevention)
Agency for relations with the public administration unions (ARAN)	• collective bargaining with trade unions on legal aspects of employment contracts (four-year agreements) and wages (two-year agreements)
Public Administration Information Technology Agency (AIPA)	• introducing and co-ordinating the use of information technology • developing standard computer networks in public administrations.

JAPAN

A.   Main tendencies and overall priorities,

B.   Context affecting public management, and

C.   Strategies and processes for planning and carrying out public management reforms

In Japan, administrative reform has been recognised as one of the most important policy issues in the field of public management to be actively promoted. The government of Japan has been working actively to reform its administrative systems and to make them more simplified, more efficient, more responsive to changes and to be more trusted by the public. Particularly since 1981, with the establishment of the Second Provisional Commission for Administrative Reform (PCAR) and three Provisional Councils for the Promotion of Administrative Reform (PCPARs) in succession, the government has adopted and implemented a series of administrative reform measures. Recently, in response to the final Report of the Third PCPAR, the government established the Administrative Reform Promotion Headquarters (ARPH) in January 1994, headed up by the Prime Minister and composed of all Cabinet ministers. Moreover, in December 1994, the Administrative Reform Committee (ARC) was established under the Prime Minister's Office to promote administrative reform in response to the report.

Significant measures implemented successfully to date include those related to management of the national administration, control of national public employee staffing levels, deregulation, decentralisation, reform of public corporations, enactment of the Administrative Procedure Law, and so on.

E.   Human resources management

Personnel measures regarding senior officials

A number of personnel measures have been put into place with the aim of promoting understanding and co-operation between ministries and agencies and enhancing the abilities of senior government officials:

a)   Based on "Regarding the Promotion of Personnel Exchanges among Ministries and Agencies" (Cabinet Decision, 22 December 1994), the promotion of personnel exchanges among ministries and agencies is being actively pursued by the Cabinet Secretariat and the Management and Co-ordination Agency (MCA). The Cabinet Decision requires of government officials work experience in at least two organisations (other ministries and agencies, international organisations, etc.) prior to promotion to division director level, and encourages interchanges of high-ranking officials among ministries and agencies.

b)   In response to an advisory commission report on the training of senior officials, the National Personnel Authority is formulating a training program designed for participation within the first year by those recruited to the national senior services.

Employment policies regarding aged personnel

In view of the steady ageing of the population, a number of issues regarding the national public personnel management have been brought to the fore by the National Personnel Authority. The Authority, taking into account the scheduled reform of public pension schemes, proposed in its 1993 report to the D*iet* and Cabinet three principles to be followed in future policy formulation in this area:

- introduction of a new re-employment system;
- consideration of part-time work; and
- co-ordination of employment and pension schemes.

The National Personnel Authority is now going to establish relevant policies in line with these principles, accompanied by possible changes to other aspects of the current personnel management system.

At a Cabinet meeting on 25 March 1994 the government decided its basic policy position on the ageing of the population: to further consider the re-employment of officials in their early sixties, with examination of various issues concerning the rapidly ageing population, measures for the employment of older people in the private sector, the relationship between employment and pensions, and the need for administrative and financial reform. One policy change adopted to date had been to raise the entitlement age for full pension payment to sixty-five years.

A committee was established in June 1994 (the "Examination Committee on Employment Problems of Aged Officials in the Public Sector") to further consider the issues arising from the above Cabinet Decision.

G.   Performance management

In the context of the recent rapid progress of internationalisation and use of information technology and the change in citizens' awareness, "a more impartial and transparent public administration" has been put forward over the last decade as a reform concept to secure the confidence of citizens. Under this concept, the government has made efforts to pursue a more impartial and transparent public administration. Significant efforts have been directed towards creating more impartial and transparent administrative processes, promotion of personal data protection, improving government information disclosure, and so on.

To ensure fairness and transparency in public administration, a general law concerning previous procedures for administrative actions has been requested for some time. After intensive discussions, the Third PCPAR submitted to the Prime Minister: the "Report concerning the arrangements for fair and transparent administrative procedure law" (December 1991). According to this report, the government has prepared the Bill and submitted it to the D*iet* in its 126th session in May 1993. The Bill has been acted on by the D*iet* and was promulgated on 12 November 1993. The "Administrative Procedure Law" was put into effect on 1 October 1994. The Law provides basic principles and guidelines for matters related to procedures for dispositions, administrative guidance and notifications. According to the follow-up reports issued by the MCA, in most areas of public administration the Law has generally been applied as intended.

The move to enhance public access to government information has recently gathered momentum. The government has implemented several measures such as establishing "Counter Services for Reference of Official Documents" in each ministry and agency, laying down the "Criteria Applicable to Administrative Information Disclosure", etc., in order to promote access to government information. In addition, the ARC was set up in December 1994, with responsibility, *inter alia*, for examining legal and administrative aspects of public access to government information. In April 1995 the Expert-Committee on Access to government Information submitted an interim report on legal aspects of the issue to the Administrative Reform Committee, with the aim of finalising the report for the Prime Minister by December 1996 and for subsequent public release.

H.   Changing structures of the public sector

In line with administrative reform, the size and role of the government has been reviewed in various ways including through improved management of the administration, containment of staffing levels of the central government, promotion of decentralisation, reform of public corporations, etc.

The government of Japan has long maintained the policy of curbing the expansion of administrative organisations and simplifying and making more efficient the existing administrative machinery through such methods as the so-called "scrap-and-build" principle, which requires existing organisational units to be dissolved before new ones can be created. Owing to these efforts, the number of central administrative bodies (offices, ministries, committees and agencies) has remained almost the same over the last 20 years and the number of bureaux and secretariats associated with these bodies has stabilised at 128 since the 1980s. Furthermore, the government has been engaged for some years in reducing national public employee staffing levels through implementation of the Total Staff Number Law and the Personnel Reduction Plans, resulting in a reduction of more than 44 000 national public employee positions since the end of financial year 1967.

Second, with regard to the relationship between the central and the local levels of government, it is necessary to promote decentralisation in order to enhance the administrative autonomy and independence of local public entities. As the Decentralisation Promotion Law suggests, the basic ideas for promoting decentralisation are regarded as aiming at clarifying both national and local roles, increasing the independence and self-responsibility of local public entities, and bringing about regional communities full of vitality and regional characteristics.

In December 1992, the government decided to introduce a new system, the "Special Scheme for Promoting Decentralisation", under which more than 30 municipalities were designated to be "Pilot Municipalities". Furthermore, the government decided the "Fundamental Principle for Promoting Decentralisation" on 25 December 1994, which contains basic philosophies, a set of basic principles and measures to promote decentralisation. In accordance with this Cabinet Decision, the government submitted the Bill concerning the promotion of decentralisation to the Diet. The Decentralisation Promotion Law came into effect on 3 July 1995 and, on the same day, the Decentralisation Promotion Committee was established. The Committee should recommend to the Prime Minister concrete guidelines for making a Decentralisation Action Program after wide-ranging and careful deliberation under the Committee as well as its two sub-committees. The Committee has made public its interim report on 29 March 1996, which set forth the background and reasons for promoting decentralisation, basic principles and the direction of further deliberation, etc.

In addition, the MCA has conducted a survey of central government involvement in local affairs with respect to local public entities every year since 1988.

As another aspect of reviewing the role of the public sector, public corporations should be taken into consideration. There were 92 public corporations in Japan as of 1995. Public corporations were established in order for the government to have independent corporate bodies with autonomy and flexibility and to operate its enterprises which are relatively suitable for corporate management. However, corresponding to changing social and economic conditions, it has become necessary to consolidate and rationalise these corporations from the perspective of simplifying and streamlining public administration.

The government decided in February 1994 to review the role and *raison d'être* of these public corporations, based on the change in social and economic circumstances, in accordance with the Final Report of the Third PCPAR. Based on the February Cabinet Decision, each ministry or agency reviewed all public corporations within its own jurisdiction with the prospect of rationalisation and reorganisation. As a result, Cabinet Decisions on consolidation and rationalisation of public corporations were adopted in February and March 1995 which included in principle agreement to consolidate sixteen public corporations into eight and abolish or privatise a further five within three years. A Cabinet Decision concerning financial disclosure requirements for public corporations was made on 19 December 1995.

I.   Regulatory management and reform

The government of Japan has been systematically promoting deregulation, recognising that deregulation is a theme to make Japanese economy and society open to the international community and to transfer itself into a free economy and society built upon the principle of free market and self-responsibility. The government is grappling with deregulation with a view to reducing the burden on citizens and companies through simplification of administrative processes, elimination of economic friction with other countries by promoting imports and expanding domestic demands, and improvement in the quality of citizens' lives through for example expanding the range of choices corresponding to the diverse needs of consumers.

Since the "Emergency Economic Countermeasures" decided at the Ministerial Conference on Economic Measures on 16 September 1993, the government has been progressively promoting deregulation through several cabinet decisions such as the "Fundamental Principles of Administrative Reforms" of 15 February 1994 and "Guidelines for the Promotion of Deregulation" of 5 July 1994. In order to promote deregulation more comprehensively and systematically, the government adopted a five-year "Deregulation Action Program" on 31 March 1995, in accordance with the final report to the third PCPAR. In the program, 1 091 items in 11 areas were included as specific deregulation measures including about 720 newly incorporated items. The programme has become now a three-year programme until the end of the 1997 financial year by the "Emergency Economic Measures to cope with the Yen Appreciation" decided at the Ministerial Conference on Economic Measures on 14 April 1995. In the process of compiling the programme, special efforts were made to guarantee transparency through extensive consultations with interested parties such as citizens and companies within Japan and abroad, and hearings by ARPH.

The programme was revised on 29 March 1996, retaining its transparency and treating with the highest priority the views of the ARC. The revised programme contains 1 797 specific measures including 569 newly incorporated items. Approximately three-quarters of items in the existing programme have already been implemented.

In addition, the MCA has been conducting annual surveys of permissions, authorisations, etc., since 1985, which show a general trend towards annual increases, although a reverse of this trend was witnessed to the end of March 1995.

J.   Other

It should be also mentioned that Japan has a system of Administrative Inspection and Administrative Counselling which is conducted by the MCA.

Administrative Inspection serves as the government's internal control and self-improvement function. The MCA inspects the actual state and problems of administrative operations by the national government and then makes recommendations for reform policies to the administrative organs concerned. The aim of the administrative inspection system is to examine public administration with a view to: 1) ensuring appropriate execution of laws, government ordinances and the budget, and 2) dealing with change, ensuring comprehensiveness, simplicity and efficiency, and keeping the trust of the citizen.

In addition, the MCA conducts administrative counselling with the objective of resolving complaints and opinions and demands by assuming a fair, objective and third-party stance. The MCA accepts complaints, opinions and demands concerning public administration from the public, examines their reasons and makes recommendations for resolution of the issues to the administrative organs concerned. The MCA receives almost 230 000 cases every year.

Mr. Mabito Yoshida
First Secretary
Japanese Permanent Delegation to the OECD
11, avenue Hoche
75008 PARIS
Tel.: (33-1) 53 76 61 43
Fax: (33-1) 45 63 05 44

Annex A

PRINCIPAL RECENT PUBLIC MANAGEMENT DEVELOPMENTS

1993

April
- "Guidelines for Implementing Special Scheme for Promoting Decentralisation" was agreed at the meeting of Administrative Vice-Ministers.

September
- "Emergency Economic Countermeasures" was adopted at the Ministerial Conference on Economic Measures.

October
- Report of the Third PCPAR (Final Report).

1994

February
- "Fundamental Principles of Administration Reforms" was adopted at the Cabinet meeting.

March
- "Regarding the Employment of Aged Officials in the Public Sector" was adopted at the Cabinet meeting.
- "Guidelines for the Promotion of Deregulation" was adopted at the Cabinet meeting.

July
- Administrative Procedure Law was put into effect.

October
- The Administrative Reform Committee started its work.

December
- "Regarding the Promotion of Personnel Exchanges among Ministries and Agencies" was adopted at the Cabinet meeting.
- "Fundamental Principle for Promoting Decentralisation" and "Fundamental Principles of Administrative Reforms" were adopted at the Cabinet meeting.

1995

February
- "Regarding Consolidation and Rationalisation of Public Corporations" was adopted at the Cabinet meeting.

March
- "Deregulation Action Program" was adopted at the Cabinet meeting.
- "Concerning Merger of the Japan Export-Import Bank and the Overseas Economic Co-operation Fund" was adopted at the Cabinet meeting.

April
- "Emergency Economic Measures to cope with the Yen Appreciation" was adopted at the Ministerial Conference on Economic Measures.

July
- Decentralisation Promotion Law was put into effect.
- The Decentralisation Promotion Committee started its work.
- "Review of Advisory Councils" was adopted at the Cabinet meeting.
- "The First Opinion concerning Promotion of Deregulation" was submitted by the Administrative Reform Committee.
- "Financial Disclosure of Public Corporations" was adopted at the Cabinet meeting.
- Fundamental Principles of Administrative Reforms" was adopted at the Cabinet meeting.

1996

March
- "The Revision of the Deregulation Active Program" was adopted at the Cabinet meeting.

Annex B

INSTITUTIONAL RESPONSIBILITY FOR PUBLIC MANAGEMENT IMPROVEMENT

ORGANISATION	TASKS AND RESPONSIBILITIES	OTHER INFORMATION
Prime Minister's Office – Management and Co-ordination Agency (MCA)	• personnel management (co-ordination and integration of policies and programmes, etc., developed by ministries and agencies for personnel management of their own national public employees, etc.) • management of administrative organisation • control of total staff numbers • management of public corporations • administrative inspection	Set up in 1984 to co-ordinate government functions.
Cabinet Secretariat	• co-ordination function for government policy	
National Personnel Authority	• personnel management (recruitment, remuneration, training, working conditions, grievance procedure, etc.)	A commission-type body with semi-independent status under the jurisdiction of the Cabinet and reporting to the Cabinet.

Annex C

KEY PUBLIC DOCUMENTS ON PUBLIC MANAGEMENT ISSUES AND DEVELOPMENTS

Administrative Management and Reform in Japan (Summary of the 1995 Annual Report of Management and Co-ordination Agency), March 1996, The Institute of Administrative Management.

LUXEMBOURG

A. Main tendencies and overall priorities,

B. Context affecting public management, and

C. Strategies and processes for planning and carrying out public management reforms

Administrative reform

The Luxembourg government, acting on a report drawn up by a senior civil servant, has recently approved a major programme of administrative reform. As in other EU Member States, the government is convinced of the need for such action in that the art of public administration or, to be more accurate, management, is now called upon to meet needs and circumstances considerably more complex than those prevailing thirty years ago.

Budgetary constraints, the need for public administrations to improve their competitiveness and productivity in response to the trend towards the Europeanisation if not globalisation of economies, the penetration of new technologies, the challenges of the information society, as well as the pressing need for organisations to renew themselves periodically, have prompted the government to seek measures that will allow public management systems to respond and adjust more effectively to socio-economic changes.

In view of the considerable growth in the importance of the public sector, to the extent that the efficiency of public management now has an impact on both the efficiency of the economy in general and on the ties ensuring social cohesion, the government, if it wishes to offer a promising future to forthcoming generations, is obliged to review the structures, management processes and attitudes with regard to citizens of its administrations. It is the duty of the government to provide the country with an Administration that is both efficient and effective at all levels of government and that delivers high-quality public services.

The main directions in which the government wishes to focus all of its reform projects are as follows:

- **externally oriented reforms**, focusing on users and aimed at improving the quality of the public service;
- **internally oriented reforms**, focusing more on the internal organisation of the Administration and its managerial methods, the improvement and adjustment of which will necessarily improve the quality of the public service.

With regard to externally oriented reforms, the government has based its action on a number of principles: public services should be fair, unbiased, available at all times, accessible, open to the environment, uncomplicated and, lastly, transparent. On the basis of these general principles, the government is considering a number of practical measures to be implemented in the short and medium term, notably the publication of a users' charter, the creation of a reception office, the requirement that public servants in contact with the public identify themselves, modification of flexi-time arrangements, publication of a users' guide, creation of a national videotex network providing information on government administrations, creation of a sales outlet for government publications, installation of a complaints box in ministries and public administrations, and the codification of legislation.

The most noteworthy internally oriented initiatives currently in progress are as follows:

- overhaul of public accounting and financial management procedures;
- conversion of the computerised payroll management system into a computerised personnel management system;
- adoption of a more dynamic approach to the management of public property assets
- development of an IT concept for government;
- merging of the *Gendarmerie* and the police force;
- analysis of the organisational modes of public services;
- comprehensive analysis of all procedures;
- revision of existing mechanisms for the recruitment of public servants;
- improved integration of trainees into the Administration;
- review of the training programme.

Size and structure of the public sector

In order to restrict wage costs, the replacement of public employees in 1996 and 1997 continued, and will continue, to be suspended but not frozen for a period of two to four months. At the same time, as part of the introduction of a restricted intake policy in 1996, the government has decided to limit staff increases in 1996 and following years to 100 units a year.

Wage costs have evolved as follows over the past few years (data provided by the I*nspection générale des Finances*):

1992: LF 30.2 billion;
1993: LF 29.4 billion;
1994: LF 29.8 billion (provisional accounts);
1995: LF 32.0 billion (provisional accounts);
1996: LF 34.0 billion (final budget);
1997: LF 34.1 billion (draft budget).

E. Human resources management

The impact of the main trends and overall priorities on human resources management is described above.

Review of the training programme

In response to a strategy paper already drawn up two years ago, and recently revised and released as an intermediate report, the government intends to draw up an action plan for 1997 aimed at substantially broadening the existing supply of vocational training courses available and at developing a new concept of general training courses for trainees which will take account, in particular, of some of the following fundamental requirements:

- training courses must inculcate an administrative culture in trainees;
- training courses must meet the general administrative training needs of trainees as well as the specific needs of administrations;
- trainees must play an active role during the training period, hence the need to organise discussions, group work and presentations by individual trainees;

– trainees must be initiated into contact with the public; particular importance is therefore to be attached to courses with a psychological content (receiving the public, informing the public, answering the telephone, management of complaints by the public);

– trainees must be introduced to group and team work through seminars to be organised on certain topics (personal organisation, administrative organisation, etc.);

– instructors, who must be properly qualified, will supervise the trainees and provide instruction based on teaching methods and practices that place the trainee at the centre of the training course/ session; the instructors must therefore themselves be properly trained as teachers ("train the trainer");

– trainees must be introduced to the realities of public administration work by means of courses which alternate theory with practice on a daily basis (case studies, etc.);

– the subjects to be taught are to be grouped into modules which allow the trainee to understand the purpose of the course (law and economics, administrative culture, administrative language, etc.);

– in order to ensure that training courses remain relatively flexible, trainees must be able to choose from a series of options those courses which are best suited to their future career needs; new subjects are to be introduced into the programme (receiving and informing the public, communication, settling disputes), whereas others are to be withdrawn or shortened;

– the theoretical part of training courses is to be limited to a number of basic and general subjects to be supplemented by "typical" practical exercises;

– trainees will be continually assessed by means of written, oral and practical tests as well as examinations in theory (particular emphasis will be placed on reports, research work and the drafting of papers);

– trainees will be introduced to the reality of administrative work by means of visits to government administrations and institutions;

– the Administrative Training Institute must not remain closed to the outside world; visits and talks by guest speakers are to be included in the training programme (*e.g.* visits to a firm as part of the introduction to business in Luxembourg).

Opening up the Luxembourg civil service to nationals of other Member States

In a judgement made by the European Court of Justice on 2 July 1996, the Grand Duchy of Luxembourg was declared to have failed to meet its obligations to the Community by refusing to open up its public service to nationals from other Member States of the European Union in "priority" sectors of the public service covered by a general and systematic action initiated by the Commission in 1988 with a view to removing all nationality-based restrictions on the free movement of workers in the sectors in question.

In this particular case, the sectors concerned were:

– organisations managing services of a commercial nature (public transport, distribution services for electricity, gas and water, inland transport, post and telecommunications);
– operational services in the public health sector;
– teaching in state-run schools;
– civil research in public establishments.

The judgement did state, however, that the sectors concerned are not entirely subject to the obligation to ensure the free movement of workers. Even in these sectors, the Grand Duchy of Luxembourg will still be able to reserve certain posts for its own nationals. It can only do so, however, if the civil servants' and public employees' posts concerned involve direct or indirect participation in the exercise of powers conferred by public law and duties designed to safeguard the general interests of the State or of other public authorities. The Court of Justice took account, to some extent at least, of the argument that national identity must be safeguarded in view of the specific demographic situation of the Grand Duchy of Luxembourg. It considered this need to be a legitimate goal recognised under Community law (since Maastricht this principle has been incorporated in the preamble to the revised Treaty on European Union). According to the Court of Justice, however, national identity may be protected by means other than those of exclusion, as a general rule, of the nationals of other Member States. The Court then makes reference to the **conditions of recruitment**, and notably those pertaining to training, experience and language skills, which nationals of other Member States are obliged to meet in the same way as nationals of the home country.

Since the Court of Justice ruled that it was not competent to grant the Grand Duchy of Luxembourg a grace period in which to comply with European law, it is clear that the government will rapidly have to amend the legislation that currently reserves access to posts in the civil service in the country to Luxembourg nationals.

Reform of the pension regime in the public sector

At the end of 1995 the government commissioned an actuarial study of all existing pension schemes in Luxembourg. With regard to the public sector, the study emphasised, *inter alia*, the important role played by the trend in employment. In 1994 there were approximately three active civil servants for each retired civil servant. Assuming that the employment trend in the public sector remains constant at 0 per cent, and that salaries and pensions rise at an average annual rate of 1.5 per cent, the study predicted that this ratio would fall to two active civil servants per retiree by the year 2030. The study also calculated the ratio, from the standpoint of the non-contributory sector, between current pension expenditure and expenditure on wages not exceeding the upper limit for pension contributions by the contributory sector, which was then used to calculate the percentage share of expenditure devoted to pensions. In 1994, this share amounted to 44.35 per cent and by the year 2015, provided that the proportion of wages above the contribution ceiling remains constant, could even rise to as high as 47.31 per cent.

The government is currently reviewing the policy implications of this study and, in particular, is considering new policy approaches to be adopted towards changes in the pension regime in the public sector.

F. Budget process and management of financial resources, and

G. Performance management

See Sections A, B and C.

Mr. Pierre Neyens
Director of State Administration and Personnel
Ministry of the Civil Service
Bâtiment "Le Royal Arsenal"
12-14, Avenue Emile Reuter
111-2011 Luxembourg
Tel.: (352) 478 3123
Fax: (352) 478 3122

Annex A

PRINCIPAL RECENT PUBLIC MANAGEMENT DEVELOPMENTS

1983
– Administrative Training Institute created.

1986
– Law on automatic promotion of public servants in entry grades after a certain number of years.

1990

– Government adopts a policy to equip all public administrations with the requisite office automation facilities in order to promote the optimal management of human and material resources.

1992
– Post and Telecommunications administration becomes a public enterprise with administrative and financial autonomy.
– Wage agreement, subsequently made into law, between the government and the largest public service union, including a number of measures modifying salaries, pensions and certain bonuses.
– Approval by the Council of State of a report on improvements to recruitment procedures. Some of the report's proposals have been included in draft legislation.

Annex B

INSTITUTIONAL RESPONSIBILITY FOR PUBLIC MANAGEMENT IMPROVEMENT

ORGANISATION	TASKS AND RESPONSIBILITIES	ADDITIONAL INFORMATION
Ministry for the Public Service	• administrative reform, particularly in terms of office automation and computer-based personnel management systems	In accordance with a Grand-Ducal Decree of 1989 with regard to the organisation of ministerial departments.
– State Personnel Administration • Division for administrative Organisation	• gives an opinion on projects relating to the organisation or re-organisation of managers of public employees working in government administrations and public establishments over which the State has oversight; examines the possibilities for harmonisation and related co-ordination • prepares medium or long term administrative reform projects, according to guide-lines laid down by the government • collects statistical data relating to public employees • acts as a secretariat for the Administration	
– Commission on cost-cutting and streamlining	• proposes measures to reduce the number of public employees and to streamline working methods • proposes measures to eliminate abusive or excessive spending	Created in 1974

MEXICO

A. Main tendencies and overall priorities

President Zedillo's government announced in May 1996 the Programme to Modernise the Public Administration 1995-2000, the general objectives of which are to improve the efficiency of the public administration and to implant a deeply rooted service ethic, whilst fighting corruption and lack of accountability through prevention and promotion activities. Four sub-programmes are planned: *a*) participation by citizens and consideration of their needs; *b*) administrative decentralisation and/or devolution; *c*) measurement and evaluation of public management; and *d*) enhancement of the status, professionalism and conduct of public servants in the civil service.

The Mexican Congress has under consideration a Presidential proposal aimed at establishing a Supreme Federal Auditing Office. This body would operate independently, be of top technical and professional quality and would have the legal authority to proceed in making an impartial, reliable and credible rendering of accounts. In the meantime, the executive branch has continued to move ahead in strengthening internal comptroller's offices in federal government agencies and in responding to the complaints of citizens. Extensive simplification and deregulation efforts to prevent misconduct and abuses caused by bureaucratic practices and imprecise standards are also being carried out.

B. Context affecting public management

The major constraints affecting the Mexican public administration are the following:

Limited capacity of the State to attend the growing demands of the citizens. Public institutions are characterised by acting in a high-handed way, there is a lack of efficient response mechanisms to citizens' complaints, and a lack of definition of minimum standards for the quality of public services. There has not been any co-ordinated policy to remove red tape and modify administrative procedures in order to facilitate the interaction between public officials and citizens. In order to comply with government regulations, citizens have to come to public offices; alternative methods such as mail, fax or telephone are not used.

Excessive centralism. Even though the legal structure of the country defines it as a federal state, Mexico is still a highly centralised country. Because of a deeply rooted tradition of paternalistic policies, the Mexican public expects the federal government to solve local problems and provide for local needs. Not only is the government not always capable of doing so, but federal decision-making often does not include local involvement. This has led to several attempts to improve co-ordination between federal and state governments in the operation of programmes. Another problem is the lack of delegation of power within the ministries. Public officials have insufficient power to take decisions. This has caused severe delays in the decision-making process as well as in the approval of permits, licenses and other government approvals.

The lack of mechanisms to evaluate the performance of the public sector. Currently programmes are evaluated in accordance with the budget spent and not in accordance with objectives attained due to an overall fiscal discipline priority. Managers are penalised for overexpenditure and all resources not utilised

Activities at federal level

Following the experience gained when basic education was decentralised in 1992, efforts have been made to take the process further.

According to the recently published Programme to Modernise the Public Administration, the main objectives of decentralisation are to:

– strengthen the *Pacto Federal* by transferring functions and decentralising authority, in order to promote regional development and economic decentralisation, improve public services, reduce costs and bring decision-making closer to its point of impact, with the ultimate aim of providing a better service to the public; and

– give public institutions the flexibility to adapt to new situations, with clearly defined objectives and functions, and to promote on-going rationalisation of these bodies to reduce the excessive cost of bureaucracy.

Steps have recently been taken to decentralise various programmes relating to social development, health, agriculture, rural development, communications, and the environment.

I.   Regulatory management and reform

Economic deregulation

Objective

Improve the efficiency of regulations by ensuring that the health and safety of Mexican citizens, environmental protection and consumer interests are effectively protected at the lowest possible cost for businesses in Mexico. This is achieved by simplifying and repealing inefficient regulations, reducing authorities' response times, and increasing transparency through the adoption of regulatory best practices by all regulatory authorities.

Legal basis

On 23 November 1995 President Zedillo launched the most comprehensive deregulation programme in Mexico's history, the Agreement for the Deregulation of Business Activity, which cuts red tape and other bureaucratic obstacles that slow or inhibit business growth and new business start-ups. The agency responsible for its implementation is the Ministry of Commerce and Industry.

– The development of legislative reforms to improve Mexico's regulatory framework, so that businesses may operate easily and efficiently. Proposals are developed to modify laws, decrees, agreements, administrative guidelines, and any other type of legal vehicle on which business regulation is founded in order to minimise the regulatory burden on businesses.

– The review of the stock of all existing business formalities – which are procedures related to the authorisation and/or certification of business activities that involve the exchange of information between businesses and regulatory agencies. All federal regulatory agencies have been required to submit the complete inventory of their business formalities for a review in which inefficient formalities are amended or repealed. The remaining formalities are included in a Federal Register of Regulatory Business Formalities. This Register will include *all* of the information and forms that the Federal Government will be allowed to require of businesses, thereby giving entrepreneurs increased certainty with regard to regulatory requirements. Any new business formalities must be approved before being included in the Register.

- The review of all new administrative or legislative proposals. All administrative and legislative proposals that could affect business activity are reviewed. This curbs the development of new regulations and ensures that they are in full compliance with the criteria specified by the Agreement. By the end of 1996, a regulatory impact statement will be required of all new regulatory proposals.

- The co-ordination of deregulatory activities between federal and state authorities. In November 1995, all 31 states signed deregulatory co-operation agreements with the federal government, and, as of August 1996, 18 states have adopted similar approaches to the Agreement for the Deregulation of Business Activity (*i.e.* each state will develop its own register of business formalities and will review all new regulatory measures). Many of these states have also signed agreements with their municipalities in order to ensure that the deregulation process permeates all levels of government.

Ambassador José Luis Bernal
Mexican Delegation to the OECD
4, rue Galliéra
75116 Paris
Tel.: (33-1) 53 67 86 05
Fax: (33-1) 47 20 07 91

Annex A

PRINCIPAL RECENT PUBLIC MANAGEMENT DEVELOPMENTS

1976
- Organic Law on Federal Public Administration, the main impact of which was to incorporate all the provisions applicable to central and semi-public administration in a single legal instrument.
- Creation of the Ministry of Budget and Planning, responsible for giving institutional form to planning, programming and budgeting practices, with the aim of linking up decisions on action with those on expenditure. This led to the introduction, throughout the Federal Public Administration (FPA), of individual programme budgets.

1979
- Under the National Fiscal Co-ordination System, a detailed definition of federal government participation in federative agencies was one of the major achievements of the Fiscal Co-ordination Act.

1982-88
- In late 1982, creation of the Ministry of the Comptroller-General of the Federation (now the Ministry of the Comptroller-General and Administrative Development). Primarily its mandate was to audit and inspect federal government expenditures and their consistency with the budget. Another new feature was the establishment of the National System for Public Management Monitoring and Assessment.
- Entry into force of the reform of the Organic Law on Federal Public Administration on 1 January 1983, laying the foundations for a restructuring process.
- Approval of a new system of rules for the FPA's planning functions, in the form of amendments/ additions to Articles 25, 26, 27, 28 and 73 of the Constitution, and publication of the Planning Act,

consolidating the National Democratic Planning System. The three aims were to harmonize development planning and make it more consistent and systematic, to enable every social group and region in the country to participate, and to help co-ordinate the work of the three tiers of government.

- In 1985, launch of a Simplification Programme for the Federal Public Administration. The aim was to make government procedures shorter, simpler, more flexible and more transparent, so as to respond rapidly and adequately to the growing demand for a better public service and take greater account of user needs.
- Entry into force on 15 May 1986 of the Federal Act on Semi-public Agencies, offering such bodies greater management autonomy in exchange for clear commitments on performance evaluation.

1988-94

- Creation of the Social Audit Programme, allowing the public to assist the authorities and participate in the monitoring of social schemes such as the National Solidarity Programme, the food subsidy programme under the National System for Family Development (DIF), and the Programme of Direct Support for Farmers (PROCAMPO).
- To further the development of the FPA, introduction of a National Modernisation Programme for Public Enterprise (1990-1994), confirming the transfer of managerial autonomy to semi-public agencies and thereby enhancing their efficiency.
- To foster integration and reinforce fiscal policy, merger of the Ministry of Finance and Public Credit with the Ministry of Budget and Planning in February 1992.
- In 1992, the Ministry of Urban Development and the Environment became the Ministry of Social Development, with responsibility for social development and the alleviation of poverty.
- In December 1993, the Bank of Mexico became independent.

1995-96

- 1995 draft Expenditure Budget adopted the same rationale, principles and goals as the initiative underlying the reform of the Organic Law on Public Administration, namely:
  - reorganisation of the Ministry of Social Development to focus on the fight against poverty;
  - the Ministry of the Comptroller-General of the Federation became the Ministry of the Comptroller-General and Administrative Development, the main aim being to modernise the Federal Public Administration;
  - the Ministry of Energy, Mines and Semi-public Industry became the Ministry of Energy, responsible for formulating national energy policy and planning/regulating the sector;
  - the Ministry of Fisheries became the Ministry of the Environment, Natural Resources and Fisheries, taking over the responsibilities formerly attached to the Ministries of Agriculture and Water Resources, Social Development, and Energy, Mines and Semi-public Industry.
- In December 1995, the Social Security Act was amended to enhance health service provision and improve the collection and redistribution of fiscal resources. More specific aims were to extend coverage to more people, increase pensions at regular intervals and increase the overall level of saving via the Pension Fund Departments (AFORES).
- In May 1996, the Programme to Modernise the Public Administration was launched to turn the FPA into an efficient, service-oriented organisation, and to fight corruption and lack of accountability through prevention and promotional measures, while at the same time taking firm, flexible and efficient corrective steps.

Annex B

INSTITUTIONAL RESPONSIBILITY FOR PUBLIC MANAGEMENT IMPROVEMENT

ORGANISATION	TASKS AND RESPONSIBILITIES
Ministry of the Comptroller General and Administrative Development	• organise and co-ordinate the integral administrative development of departments and agencies of the Federal Public Administration (FPA) to make efficient use of human capital and technical resources, with a view to decentralising government and reducing bureaucracy • approve the organisational and professional establishments of FPA departments and agencies and any changes thereto, and keep appropriate records for the purpose of developing and modernising human resources
Administrative Development Unit	• draw up and put forward a National Development Plan for the FPA • propose integral administrative development policies for FPA departments and agencies • give its opinion on the draft rules for human resource management drawn up by the Ministry of Finance and Public Credit • approve, in conjunction with the Ministry of Finance and Public Credit, proposals for the organisational and professional establishments of FPA departments and agencies, and any changes thereto; to keep appropriate records and set up the necessary information systems • conduct studies and programmes with a view to enhancing governmental management, simplifying/automating formalities and procedures, and decentralising functions • design and promote measures and schemes to enhance productivity, encourage training and foster a service ethic in the civil service • draw up criteria for new incentive schemes for civil servants who have achieved their performance targets • provide FPA departments and agencies with assistance on administrative development • draw up, co-ordinate and supervise the system for assessing administrative development in the FPA • determine performance-assessment methods and models for public service provision in FPA departments and agencies • measure performance in relation to the targets set by FPA departments and agencies

ORGANISATION	TASKS AND RESPONSIBILITIES
	• monitor FPA administrative development programmes, and to compile and publish the results of the administrative development process implemented by the departments and agencies
Ministry of Finance and Public Credit – Directorate-General for Regulation and Administrative Development	• design, co-ordinate, supervise and assess the professional civil service • propose provisions regarding job grades, salary scales, pay, service provision, individual functions, and staff management and development in general

Annex C

KEY PUBLIC DOCUMENTS ON PUBLIC MANAGEMENT ISSUES AND DEVELOPMENTS

National Development Plan 1995-2000.

Decree establishing the Federal Expenditure Budget.

Programme to Modernise Public Administration 1995-2000.

NETHERLANDS

A.   Main tendencies and overall priorities, and

B.   Context affecting public management

In the 1980s the main objective was to improve *coherence and integration*, this being the central issue for public management in the Netherlands. Emphasis was placed on the search for new methods and structures for government planning and for co-ordinating decision-making. Subsequently, the focus of attention shifted to the *size* of government and how to reduce it.

In the period 1992 to 1994, the quantitative reduction target was linked to a discussion on content, *i.e. core tasks*. On the basis of an analysis of core tasks – aimed at identifying the core business of government departments – the tasks of the government have been reviewed and, where necessary, reallocated or reduced. (The annexed tables show changes in the employment structure of the Netherlands public sector, 1991-1995.)

This core task analysis also embodies a significant qualitative element: the government should carry out its tasks at the correct level, as close to the public as possible. Wherever possible, central government must therefore transfer tasks to the two other levels of government with directly elected representatives: the provinces and the municipalities. This strengthens the mechanism of accountability to elected representatives. The decentralisation operation of 1991 aimed to save 8 billion guilders through decentralisation and helped to reduce the size of the central government apparatus.

Since the first coalition government of liberals and social-democrats took office in the Netherlands in 1994, there has been another shift of emphasis. In addition to reducing responsibilities and size, the present government is seeking to restore the *primacy of politics*. This does not mean that activities which have already been hived off or transferred to other bodies must be returned to central government. Rather, it involves reformulating the requirements to be met in respect of steering and supervision by the administrators concerned, and improving the manner in which account is rendered to elected representatives.

C.   Strategies and processes for planning and carrying out public management reforms

D.   Policy-management capacities, and

H.   Changing structures of the public sector

As part of the effort to restore the primacy of politics, the government has laid down in legislative instructions the requirements to be met by statutory regulations, and administrative authorities with autonomous powers are being established. A co-ordinating team from the Ministry of Finance and the Ministry of the Interior assesses the proposals for setting up such bodies in the light of these guidelines.

The existing (253) *autonomous administrative authorities* are screened by the ministers concerned. Where necessary, this leads to review of the manner in which the government task concerned is carried out and to improvements in steering, supervision (by the minister responsible) and organisation. A report on these measures will be presented in 1996.

The government is reorganising the existing system of around 130 *advisory bodies*, so that the advisory system is more geared to political requirements, and focuses on strategic questions and the main policy elements. The new system will consist of over 20 advisory bodies, which will give advice on broader policy areas and a number of core ministry tasks.

A Revision Act reorganising the old system and a Framework Act setting out the main elements of the new system were recently ratified by parliament. Legislation for setting up the individual advisory bodies has been partly established.

The creation of more strategically oriented core ministries will be advanced by improving the steering and supervision of semi privatised bodies (discussed in Section F), the progressive transfer of tasks to other levels of government, and the reorganisation of the system for providing strategic advice by setting up bodies for that purpose. The government will continue the formation of smaller strategic policy and administrative centres in the ministries. In 1996 it will report to parliament on the current state of affairs and determine the main points of attention for the future.

E.   Human resources management

Current themes are personnel age structure, personnel mobility and the introduction of an average 36-hour working week.

The *average age* of civil servants still shows a general upward trend. The workforce is ageing. The percentage of young people below the age of 25 has fallen from over 12 per cent to under 3 per cent of the workforce during the last 10 years. This phenomenon is partly the result of the decline in the size of government and the falling number of jobs on the lowest scales. In the long term, an increase in the proportion of older staff in the civil service will have implications for the level of personnel costs. It will also hinder the influx of new and younger staff. Furthermore, staff mobility will stagnate, resulting in inadequate career prospects. In 1997 Parliament will be informed of the policy options, so that the effects of the ageing workforce can be guided in a positive direction. The views and desires of staff and managers regarding their work in later life are currently being studied.

Various initiatives are being taken to promote *mobility*. In late 1995 the Office for Training of the General Administrative Service became operational. One of its activities is to fill vacancies and promote the mobility of senior civil servants. In co-operation with other ministries, the Ministry of the Interior is also developing plans to promote the mobility of middle management, partly to increase the employability of staff. A manual has been drawn up for ministries to encourage the introduction of employment pools. These make it possible to lend and borrow staff, are aimed at the advancement of the staff concerned, and can help to accommodate peaks in the workload.

The "interim placement" mobility instrument is also commonly used in the civil service. Its most important features are that staff switch jobs on a voluntary and temporary basis, are guaranteed the right to return to their old posts, and preserve their legal status. Finally, mobility meetings are organised in the provinces for decentralised government services established there to promote regional mobility.

F.   Budget process and management of financial resources

The present government employs a *new budgetary system*. The key feature of the new system is that limits have been established for net public spending for 1995 to 1998. Three sectors are distinguished:

the central government budget in the narrow sense, social security and the health care sector. (The net expenditure must remain within the stipulated limits for these sectors.) The spending limits are expressed in real terms. This means that the spending limits expressed in guilders are continually adjusted if general nominal trends deviate from the forecasts contained in the coalition agreement.

In the new budgetary system, the budget deficit is no longer a target to be met each year, but a parameter for budgetary policy. The deficit should remain below the stipulated ceiling. No measures need to be taken provided the deficit remains below the ceiling. The chance of the ceiling being exceeded is limited by the fact that the calculations in the coalition agreement were based on conservative assumptions.

To assess whether the budget deficit remains below the agreed ceiling, the policy-related budget deficit is used. This deficit does not take account of incidental factors such as proceeds from the sale of state holdings and revenue from cash transfers. The changes in the budgetary system make budgetary decisions more stable, since it is no longer necessary to respond to every change in macro-economic forecasts.

In addition to the changes in the budgetary system, the stability of budgetary policy is also being improved by streamlining the budgetary process. The key feature is that the government takes general decisions on public expenditure in the spring. To prevent subsequent macro-economic developments reopening the decision-making procedure, a certain safety margin should be taken into account in spending estimates when making decisions in the spring. If macro-economic developments result in the spending limit being overrun to some extent, this problem can be raised when making decisions the following spring.

In the field of *financial management* there is growing interest in putting central government activities on a commercial footing. The aim is to make the relationship between funds deployed and the resulting activities, services and effects more visible. This makes it possible to steer the government in a more result-oriented fashion, and provides a lever for improving efficiency. Instead of providing an insight into "expenditure for input", the aim is to provide more insight into "costs for output", and, as far as possible, the effects of policy. In previous years, a number of important measures have been taken to improve management. These are now being broadened and deepened.

The year 1994 saw the launch of the first *agencies*. An agency is a semi-privatised service within the public sector, having public tasks, which has broader powers concerning the deployment of resources than other services. This is because the agency's objectives can be achieved more efficiently in this way. The most important power is the use of a cost accrual system. The government plans to introduce further agencies in a controlled fashion. A service can switch to the cost accrual system if this would improve its management. Other services can improve efficiency by means of other instruments, such as indicators, policy evaluation and studies of financial renewal. The use of these instruments is steadily increasing. For example, estimate indicators are increasingly being used in the budget and financial statements, and in the years ahead attention will also be paid to efficiency and effectiveness indicators.

G. Performance management

In 1995 the government presented its policy document on the provision of *information*, entitled "Back to the Future". It describes how the provision of information and related technologies can help to improve the accessibility and transparency of the government for the public. On the basis of this policy document, experiments and pilot projects are being developed for the creation of integrated government information centres. These pilot projects relate to three fields involving the provision of services and information: real estate, the elderly and disabled, and the "know your rights" information pillars.

Since these services are mainly offered at local level, these pilot projects involve co-operation between local and national government. The projects will be accompanied by research and evaluations aimed mainly at the further development of the administrative and organisational aspects of the application of information technology. Attention will also be devoted to the further expansion of these initiatives so that other services suitable for this approach can be identified. In the event of further expansion, explicit attention will be paid to the aim of gearing public services more to public demand.

The initiatives to set up government information centres have been placed in a broader context of *quality improvement* of government activities. For instance, the possible use of "Total Quality Management" models by the public sector is being assessed, the translation of qualitative agreements into quality charters (comparable with the Citizen's Charters in Great Britain) is being encouraged, and the police monitor (an instrument for improving the quality of the police organisation with the help of information from the public) is being applied.

The use of information technology will also lead to innovative approaches outside government activities that involve the provision of services. For example, the use of information technology for stimulating public participation in the preparation of political decisions will be tried out in experiments with electronic consultation. In addition, new policies are being prepared for improving the active and passive availability of government information. Issues relevant to performance management are also discussed inSection F.

I.   Regulatory management and reform

Deregulation and *ex ante* impact assessment are the two main tendencies in regulatory management in the Netherlands.

At the beginning of the present government's term of office, a programme was launched for reviewing existing bodies of legislation, under the watchwords: market functioning, deregulation and quality of regulation. Every year about ten projects are set up, which develop proposals for regulations which are less burdensome and easier to enforce.

The main feature is the linking of economic and judicial aspects. By promoting market forces and competition, political objectives can sometimes be achieved more effectively than by imposing compulsory rules. On the other hand, more transparent and consistent rules, which are easier to enforce, will strengthen competition. Another important feature is organised political commitment. At the start of every project, documents are drawn up in which the minister responsible states his commitment to the project. When the proposal has been finalised, he immediately gives his opinion, so that the government can reach a decision and order the implementation of the proposal.

Last year, proposals included food regulation, noise nuisance, the use of market forces in education and hospital regulation. An important general theme was standardisation and certification, as an alternative to quality regulation. Next year, proposals will include product legislation, competition clauses, bailiffs, competition in health care, water pollution and construction legislation.Several activities are being carried out to *assess the effects* of intended regulations during the preparatory phase. They are designed to ensure that greater account is taken of the interests on which the regulations are based.

A working party has been set up to select subjects which qualify for assessing the effects of regulations, and to indicate the questions to be answered. The questions concern effects on companies, effects on the environment, effects on the workload of the judicial system, and the enforceability of the proposed regulation. To answer these questions, instruments such as questionnaires are developed to assist the officials concerned.

On the instructions of the Ministry of Justice, an institute has been developing simulation techniques for regulations and a policy paper on the evaluation of legislation has been drawn up.

Projects have been launched for involving the judiciary in the preparation of regulations, mainly concerning enforceability and workload.

Mr. Guus Bronkhorst
Counsellor for International Affairs
Ministry of the Interior
P.O. Box 20011
NL-2500 EA The Hague
Tel.: (31-70) 302 75 26
Fax: (31-70) 302 61 50
E-mail: guus.bronkhorst@cs.minbiza.nl

Annex to Sections A *and* B

EMPLOYMENT STRUCTURE OF THE NETHERLANDS PUBLIC SECTOR

Table 1.   **Public Employees in Ministries***

	1991	1995
Agriculture (Conservation of Natural Scenery) and fisheries	11 883	10 939
Defence	24 088	
Economic Affairs	5 498	4 935
Education and Science	3 446	2 348
Finance	32 955	30 184
Foreign Affairs	3 198	2 844
General Affairs	392	318
Interior	2 489	2 770
Housing, Physical Planning and Environment	7 506	4 429
Justice	23 570	21 033
Social Affairs and Employment	2 661	2 148
Transport and Public Works	15 838	13 725
Welfare, Health and Cultural Affairs	7 432	5 868
Higher Courts of State		1 524
Cabinet of Dutch Antilles and Aruban Affairs		84
Total	**140 956**	**103 149**

* Since the creation of sectors of government (see Table 2), the counting method has been slightly changed.
Source: Ministry of the Interior, DGMP/AO.

Table 2. **Total Employment by Sector of Government***

	1991	1995
National	144 552	103 149
Education and Science	302 930	269 712
Defence	101 864	92 249
Police	30 883	40 892
Judiciary	1 538	2 054
Municipalities	196 017	155 726
Provinces	13 951	12 310
Polder and Water Boards	7 815	7 903
Common Regulations (between municipalities)	21 222	17 744
Total	**820 772**	**701 739**

* The data in these tables indicate the number of full time jobs, not the number of employed persons, who can be working part time.

Source: Ministry of the Interior, DGMP/AO.

Annex A

PRINCIPAL RECENT PUBLIC MANAGEMENT DEVELOPMENTS

1993

- Appearance of the report of the special committee on issues concerning advisory bodies, entitled "Tailor-made advice". It called for the revision of the system of advisory bodies.
- The government presented its action plan for the revision of the advisory system.
- Publication of the policy document of the fourth external committee on political, administrative and constitutional renewal, entitled "Towards core ministries". It called for the formation of smaller, strategic administrative centres.
- Report of the secretaries-general, entitled "The organisation and working methods of the civil service", which analysed the core tasks of each ministry.
- Application of broader rules of budgetary discipline (internal cabinet agreements regarding the containment of public spending), such as the introduction of the end-of-year margin, with a view to enhancing efficiency.
- Start of policy aimed at ensuring that charges cover costs.
- Nearly all ministries have set up a policy evaluation programme. The budget looks at current, planned and completed evaluations.
- Start of projects for the introduction of indicators for the cost of implementing regulations.

1994

- Coalition agreement, which included proposals to establish core ministries, restore the primacy of politics and steer organisations at arm's length more effectively.
- Publication of *People and management in the civil service*, the first annual report on personnel management in the public sector.
- Launch of the first four agencies.
- Control of the integrated operating budget by integrating expenditure on personnel and equipment.
- Conclusion of the integrated subsidy policy and charges policy.

- Adoption of the principle that no further rental or lease contracts will be concluded, unless it can be shown in specific cases that it is more efficient than purchase.

1995

- Achievement of the target of the efficiency operation (reduction in the number of civil service jobs by 5 957, among other things by reducing support staff).
- Policy document and government position paper on how to semi-privatise bodies in a responsible fashion. They specified the conditions under which independent powers can be assigned to central government bodies.
- Government position paper on autonomous administrative authorities and ministerial responsibility.
- Government policy document entitled "Back to the future", on the use of information and information and communications technology in the public sector.
- Start of the operation to screen autonomous administrative authorities (253 bodies are to be assessed by the government, especially ministerial powers and responsibilities, steering, supervision, and organisation).
- Introduction of the General Administrative Service: improvement of the quality and mobility of public servants, the first phase being aimed mainly at senior ministry officials.
- Launch of three new agencies.
- Increase of the end-of-year margin by 0.25 per cent to 1 per cent.
- As part of the review procedure, inter-ministry policy studies are started, the central theme being financial reform. The primary aim of the studies is to explore the scope for improving the systems for financing government services. This mainly involves improving the system's incentives which affect the behaviour of executive bodies and of members of the public and organisations which make use of the services, with a view to improving the effectiveness, efficiency and transparency of policy.

1996

- Acceptance by Parliament of the Framework Act on advisory groups and the Act amending the advisory system. The Acts laid down the main features of the new advisory system to be introduced in 1997.
- Introduction of instructions (for regulations) concerning autonomous administrative authorities.
- Report on the screening of autonomous administrative authorities (planned for autumn 1996).
- Launch of six new agencies.
- Introduction of more stringent rules for contract management and equipment management.

Annex B

INSTITUTIONAL RESPONSIBILITY FOR PUBLIC MANAGEMENT IMPROVEMENT

ORGANISATION	TASKS AND RESPONSIBILITIES
Ministry of the Interior – Directorate General for Management and Personnel Policy (DGMP)	• co-ordination of personnel policy; salary negotiations, number of posts, job descriptions, training and staff development • initiation of modernisation schemes (*e.g.* decentralisation, mobility and management development)
– Directorate General for Public Administration	• co-ordination for organisational matters of central and decentral governments and the relations between the different layers of government, including decentralisation • co-ordination of the policy on information technology in government
– Office for the Senior Public Service	• enhancing professionalism and integrity of the public service by measures aimed at mobility, knowledge intensification, career development instruments, research and infrastructure
Ministry of Finance	• financial management, financial control of re-organisation
Ministry of Justice	• regulatory policy and reform

NEW ZEALAND

A. Main tendencies and overall priorities

A solid foundation for the State sector management framework has been set in place over the last ten years, particularly through the enactment of the State Owned Enterprises Act 1986, the State Sector Act 1988 and the Public Finance Act 1989, and through the maintenance of an open and information-rich management system. As this decade of radical change to New Zealand's State sector structures, systems and processes comes to an end, it is possible to identify a number of areas where further work and effort will be required in order to maximise the gains from those reforms. For example, there is a need to study what has been learnt about accountability systems and governance arrangements in the Public Service and wider State sector, so as to minimise compliance costs and disincentive effects on agencies, while maximising their effectiveness.

Another element of the original formula that has taken some time to crystallise into a practical form is the set of issues bound up in "ownership". The architects of the reforms saw ministers having two interests as managers of the State – one as 'purchasers' of goods and services from departmental and other suppliers, and the other as "owners" (or, more properly as 'stewards') of the agencies of the State. Work undertaken recently has identified four ownership dimensions:

a) *strategic alignment*: ensuring that the government's institutional arrangements suit its objectives, complemented by a co-ordinated approach to business across the whole of government;
b) *integrity of the public service*: ensuring that the collective management conditions needed for coherent government are in place and are complied with;
c) *future capability*: the investment in, and management of, strategically important resources to enable the public service as a whole, and departments individually, to deliver on expected future business demands;
d) *cost effectiveness over the long run*: ensuring that departments produce required outputs cost effectively over time.

Departments, in concert with the agencies at the centre of government, are currently working to ensure that ministers are provided with a reliable means of gaining assurance that departments are in the right shape to ensure effective government and are being managed with the future in mind. This will be done through enriching existing management processes, rather than creating a new kind of accountability process.

B. Context affecting public management

In a 1993 referendum, New Zealanders voted to replace the traditional first-past-the-post (FPP) electoral system with one based on Mixed Member proportional representation. In the future, therefore, it is less likely that a single political party will obtain a majority of seats in the New Zealand House of Representatives.

The implications for the public service of this change in the electoral system are mixed. At a constitutional level, things will remain the same. The public service will continue to be non-partisan, independent and bound by the law. It will continue to serve the government of the day with professionalism and integrity by providing it with free and frank advice and by executing its decisions.

Any impact on the public management reform programme will arise from the consequences of the changing dynamics of the political process, and their parliamentary manifestation. For example, the following are more likely to occur: more than one party represented in government; the possibility of more frequent changes of administration; coalition-building and maintenance; and less certainty over getting legislation passed or policy proposals advanced.

C. Strategies and processes for planning and carrying out public management reforms

As central agencies, the State Services Commission, the Treasury and the Department of the Prime Minister and Cabinet are the key advisors to the government and co-ordinators of its business. The heads of these agencies advise and support the group of Ministers responsible for considering major policy issues and developing and managing the government's strategic policy directions. They meet regularly to discuss and deal with matters relating to the overall management, performance, and co-ordination of the public service.

In addition to this ongoing activity, the State Services Commission, in conjunction with other departments, periodically undertakes or supports independent, long-term reviews of both the State sector as a whole and significant management issues within it. System-wide reviews were completed in 1991 (Steering Group, *Review of State Sector Reforms*) and 1996 (Allen Schick, *The Spirit of Reform: Managing the New Zealand State Sector in a Time of Change*).

D. Policy-management capacities

One significant recent development in this area has been a study on how an applied social science research capacity could best be provided in New Zealand. The review team concluded that there were generic gaps in government's social science research activities. In response to the report, a co-ordinated departmental process has also been launched to:

a) periodically develop forward-looking strategic analysis drawing out the implications of government strategy for long-term and cross-portfolio applied social science research and evaluation that will be required to support policy advice assessing future policy options and new and existing programmes, as an aid to forward planning and co-ordination;

b) advise on identifying and addressing gaps in social science research;

c) investigate options for optimising the range and accessibility of statistics relevant to applied social science research;

d) develop and assess options for a comprehensive and easily usable information system providing ready access to information about policy-related research and evaluation;

e) consider means of encouraging proactive development of the infrastructure where this is needed to meet the government's requirements for social science research.

E. Human resources management

The State Sector Act 1988 and the Employment Contracts Act 1991 significantly altered the public service's approach to human resource management and industrial relations. Under the State Sector Act, service-wide bargaining ended as individual chief executives (CEs) became the employers of their departmental staff. The CEs themselves, and their most senior managers, were placed on fixed-term contracts. Under the Employment Contracts Act, which applies to both the private and State sectors, union membership is voluntary, and every employee's conditions of employment are set out in an employment contract with their employer – either on an individual or a collective basis. Public service CEs and their managers now have very much the same latitude – and accountability – in personnel matters as their private sector counterparts.

A Management Development Centre was established early in 1996, under the collective oversight of CEs, to cater for the needs of public sector managers. Its objective is to increase the size and quality of the senior management pool across the public service. In addition, a Public Sector Training Organisation was established in May 1995. Its role is to identify and publish the key competencies needed in public sector occupations, and co-ordinate sector-wide training. Departments continue to have freedom to develop and implement their own training strategies.

F. Budget process and management of financial resources

The strategic phase at the start of the annual budget process was "rolled over" and developed further. A special meeting of all ministers held in September 1995 confirmed: the government's Strategic Result Areas (see below) for the period 1994-97; strategic priorities for the 1996 budget to be reported in the 1996 Budget Policy Statement (BPS), issued in February; and overall shape of the Budget itself (delivered in May).

The regime introduced through the Fiscal Responsibility Act 1994 has been further bedded in, enabling a more informed debate about the overall direction of fiscal policy and the appropriate balance between the major fiscal aggregates. Documents required by the Fiscal Responsibility Act are closely integrated. For instance, the three-year fiscal intentions set out in the BPS are informed by a mid-year economic and fiscal update (EFU) released in the preceding December. At the time of the budget, the government publishes a fiscal strategy report and a further EFU. Any departures from the intentions and objectives specified in the most recent BPS must be explained.

The move under the Fiscal Responsibility Act to preparing forecasts in accordance with generally accepted accounting practice means that the government has an accrual-based budgeting system that is on the same footing as its ex-post aggregate reporting.

Significant changes have been made to the format of the estimates of appropriation over the last few financial years, with the aim of ensuring they focus clearly on information supporting requests for appropriations in each vote, for which ministers are accountable to Parliament. Information about expected performance of departments is presented in Departmental Forecast Reports and may be compared with results disclosed in year-end audited Annual Reports.

Following recent changes to Parliament's rules, members of Parliament who are not ministers are able to introduce bills and propose amendments to bills or changes to votes that have an impact on, respectively, the Crown's fiscal performance or position, or the composition of votes. Previously, these would have been ruled out of order. However, the principle of government control of Crown finances is protected by a new financial veto procedure. This allows the government to veto such bills, amendments and changes if they would have a more than minor impact on the Crown's fiscal aggregates or on the composition of a vote.

Three other developments to note are:

a) Departments and Crown entities that seek injections of capital are required to prepare strategic business plans and sound business cases to support their bids.

b) The Treasury has instituted a programme of financial management reviews aimed at assessing and enhancing departmental performance. The first reviews addressed costing systems and user charges, and financial reporting.

c) In July 1996 the Local Government Act 1974 was amended to impose on local authorities transparency and accountability disciplines (effective by 1 July 1998) similar to those applied to central government under the Fiscal Responsibility Act.

G.   Performance Management

Performance management in the New Zealand public service is based around a number of management processes and instruments:

a) the strategic management process – a structured process of interaction on strategic issues amongst and between Ministers and CEs, which results in high level objectives – consisting of Strategic Result Areas (SRAs), Key Result Areas (KRAs), and CE performance agreements;

b) departmental purchase agreements;

c) Departmental Forecast Reports (DFRs) and Annual Reports.

The new arrangements for strategic management and co-ordination of the State sector were bedded in further. They start with the government declaring its political priorities and these being translated into higher-level deliverables within the assumptions of the medium-term budget strategy as SRAs. SRAs are selected points of leverage; that is they do not cover the entire business of government. Those strategic results which are identified as being of highest priority are framed in such a way that relevant departments can draw up KRAs which will contribute towards those SRAs. These KRAs become a focus for departmental planning, and as the year goes by, they provide a focus for assessing performance. Individual KRAs can also be developed for departmental management purposes, covering aspects regarded as critical to a department's performance and its strategic capability to deliver its goods and services.

The Chief Executive performance agreement is a key accountability document between a minister, on behalf of the government, and his or her chief executive. It provides a basis for specification and review of performance in terms of the government's purchase and ownership interests and priorities in a department. The 1996-97 performance agreement guidelines require the specification of KRAs and additional personal requirements the chief executive will give priority to, and undertakings to deliver on the departmental purchase agreement (see below) and to work in accord with the government's collective ownership interests.

Before performance agreements are finalised, draft KRAs are reviewed by the State Services Commissioner, in order to assess the degree of:

a) strategic alignment (are they linked to SRAs or other government goals?);

b) significance (do they reflect priority areas?);

c) specification and assessability (do they define a discrete product/objective whose delivery can be demonstrated?);

d) coherence (do they mutually reinforce the KRAs of other departments which contribute to the same SRA?);

e) consultation (with ministers and other chief executives); and

f) collective interest (is this advanced, or at least not compromised by the KRAs?).

At a departmental level, the goods and services to be supplied by a department to a minister are set out in a purchase agreement. These agreements specify the quality, quantity, price and timeliness of each output to be supplied. The arrangement allows a minister to make considered and deliberate decisions as to what he or she wishes to purchase each year (within budgetary priorities agreed by Cabinet), and, where there is scope for competition, to select the best supplier.

H. Changing structures of the public sector

The overall purpose of structural reform activity is to significantly improve the performance of the State sector, first by removing any functions that the government considers to no longer be the business of the State or that could clearly be better performed elsewhere, and then by ensuring the agencies responsible for the remaining functions are structured to deliver their services as efficiently and effectively as possible.

Following a period of corporatisation of commercial activities, in a number of the remaining departments policy and service delivery activities have been separated to reduce or eliminate conflicts between these functions. The public service is now appreciably more focused on policy advice and on what continues to be seen as the core regulatory and related functions of the government. Crown entities, under the control of Government-appointed Boards, perform many of the funding and service delivery functions previously carried out by public service departments – in the transport and science sectors for example – while structural changes in the health and education sectors have introduced concepts of "purchase and supply" into previously heavily demand-driven sectors. Beyond this are the State-owned enterprises (SOEs) operating on fully commercial lines. Little is static in this new State sector, and changes and refinements are being made or considered continuously. For example, recent changes include the decision to split the Public Service Department of Survey and Land Information into a SOE and a department with a narrower focus, and to sell three SOEs to private interests.

I. Regulatory management and reform

On 1 January 1996, the Compliance Cost Assessment Framework came into effect. The Framework contains two specific mechanisms:

a) Papers for Cabinet must now include a Compliance Cost Statement. The Compliance Cost Statement identifies the compliance cost implications of a proposal and, if possible, quantifies those costs.
b) Where it is considered there is a risk that substantial compliance costs will be imposed, departments must prepare a Compliance Costs Assessment report.

The Framework is designed to ensure that unnecessary new compliance costs are avoided, and to reinforce compliance cost reductions achieved by particular reform measures. It does not promise the elimination of compliance costs but provides an assurance that compliance costs, along with other costs and benefits, will be considered in the policy development process.

Mr. Michael Webster
State Sector Development Branch
State Services Commission
P.O. Box 329
WELLINGTON
Tel.: (64-4) 495 67 20
Fax: (64-4) 495 66 71

Annex A

PRINCIPAL RECENT PUBLIC MANAGEMENT DEVELOPMENTS

1986
- State Owned Enterprises (SOE) Act specified the principles governing the operation of SOEs, authorised the formation of companies to carry on certain government activities, and established requirements about the accountability of SOEs, and the responsibility of Ministers.

1988
- State Sector Act enacted with the goals of: enhancing efficient and effective public service management by increasing managerial autonomy and more clearly defining accountabilities; preserving the values of service to the community and integrity; and ensuring that the State is a "good employer".

1989
- Public Finance Act introduced a new legal framework covering the use of public resources, including: Parliamentary scrutiny of the government's management of the Crown's assets and liabilities, and expenditure and revenue proposals; the establishment of banking arrangements for public and trust money; and the specification of minimum accrual-based financial reporting obligations of the Crown, departments and Crown entities designed to disclose the effectiveness and efficiency of the use of financial resources in departments and Crown entities. The Act also introduced a markedly different basis of appropriation.

1990
- Public Service Code of Conduct issued, detailing minimum standards of integrity and conduct of public servants in their work.

1991
- Major review of State sector reforms, covering: parliamentary accountability; the collective interest; strategy formulation by Cabinet; risk management; the relationship between ministers and CEs; the role of central agencies; senior management development; and human resource and financial management.
- Employment Contracts Act provided a new legal and institutional framework for industrial relations in both the private and public (State) sectors.

1992
- Significant restructuring of public service departments, with the creation of Crown entities in the health, science, housing and transport sectors.

1994
- Fiscal Responsibility Act enacted to improve the conduct and transparency of fiscal policy by specifying principles of responsible fiscal management and by strengthening the reporting requirements of the Crown.

1995
- Guidance issued on public service principles, conventions and practice, and on the implications for the public service of the changing electoral system.

1996
- New rules (Standing Orders) for the operation of the House of Representatives came into effect, including changes to the annual financial cycle. Major review of the State sector management framework, covering: structure of the State sector; organisational capacity; managing public money; and accounting for results.

Annex B

INSTITUTIONAL RESPONSIBILITY FOR PUBLIC MANAGEMENT IMPROVEMENT

ORGANISATION	TASKS AND RESPONSIBILITIES
State Services Commission	• appoints and develops heads of departments (chief executives), and operates the chief executive performance management system • promulgates and maintains appropriate values and standards of behaviour (including constitutional aspects) for the public service • provides assurance to the government that the State sector has the capability in terms of people, information, management structures and systems to deliver the government's strategic objectives • advises the State Services Commissioner and the government on the performance of public service departments and agencies • advises the government on appropriate conditions of employment in the education sector, acting as the government's bargaining agent • is responsible for administering the provisions of the State Sector Act 1988
Treasury	• advises on the contents of the government's annual Budget and prepares the budget documents and associated legislation • accounts for the revenue, expenses, assets and liabilities of the Crown and produces the Crown's financial statements • manages the Crown's public debt and Treasury-managed financial assets • reports on expenditure proposals before the government, disburses funds to departments and monitors spending against appropriations • analyses and reports on the macroeconomic situation and outlook, and provides economic policy advice • provides policy advice, usually in a second-opinion role, on specific sectors of the economy and on appropriate interventions to achieve policy outcomes • participates in more general reviews of policy issues where there are resource implications • implement specific and financial policies

ORGANISATION	TASKS AND RESPONSIBILITIES

Department of the Prime Minister and Cabinet

- advises the Prime Minister on policy and constitutional issues
- helps to ensure there is a high quality and effective process of decision making by the government through the provision of secretariat services to the Cabinet and the Executive Council
- reviews, on an annual basis, progress against the government's Strategic Result Areas (the agreed policy priorities for government departments set by Cabinet)
- contributes to the effective co-ordination of the work of the government across departmental lines, and tests the quality of advice coming from departments

Annex C

KEY PUBLIC DOCUMENTS ON PUBLIC MANAGEMENT ISSUES AND DEVELOPMENTS

State Sector Act 1988.

Public Finance Act 1989.

Public Service Code of Conduct, State Services Commission, 1990.

Employment Contracts Act 1991.

Review of State Sector Reforms, Steering Group on Review of State Sector Reforms, 1991.

Review of Accountability Requirements, Report of the Working Party to the Advisory Group, 1994.

A Profile of the Public Service in New Zealand, Commonwealth Secretariat, 1995.

Fiscal Responsibility Act 1994: An Explanation, The Treasury, 1995.

Public Service Principles, Conventions and Practice: A Guidance Series, (in nine parts), State Services Commission, 1995.

Purchase Agreement Guidelines with Best Practice for Output Performance Measures, The Treasury, 1995.

Strategic Result Areas for the Public Sector: 1994-1997, Department of the Prime Minister and Cabinet, 1995.

Taking Care of Tomorrow, Today: A Discussion of the Government's Ownership Interest in Departments, Parts I and II, Interdepartmental Working Group on Ownership, 1995.

Working Under Proportional Representation: A Reference for the Public Service, State Services Commission, 1995.

Chief Executive Performance Agreement: Proforma and Guidelines 1996-97, State Services Commission, 1996.

OECD Economic Surveys 1995-1996: New Zealand, OECD, 1996.

Putting it Together: *An Explanatory Guide to the New Zealand Public Sector Financial Management System*, The Treasury, 1996.

State Sector Reform: A Decade of Change, State Services Commission, 1996.

The Spirit of the Reform: Managing the New Zealand State Sector in a Time of Change, Allen Schick, State Services Commission, 1996.

Government Reform in New Zealand, Graham C. Scott, IMF Occasional Paper, N. 140, 1996 (forthcoming).

NORWAY

A. Main tendencies and overall priorities

The basic objectives of the Norwegian public administration are to contribute to full employment, social equalisation, welfare and security. The priorities of the Ministry of Government Administration in order to fulfil these aims are to secure a user-oriented, quality-conscious and efficient public administration, and a skilled and adaptable civil service with good management.

The task of devising and implementing administration policy will become more demanding in the years ahead. The restructuring that has taken place up till now must be consolidated, and the foundation must be laid for the continuation of a strong public administration.

B. Context affecting public management

Many areas of our society are under-going sweeping, rapid-paced change. Internationalisation leads to the dismantling of trade barriers and greater competition. The basis for the governance of society is changing. At the same time, increased competition, the implementation of information technology and new management techniques will help us to use our resources more effectively. One of the main challenges facing the public sector is to respond to the changes taking place by designing new strategies to deal with them.

The efficacy of the instruments of the welfare state has become the subject of debate. Our challenge is to find instruments that reach and assist those who need them the most.

A strong public administration is an important tool for ensuring both equal distribution and democratic development.

C. Strategies and processes for planning and carrying out public management reforms

Traditional methods of public control and use of policy instruments are now being adopted to new, challenging framework conditions. As a result of internationalisation and advances in technology, public services in many areas are subjected to the forces of competition. Two means are used to deal with this trend. The first is to give the agency in question the authority and framework conditions that are appropriate to a competitive environment. The second is to create a stronger statutory framework by means of acts of legislation, regulations and concessions.

The need for efficiency and new forms of management and association means that public agencies and their staff must be prepared for restructuring and down-sizing. It has been a priority for the government to deal with restructuring without having to resort to dismissals. Up till now, this endeavour has been largely successful. In situations where staff reductions have been necessary, human resource development measures have been targeted either towards the needs of other central government or municipal agencies or towards enhancing the individual employee's skills. It is, however, regarded as important that job security is not perceived as a shield against change.

In 1994, the Norwegian Government's Information Policy was launched. The principal aims are to:

– ensure that each resident and enterprise has genuine access to information on public sector activities;
– ensure that every resident is informed of his or her rights, obligations and opportunities;
– secure general and equal opportunity to participate in the democratic process.

The information policy is based on five principles, which must be viewed in relation to each other:

1) *Communication*. The communication principle implies that the administration and its users are regarded as equal partners, who alternate as senders and receivers of information.
2) *Active information*. This principle means that the administration itself must inform the public, actively and systematically.
3) *Comprehensiveness*. The principle of comprehensiveness implies that information from central government must as far as possible be co-ordinated, so that receivers perceive it as a whole.
4) *Line management*. Whoever is responsible for results in a particular area must not only have the resources and tools at his or her disposal with which to achieve the objectives, but also have the authority to use them.
5) *Information as a management responsibility*. The principle of information as a management responsibility implies that although managers may delegate particular tasks, they cannot delegate responsibility for information.

D.   Policy-management capacities

To strengthen co-ordination of activities relating to the european Union, such as matters concerning the european Economic Area, a central government decision-making structure has been established consisting of twenty inter-ministerial subcommittees and one overarching co-ordination committee with representation from all the ministries.

A trial project involving government service office was initiated by the government in 1992. The aim was to co-ordinate local and central government services from a variety of sectors through a single joint office. The goal has been to improve the availability and quality of services, to maintain local services at similar levels from one place to another, to achieve optimal utilisation of resources and to promote viable local communities.

E.   Human resources management

Expertise is and will remain a decisive factor if the public administration as a whole and each individual employee is to succeed in meeting the new challenges and providing good services to users. The ministry is therefore focusing its efforts on encouraging human resources development throughout the public administration. The ministry has drawn up a strategy that emphasises the need to tie human resource development more closely to the goals and challenges of the various agencies.

The central government must be prepared to face the challenges of restructuring for many years to come. We are therefore already evaluating new models for creating a more long-term policy for mobility. We must move from a situation in which employees spend their entire working lives at one work-place, to a situation in which moving from job to job becomes the norm. This is the trend we are already seeing to-day. As outlined in section C above, it has been a priority for the government to deal with restructuring without having to resort to dismissals.

Since 1990 a new performance-oriented top management pay system has been in operation in the civil service. A new and more flexible civil service pay system has been in use since 1991. The effects of both systems have been studied through evaluation projects. As regards the general pay system, evaluation shows that one of the effects has been a development towards more equal pay between men and women. The ministry will continue to follow the development in this field in the coming years.

The demographic development indicates a considerable increase in the number of older employees during the next 15 years. As the government has decided a general policy of developing people instead of retirement, this has an impact upon the policy regarding older employees, which in the government sector are supported in various ways to continue their career development. Measures like flexible or graduated retirement are also being investigated.

Increasing attention has also been paid to ethical issues in business and industry as well as in public administration. A report by a working group was in 1993 presented to the Ministry of Government Administration. The report gives an account of ethically important public service values and statutory provisions. It also draws attention to some of the problems in the form of ethical dilemmas and "grey zones" that may be met by persons exercising administrative authority and administrative discretion. Proposals are submitted for ways in which the agencies themselves can address such issues.

Another question that the ministry is facing is the employment of immigrants, which to-day is low, particularly as regards persons of a non-western ethnic background. A project will now be started up with the aim to increase the number of immigrant employees, running over a 2-year period, and including various activities aimed at influencing the attitudes of government sector employers, the trade unions concerned and the immigrants' organisations.

Reducing the overall sick-leave rate among employees in the government sector has been the goal of a project which was starting up in 1991 and is still running. According to an agreement between employers and trade unions in the government sector, focusing on the working environment will be given high priority.

In agreement with the confederations for government employees' unions (including the Norwegian Union of Teachers), the Ministry of Government Administration has offered advice and economic support to try to change the vocational training systems in the individual agencies. The aim is to give the employees a broader and more flexible vocational training for working as skilled employees both in public and private sectors. The education leads to a common craft certificate recognised in all sectors.

The long-term goals and principles of the public administration will not be lost sight of. These are that the public administration must act consistently, ensure equal treatment, openness and transparency, give all parties the opportunity to be heard in the decision-making process, facilitate the participation of both women and men in society, and enable employees to participate in decisions involving the workplace.

F.   Budget process and management of financial resources

From 1997 a new set of regulations will be implemented, regulating the financial transactions of all government agencies. This will be the main document concerning governmental accounting. These rules aim at a more effective management of governmental resources and a clearer orientation towards goals and resources. A significant new element is that as well as the reporting of the agency's financial results the reporting of obtained performance is also required. The new rules will consist of both a section of formal and binding regulations as well as a section of guidelines and more technical instructions.

There is also ongoing planning of a new system for the payment of governmental expenditures and incomes. One element of this reform is that all financial transactions of an agency will be transmitted to the bank electronically, while the bank draws the necessary amount of money from the Norwegian Central Bank on a daily basis. In this way the central administration will achieve a substantial reduction of costs.

G. Performance management

For some time, the government has emphasized the role of performance management as an aid to restructuring and a means of enhancing the utilisation of resources. In recent years, the ministries have invested considerable resources in improving the application of performance management techniques in their respective areas. The introduction of new budget regulations for the central government (discussed in Section F above) will co-ordinate and consolidate the measures that have been developed in this field during the 1980s and 90s. These regulations are based on the obligation to identify goals beforehand and to report targets that have been achieved afterwards. The principles of identifying goals, performance monitoring and evaluation will also be incorporated into government grant schemes.

The introduction of the new budget regulations will pose a challenge in that performance management must be adapted specifically to the tasks and nature of the individual agency. Previous experience shows that such differentiation is essential if the work of the individual agency is to become genuinely result-oriented.

H. Changing structures of the public sector

We have become accustomed to a situation in which government agencies provide services within many sectors. Governance is exercised by means of direct instructions to these agencies. However, as a result of internationalisation and advances in technology, public services in many areas are now subjected to the forces of competition, and must conform to the same rules and parameters as members of the private sector. The telecommunications sector is perhaps the clearest example of this.

The ownership management involves the state as a market player, whereas the development and application of regulations and concession schemes involves the state as a regulatory authority. These two roles must be kept separate from one another, or there will be speculation as to whether the state as a regulatory authority is showing favouritism to its own ownership positions.

Due to changes in the external framework, political control must be organised in a different manner from before, which is more conscious of the division between politics and management within the ministries and which uses performance management as a tool to aid restructuring and improve efficiency. And the results of the restructuring that has taken place, for example the new markets for energy, telecommunications services, civil aviation and pharmaceutical products, are that these changes have brought about positive outcomes in the form of lower prices and better use of resources.

I. Regulatory management and reform

In order to improve the methodical basis of the benefit and cost calculations, as regards both reforms and concerning public enterprises and projects, the government has established an independent calculation committee, which is charged with the task of evaluating methods to disclose the real costs of the implementation of new reforms. The committee is to work out a proposal of practical guidance regarding benefit and cost calculations in connection with assessments of projects, reforms and enterprises in the public sector. The aim is to arrive at the construction of a detailed model and a check list to be used by the ministries and agencies, as well as by all investigation committees charged with calculating the economical consequences of official studies and proposals. Such a check list will, together with the governmental planning instructions, contribute to the economical consequences of regulatory reforms being more soundly deliberated. The committee is expected to finish its work before the end of 1996.

J.   Other

Another aspect of user orientation involves establishing simpler reporting arrangements for the business sector. The Central Co-ordinating Register for Legal Entities has now been established, and a database over reporting requirements is being prepared. Together with an accompanying co-ordinating body, this register is intended to prevent double registration, ensure the re-use of data, initiate changes in regulations and assist government agencies in designing new reporting requirements. A central aim is to establish an effective flow of information between the public administration and the business sector, by means of electronic data interchange among other things.

Information technology can also be used to facilitate communication across traditional organisational boundaries. This will enable the public administration to provide more uniform services to users regardless of the overlying administrative organisation. Moreover, this technology should be used to make the public administration more accessible than has previously been the case. For example, open documents can now be made available to the public far more easily. The government's electronic information database ODIN has been available on the Internet since August 1995. ODIN (the database for public documentation and information in Norway) provides the general public with access to speeches, press releases and publications issued by the government and the ministries.

Mr. Odd Bøhagen
Deputy Director General
Royal Ministry of Government Administration
P.0. Box 8004 Dep.
N-0030 Oslo
Tel.: (47-22) 24 48 20
Fax: (47-22) 24 95 16

Mr. Terje Dyrstad
Deputy Director General
Royal Ministry of Government Administration
P.O. Box 8004 Dep.
N-0030 Oslo
Tel.: (47-22) 24 49 75
Fax: (47-22) 24 95 17

Annex A

PRINCIPAL RECENT PUBLIC MANAGEMENT DEVELOPMENTS

1993

- Report to the Ministry of Government Administration on the values, attitudes and attitudinal development in the public administration.
- Public Sector Management Reform in Norway – Recent Developments.
- Guiding lines from the Ministry of Government Administration for the readjustment and restructuring of the government sector.
- The use of executive committees in the central government administration.

1994

- Statement to the *Storting* on administration policy – by Minister of Government Administration.
- Central Government Information Policy. Main Principles.

1995

- Guidelines for establishing governmental standards for information technology (IT) in the public administration.
- Guidelines for management and monitoring of subordinate agencies.
- To regulate or not – checklist for use when deciding on instruments and new regulation.
- Organisational forms of central government undertakings in Norway.
- Strategic plan by the Ministry of Government Administration for competence development in the government sector.

1996

- Statement to the *Storting* on administration policy – by Minister of Government Administration.
- Working group report to the Ministry of Government Administration recommending various measures to strengthen the international competencies of the government sector – July 1996.
- Older government employees: Guidelines from the Ministry of Government. Administration as regards measures concerning senior employees in the government sector.
- At the request of the *Storting*, a report will be delivered by the Ministry of Government Administration on the effects of the top management pay system. The report will be forwarded to the *Storting* in the ministry's budget proposal for 1997.

Annex B

INSTITUTIONAL RESPONSIBILITY FOR PUBLIC MANAGEMENT IMPROVEMENT

ORGANISATION	TASKS AND RESPONSIBILITIES
Ministry of Government Administration – Department of Administration Policy – Department of Government Employer Affairs	• initiate, monitor and co-ordinate public management reform • personnel policy, salaries
Directorate of Public Management	• external agency of the Ministry of Government Administration
Norwegian Central Information Service	• advice and assistance to the government, ministries, and agencies on financial management, corporate planning, introduction of IT, management development, organisational development, service improvements, training and development
Ministry of Finance	• budgetary reform and the introduction of performance measurement in the budgetary process
Ministry of Municipal and Labour Affairs	• questions relating to local government

PORTUGAL

A. Main tendencies and overall priorities

Over the past ten years, public management reform in Portugal has been an integral part of the structural adjustments that are vital to achieving a general improvement in economic efficiency; this reform has been driven by three main aims:

- to improve the relationship of the administration with citizens;
- to improve public management; and
- to simplify procedures, making them less bureaucratic.

The aim has thus been to create an internal dynamic for modernisation and for a client-oriented approach to service quality. A further aim has been to provide greater safeguards for citizens and to involve them more closely in the administration's decisions and in the process of administrative change. Efforts have also focused on making greater use of new technologies, encouraging training, and improving the image of public servants by calling attention to their strengths and reforming the terms of their employment.

The plans for change, centred on the main framework documents – the Government Programme and the "Major Options" of the 1996 Plan – are based on the following priorities for the coming years:

- to design a model of public administration that is democratic, open to participation, as unbureaucratic as possible, non-partisan and non-politicised;
- to create a public administration dedicated to the harmonious development of the country and attentive to the needs of citizens and economic agents;
- to organise an efficient, effective and quality public service which will be a catalyst for more effective government action and faster socio-economic development;
- to provide citizens and economic agents with the guarantee of simplified administrative procedures, receptiveness, greater participation and responsiveness, faster and more detailed information, a reduction in bureaucracy-related costs, as well as the strengthening of the mechanisms of interprofessional relations;
- to qualify, improve, encourage and professionalise the human resources of the public service through a coherent and appropriate career development, pay and vocational training policy;
- to focus on a results-oriented approach rather than formal controls; and
- to develop and extend the use of multimedia resources and leading-edge information technologies in order to improve management and communication, and to strengthen citizens' rights in relation to the administration.

B. Context affecting public management

Modernisation of public management therefore continues to be a priority and a challenge for Portugal. The modernisation drive is largely the result of:

- the strategic significance of the manifestly important functions of the public administration;
- the great economic importance of the public administration as a service provider and a consumer;
- the weight of the public administration in the labour market;

- pressure from within – more and more services of a higher standard – and from outside, especially having regard to European integration and the adoption of a single currency, requiring strict budgetary control of public spending.

These factors inevitably mean that even more attention has to be paid to public management reform in order to increase the productivity of the public services and improve the quality of the services provided to the public in general and to economic agents in particular.

One of the most important short-term factors is the strengthening of citizens' rights.

Key points with regard to developments in public management reform include the election of the new government led by António Guteres (Socialist Party) and approval of the Government Programme by the Assembly of the Republic.

C. Strategies and processes for planning and carrying out public management reforms

The composition of the new government indicates improved co-ordination between the bodies responsible for promoting public management reform. Following the creation of the Secretariat of State for Public Administration, under the Minister directly answerable to the Prime Minister, the Directorate General of Public Administration (DGAP), previously part of the Ministry of Finance, and the Secretariat for Administrative Modernisation (SMA) have been brought under the umbrella of this Secretariat of State. This has served to strengthen the role of government at the centre in this particular area.

In structural terms, another aspect that needs to be considered in Portugal is regionalisation, currently high on the political agenda, given its obvious repercussions on the organisation, size and functions of the public administration. In this context, the quantitative and qualitative role of the bodies currently promoting, monitoring and supervising public management will of course have to be redefined.

E. Human resources management

Of particular note, as far as human resources management is concerned, are the talks taking place at the moment between the government and the trade unions to address certain aspects of the rules governing the employment of public servants. The bargaining process is a complex one involving collective bargaining rights; the rules governing public service employment; career structures; remuneration and terms of employment of managerial staff; recruitment and selection; assessment; etc.

The process also includes an in-depth survey to obtain an accurate picture of current human resources in the public administration, in both quantitative and qualitative terms.

As far as the terms of employment of managerial staff are concerned, arrangements have been worked out to replace the current system of simple appointments with recruitment by competition (at least for grades three and four – department directors and heads of division).

F. Budget process and management of financial resources

The Ministry of Finance is finalising its Revenue Project, due to be launched by pilot schemes in January 1997.

The project includes two interactive systems, linked essentially by electronic communication: the revenue management system and the collection control system.

The benefits, when the whole project is fully up and running, will be:

- simplification of collection arrangements by means of a single collection document;
- decentralisation of the departments responsible for revenue administration, settlement and accounting;
- centralisation and integration of all information on State revenue budgeting and accounting; and
- integration of the Treasury and the financially autonomous departments.

The revenue management system will be implemented by a local application in revenue-administering departments and by another central application which will be the responsibility of the Directorate General of Public Accounts. The local system includes an accounting module, as well as a revenue administration module which will be used to produce the single collection document.

The collection control system also includes a local application in departments with "cashier" functions, and a central application which is the responsibility of the Directorate General of the Treasury.

G. Performance management

Programmes to improve quality in public services have been developed during 1995. One of these programmes, noteworthy because of its scope, is that covering the entire Ministry of Finance. Another aspect of the quality drive has been the Quality Charters which have been approved in various public services. These charters include specific service standards.

Improving service quality is also one of the aims of the management review which is due to start this year under the auspices of the Secretariat for Administrative Modernisation (SMA) and the Directorate General of Public Administration (DGAP). Among the actions taken in the field of new technology application, the following may be mentioned:

- development, improvement and extension to more access points in the country of the interdepartmental and citizen-oriented information system (INFOCID) and the increased importance to be given to the information service for business support (SIAE) component accessible on the Internet [http://www.infocid.pt];
- approval of legislation setting out the main rules for co-ordinating the use of information technologies in the public administration;
- participation in the Euro-Mail project, with the planned installation of a national server in the Informatics Institute for electronic mailing between the Portuguese public administration and other European administrations;
- organisation of the fourth meeting of information and computer systems managers in the public administration, entitled: "Information technologies – the right solutions for the public administration";
- publication of a technical computer security manual produced by the Informatics Institute and the National Security Authority; and
- development of a contracts management system module (SGC) as part of the reform of Public Accounting and the Treasury, to provide a computer tool for the financial control of public contracts.

H. Changing structures of the public sector

Regionalisation, which is considered a high priority on the reform agenda, is discussed in Section C above.

I.   Regulatory management and reform

Among the measures due to be implemented in 1996 in the field of regulatory reform is the initiative to encourage a reappraisal of all the regulations relating to procedures for issuing licences and permits required by central government (about 1 500). The aim is to modernise the legislation, abolish licence and permit requirements that are out of step with modern-day reality and, where appropriate, to delegate authority for these administrative procedures to other departments, other tiers of government or other private, non-profit organisations.

The year 1995 saw the start of the process of amending the Code of Administrative Procedure in the light of the lessons learnt over the three years it has been in force. The Code of Administrative Procedure was enacted as a government decree in 1991. However, it was made obligatory that the code would be reviewed and revised in 1995, so as to learn from its use and incorporate the results of practical experiences. This operation has been launched with the creation of a commission to evaluate the experience. The revision has now been completed.

Dr. José Fernando Orvalho Silva
Director
Secretariado para a Modernizaçáo Administrativa
(Secretariat for Administrative Modernisation)
Rua Almeida Brandáo, 7
P-1200 Lisbon
Tel.: (351-1) 392 15 32
Fax: (351-1) 392 15 99

Annex A

PRINCIPAL RECENT PUBLIC MANAGEMENT DEVELOPMENTS

1993

- Inauguration of the first INFOCID (interdepartmental and citizen-oriented information system) kiosks.
- Organisation of the first national "Quality in Public Service Awards".
- Organisation of the seminar "Quality in Public Services: Commitment to the Citizen" with the backing of the OECD Public Management Committee.
- Continued development of public accounting reform strategies.
- Publication of the "Public Service Deontological Charter".

1994

- Publication and presentation at meetings and seminars of the report "Renovating the Public Administration: a Challenge and Commitment" produced by the Commission for Quality and Rationalisation of the Public Administration. The report's proposals focused on four main areas for developing the process of modernising the public administration: withdrawal of the State, relations with citizens, organisational and managerial flexibility.
- Drafting, presentation and publication of the "Public Service Quality Charter", with the Prime Minister's personal backing.
- Organisation of the second seminar on new technologies in administrative modernisation.
- Continued implementation and development of public accounting reform strategies.
- Publication of a study on the impact of information technologies on the Portuguese public administration.
- Approval and implementation of PROFAP II (Integrated Programme for Training in Public Administrative Modernisation), jointly funded by the European Union.
- Development and improvement of INFOCID which now includes the SIAE (information service for business support).

1995

- Approval and publication of a number of Sectoral Quality Charters setting out the commitments of the respective public services to their customers.
- Continued extension of INFOCID to more access points in the country and new fields of information.
- Survey into the different procedures for issuing licences and permits (about 1 500) by central government, laying the foundations for a huge programme to cut down bureaucracy in this area.
- Organisation of a seminar on "Modernisation, Quality and Improvement of the Public Services", with the collaboration of the OECD PUMA Committee and the participation of 2 000 or so civil servants.
- Formation of a new government following the parliamentary elections. This government includes a Secretariat of State for Public Administration incorporated into the Presidency of the Council of Ministers; the main thrust of the government's programme in this area is to reduce bureaucracy, improve relations with the public, rationalise and improve management, vocational training, bargaining and interprofessional relations.
- Production by the PUMA Committee of a case study on the process of administrative modernisation in Portugal.

Annex B

INSTITUTIONAL RESPONSIBILITY FOR PUBLIC MANAGEMENT IMPROVEMENT

ORGANISATION	TASKS AND RESPONSIBILITIES	OTHER INFORMATION
Secretariat for Administrative Modernisation (SMA)	• steer modernisation, with focus on simplifying administrative procedures • introduce flexibility into personnel management • support the Quality Programme • INFOCID executive body	Created in 1986; under Secretary of State for Public Administration
Directorate General of Public Administration	• management of human resources and organisational adjustment • permanent system for controlling staff members	Now under the Secretary of State for Public Administration
Legal Centre (CEJUR)	• regulatory reform	Previously Technical Study and Legislative Support Centre (CETAL)
Informatics Institute	• introduction and use of information technologies	
Directorate General of Public Accounts	• reform and modernisation of State financial management • budgetary reform	
Court of Auditors	• control of public spending	Independent court

SPAIN

A. Main tendencies and overall priorities

Main tendencies and overall priorities include the following:

- promote the progress of the Autonomous Government by handing over more powers to the Autonomous Communities (ACs);

- adapt the State Government taking into account:
  - power reallocation with ACs;
  - meeting of the Maastricht criteria;
  - improvements in efficacy/efficiency.

- improve the quality of public services by means of an open, informative, participative assessment and public report.

B. Context affecting public management

The context includes:

- the modernisation and simplification of public administration, based upon an austerity deal, are main targets for the "*Partido Popular*" new government;
- the "Single Administration" ("*Administración Única*") is the key programme: avoiding duplications and establishing responsibilities in different levels of the Public Administration;
- the Government and Administration Act will be passed in the next months, and a Quality Plan will be implemented to evaluate the efficiency of Public Services;
- negotiation/agreement with Autonomous Communities.

C. Strategies and processes for planning and carrying out public management reforms

The following are some of the initiatives that are meant to improve management practices and quality of the services rendered:

a) Enactment of a Royal Decree (9 February 1996) that regulates the administrative information services and citizen information services, setting up a territorial net of offices in which the citizens can receive information, start administrative proceedings and submit initiatives and suggestions to improve the service quality. This rule also provides for the "Book of Complaints and Suggestions", that will always be available to the users of public services, as a means to receive and analyse what they think of them.

b) Publication in the State Official Journal and in other media of the "List of Practices of the State General Government", that contains the information about the most significant issues that concern citizens (rights, benefits, services, subject, regulations, effects, etc.) of almost 2 000 practices dealing with the daily activity of the State Government.

This List is supplemented with a computerised "Handbook of practices, benefits and services" which is transmitted though the territorial net of information offices, as well as through the so-called "information superhighway"; it facilitates the administrative operations carried out by the citizens, by giving them all the necessary information about all the matters concerning the State General Government, from any information office. Fourteen offices have been opened since.

c) As a means for the citizens to be able to reach all the levels of the government and as a co-operation tool between them, the Cabinet approved (13 March 1996) the bases for the Agreements with Local Corporations that allow the citizens to file documents and communications in the registries of the local bodies addressed to entities of the State government, therefore enabling its accessibility by the population living in rural or scattered areas.

Nine Agreements have been subscribed up to now and Agreements with 61 Town Councils of multiple provinces are being executed.

d) We must mention the Royal Decree (16 February 1996) that regulates the use of electronic, informatic and telematic techniques for the State General Government as an example of innovative applications of technologies, giving effect to the procedures and documents made with this type of media and supports; establishing the guarantees of use and enabling Government-citizen communication by technical means (fax, e-mail, etc.).

Throughout 1995 an initiative to promote better public service quality has been undertaken, acting through transparency, information, participation, assessment and publicity of results. This initiative lies in the preparation of a Royal Decree Bill on Letters of Services and Systems of Quality Assessment in the State Government.

The bill has not yet taken shape, but we think that it may set up a series of measures that will lead to the improvement and assessment of the quality of Spanish State Governments.

e) Finally, we should point out as an innovative initiative in this area, the creation, in December 1995, of a "Negotiating Table with the citizens", in which representatives of the Consumer and User Associations participate with the Ministry for Public Administration in the discussion and assessment of the quality of public services.

The most important reform initiatives related to information and communication technologies are the following:

a) Data Form to exchange information between governments.

A global data form has been defined for the governments (State general, autonomous and local) that functions as common reference for the exchange of information and that is the centre of the information systems in all the fields: internal system; population, economic management, contracts, taxes, territory, citizen protection, social services, documents management. This data form has been designed by nine Ministries, nine Autonomous Communities, 15 county councils, 26 town councils, 3 universities and 5 public companies. Its content is currently available on CD-ROM.

b) Message processing system to support the organisation.

This is a corporate e-mail used by governments, based in Rule X.400(88) for the exchange of messages and documents. The system currently has about 14 000 mail boxes connected through 30 nodes to the central MTA. There are currently six Autonomous Communities and 12 ministries connected, despite the fact that the system is still being implemented.

c) Technical Guides for the Acquisition of Computer Goods and Services.

Its aim is to facilitate the task of the public buyers with a tool that helps them draw up contracts on their technical, ruling and procedural matters. The guides are available in a software package for Windows®.

E. Human resources management

The most significant practices and initiatives carried out since 1993 can be summarised as follows:

a) Government-unions agreement about working conditions in the civil service.

This agreement was executed on 16 September 1994 and will be in force during 1995-97; it mainly refers to the following matters: wages (maintenance of purchasing power, negotiation of wage conditions), increase of productivity, public contracting policies within a limited budget, validation of temporary jobs, administrative career, inside promotion aids, financing of training programmes, training programmes offers, social activities, labour health and welfare benefits, working week and working hours, holidays, absenteeism and mixed bodies of government/unions participation.

The agreement means, in relation to wages, that the social negotiators accept linking civil servants' wage conditions to the development of economic factors and to the fact that the objectives established in the Convergence Programme are met.

Therefore, this involves that the implicit guarantee of maintaining the purchasing power of civil servants' wages will disappear and will be replaced by a system in which those very same wages are fixed according to how the financing forecasts of the general budgets are met, to how the increase of civil servants' productivity will be assessed and how the wages and employment will grow in the country as a whole.

b) Employment Plans

The existence of a limited budget makes it difficult for the government to rely on outsourcing; therefore, it has to manage more effectively its current human resources.

The employment plans are an initiative designed to optimise the government's human resources; they were established on 29 December by Law 22/1993, covering fiscal measures, reform of the civil service legal system, and unemployment benefits. The following measures may be included in an Employment Plan:

- forecasts for the change of organisational structures and jobs;
- no more outsourcing for the affected work-place;
- reallocation of surplus employees to other work-places that need personnel;
- creation of training and capability courses;
- authorisation of tenders to enable the mobility of personnel with a limited work-place;
- part-time jobs;
- specific internal promotion measures.

c) Enactment of new Access, Provision of Jobs and Professional Promotion Regulations (Royal Decree 364/1995, of 10 March) and Administrative Situations Regulation (365/1995, of 10 March).

The significant changes caused by the fiscal measures, the reform of the civil service legal system, and the unemployment benefits Law 22/1993 (of 29 December), came into force in order to improve human resources performance, subjecting its planning and management to more flexible and efficient strategies. In particular, the implementation of the Employment Plans required the reform and update of the rules that contained the regulations related to access to the civil service, administrative career, provision of jobs, and administrative situations of civil servants.

d) Ongoing Training Programmes

Since the approval of the government-unions Agreement of 16 September 1994, the civil servants become a party of the tripartite ongoing training agreements (government-trade unions and companies). These agreements deal with the use and allocation of the funds collected from certain taxes paid by the employees.

This involves the participation of all the administrative and social representatives in the preparation of an ongoing training programme as the best guarantee to obtain more efficient results and with the purpose of offering quality public services to the citizens.

The Ongoing Training General Committee is involved in the planning of these training programmes that are made up of specific training programmes that are set up by the different representatives involved and that contain the training actions which will be financed by the Ongoing Training Funds.

e) Resolution of 15 February 1996 of the State Secretary for Public Administration and the State Secretary for Finance for re-entry into active service and allocation of jobs.

This Resolution streamlines the existing procedures applied to approve re-entry into active service of those civil servants who were in different administrative situations so that such re-entry is made by fulfilling similar requirements in all the Ministries.

f) Regulation for personnel working for the Post Office Autonomous Body (Royal Decree 1638/1995 of 6 October).

This Regulation carries out the adaptation of the civil service regulation to the special characteristics of the management of this autonomous body.

g) Human Resources Documentary Data Bases

The General Directorate of Civil Service of the Ministry for Public Administration has been offering since 1993 the human resources managers of the different Ministries and the marginal governments a service that enables access by CD-ROM to the criteria that, due to a great number of consultations related to human resources, have been set up by the General Directorate of Civil Service, as well as many judgements of the Courts of Justice on the same matter.

h) Access of nationals of other member States of the European Union to certain sectors of the Spanish civil service.

During 1993 a rule classified as Law (17/1993) was enacted, and was later extended by a Regulation which, under article 48 of the Treaty of Rome, allows the access of nationals of other member States of the European Union to certain sectors of the Spanish Civil Service: post office, health care, education and research.

i) Government-unions agreement on the arrangements for negotiation of the government collective bargaining agreements of 7 February 1995.

With this agreement we try to group and unify as far as possible the labour relationships of the personnel working for the government by fixing minimum criteria that must be met by all the collective bargaining agreements executed in different sectors.

j) Follow-up of the implementation of coexisting official languages in the marginal governments.

By issuing an annual report, the Directorate General of Civil Service of the Ministry for Public Administration analyses the degree of implementation of the languages that, together with the Spanish language, coexist officially in Spain: Basque, Galician, Valencian and Majorcan languages.

F.   Budget process and management of financial resources

The actions of the officials in charge of public finance in Spain, during the latest fiscal years and in their middle term forecasts, both during the previous and present political terms, are focused on the fulfilment of the objectives set up in the reviewed Convergence Programme, whose implementation in relation to the budget started in 1994, was stressed in 1995 and is reinforced by the extension of this budget for 1996.

The main objective of this programme involves the reduction of the deficit from 7.5 per cent reached in 1993 to 3.0 per cent in 1997 with a decrease of 4.5 points during that period. This required and will require important measures in order to obtain a greater rigour and efficiency in budget control. The most important are the following:

– prohibition of recognising monetary obligations exceeding the credits approved, establishment of limits and monthly control by departments thereof, and the automatic offset of lower revenues and excess costs; application to the deficit of any excess economic rights;
– co-responsibility agreements with the Autonomous Communities to restrain the deficit, adopting similar measures to those taken by the central government;
– in 1995 and 1996 credit reserves are established to offset costs variations and certain credit residuary funds are declared unavailable.

The Convergence Programme objectives that led the economic-budgetary actions of the outgoing government have been taken again by the new government following the 3 March elections, which seeks to meet the desired objectives by taking new and significant measures that can be summarised as follows:

– restructuring and streamlining of administrative structures from the budgetary point of view of reducing costs and improving efficiency;
– promotion and reinforcement of the means to control costs, emphasizing the State General Control and creating a Budget and Costs Secretary, and a Budget Bureau directly run by the President, that must advise on the establishment of the budget policy and enforcement control;
– preparation of a new Budget General Law.

The measures involve more deregulation and preservation, with a tendency to reduce taxation, promote tax bases by improving management activity and the fight against fraud, reorganisation and reduction of subsidies and tax costs, that together with the cutbacks may meet the Convergence Programme objectives.

G.   Performance management

See the information in Section C above.

H. Changing structures of the public sector

Decentralisation implications for central management include the following:

a) Structures

The decentralisation in favour of the Autonomous Communities is a gradual process that started in 1978 and is not finished completely yet, even though it is in a very advanced stage today. There is no doubt that the decentralisation process required and will require in the future a new organic adaptation of the general government (hereinafter, central government); however, we have to bear in mind the fact that decentralisation being a gradual process, it involves a slow adaptation of the structures. Changes to the central government are still occurring, therefore, in relation to the matters being transferred to the Autonomous Communities, affecting their size and functions.

The future role of the different structures of the central government shall be of a specific nature according to the administrative functions assigned to each of them, but, in general, these are the main tendencies:

- preparation of normative projects and establishment are important measures, in those matters that constitutionally are assigned to the State;
- guarantee that all Spaniards have equal rights, irrespective of the Autonomous Community or municipality where they live;
- preservation of international relations and especially with the European Union, with respect to the configuration of the Spanish stance and the guarantee of compliance with community law;
- promotion and preservation of co-ordination functions and arrangement of co-operation mechanism functions, settling the necessary means to guarantee interterritorial communication;
- promotion of the use of new techniques and procedures, in general and in the different administrative performance areas, carrying out surveys which concern the territory as a whole.

b) Inter-administrative co-ordination and collaboration

- The development of a decentralised State, called "Autonomous State" in Spain, can bring about serious communication difficulties between the governments.

These difficulties, however, are characteristic of a first stage in the development of this pattern, and solutions have been sought and found throughout the years. Gradually, the government has been promoting and developing the collaboration principle, with a double sense, as a guideline to the political behaviour and as an interadministrative co-operation technique. This principle has been developed by the meetings of 24 Local Conferences; they are co-operation bodies in which the central government and the governments of the 17 Autonomous Communities take part, chaired by the corresponding minister, and where the main issues of interest for both parties, needing the collaboration of both governments, are discussed.

With respect to local government, the pattern is not homogeneous because the power resides in the Autonomous Community and the dimensions and needs of the local government are different for each Autonomous Community, and for each material sector of administrative measures.

- The meetings of the co-operation bodies mentioned have established the so-called Local Conferences, as well as the support bodies thereof. They consider local policies in which the central government and the Autonomous Community governments take part. In these policies, usually considered as plans or programmes, the interested governments reach an agreement to avoid double administrations with respect to objectives and activities to be done, co-financing and the creation of follow up and assessment mechanisms of the policies that are being carried out.

- As a complement to the discussions of Local Conferences, a significant increase in the number of meetings of these Local Conferences can be seen in recent years, as well as greater detail in the issues dealt with. Therefore, it is common that the central government informs the Autonomous Communities about measures and the European Union's plans, so the Autonomous Communities are heard prior to the formulation of the Spanish stance. Likewise, it is common that the details of the main normative projects of the State are discussed with the Autonomous Communities prior to action by the legislative bodies, even where it is clearly a State matter.

- Obviously, the need or convenience to carry out these consultations affects the role given to the central government, so that by the existing collaboration mechanisms it carries out the task of aggregating or adding the corresponding interests of the different regional governments.

c) Outlook for the administrative system as a whole. We can take into account the following three issues:

- The need to create a financing system of the Autonomous Communities in which the "tax co-responsibility" principle is met. That is, not only that the Autonomous Communities be responsible for the costs of the finance amounts handed over by the central government, but also the collection of these amounts. This issue is specially important in relation to health costs of the Autonomous Communities.

- Even though it is not an administrative but basically a political matter, the need to complete the transfer of means and services to the Autonomous Communities. Even though this issue has been supported in recent years, it is essential to complete the process before the central government is rearranged.

- The need to limit and determine the role of the municipalities in relation to the Autonomous Communities. Nevertheless, this is not felt with the same intensity in all issues, only in some, and only affects some municipalities, especially the most important municipalities and those with greater social claims.

d) Organisational Restructuring with significant effect on the economic public sector.

- Autonomy Law of the Bank of Spain. This was approved in 1994 but it is included herein due to its importance. Its aim is to give the Bank of Spain the autonomy that the Maastricht Treaty gave the monetary institutions that will make up the European system of Central Banks.

- Creation of the National Electronic System Commission as a regulating body of the national electric system that will control the objectivity and openness of its operation.

- Elimination of the National Institute of Industry and the National Institute of Hydrocarbons and their replacement by two new bodies: the Industrial State Agency and the State Association of Industrial Corporations. The object of this restructuring is to globally rationalise the management of the public industrial corporations. The Agency is in charge of the companies subject to restructuring plans or industrial reorganisation, or companies partially not subject to the system of free competition established by the EU. The State Association is made up of corporations run by the State and the remaining public companies that were previously managed by the eliminated bodies.

- Elimination of two public entities in charge of the allocation of community subsidies related to agricultural policy and their replacement by a new entity, called the Spanish Agricultural Guarantee Fund, as a co-ordinating public entity established to finance the common agricultural policy, in charge of the negotiations with the European Commission and the enforcement of community regulations.

Mr. Emilio Casals Peralta
Advisor for International Affairs
Ministry for Public Administration (MAP)
Paseo de la Castellana
E-28046 Madrid
Tel.: (34) 1 586 11 95
Fax: (34) 1 586 10 18

Annex A

PRINCIPAL RECENT PUBLIC MANAGEMENT DEVELOPMENTS

1988

– Beginning of the activities of the Conference of European Issues as a co-ordinating body between the central government and the Autonomous Communities related to the community process.

1990

– Approval of two Agreements, one of them for the regulation of the Autonomous Communities' participation in State actions in precontencious proceedings before the European Commission and in issues related to the European Court of Justice, and another about State Subsidies.

1992

– Autonomous Agreements of 28 February 1992 to extend the powers of the Autonomous Communities that became autonomous under Art. 143 of the Spanish Constitution, and had to wait a period of time in order to extend their power level.
– Transfer of the Autonomous Communities' powers Organic Law 9/1992 of December 1992.
– Institutionalisation Agreement of the Conference of European Issues of 29 October 1992.

1993

– Completion of the first stage of the State Government Modernisation Plan.
– Ministry rearrangement after the general elections, with 16 Ministries.
– Creation of the Data Protection Agency as an independent body in charge of the enforcement of data protection laws.
– Law 16/1993 of 23 December, that introduces Directive 91/250/EEC of 14 May 1991 on legal protection of software to Spanish law.
– Filing of the first two reports of the Public Service Quality Control Agencies (April and December).

1994

– Reform of the Statutes of Autonomy of the Autonomous Communities that became autonomous under article 143, (Asturias, Cantabria, La Rioja, Murcia, Aragón, Castilla-La Mancha, Extremadura, Baleares, Madrid and Castilla-León).
– Agreements of the Conference of European Issues related to the approval of internal rules, extension of its powers to the activities outside the Autonomous Communities, especially to the relationship with the European Council and to the internal participation of the Autonomous Communities in the European issues through Local Conferences.
– Government-Unions Agreement, on labour conditions that affect wages increase, negotiation of collective bargaining agreements, ongoing training, social action plan, etc.
– Establishment of Labour Plans to rationalise the use of human resources in the Government and upgrade its performance.
– Bank of Spain's Autonomy Law pursuant to the Maastricht Treaty on Central Banks' autonomy.

- Reduction of the number of Ministries from 16 to 15, unifying the Ministries of Justice and Internal Affairs.
- Royal Decree 1332/1994 of June 20 by which certain aspects of the Organic Law 5/1992 of October 29 on Regulation of the Computerised Processing of Personal Data is developed.
- Second stage of the State General Government Modernisation Plan, with 165 projects planned based on four strategic measures: information improvement to citizens, improvement of service quality, rationalisation measures of internal management and efficacy and costs reduction measures.
- Third Report of the Public Service Quality Control Agency (April). Submitted to the Parliament and to the media.

1995

- Approval of the Statutes of Autonomy of Ceuta and Melilla, Organic Laws 1/1995 and 2/1995 of 13 March respectively.
- Elimination of the National Institute of Industry and the National Institute of Hydrocarbons, replaced by the State Industrial Agency and the State Association of Industrial Corporations, to rearrange the management of the State corporations into public companies.
- Establishment of a Spanish Agricultural Guarantee Fund to co-ordinate the European financing of the common agricultural policy.
- Government Contract Law that includes the community directives related to contracts.
- Approval of Law 12/1995 of 11 May, that regulates the incompatibility system of the government staff and the senior officials of the State general government.
- Approval of Royal Decree 1410/1995 of 4 August, that regulates the registries of senior officials' activities, property and patrimony rights.
- Fourth Report of the Public Service Quality Control Agency (December). Sent to the Parliament and submitted to the media and, consumer and user associations.
- In order to develop the co-operation principle (central government-regional governments), certain steps have been taken to promote, improve the operation and new creation, in some cases, of Local Conferences, as bodies that develop the co-operation principle. Currently, there are 24 Local Conferences that have held 145 meetings throughout the year. These first level bodies are complemented by other supporting bodies – specialised commissions –, up to a total of 383 co-operation bodies.
- Other essential co-operation tools are the collaboration agreements. 1070 agreements have been subscribed with the Autonomous Communities during 1992/95.
- Transfer process to the Autonomous Communities of, in the Autonomous Agreements scope of 1992, the exclusive powers, legislative and executive development powers or just the executive powers related to: broadcasting; mines; civil engineering; gambling; associations; show business; co-operatives; labour law; international fairs; foundations; welfare benefits; universities, rural development, official or professional associations; etc. This process has been completed in the period 1993/95 with 204 transfers involving 207 446 million in material and 13 788 workers, respectively, excluded from this latter case, the employees directly working for the universities.

Annex B

INSTITUTIONAL RESPONSIBILITY FOR PUBLIC MANAGEMENT IMPROVEMENT

ORGANISATION	TASKS AND RESPONSIBILITIES	OTHER INFORMATION
Ministry for Public Administration (MAP)	• promotion of administrative modernisation • improvement of citizen-administration relations	For policy on salaries, these two ministries exercise joint responsibility specifically for remuneration of posts occupied by officials, and for the supervision of remuneration for employees as established in collective agreements
Ministry of the Economy and Finance	• prepares the State budget • controls public expenditure, including salaries of public servants	

SWEDEN

A. Main tendencies and overall priorities

Owing to Sweden's economic difficulties of late, reforming the budget process is among the most important reforms of administrative policy. Management of public administration by results has undergone and is undergoing further development. Delegation of decision-making power from the government to the agencies with respect to the funds for attaining their objectives has been far-reaching, and comprises organisation, staff, premises and the utilisation of financial resources. Simultaneously, major changes in the agencies' structure have been implemented during the 1990s, in such forms as the corporatisation of State-owned enterprises.

The municipalities, which have been given greater freedom from the State in terms of finances and organisation over the past few years, have in turn decentralised decision-making to committees and boards.

In several areas of importance for administrative policy, evaluations are currently under way. These relate to the forms for organisation and control of public administration, the work of municipal modernisation and also a new Organisation for State Employers. the forms for organisation and control of public administration are being evaluated by a Public Management commission which is due to release its report in Spring 1997. Its task is to assess if the current forms for organisation and control of the public administration in the State are in line with the goals adopted by the government and the *Riksdag* (the Swedish Parliament). It is also expected to present its views concerning the direction of the long-term work on structural change in the public administration.

B. Context affecting public management

Public administration is facing new challenges. The situation in public finances demands better management of the resources that are available. Internationalisation is modifying the preconditions for work in public administration. New, more complex social problems require different types of input and new working methods. Greater quality and flexibility in public services are being required as a result of the overall development of society.

During the early 1990s, Sweden underwent a period of sharp deterioration in general economic trends. Results of this include major deficits in public finances and a massive increase in government debt. In the light of this situation, the government and *Riksdag* have resolved on certain budget policy restrictions, guided partly by the European Union convergence (Maastricht) criteria for the European Monetary Union.

The following budget policy objectives will govern the scope of the public sector over the next few years:

– the debt ratio (government debt as a proportion of GDP) is to be stabilised in 1996;
– the deficit in public-sector financial saving will not be permitted to exceed 3 per cent of GDP in 1997;
– public finances are to be in balance by the year 1998.

The scope for further tax rises is severely limited.

C.   **Strategies and processes for planning and carrying out public management reforms; and**

D.   **Policy-management capacities**

Strategies for public management reform and main initiatives affecting policy-management capacities are the evaluations referred to in Section A and the budgetary and financial reforms highlighted as priorities in Sections A, B and F.

E.   **Human resources management**

New leadership policy

At the beginning of 1995 the Swedish government adopted a more distinct leadership policy, and formulated a strategy for the recruitment, induction, continuous leadership training and mobility of senior officials in public administration. This policy is to focus mainly on the heads of government agencies, since these are government-appointed. Other appointments, including those of Deputy Directors-General, should in most cases be delegated to the agencies.

One specific element in the government's leadership programme is to intensify and develop contacts between ministers and government agencies' heads through a regular *dialogue concerning goals and results*. This is a very important instrument for the government's control of the agencies within the framework of the new budget process. The dialogue takes the form of regular discussions and concerns the goals of the agency's activities, the results achieved, their impact and costs, etc. In addition, areas of strategic importance for the agency's future activities are discussed and defined. Other matters discussed include the personal situation of the agency's head, plans for the future and the need for further leadership training.

New concept of employer co-operation

As a consequence of the greater responsibility for human resources management laid upon the agencies, the government has decided to charge them with substantially increased responsibility for their collective employer's role. In 1994, the government restructured the Swedish Agency for government Employers as an agency formed, directed and financed by the other government agencies. Consequently, the government and *Riksdag* no longer directly influence the content of collective agreements establishing salaries and other general terms of employment for government employees. The new organisation is thought to strengthen the employer's position in central negotiations, since it enjoys strong collective support from the agencies.

A new agreement on general terms of employment has also been signed. This provides scope for modernisation, adjustment to local business conditions, fewer and less detailed regulations, and simplification. It also allows for single agencies to determine their own level of pay rises and scope for pay distribution.

F.   **Budget process and management of financial resources**

Over the past few years, Sweden's *Riksdag* and government have taken several decisions aimed at reforming and strengthening the budget process, and this endeavour should also be regarded as an element in the work of improving public finances, which is an area highlighted as a priority in Sections A and B. One such decision is to introduce a *framework-budget model* for handling budget proposals in the *Riksdag*. The model means that the *Riksdag* will first decide on the overall level of spending and then determine its distribution among various purposes. A decision has also been taken that the government's budget proposals should come within a set *expenditure ceiling* for the public sector. This expenditure ceiling is defined in nominal terms, spans three years, and covers the entire public sector (the State excluding interest payments on government debt, social-insurance schemes and the municipalities). For the State sector, it is divided into spending areas. As far as the municipalities are concerned, the expenditure ceiling rests on an agreement between the government and the municipal sector. With the introduction of the ceiling, open-ended or draft appropriations as a form of appropriation have been abolished.

For some time, all the agencies have been providing annual and interim reports, and there is also monthly and quarterly monitoring of expenditure in real terms against the national budget. The annual reports include both performance reports and financial statements. The entire annual report is audited by the National Audit Office. The observations of the audit have been reported to the *Riksdag* since 1994. This has had a highly beneficial effect on the government agencies' financial behaviour. An annual report for the State is submitted to the *Riksdag* annually.

G. Performance management

Experience to date shows that the reforms concerning management by results were necessary, and that the new forms of control have provided a better basis for the government's continuous monitoring of State activities. Management by results has had the greatest impact when it comes to the government's control of the agencies' administrative appropriations within the framework of the budget process. Attempts are under way to apply management by results to transfers and other specific-purpose appropriations to a greater extent.

The documentation that the government receives from the agencies as a basis for its reassessment of activities is not yet, however, fully satisfactory. Experience of formulating objectives shows that the general objectives can easily be defined, but that the difficulties lie in breaking them down into targets that are sufficiently specific and capable of being followed up. These difficulties may be partially surmounted if management by results is now *adapted to activities* to a greater extent. Central regulatory frameworks must exist in order to make the behaviour of the government Chancery and the agencies fundamentally uniform. Such a framework has been put in place in the form of the Government Ordinance Concerning the Annual Reports of State Agencies, etc. These sets of regulations, however, have recently been changed in order to be flexible enough to permit the instruments of management to be adapted to the distinct conditions of the various activities. The government is conducting a pilot project involving adaptation of management by results to specific authorities. Experience is largely positive. The ambition is for the management prescribed in the Government approval document for the year 1997 to be adapted to activities and improved.

Information Technology

The government has resolved that the provision of information in the Swedish public administration over the next few years should be characterised by:

- an open electronic infrastructure, as a joint basis for establishing information systems for public administration;
- efficient information systems that create opportunities for structural changes in public administration, while simultaneously enabling urgent social needs to be met in a better way;
- general sectorial overviews of agencies' information processing and use;
- new forms for collecting and disseminating information that make things easier not only for the agencies but, importantly, for the providers and recipients of information;
- consideration of the requirements imposed on the agencies' information processing in European co-operation regarding public administration; and
- simultaneous consideration of the stringent requirements concerning security and protection for personal integrity.

H. Changing structures of the public sector

Structural changes

The rate of change in the State sector is now very rapid. This has applied particularly since the beginning of the 1990s. Demands for modernisation and greater economy have helped to bring about major changes in the organisation and functioning of the State more rapidly than ever before. Such changes have involved abolishing, amalgamating and corporatising government agencies. Part of this work has been the task of finding the right forms for State activity. It has been decided that this should take place in agency form. In exceptional cases, when this form is not suitable, limited companies or non-profit-making associations are to be used. More is said about other aspects of agencies in the sections above.

Corporatisation is the type of change that has the greatest financial and staff consequences. This category includes several of the major State-owned enterprises that have become limited companies (including the Swedish National Defence Factories, the Swedish State Power Board, Swedish Telecom and Sweden Post). Approximately 100 000 employees have been concerned by the corporatisation. The foremost motives for corporatisation have in most cases been to improve the scope for running the activity more efficiently on a competitive market, and to obtain a better yield on what are, in many cases, the large amounts of capital managed. To guarantee competitive neutrality, independent supervisory agencies have been created for the telecommunications, postal service, and electricity markets.

The municipalities

Important reforms in the structure of local government have been implemented in the 1990s. The new Local Government Act entitles all the municipalities to choose their own organisational structure. Another change is the new State funding system, whereby numerous special State grants for certain activities have been combined in a general State grant. This has permitted local priorities to dictate the use of State grants, without the State imposing any restrictions. It should also be made clear that the switch to general grants has been linked with a general reduction in State grants to the municipalities.

Since 1992, several steps have been taken to modify the division of responsibility between different levels of government. The principle has been established that all transfers of responsibility between the State and the municipal level should be subject to comprehensive financial regulation. Improved follow-up systems regarding local activities and finances have been introduced at national level. In a few cases, where local variations are undesirable or more efficient administration might be expected, centralisation has taken place.

The assembly – *i.e.* the central decision-making body in a municipality and county council with the task of deciding on matters of principle, etc. – is free to vest in a committee the power to decide in all other matters. In the past few years, many municipalities have decentralised most of their powers to committees and boards.

Under Swedish law, legal authority regarding resident individuals and firms must be exercised by the municipality. All other matters, such as technical services, may be contracted out. In a few cases, almost all activities in the technical-service sector have been contracted out to private firms. In most cases, services of this kind were previously produced largely by public enterprises, but in the past few years private companies have increasingly entered the market. In the past five years, State regulations have been changed to allow education, child care, care of the elderly, etc., to be run by private contractors. In these sectors, some six per cent of total service volume is currently being provided by private producers under contract. In many cases, this has reduced costs for the service contracted out, and boosted productivity in the municipal organisation.

Joint efforts on the part of the State, municipalities and county councils have been initiated to modernise public administration through greater use of information technology. The purpose is to eliminate various types of obstacles and pave the way for rational and reliable use of information technology in public administration.

I.   Regulatory management and reform

Extensive work on improving the quality of regulation has been in progress for several years. This work encompasses laws and government ordinances, and also the agencies' statutes. The work is shaped by current political and administrative concerns, and is part of the endeavour to achieve management by objectives and results. The work is gradually more influenced by similar work carried out within the EU.

At present, employment and balance in public finances are two of the primary underlying concerns of this policy.

The work follows a programme to improve the quality of regulation manifested in a "Checklist for Rule-makers".

Mr. Per Högberg
Principal Administrative Officer
Ministry of Finance
Drottninggatan 21
S-10333 Stockholm
Tel.: (46-8) 405 14 36
Fax: (46-8) 24 62 13

Annex A

PRINCIPAL RECENT PUBLIC MANAGEMENT DEVELOPMENTS

1993

- Government's introduction of the following changes in its financial control of the agencies:
  - a new accrual-accounting model;
  - the frame-appropriation technique;
  - interest accounts; and
  - a loan model for investments in fixed assets.
- Government's adoption of criteria for corporatisation of State activities.

1994

- *Riksdag* resolution on a framework-budget model for its own budget work; first resolution on a four-year mandate; resolution that the government should normally appoint only an agency's head; new Organisation for State Employers *controlled* and financed by government agencies.

1995

- *Riksdag* resolution in principle that the government's budget proposals be submitted in the form of an expenditure ceiling for the public sector; government adopts new leadership policy; new agreement for the State labour market providing scope for modernisation, etc.; pilot project of adapting management by results of agencies to their activities; government lays down principles for suitable forms of state activity.

1996

- *Riksdag* resolution on implementation of expenditure ceiling.

Annex B

INSTITUTIONAL RESPONSIBILITY FOR PUBLIC MANAGEMENT IMPROVEMENT

ORGANISATION	TASKS AND RESPONSIBILITIES	OTHER INFORMATION
Ministry of Finance	• budgetary reform, budget development, personnel policy, salaries, pensions • overall responsibility and co-ordination of public management reforms	An independent Expert Group on Public Finance (ESO) conducts studies related to budgetary and economic policy-making (*e.g.* productivity in the public sector).
– Swedish Agency for Administrative Development (SK)	• public sector review and reform in general • implementation of public management reforms at agency level	
– Swedish Agency for Government Employers (AgV)	• employer policy responsibility • collective agreements, establishing salaries and other terms of employment for government employees	
– National Audit Bureau (RRV)	• development of methods regarding result-based management	
Ministry of Justice	• regulatory quality and handbooks	
Ministry of Interior	• regional and local administration, community development, consumer protection	
Ministry of Industry and Commerce	• regulatory reviews and reforms aiming to a better functioning market	

Annex C

KEY PUBLIC DOCUMENTS ON PUBLIC MANAGEMENT ISSUES AND DEVELOPMENTS

Swedish Local Government – Sören Häggroth mfl.

The Swedish Local Government Act – Ds 1995:19.

Structure and Operation of Local and Regional Democracy: Sweden, Council of Europe, 1994.

Papers on public sector budgeting and management, Budget Department, Swedish Ministry of Finance: Vol. 1: *In search of results and financial incentives*, 1994; Vol. 2: *Annual performance accounting and auditing in Sweden*, 1995; Vol. 3: *Productivity in the public sector in Sweden*, forthcoming 1996.

Governing Sweden, Swedish Agency for Administrative Development, Torbjörn Larsson, 1995.

The Public Sector Labour Market in Sweden, Swedish Ministry of Finance.

Top Managers' Forum, Joint-action to modernise public administration with assistance of IT, Swedish Ministry of Finance.

Leadership in Government Administration, Swedish Ministry of Finance, 1995.

Productivity Trends in the Public Sector in Sweden, Expert Group on Public Finances, 1996.

SWITZERLAND

A. Main tendencies and overall priorities

The impetus for reform of the federal State, its government and its administration is the Federal Council's determination to strengthen its role as the supreme executive authority of Switzerland. In particular, the Council's intention is to bolster its operations as a collegiate governing body.

There are two phases to this vast project, the first consisting in reorganising federal executive power, the second in reapportioning responsibilities between the federal State and the cantons and among the legislative, executive and judicial branches of the federal government.

"Governmental Reform 1993" ("GR93") is the name of the first phase, the essential aim of which is to relieve the Federal Council of routine or technical tasks, thereby enabling it to devote more time to policy issues. The other component of GR93 involves redistributing tasks within the Federal Council, whose members head government departments and the Federal Chancellery, and bringing working methods up to date. As a result, a new style of public management has been making its way into the Swiss federal administration.

GR93 will culminate in a new law on the organisation of the government and the administration (LOGA), investing the Federal Council with the powers and resources it needs. The Council will, in particular, be authorised to transfer tasks amongst its members without having to seek parliamentary approval. It is also proposed to give service mandates to administrative units and institute Secretaries of State to relieve the burden on Federal Councillors.

This last item met with such opposition that the LOGA was voted down in a popular referendum on 9 June 1996. Even so, driven by the imperative need to consolidate federal finances, the political authorities have manifested their determination to carry out the reforms to the end. This is why the government is pursuing its efforts, preparing the legislative amendments that are needed but that are also acceptable to Parliament and Swiss citizens alike.

Governmental reform is therefore continuing to focus on the following four major areas:

- redistributing the portfolios of members of the Federal Council, thereby instituting a new division of powers within a collegiate body that brings together representatives of Switzerland's leading political forces;
- issuing the first service mandates, which *inter alia* would mean greater delegation and so-called overall budget management;
- introducing the principles of new public management into each sector, to enhance the transparency of federal government operations and respond better to the expectations of citizens as taxpayers and service users;
- adapting senior administrative offices and control bodies to the restructuring and new working methods stemming from the reforms.

It should be noted that all of these endeavours require a number of legislative or regulatory changes that go further than the aforementioned LOGA.

The second phase will lead to a revision of the federal constitution. This has already begun, with consultations on a draft new constitution which has aroused an unexpected amount of interest, some 10 000 members of the public and 500 organisations and associations having taken part in the discussions.

It is noteworthy that the cantons and governmental political parties seem to approve the thrust of the revision. In particular, the proposed constitution would transfer a number of tasks from the federal authorities to the cantons and bring the rights of the people more into line with a changing population; at the same time, it would make laws of greater complexity subject to a vote by the people in their sovereign capacity.

The houses of Parliament will, in the autumn of 1996, be formally presented with a message from the Federal Council in support of the new constitution that they will be called upon to adopt.

B.   Context affecting public management

C.   Strategies and processes for planning and carrying out public management reforms; and

D.   Policy-management capacities

Information given in Section A, applies also to Sections B, C and D.

E.   Human resources management

There can be no administrative reorganisation without updating personnel management tools. An important first step in this direction was taken when the 1927 law governing the status of civil servants was partially revised. The chief amendments, which entered into force on 1 January 1996, were the following:

– pay mechanisms were made more flexible, in particular through the introduction of merit-related components (opportunities for individual rewards and performance-related adjustment of ordinary increases);
– a joint body was created to hear appeals of initial decisions involving performance-related components of pay;
– delegation of authority was strengthened with regard to staff appointments and promotions;
– a legal framework for personnel management measures was created ready for any restructuring of services.

In conjunction with these changes, the Federal Office of Personnel dispensed unique, tailor-made training for managers in the federal administration. The goal of this training was essentially to teach management techniques involving the setting of objectives – an essential corollary to performance-related pay. Other further training courses for civil service managers focus on interviewing techniques and other vital tools for personnel administration.

F.   Budget process and management of financial resources

The proposed review of subsidies

Section 5 of the federal law that governs financial aid and allowances (the Subsidies Act) requires the Federal Council to conduct periodic reviews (at least every six years) of all financial aid and allowances, to ensure that subsequent legislation complies with the principles of the Act. The Federal Department of Finance (FDF) is responsible for the reviews, in association with the other government departments. Preparation of the reviews themselves, as well as of reports on their outcomes, is delegated to the Federal Finance Administration. In 1995, federal subsidies amounted to SF 25 billion, or 5/8 of aggregate federal expenditure.

The Federal Finance Administration's objectives for the review were as follows:

– The first step, as an essential starting point for a systematic review, would be to draw up an exhaustive and detailed list of all subsidies (including a whole series of tax concessions). Each subsidy would be described in terms of its main characteristics (type, amount, recipient, purpose, rate of subsidy, method of intervention, etc.).

– The review itself would be conducted in accordance with the criteria laid down in Section 6 et sequence of the Subsidies Act, and with the help of the relevant specialised services.

– The review/evaluation of subsidies would show:
  • where the basic legislation needed to be amended;
  • where amounts could be reduced or effectiveness increased;
  • how changes could be effected.

– Review of all subsidies would be completed in 1997.

In the spring of 1996, the Federal Finance Administration finished recording all of the data and established a new system for the retrieval of information about subsidies that is comprehensive, transparent and up to date. About 500 subsidies were entered. The evaluation proper is to be carried out in two stages, owing to the large number of federal subsidies as well as a shortage of available manpower. Each subsidy is to be evaluated in terms of the following aspects:

– Preconditions (*inter alia*, the benefits to Switzerland, the division of tasks between the federal government and recipients, the personal contributions required of applicants, how tasks would be carried out if financial aid were absent).

– Conditions of implementation (*inter alia*, a minimum of expense and of administrative formalities, services performed by recipients themselves, time limits, effectiveness and efficiency of outcomes, whether the amount of aid could be set in the aggregate or on a flat rate basis).

An initial partial report will be submitted to the Federal Council in the autumn of 1996, containing an exhaustive list of subsidies and the results and proposals arising from the first reviews.

This first step in the evaluation process has shown that over 85 per cent of the subsidies examined require some sort of change (elimination, transfer to the cantons, reduction of contribution rates, time limits, introduction of flat rate amounts or overall solutions, tighter management, further evaluation, a new division between the Confederation and the cantons, and so on).

The new financial equalisation project

Financial ties between the Confederation and the cantons are complex and entangled. The main problems that have come to light are a widening of financial disparities between cantons, an absence of specific policy objectives in the realm of financial equalisation, an over-centralised system of transfers, overlapping jurisdiction between the Confederation and the cantons, diminished cantonal autonomy for performing tasks and using resources, and a system of subsidies that on the whole is not very effective. A fundamental overhaul of the system is imperative.

In 1994, the Federal Council gave the go-ahead for work on a new system of financial equalisation. To date, the project has been carried out by the Federal Department of Finance in tandem with the Conference of Cantonal Finance Directors.

Guidelines for the reform were presented to the Federal Council in March 1996 and submitted for consultation. The Council will take further decisions as to the project's future in the autumn of 1996. The broad outline of the reform is as follows:

– Relations between the Confederation and the cantons in the realm of financial policy should be based as much as possible on the principle of subsidiarity:

● Cantonal tasks should be funded by the cantons and national tasks by the Confederation. Accordingly, a new division of tasks between the Confederation and the cantons is being proposed in some thirty areas.

● Whenever cantonal tasks are of benefit to more than one canton, the expenditure should be financed jointly by an association of those cantons.

● Where collaboration between the Confederation and the cantons is crucial, the respective role and powers of each level should be clarified. Tasks should be carried out more effectively, using appropriate collaborative mechanisms and types of subsidy. The Confederation's role should be limited to one of strategic leadership, while the cantons should enjoy wider operational latitude. Subsidies should be more general and linked to multi-year programmes.

– The cantons' financial capacity should be reinforced so that all of cantons are in a position to meet their own responsibilities, as the principle of subsidiarity demands.

● To this end, the portion of federal subsidies that is graduated according to ability to pay (which is not very effective from an equalisation standpoint and mixes up incentives and equalisation) should be replaced by unearmarked transfers targeted at the financially weakest cantons, so that they might attain a certain level of resources.

● A new system of intercantonal financial equalisation should be put in place – one that is politically manageable, effective and capable of keeping financial disparities between the cantons under control.

● Financial equalisation should be based on a new indicator that measures the cantons' potential financial resources.

Together, these reforms seek to revitalise federalism while promoting national cohesion thanks to a more effective system of financial equalisation. Moreover, by attributing tasks to a single level of government as clearly as possible and reforming the mechanisms of subsidy, substantial savings should be generated for the Confederation and the cantons alike.

G.   Performance management, and

H.   Changing structures of the public sector

In order to achieve greater efficiency and flexibility, the structure of the federal administration is to be updated in line with the principles of new public management (NPM). These principles lead to an organisational model that involves:

– Redefining the roles of policy management and administrative responsibility.

– Decentralising tasks, powers and responsibilities. The desired model is that of a "holding company" comprising four concentric circles. Offices and services of the administration would be "attributed" to a circle according to their need for legal and strategic autonomy, with the innermost circle grouping together services that perform tasks of co-ordination and direction, and the outermost containing joint public/private-sector enterprises and private firms that perform tasks assigned to the Confederation. The main focus of NPM is on services lying within the second circle, *i.e.* "agencies", managed by means of service mandates and overall budgets; these services have no legal personality of their own and remain entirely within the administrative sphere. The new steering instruments give them a measure of autonomy.

– Piloting services and outcomes.

– Strengthening the links between planning, implementation and control.

– Introducing elements of markets and competition.

On 7 March 1996, the Federal Council decided that preparation and implementation of NPM tools would constitute an ongoing project which would be co-ordinated with reform of the government and the administration. The Council therefore gave the go-ahead for management by means of service mandates and overall budgets. A number of trials have already been conducted in two pilot offices. Other such offices will be designated so as to initiate application of the principles of NPM in their respective sectors in 1997.

NPM constitutes an approach to staff development and to organisation that differs from traditional schemes for rationalisation and cost-cutting in public administration in that it is expected to improve productivity in the medium and the long term. In addition, it will lead to profound cultural changes and a transformation of staff motivation.

Mr. Beat Bürgi
Swiss Delegation to the OECD
28, rue de Martignac
75007 Paris
Tel.: +33 (1) 49 55 67 74
Fax: +33 (1) 45 51 01 49

Annex A

PRINCIPAL RECENT PUBLIC MANAGEMENT DEVELOPMENTS

1993

- The Federal Council's message regarding the new law on the organisation of the government and the administration (LOGA) is published.

1994

- The continued existence of the Federal Council's Administrative Control Service, which was created in 1990, is confirmed, in accordance with its mandate.
- A governmental reform delegate is appointed by the Federal Council.

1995

- The Federal Council sets general rules for the delegation of tasks and powers at the federal level and launches a programme to bring all regulations in line with the new rules.
- The Federal Council gives itself the means for systematic and periodic control of the tasks of all bodies placed under its supervision, thereby amending the mandate of its Administrative Control Service.
- The Federal Council issues a supplementary report on the LOGA.
- Guidelines for the State's future service contracts are adopted, and the first bodies to enter into such contracts are stipulated.

1996

- In June, the LOGA was rejected in a referendum because of the Secretaries of State it would create.
- The final EFFI-QM report is submitted, and the Federal Council so informs the parliamentary management committees.

Annex B

INSTITUTIONAL RESPONSIBILITY FOR PUBLIC MANAGEMENT IMPROVEMENT*

ORGANISATION	TASKS AND RESPONSIBILITIES	OTHER INFORMATION
Federal Council	• responsibility for reform	Presentation to Parliament.
High Directorate for Reform	• strategy and timetable for reform	2 Federal Councillors and the Chancellor.
Federal Chancellor	• management of Phase I reforms	Proposals to the Federal Council for an overhaul of executive power.
Reform Delegate I	• preparation of Federal Council decisions	Preparation of reports and search for resources.
Outside Consultant	• proposal of a new organisation chart	Adjustment of the balance of resources and expenditure among departments.
Head of the Federal Department of Finance	• pilot projects	Overall budget management and service mandates.
Head of the Federal Department of Justice and Police	• management of Phase II reforms	Preparation of a new federal constitution and presentation to the Federal Council.

---

* See also "*Réforme gouvernementale et constitutionnelle*", Section II, Part A, Chapter I of *Rapport sur le Programme de législature* 1995-1999 of 18 March 1996 (http:/www.admin.ch/ch/f/cf/rg/lp1995/ii_a_1.html).

TURKEY

A. Main tendencies and overall priorities

The need to improve public management in terms of organisation, operation and personnel structure in order to adapt to changing conditions is increasing. Within this framework, re-evaluation of the role of the state with respect to public services, reducing the size of the state and its structures, making them more functional, and establishing a citizen-oriented administration, remain important.

A new wages regime will be put into effect. Its objectives are to establish a balance among public personnel in terms of wages, additional payments, social rights and benefits; to remove differences in wages at institutional and sectoral levels among personnel who are of the same grade; to introduce the principles of career, merit, transparency and equal pay for equal work based on job definition without distorting hierarchy; and to codify legislation.

Administrative methods and procedures need to be simplified. Practices based on citizens' declarations rather than on certified proof will be further developed in the units providing direct service to the public. The role of the state will be redefined within the framework of globalisation and work towards European integration. All public agencies and institutions will be given a harmonious structure to conform with the task they undertake; unnecessary formalities will be abolished.

C. Strategies and processes for planning and carrying out public management reforms

The State will reduce its economic activities, and avoid granting subsidies, thus eliminating pressure on financial markets. It will provide general guidance to remove medium-term uncertainties by forming the most appropriate macro-economic environment for efficient resource allocation.

Public duties and powers of central administrations will be revised according to the principles of deconcentration and decentralisation. In this context, certain services provided by central administrations will be transferred to the authority and responsibility of local administrations and provincial units starting with Special Provincial Administrations. Amendments will be made in related laws.

A new supervisory system will be established in order to evaluate performance. This will be done after the review of central supervisory agencies and supervisory units of line agencies and institutions.

In order to settle effectively and rapidly disputes and difficulties which citizens encounter with the public administrations, an Ombudsman system will be established. This has arisen from the need for an independent body other than the judiciary to defend citizens' rights and control excesses by the administration.

Within the framework of "The Principle of the Separation of Powers" several rules and regulations have been introduced to clarify the functioning of legislation and jurisdiction. However, some uncertainties have been observed in the implementation of public service rules and regulations. In order to clarify these a project on "the Administrative Procedures Law" has been launched by the Administrative Development Department of the Prime Ministry. This project will be carried out between 1 January 1997 and 31 December 1998.

D. Policy-management capacities

No significant initiatives.

E. Human resources management

A standard package with a wide scope to solve problems of the public personnel regime will be prepared and implemented with the contribution of all institutions concerned.

Public sector employment will be reviewed in terms of numbers, quality, efficiency and the level of wages. Manpower planning will be undertaken in order to equip the public administration with sufficient quality and quantity of personnel and to use them effectively. Standard positions based on job analysis will be introduced to increase efficiency, and a public manpower inventory will be made to evaluate the present in the light of desired targets.

The present system of wages will be abolished by removing the inequity of wages and additional payments, and some social rights and benefits will be removed. A new system of wages will be introduced in order to create a balance between wages, social rights and benefits. The implementation of the principle of equal pay for equal work will be improved.

Flexibility in work rules and methods will be introduced and their scope will be clarified.

Financial and social rights of public personnel with civil servant status will be arranged in a single law through codification in legislation; therefore, more transparency will be ensured.

More effective training will be provided to civil servants to be appointed in administrative posts. Appointments, qualifications, wages and dismissal will be regulated by special arrangements. Those not meeting the required performance levels will be shifted to other public duties appropriate with their education and qualifications.

F. Budget process and management of financial resources

The government has launched a programme to set up a modern fiscal management system which will enable it to improve the management of its financial and budgetary practices.

The objective of the Public Financial Management Project is to enhance the efficiency and effectiveness of tax administration, expenditure and personnel management, and customs operations. The reform aims at modernising the institutional and technical framework of public financial management.

Within the context of the Public Expenditure and Personnel Management component, various initiatives will be set up to strengthen the government's budget usefulness as a fiscal policy instrument, such as modernising budgetary and accounting control procedures, making the budget code and programme structure and chart of accounts more suitable for economic analysis, and introducing accrual accounting and performance audit systems.

While strengthening budgetary discipline, greater budget execution responsibility will be devolved to spending agencies.

As part of the fiscal reform process, an integrated suite of modern computer based information systems will be implemented to support the core expenditure management processes. It is expected that the implementation of these systems would improve the efficiency of public resource allocation and use. A

Financial Ledger System, to be located in the Ministry of Finance, will support the financial reporting and multi-year budgeting.

G. Performance management

Particularly for jobs related to service provision, public agencies and institutions will define clear targets. Personnel carrying out the relevant activities will be informed in the light of these targets, of expenditure limits and deadlines. Although performance levels will be fixed, units will be allowed to select appropriate methods to be followed to reach these targets.

Some legislation [relating to supervisory responsibilities and functions of the Grand National Assembly of Turkey (GNAT), and of supervisory units] will be revised in order to introduce performance management into the public sector. Additionally, a law related to the establishment of the Ombudsman system will be put into force.

With a view to benefiting consciously from modern technology in public administration, importance will particularly be given to widening the use of computer systems.

H. Changing structures of the public sector

In view of decentralisation policy, a number of laws will be modified to give more authority and financial resources to metropolitan governments, municipalities, villages, and Special Provincial Administrations.

Mrs. Reyyan Ödemis
Head, Foreign Relations Department
Prime Ministry
Basbakanlik Dis Iliskiler Baskanligi
Basbakanlik Ek Binasi
Mesrutiyet Cad. No.24, Kat. 5
Kizilay
06640 ANKARA
Tel.: (90-312) 419 11 52
Fax: (90-312) 419 11 56

UNITED KINGDOM

A. Main tendencies and overall priorities

Continuity – commitment to the maintenance of a permanent Civil Service, based on the values of integrity, political impartiality, objectivity, selection and promotion on merit, and accountability through ministers to Parliament.

Change – a continued improvement in the performance of the Civil Service within the framework of two key disciplines:

- the commitment under the Citizen's Charter to clear standards of service for users and to a clearer definition of output targets; and
- continued tight control of the costs of running the Civil Service.

B. Context affecting public management

Twin pressures for change are a desire for improvement in the quality and delivery of services coupled with resistance to higher taxes.

C. Strategies and processes for planning and carrying out public management reforms

The United Kingdom government has been subjecting all its activities to searching scrutiny by addressing a series of "prior options" questions.

1. *Does the work need to be done at all?* If not, the work should be abolished.

2. *If the work is necessary, does the government need to be responsible for it?* If not, privatisation should be considered.

3. *If the government does need to be responsible, does the work have to be performed by civil servants, or could it be delivered more efficiently and effectively by the private sector?* A competition should be held to establish who can deliver the service in the most efficient and effective way. The basis of the decision will always be best value for money.

4. *Where the job must be carried out within government, is the organisation properly structured and focused on the task?* The Next Steps principles of clear accountability and delegation should be applied (see Section G). A range of techniques may be applied to improve efficiency (see Section G).

D. Policy-making capacities

No significant initiatives.

E. Human resources management

Civil Service Code

The Civil Service Code came into force on 1 January 1996. It is a clear and concise statement of the responsibilities of civil servants and is part of civil servants' terms and conditions of employment. As well as restating the integrity and loyalty to the government required of civil servants, its express prohibitions include:

- deceiving Parliament or the public;
- misuse of official positions; and
- unauthorised disclosure of confidential information.

The Code provides a right of appeal to the independent Civil Service Commissioners on matters of propriety, conscience, etc., if the problem cannot be resolved within the department in question.

Delegation of Civil Service management to departments

From 1 April 1996, ministers and office holders in charge of departments have had considerable scope to develop terms and conditions of service of their staff. This allows them to set conditions of employment to suit their own particular circumstances and thereby achieve better value for money.

Senior Civil Service

Following reviews of departmental senior management structures (leading to substantial delayering and reductions in numbers of posts), the old grading system was abolished and a new Senior Civil Service was created on 1 April 1996. It numbers just under 3 000 members and is a group of senior managers and advisers who, while employed and managed by their own departments, have a broader identity as part of a cohesive group at the top of the Service and are covered by a common framework. The framework has a number of important features:

- a central framework of nine overlapping pay bands;
- a common job weighting system;
- a personal formal written contract; and
- a senior common appraisal system.

The possibility of wider or open competition must be considered for all Senior Civil Service vacancies. In recent years around 30 per cent of vacancies at the top three levels of the Service have been openly advertised outside the Service.

Development and Training White Paper

The White Paper *Development and Training for Civil Servants: A Framework for Action* was published on 1 July 1996. It sets out a new programme for action on training and development across the Civil Service.

The key commitment is to Investors in People, the national standard for organisations that take the training and development of their staff seriously. The government has set a target that by the year 2000, all civil servants will be employed in organisations recognised as Investors in People. In addition, there will be a new drive to raise the levels of skills and awareness of staff, through the development of a stronger managerial culture; the development of an increasing number of civil servants with specialist expertise; an increase in awareness training and development opportunities; and a flexible approach to recruitment at all levels. The paper also emphasizes the role of the individual in seeking development and training opportunities, actively supported by line and top management.

F.   Budget process and management of financial resources

The government's policy is to set an overall ceiling for public spending; to focus resources on core activities; to utilise choice, competition and market forces in provision of services; and to see maximum output from a given input, *i.e.* maximum value for money. Key financial management tools used are the Private Finance Initiative; privatisation; strategic contracting out; market testing; development of customer/contractor relationships, internal markets, service level agreements, delegated budgets and other market mechanisms/operational flexibilities; performance indicators and targets; closer linking of performance to reward; strategic planning; efficiency scrutinies of specific areas; and policy evaluation.

Private Finance Initiative

In November 1994 the Chancellor of the Exchequer announced that HM Treasury would not approve any capital projects unless private finance options had been explored. The initiative is based on government purchasing rather than providing services. But the private sector must genuinely assume an appropriate amount of the risk; and projects must represent good value for money for the taxpayer.

Resource accounts and budgetary control

Proposals contained in July 1995 White Paper. From 1998-99 all departments will produce resource accounts which will link input cost to output achieved and show departmental assets and liabilities. By 2000, the planning and control of public expenditure will be based on both cash and accrual measures.

G.   Performance management

Next Steps

The 1988 Efficiency Report recommended that, in order to deliver government services more efficiently and effectively, agencies should be established to carry out executive functions of government within a policy and resources framework set by a department.

127 agencies are now in existence – within the Home Civil Service, the Northern Ireland Civil Service and the Forestry Commission – with nearly 387 000 civil servants (72 per cent) working in them. 37 more candidates have been announced and the launch programme is expected to be complete by the end of 1997.

Each agency, headed by a chief executive, has an individual framework document setting out aims and objectives, responsibilities of ministers and chief executives and other operational arrangements. Agencies are set key annual targets by Ministers, covering quality of service, financial performance, efficiency and throughput. Performance against these targets is published annually in the *Next Steps Review*.

From 1996 the *Next Steps Review* will report on progress towards developing benchmarking of organisational performance.

Citizen's Charter

The Citizen's Charter was launched by the Prime Minister in 1991 as a ten-year programme to raise the standard of public services and make them more responsive to the wishes and needs of their users. The six principles of the Citizen's Charter are:

– standards;
– information and openness;
– choice and consultation;
– courtesy and helpfulness;
– putting things right;
– value for money.

There are now 42 main charters, covering all the key public services, setting out the standards of service people can expect to receive. There are more than 8 000 local charters covering local service providers such as general practitioners (GP) practices, police forces and fire services. Once standards are met, they should be raised and new ones added to cover additional areas of importance.

Performance tables for schools, hospitals, local authorities and police forces give people the opportunity to see how their local services are performing. The tables are expanded and developed each year in the light of public reactions and are now available free on CD-ROM, as well as on paper.

The Charter Mark Awards Scheme recognises excellence and innovation in public service. Members of the public play an increasingly important part in the scheme by nominating organisations for an award. There are now 417 Charter Mark holders. Over 15 000 nominations were received in 1996.

In June 1995 the Citizen's Charter Complaints Task Force issued its final report on the way in which public services in the United Kingdom handle complaints. The Task Force made a number of recommendations and produced a Good Practice Guide for use by managers and staff.

Competing for Quality

The Competing for Quality programme, launched in 1991, identifies activities which may be suitable for strategic contracting out and market testing. From April 1992 to March 1995 £2.6 billion of activities were reviewed. If the programme is managed well and performance matches expectations, annual cost savings should be around £540 million – average savings of 20 per cent. A report on a review of the Competing for Quality initiative was published in July 1996. The report's findings reinforced the benefits of competition.

Departments now produce their own Efficiency Plans showing how they will deliver key outputs within running costs limits. There is a continued strong commitment to competition, with well over £1 billion of Competing for Quality planned for 1996-97.

H.   Changing structures of the public sector

Privatisation

Since 1979 the government has pursued a policy of transferring organisations that no longer need to be owned by government to the private sector. In 1996, privatisations that have taken place or are planned include the railways: HM Stationery Office; Chessington Computer Centre; the Occupational Health and Safety Agency; the Building Research Establishment; the Natural Resources Institute; the Transport Research Laboratory; the Laboratory of the Government Chemist; the Teachers' Pensions Agency; AEA Technology; Recruitment and Assessment Services and British Energy.

Next Steps

See Section G above.

I. Regulatory management and reform

The Deregulation Initiative is designed to help increase competitiveness and encourage enterprise by improving the United Kingdom's regulatory framework. It promotes fewer, better, simpler regulations and paperwork at home and in Brussels, and it encourages more business-friendly enforcement. The Initiative is co-ordinated by the Deregulation Unit in liaison with the Deregulation Task Force of representatives from business and charities. Each department has an appointed Deregulation Minister and a Departmental Deregulation Unit.

The Deregulation and Contracting Out Act 1994 provides a mechanism to change primary legislation for removing or reducing burdens on business, provided necessary protection is not removed. The Unit has amended or repealed over 643 regulations and the total is expected to rise to over 1 000 by the end of 1996. The Unit has introduced Risk and Cost Assessments, and Implementing European Law Checklists.

J. Other

Open government

The government's Code of Practice on Access to Government Information came into effect on 4 April 1994. It commits departments to answer requests for information, but also to provide:

- facts and analysis with major policy decisions;
- explanatory guidelines about departments' dealings with the public;
- reasons with decisions; and
- information under the Citizen's Charter about public services; what they cost, targets. performance, complaints and redress.

Information technology

In November 1995 the government established a Central Information Technology Unit whose principal task is to advise the Ministers on the development of an IT strategy to enable the government to improve the efficiency of the government's internal processes, and improve the efficiency and quality of services it supplies to businesses and the citizen. The unit also has responsibility for the application of the Private Finance Initiative to IS/IT projects.

A draft strategy for the use of IT by government will be published as a Green Paper in autumn 1996.

Ms. Hilary Douglas
Under Secretary
Office of Public Service
Cabinet Office
Horse Guards Road
London SW1P 3AL
Tel.: (44-171) 270 61 29
Fax: (44-171) 270 19 73

Annex A

PRINCIPAL RECENT PUBLIC MANAGEMENT DEVELOPMENTS

1979
- Range of measures launched to reduce size of State-controlled sector.

1981
- Civil Service Department disbanded. Responsibilities transferred to HM Treasury (HMT) and newly-formed Management and Personnel Office within Cabinet Office.

1982
- Financial Management Initiative introduced.

1984
- *Government Purchasing: Review of Government Contract and Procurement Procedures* published. Central Unit on Purchasing set up – charged with reporting annually on progress against vfm targets.

1985
- White Paper *Lifting the Burden* published spelling out the need for deregulation.
- Top Management Programme launched.

1986
- Multi-departmental Review of Budgeting completed including encouragement to develop budgeting as a management tool for improving resource allocation.
- White Paper *Building Business… Not Barriers* published.

1987
- Management and Personnel Office reconstituted as the Office for the Minister for the Civil Service, giving support as part of Cabinet Office to the Prime Minister.

1988
- Next Steps initiative launched.
- Progress report on budgeting reforms published.
- White Paper *Releasing Enterprise* published reporting progress on deregulation and making proposals for further action.

1989
- HMT document published outlining 21 management flexibilities available to departments and agencies.
- New career arrangements for IT and Purchasing and Supply staff aimed at increasing professionalism.

1989-1990
- Challenge funding introduced to improve the performance of department in training senior managers. Measures introduced to develop more flexible framework for recruitment, development and training.

1990
- First *Next Steps Review* published.
- Series of equal opportunities initiatives launched.
- Efficiency scrutinies and policy reviews continue

1991

- *Making the Most of Next Steps* published – on relationships between departments and agencies.
- Citizen's Charter programme launched.
- White Paper *Competing for Quality* published.
- HMT document published outlining 40 management flexibilities available to departments and agencies.
- Booklet *Cutting Red Tape for Business* published reporting progress on the Deregulation Initiative.

1992

- Office of Public Service and Science (OPSS) created within the Cabinet Office.
- Charter Mark Competition launched to reward excellence in implementing the Citizen's Charter.
- Civil Service (Management Functions) Act to facilitate delegation of management responsibilities.

1993

- Programme of Fundamental Expenditure Reviews launched.
- Efficiency Unit Report on Career Management and Succession Planning published.

1994

- Civil Service White Paper *Continuity and Change* published.
- Central funding scheme introduced to help departments meet costs of early departures.
- *Next Steps: Moving On* published.
- Code of Practice on Access to Government Information introduced.
- Private Finance Initiative launched.
- All government departments committed to taking forward plans to become Investors in People.
- First *Competitiveness* White Paper published.

1995

- OPSS loses responsibilities for science and becomes OPS.
- Civil Service White Paper *Taking Forward Continuity and Change* published.
- Departments to prepare efficiency plans each year.
- Public Sector MBA programme launched.
- Efficiency Scrutiny of Management Information Systems published.
- *Burdens of Bureaucracy* efficiency scrutinies published.
- White Paper *Resource Accounting and Budgeting in Government* published.
- Central Information Technology Unit set up within OPS.
- Remaining HMT responsibilities for Civil Service management transferred to OPS(S). (Joint responsibility for pay and grading until April 1996.)

1996

- Civil Service Code comes into force.
- New Senior Civil Service created.
- Delegation of responsibility for pay and grading and a wide range of other terms and conditions for all staff outside the Senior Civil Service.
- Senior Management Reviews completed.
- White Paper *Development and Training for Civil Servants* published.
- Evaluation of first three years of Competing for Quality published.
- Benchmarking initiative for executive agencies launched.

Annex B

INSTITUTIONAL RESPONSIBILITY FOR PUBLIC MANAGEMENT IMPROVEMENT

ORGANISATION	TASKS AND RESPONSIBILITIES	OTHER INFORMATION
Cabinet Office (Office of Public Service, OPS)	• promotion of competitiveness agenda • promotion of deregulation initiative • development of Citizen's Charter programme • promotion of competition in central government • implementation of Next Steps programme • promotion of best practice in interchange, development and training and equal opportunities • delegation of Civil Service management responsibilities to departments and agencies • monitoring of delegated pay and grading and other terms and conditions of service • industrial relations • advising on structure and practice of government • promotion of high standards of integrity, efficiency and merit • promotion of open government • development of IT strategy for government	OPS and Commissioners have responsibility for the general principles and the necessary central machinery for the management of the Civil Service. However, most management is carried out by departments and agencies themselves.
Civil Service Commissioners	• maintenance of principle of recruitment on merit • final court of appeal in cases of concern about propriety and conscience	
HM Treasury	• financial management including Private Finance Initiative • government purchasing • privatisation	

Annex C

KEY PUBLIC DOCUMENTS ON PUBLIC MANAGEMENT ISSUES AND DEVELOPMENTS

White Paper *Efficiency and Effectiveness in the Civil Service* (1982).

White Paper *Government Purchasing: Review of Government Contract and Procurement Procedures* (1984).

White Paper *Lifting the Burden* (1985).

White Paper *Building Business...Not Barriers* (1986).

Efficiency Unit Report *Improving Management in Government: The Next Steps* (1988).

White Paper *Releasing Enterprise* (1988).

Efficiency Unit Report *Making the Most of Next Steps* (1991).

White Paper *Competing for Quality* (1991).

White Paper *The Citizen's Charter* (1991).

Efficiency Unit Report *Career Management and Succession Planning Study* (1993).

White Paper *Open Government* (1993).

Civil Service Select Committee (TCSC) Report *The Role of the Civil Service* (1994).

The Trosa Report *Next Steps: Moving On* (1994).

White Paper *Competitiveness* (1994).

White Paper *Continuity and Change* (1994).

White Paper *Resource Accounting and Budgeting in Government* (1995).

White Paper *Taking Forward Continuity and Change* (1995).

Efficiency Unit Report *Competing for Quality Policy Review* (1996).

White Paper *Development and Training for Civil Servants* (1996).

Annually: *Next Steps Reviews* (since 1992); *Citizen's Charter progress reports* (since 1992); *Competitiveness White Papers* (since 1994)

UNITED STATES

A. Main tendencies and overall priorities

The Administration is transforming agencies into lean, flexible organisations that emphasize performance: measuring the results of programmes, not just the amount of money spent on them; making the government an effective buyer and manager, especially of complicated information systems; and providing financial accountability for government spending. Since 1993, the Administration has cut the Federal workforce by over 200 000 employees, creating the smallest Federal work-force in 30 years – and, as a share of the total civilian work-force, the smallest Federal work-force since 1931.

B. Context affecting public management

In past years, debates about government programmes were usually dominated by discussions over how much the government should spend, rather than on what the spending would accomplish. But for Americans, the debates were largely academic. For well over a decade, the public has been saying that government simply is not working. To answer the call, the Administration is making government smaller, better managed, and more efficient. It is, in fact, creating a government that "works better and costs less". The Administration is creating a government that provides better service to the American people by building on the four principles of Vice President Gore's National Performance Review (NPR) – putting customers first, empowering employees to get results, cutting red tape, and cutting back to basics.

C. Strategies and processes for planning and carrying out public management reforms

Streamlining the government

Americans want a smaller government, and the Administration is creating one. Starting with the NPR's report of September 1993, From Red Tape to Results, and continuing a year later in the Federal Work-force Restructuring Act, the President and Congress agreed to cut 272 900 full-time equivalent (FTE) personnel by the end of this decade – that is, 12 per cent in six years. (An FTE is not necessarily synonymous with an employee. Put simply, one full-time employee counts as one FTE, or two employees who each work half-time count as one FTE.) The Administration is ahead of schedule. It has cut the Federal civilian work-force by 9.8 per cent, or by over 200 000 employees, out of 2.2 million in January 1993. The Federal government now has the smallest work-force in 30 years and, as a share of the Nation's total work-force, the smallest since 1931.

Restructuring agencies

A smaller government is not an end in itself. The government must change the way it operates. In place of the highly centralised, inflexible organisations of yesterday that focused on process, the Administration is creating decentralised management structures within agencies to focus on results. In the past three years, agencies themselves have cut the number of their supervisory personnel by over

45 000, or 23 per cent of the overall cut in employees. The President's Management Council (explained below) has led efforts to restructure and eliminate unnecessary agency field offices. In many instances, agencies are consolidating their operations, allowing them to close small, inefficient field offices in some places while strengthening the services they provide to customers.

Putting customers first

In 1993, the President issued an Executive Order directing all agencies to develop a comprehensive programme of customer surveys, training, standard setting, and benchmarking to enable the government to deliver service "equal to the best in business". A year later, the National Performance Review (NPR) published the government's first comprehensive set of customer service standards. In all of its efforts, the Administration is working to ensure that government delivers better service to its customers, the American people.

The Administration is committed to empowering Federal workers, and encouraging and recognising their enterprising efforts. Managers and workers are transforming government from its preoccupation with procedures, process, and penalties to a focus on customers, partnerships, and delivering information and services rapidly. That is, managers and workers are changing the way government operates.

"Reinvention Labs"

In the past three years, the Administration has created over 200 Reinvention Labs, in which groups of employees work outside normal bureaucratic processes to achieve results. Some Reinvention Labs focus on the work of entire agencies or bureaux. Others concentrate on improving or redesigning specific processes.

The President's Management Council (PMC)

In his first year, the President asked all executive departments and agencies to name a Chief Operating Officer who would report directly to the agency head and be responsible for the agency's overall management. At the same time, to help him and the Vice President foster management reforms, the President created the PMC, comprising the Chief Operating Officers of the Cabinet departments and several other major agencies. The PMC is a catalyst and implementer of management reforms. It has contributed to the Administration's efforts to reform procurement and personnel systems, improve customer service, rationalise field office structures, and streamline the Federal work-force. It has worked closely with employee representatives and associations of government managers to make labour-management partnerships a reality. PMC members also worked closely with Members of Congress to craft buyout legislation to make the necessary government downsizing more humane.

Performance-based organisations and market incentives

Performance-Based Organisations (PBOs): In September 1995, the Vice President unveiled the next phase of Administration efforts to improve the delivery of government services, designating the Commerce Department's Patent and Trademark Office as the first agency function to be transformed into a PBO. With PBOs, the customer comes first. The Administration will transform some agency customer service functions, such as issuing patents or retirement benefits, into performance-driven, customer-oriented tasks. The agencies will get considerable flexibility to make personnel, procurement, and financial management decisions and, in return, will be held accountable for meeting measurable performance goals in delivering services to the public.

D. Policy-management capacities

Interagency councils

The President's Management Council, the Chief Financial Officers Council, and the President's Council on Integrity and Efficiency are encouraging the cross-agency dissemination of ideas, speeding the process of reforming government. These councils will be responsible for maintaining the reforms in 1997 and beyond (refer also to Section C).

E. Human resources management

The National Partnership Council (NPC) and labour-management partnerships

The Administration is encouraging a stronger partnership between Federal management and its employees. Across the government, the National Partnership Council is spurring collaborative labour-management efforts, improving customer service, and cutting costs. Since its creation in October 1993, the NPC has stimulated collaborative labour-management activities across the government, enabling agencies to accomplish their missions more efficiently and save tax dollars. Other human resources strategies are discussed in Section C.

F. Budget process and management of financial resources

Improving financial management

An efficient, effective government needs sound financial management, including management and reporting systems that produce reliable information. To develop these systems, the Administration is establishing government-wide accounting standards, producing audited financial statements, streamlining management controls and reporting, and modernising debt collection.

Government-wide Accounting Standards

To make the government's financial information more consistent, the Administration set an ambitious goal for the Federal Accounting Standards Advisory Board to recommend a comprehensive set of government-wide financial accounting and cost accounting standards by spring. Once the Administration and the General Accounting Office adopt the standards, agencies will use them as they prepare financial reports and cost information that, in turn, make the agencies more accountable to taxpayers.

Audited financial statements

The Administration has worked to increase the number of agencies with audited financial statements that earned "unqualified opinions" (that is, a clean bill of health). Under the 1990 Chief Financial Officers (CFOs) Act, several agencies and other government entities must prepare financial statements and have them audited. In 1991, only 35 per cent of these entities earned unqualified opinions. By 1994, almost 60 per cent did. The 1994 government Management Reform Act extended the requirement for audited financial statements to all activities of agencies covered by the CFOs Act, beginning in 1996. Many of the agencies, such as SSA, General Services Administration (GSA), NASA, and the Nuclear Regulatory Commission (NRC), already have complied and issued department-wide audited financial statements with unqualified opinions.

Electronic payments

The government makes payments to over 90 per cent of Federal employees and retirees through direct deposit, and pays vendors through the government-wide small purchase card and government travel card. The Administration and Congress are developing legislation to mandate that, by 1999, the government make all Federal payments electronically.

G. Performance management

The focus on results

To improve customer service and ensure that government spends money wisely, the Administration has directed agencies to manage their programmes with an eye toward achieving performance goals – that is, results. Using the 1993 government Performance and Results Act (GPRA), the Administration is working to transform the way agencies are administered and programmes are managed. Under GPRA, agencies will prepare strategic plans that are built around their missions and clearly outline their goals, and develop measures to track their progress in achieving the goals. They will publish annual performance reports to enable Congress and the public to better understand how the government is spending tax dollars and what it is achieving. These reports will give the public an annual update on our efforts to create a government that works better and costs less. Final strategic plans and goals are due at the Office of Management and Budget (OMB) in September 1997. Refer also to Section C for other relevant strategies.

Increased emphasis on customer service

Better customer service is central to the Administration's efforts to make government work better and cost less. The President and Vice President have challenged service-providing agencies to make significant, visible improvements in their customer service. A number of the agencies will make their specific commitments to improve service through the Internet and, for the first time, will take feedback from their customers through that medium.

Information and information technology

The Administration has used advances in information technology (IT) to serve customers faster, more accurately, and more reliably. It is not an end in itself, but a means for agencies to work smarter, faster, and better. By making data more easily accessible, the electronic dissemination of information not only better serves current users but expands the potential audience. Previously, for information about benefits or services, citizens typically had to visit a Federal office during business hours. Now, the government is increasingly using 1 800 numbers and on-line connections to deliver such information 24 hours a day.

H. Changing structures of the public sector

Performance-based intergovernmental partnerships

Performance-based intergovernmental partnerships are agreements between the Federal government and other levels of government based on goals and the progress toward meeting them. In exchange for commitments to specific performance levels, State and local governments receive more administrative flexibility on how to achieve these levels. Last year, the President proposed to consolidate 271 programmes into 27 "Performance Partnerships" in areas such as public health, rural development, education and training, housing and urban development, and transportation. Congress has not yet enacted legislation to implement the proposed consolidation. Other strategies relevant to structural change are referenced in Section C.

Oregon option

In 1994, the Federal government launched an interagency partnership with Oregon to achieve specific results: better health for children, more stable families, and a more capable work-force. Federal agencies are giving their state counterparts more freedom in how to spend Federal dollars, in exchange for a commitment to be accountable for achieving measurable results. The Administration recently signed a similar partnership with Connecticut to improve the state's poorest communities through economic development and neighbourhood revitalisation.

Local partnerships

Individual Federal agencies also have developed performance-based intergovernmental partnerships. The Department of Housing and Urban Development, for example, formed a partnership with the State of Texas and the City of Dallas to revitalise that city, with deadlines for achieving certain objectives and performance measures to assess success. The Environmental Protection Agency has launched an effort, "XL for Communities", giving communities the assistance and flexibility to implement their own community-designed strategies for greater environmental quality.

I. Regulatory management and reform

Changing the face of federal regulation

The President laid out his regulatory principles in Executive Order 12866 of 1993. They include:

– collecting accurate data and using objective analysis to make decisions;
– considering the costs and benefits of alternative ways to reach the goals; and
– opening the decision-making process, with meaningful input from affected entities.

Regulatory reform

Improving new regulations is only half the challenge; revising existing ones is equally important. In 1995, the President directed agencies to review, page-by-page, their existing regulations and eliminate those that were unduly burdensome, outdated, or in need of revision. The government is now eliminating 16 000 pages of regulations and improving another 31 000. By the end of 1995, agencies already had eliminated over a third of the 16 000 pages, and improved nearly 5 000 others.

J. Other

Reforming procurement

The Federal Acquisition Streamlining Act of 1994 (FASA), which the Administration and Congress developed co-operatively, includes many Administration proposals relating to purchases of commercial items and purchases considered "smaller-dollar" – that is, under $100 000. FASA allows agencies to use simplified procedures for a larger class of smaller-dollar purchases, promotes the acquisition of standard commercial items, eliminates many record-keeping and reporting requirements, focuses on past performance in choosing contractors, and reinforces the President's directive that instructs agencies to use electronic commerce to streamline procurement. More recently, and at the Administration's urging, Congress reformed the way government makes larger-dollar purchases and acquires information technology (IT) as part of the Federal Acquisition Reform Act (FARA) and Information Technology Management Reform Act, which the President signed into law earlier this year.

Streamlined negotiation process

The Administration is working to enable agencies to issue solicitations more easily and to reduce their reliance on the detailed written proposals they receive from suppliers For example, agencies might ask potential suppliers to present their proposals orally.

Commercial purchases

FASA and FARA also will simplify the procurement process for commercial products and encourage agencies to adopt more commercial practices. These laws are enabling the government to enjoy the same access to good prices and current technology that other commercial market customers enjoy.

Past performance in picking contractors

In an early initiative, the Administration encouraged agencies to use the commercial practice of comparing the past performance of competing contractors. Knowing their ability to get work depends on how well they have performed, contractors now have a strong incentive to strive for excellence.

Mr. Jonathan D. Breul
Senior Advisor to the Deputy Director for Management
Office of Management and Budget
New Executive Office Building, Room 10235
725 17th Street, N.W.
WASHINGTON, DC 20503
Tel.: (1-202) 395 56 70
Fax: (1-202) 395 69 74

Annex A

PRINCIPAL RECENT PUBLIC MANAGEMENT DEVELOPMENTS

1991

- Implementation of the Chief Financial Officers Act, including establishment of Office of Federal Financial Management in the Office of Management and Budget (OMB), and publication of guidelines and standards for financial reporting and financial accounting.
- Initial set of annual audited financial statements published by several agencies and 27 government business entities.
- Renewed focus on improving quality of government services and products.
- OMB asks Federal agencies to provide cost/benefit data for all significant regulations, thereby increasing the number of rules covered from about 80 to 500 per year.
- A "pilot regulatory budget" is tested in several industrial sectors covered by the 1990 Clean Air Act amendments.

1992

- 67 government entities and 24 government corporations complete their first set of audited financial statements.
- President initiates a moratorium on new regulations; Federal agencies required to review existing regulations to ensure that benefits outweigh costs.
- Federal Budget contains new alternative form of budget reporting: generation accounts presentation; and budget summary transmitted in January 1993 contains another alternative: the balance sheet presentation.

1993

- New Administration sets goal of cutting 100 000 government employees and reducing White House staff by 25 per cent.
- National Economic Council established in the White House to deal with domestic issues.
- Congress enacted the Government Performance and Results Act – requiring (when fully implemented in 1997) all Federal agencies to develop 5-year strategic plans, annual performance plans and report on performance.
- The President asked Vice President Al Gore to lead the National Performance Review (NPR), a campaign to "reinvent" the federal government.
- The NPR issues its report "From Red Tape to Results: Creating a government that Works Better and Costs Less".
- The President issued E.O. 12866, "Regulatory Planning Review", overhauling the regulatory system by cutting obsolete regulations, rewarding results not red tape, getting out of Washington, creating grassroots partnerships, and negotiating instead of dictating.
- The President issues E.O. 12862, "Setting Customer Service Standards", telling the Federal Government to ask customers what they wanted, listen, and respond.

1994

- Congress passes the Federal Workforce Restructuring Act of 1994 cutting the Federal workforce by 272,000 full-time equivalent positions by 1999 and providing agencies with "buyout" authority to encourage employees to leave.
- The Government Management Reform Act expands the requirement for the preparation and audit of financial statements for their entire operations to all 24 CFO agencies.
- Federal Acquisition Streamlining Act (FASA) of 1994 reforms procurement system.

1995

- The Federal Government establishes a government-wide electronic contracting system.
- The Paperwork Reduction Act is reauthorized.

    – The Unfunded Mandates Reform Act of 1995 became law, limiting Congress' ability to impose new mandates for State, local and tribal governments unless it is also willing to pay for implementing the new mandates.

1996
    – The Federal Acquisition Reform Act (FARA) of 1996 passed.
    – Information Technology Management Reform Act of 1996 establishes a Chief Information Officer in each agency and a new scheme for information technology management and acquisition within the Executive Branch.
    – The President signs the Line Item Veto Act which authorises the President to cancel discretionary spending, new entitlement authorisations and tax provisions.

Annex B

INSTITUTIONAL RESPONSIBILITY FOR PUBLIC MANAGEMENT IMPROVEMENT

ORGANISATION	TASKS AND RESPONSIBILITIES
Executive Office of the President – Office of Management and Budget (OMB)	• assistance to the President in budget preparation and formulation of government's fiscal program • improvement of management and review of government regulations and rules affecting the public • overall guidance for government contracting policies, regulations and procedures • overall guidance for government financial management policies, including financial statements, financial systems, and internal controls
Office of Personnel Management (OPM)	• operation of federal employment system, including recruitment, testing, training, and promotion • operation of civil service retirement, health, and life insurance programmes
General Services Administration (GSA)	• construction and operation of government office and general purpose buildings, purchase of supplies, logistics, and travel services, management of data processing services, and provision of telecommunications services
Department of the Treasury – Financial Management Service (FMS)	• improving the management of government financial transactions • improving the management of government credit activities; • issues Treasury checks and electronic fund transfers • maintains a central system of accounts with periodic reports on financial status • operates systems for collecting government receipts
Office of Government Ethics (OGE)	• provides overall direction of executive branch policies in preventing conflicts of interest

Annex C

KEY PUBLIC DOCUMENTS ON PUBLIC MANAGEMENT ISSUES AND DEVELOPMENTS

Creating a Government that Works Better and Costs Less: Report of the National Performance Review, National Performance Review (September 1993).

Creating a Government that Works Better and Costs Less: Status Report, September 1994, National Performance Review (September 1994).

Common Sense Government: Works Better and Costs Less, National Performance Review (September 1995).

Putting Customers First: Standards for Serving the American People, National Performance Review (September 1994).

Putting Customers First '95: Standards for Serving the American People, National Performance Review (September 1995).

Budget of the US Government, Fiscal Year 1996.

Budget of the US Government, Fiscal Year 1997.

Annex C

SELECTED DOCUMENTS ON PUBLIC MANAGEMENT ISSUES AND DEVELOPMENTS

Part IV

REFERENCE

- A statistical window on OECD Member countries' government sectors 299

- The Public Management Service (PUMA) of the OECD 320

- Glossary of selected terms 322

A STATISTICAL WINDOW
ON OECD MEMBER COUNTRIES'
GOVERNMENT SECTORS

Introduction

Glossary of Terms and Conventions

The Presence of Government in National Economies

- Table 1: General Government total outlays
- Table 2: Changes in General Government total outlays
- Table 3: General Government employment
- Table 4: Changes in General Government employment
- Table 5: Compensation of General Government employees
- Table 6: Changes in compensation of General Government employees
- Graph 1: General Government outlays and employment, 1994

Budgetary and Financial Situations

- Table 7: General Government current receipts
- Table 8: General Government net lending
- Graph 2: General Government outlays and net lending, 1994
- Graph 3: General Government gross public debt and outlays, 1994
- Table 9: General Government gross public debt

The Structure of Government Outlays

- Table 10: Structure of General Government outlays by type of outlays
- Graph 4: Structure of General Government outlays by type of outlay
- Table 11: Structure of General Government outlays by level of government

Economic Context

- Table 12: Changes in gross domestic product
- Table 13: Per capita gross domestic product

A STATISTICAL WINDOW
ON OECD MEMBER COUNTRIES'
GOVERNMENT SECTORS

Introduction

This section provides a set of statistical tables indicating the size and presence of the government sector in OECD Member countries' economies, their budgetary situations and types of expenditures. It brings together available comparable data as far as possible as stand-alone reference material for the convenience of public management practitioners and those interested in public management or governance.

The selected data for this reference section are presented in tables and graphs grouped under four headings and sequenced in order to facilitate their use.

- The first group presents data which are indications of the size and presence of the General Government sector in the economy, and its evolution over the past twenty-five years, using three indicators: general government outlays, general government employment, and the compensation of employees.
- The second group of data sets out the evolution of the budgetary and financial situations of Member countries' government sectors, also over the past twenty-five years, using receipts, deficits or surpluses (net lending), and public debt as indicators.
- The third group of data presents the structure of government outlays by type of expenditure and by level of government.
- The fourth group provides some economic context through GDP data. Much more information is available in other OECD publications, such as the *Economic Outlook*, the *Employment Outlook*, and *Economic Surveys* of individual countries.

The data have been drawn from two major OECD sources which collect and publish regularly a vast range of economic data, acording to standardized concepts and procedures. Those sources are:

- National Accounts (NA) data published annually in OECD *National Accounts*, Volume I (Main Aggregates) and Volume II (Detailed Tables);
- Economic statistics from the OECD's Analytical Databank (ADB), mainly as published bi-annually in the OECD *Economic Outlook* (June and December).

Both sources use the standardized National Accounts concept of the General Government sector (as explained in the following glossary), which enables data to be comparable from country to country. They provide information about the magnitude of the government sector, governments' presence in national economies, governments' fiscal situations and their broad types of activities; they do not allow for evaluation of internal government performance or of the results of particular public management changes. The Public Management Service of the OECD (PUMA) is exploring paths toward enriching this set of data in the medium term. In the meantime, PUMA compiles available OECD data relevant to public management for the purposes of informing its work programme.

- For purposes of this "Statistical Window", in order to be as current as possible and to include as many countries as possible, ADB data have been used where possible. NA data at the time of publishing are not yet available beyond 1994 or 1995 and cover – in the case of data on general government employment, for instance – fewer countries. Using ADB data and the most recent OECD *Economic Outlook* allows inclusion of the year 1995 and of estimates and projections for 1996 to 1998. These data are widely used in economic and financial analyses based on the OECD *Economic Outlook*. Data on the structure of government outlays by type of expenditure and by level of government are only available in NA.

– It should be noted that the estimates and projections provided in certain tables were done for the OECD *Economic Outlook* (No. 60, December 1996). As estimates and projections, these data stand to be modified by later estimates and more up-to-date data; the estimates and projections are updated in every bi-annual edition of the OECD *Economic Outlook*.

Glossary of terms and conventions

a) Definitions

"**General Government**" covers the standardized institutional sector used in the System of National Accounts (SNA). General Government includes:

- the public authority and its administration at all levels: **central** or federal, regional (**state** or provincial), **local**, and **social security** funds;
- public services provided by the government (at all levels) on a non-market basis (*e.g.* public schools, hospitals, welfare services);
- non-profit institutions providing services on a non-market basis which are controlled and mainly financed by the public authority;
- social security funds imposed, controlled or financed by the public authorities for purposes of providing social security benefits for the community, which are separately organised from the other activities of the public authorities and hold their assets and liabilities separately from them.

General Government does *not* include public enterprises. Such enterprises provide goods and services on a market basis but are controlled by public authorities. Therefore, the General Government sector is not equivalent to the concept of the larger public sector, which includes public enterprises, often used in the context of evaluating public sector borrowing requirements. Unfortunately, available data on public enterprises is insufficient for comparative purposes.

"**General Government Receipts**" – a broader concept than revenues which encompasses only tax receipts. The term is borrowed from National Accounts, whereas "revenues" is used in OECD and IMF tax statistics. In the attached tables only current receipts have been retained (excluding capital receipts). They are made up of the sum of the operating surplus, property and enterpreneurial income, indirect taxes, direct taxes, social security contributions, fees, fines and penalities, and current transfers received.

"**General Government Total Outlays**" – this concept is sometimes referred to as general government expenditures. National Accounts break down general government total outlays into:

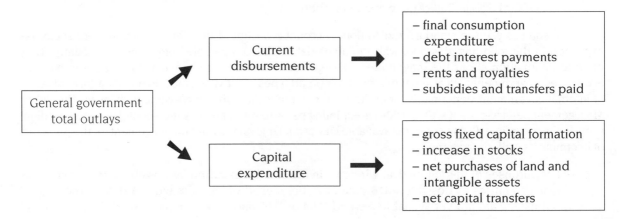

Specific components of outlays, as provided by National Accounts in terms of **"economic types" of outlays** are:

- **final consumption expenditure** – current (excluding capital expenditure) government operating outlays net of sales of goods and services and of fixed capital formation for own account;
  - *of which* compensation of employees encompasses payments of wages and salaries, and contributions paid in respect of social security, pension, income maintenance and similar schemes.

- **transfers** (current and capital transfers) – payments made in the absence of any economic exchange;
  - *of which* **social security** – benefits payed to individuals under social security schemes, usually out of a special fund;
  - *of which* **subsidies** – current government transfers or grants to private or public enterprises, mainly to offset operating losses;
  - *of which* **other transfers** – other current transfers, intangible assets and net capital transfers.

- **investments** – gross fixed capital formation plus increase in stocks (gross investment). Net investment is obtained by deducting consumption of fixed capital;

- **debt interest payments** (including net purchases of land, rent and royalties).

"General Government Net Lending" – the annual surplus (lending) or deficit of net acquisitions of financial assets over net incurrence of liabilities.

"General Government Gross Public Debt" – the gross public debt is the total of outstanding general government financial liabilities, including interest payable (the related concept of net debt deducts general government assets, two major components of which are government loans and social security funds).

"Purchasing Power Parities (PPPs)" – Purchasing Power Parity are the rates of currency conversion that equalise the purchasing power of different currencies. This means that a given sum of money, when converted into different currencies at the PPP's rates, will buy the same basket of goods and services in all countries. The PPPs are the rates of currency conversion which eliminate differences in price level between countries. Here the conversion is made in $US, and the benchmark year is 1990.

b) *Conventions for the presentation of data*

- because entries are rounded, total may differ slightly from the sum of constituent entries;
- rather than provide data for every year over a long period, data are generally provided for every five years from 1970 to 1990 and for every year since then as available;
- the data presented in the graphs derive from the figures shown in the corresponding tables; countries not appearing in the graphs are a consequence of the unavailability of data;
- calculation of average annual changes is the change over the period, divided by the number of years of the period;
- treatment of Germany: data after 1991 include the new *Länder*, except for Table 10, Table 11, and Graph 4;
- Czech Republic: data are available since 1991;
- the **conventional signs used in the tables** are the following:

. .	data not available;
–	not applicable;
(*)	estimation or projection;
highlighted in **bold**	peak year figure for the country.

Table 1. **General Government total outlays**
As a percentage of nominal GDP

	1970	1975	1980	1985	1990	1991	1992	1993	1994	1995	1996*	1997*	1998*
Australia	..	31.4	31.4	36.5	34.9	37.3	**37.7**	37.3	36.9	36.9*	36.4	35.7	34.7
Austria	38.5	45.3	48.1	50.9	48.6	49.9	50.5	**53.2**	51.8	52.5*	52.2	51.4	51.2
Belgium	41.9	51.0	58.3	**61.9**	54.3	55.7	56.2	57.1	55.7	55.0	54.5	53.8	53.2
Canada	33.5	38.5	38.8	45.3	46.0	49.2	**50.2**	49.4	47.2	46.5	45.6	44.6	43.7
Czech Republic	..	..	..	..	..	53.4	54.0*	49.7*	50.7*	49.4*	48.1	48.0	48.3
Denmark	..	48.2	56.2	59.3	58.6	59.2	61.1	**63.7**	63.6	60.9*	61.6	59.9	58.5
Finland	30.0	37.6	38.1	43.8	45.3	53.9	59.1	**60.2**	59.5	58.1	57.2	55.0	53.8
France	38.5	43.4	46.1	52.1	49.8	50.4	52.0	**54.6**	54.0	53.7	54.1	53.0	52.8
Germany	38.3	48.4	47.9	47.0	45.1	47.9	48.5	**48.5**	48.9	**49.5**	49.6	49.0	48.1
Greece	..	27.9	30.4	42.9	48.2	44.4	46.0	49.5	48.0	46.7	46.2	44.3	44.1
Iceland	..	..	32.5	35.7	39.4	40.2	**40.6**	40.4	40.1	38.8*	38.0	37.4	37.1
Ireland	..	..	49.2	**52.6**	41.1	42.2	42.8	42.8	42.9*	40.9*	39.7	39.1	38.2
Italy	33.0	41.5	42.1	51.2	53.4	53.7	53.8	**57.0**	54.2	51.8	53.4	51.7	50.6
Japan	19.0	26.8	32.0	31.6	31.3	30.9	31.7	33.7	**34.3**	35.4*	36.2	36.0	36.0
Luxembourg	..	..	..	..	..	..	..	..	..	..	..	..	..
Mexico	..	..	..	..	..	..	..	..	..	..	..	..	..
Netherlands	41.6	50.4	55.8	**57.1**	54.1	54.6	55.0	55.5	53.1	52.3	50.0	49.1	48.3
New-Zealand	..	..	..	**62.4**	57.9	54.8	54.5	51.6	48.8	47.8*	48.0	47.1	46.5
Norway	36.7	41.4	43.3	40.9	49.8	50.7	**52.0**	51.3	49.1	47.1*	44.8	44.1	42.5
Portugal	20.0	28.7	23.8	41.2	41.8	**43.9**	43.3	44.0*	42.9*	43.1*	43.5	42.6	42.4
Spain	21.6	24.3	32.2	41.2	42.0	43.4	44.4	**47.7**	45.9	44.8	43.1	41.6	40.6
Sweden	42.8	48.4	60.1	63.3	59.1	61.3	67.2	**71.0**	68.3	66.0*	65.4	62.6	60.8
Switzerland	..	..	..	..	..	..	..	..	..	..	..	..	..
Turkey	..	..	..	..	..	..	..	..	..	..	..	..	..
United Kingdom	36.7	**44.4**	43.0	44.0	39.8	40.6	43.1	43.5	43.1	43.3	41.6	40.6	40.1
United States	30.0	32.8	31.4	32.9	32.8	33.4	**34.4**	33.9	33.0	33.2	33.3	33.3	33.3

* Estimates and projections. *Source: Economic Outlook No. 60, December 1996*, OECD.

Source: Analytical Databank, OECD.

Table 2. **Changes in General Government total outlays**
Annual percentage changes from previous period in real terms

	1975-80*	1980-85*	1985-90*	1991	1992	1993	1994	1995
Australia	2.6	**6.2**	1.5	4.1	4.4	2.3	3.4	..
Austria	4.5	2.5	2.8	**5.9**	3.5	5.4	0.9	..
Belgium	**5.0**	0.9	1.5	4.1	3.7	1.4	0.0	0.5
Canada	3.7	**4.7**	2.7	2.3	2.6	−0.3	0.1	0.1
Czech Republic	..	..	..	..	..	..	..	..
Denmark	4.2	3.5	1.2	2.2	4.4	**5.3**	3.8	..
Finland	2.4	5.8	4.8	**8.6**	3.4	0.9	3.2	3.8
France	4.3	3.7	2.6	2.0	**4.5**	3.9	1.6	1.4
Germany	3.0	0.1	3.6	**20.5**	4.0	0.3	1.1	3.5
Greece	5.7	**8.3**	3.6	−4.8	2.9	4.2	0.3	−1.6
Iceland	..	2.8	**5.8**	4.3	−2.6	−1.2	3.4	..
Ireland	..	2.7	−0.4	3.4	4.4	**6.1**	..	..
Italy	5.2	**5.9**	5.1	2.9	0.2	4.8	−3.3	−1.9
Japan	**7.0**	2.9	4.5	2.0	3.7	5.7	1.8	..
Luxembourg	..	..	..	..	..	..	..	..
Mexico	..	..	..	..	..	..	..	..
Netherlands	**4.9**	0.7	2.1	2.9	2.0	0.2	−1.5	0.2
New-Zealand	..	..	..	−9.0	**1.0**	0.3	−1.3	..
Norway	**6.1**	1.5	3.2	3.6	3.5	1.4	..	..
Portugal	1.8	**14.9**	7.4	10.0	3.9	..	..	..
Spain	**7.2**	6.0	5.8	7.0	3.9	5.6	−2.0	−1.1
Sweden	5.9	2.3	1.6	0.9	**6.8**	1.3	−0.3	..
Switzerland	..	..	..	..	..	..	..	..
Turkey	..	..	..	..	..	..	..	..
United Kingdom	1.7	2.2	1.0	0.7	**6.2**	4.8	2.3	2.1
United States	1.3	3.8	2.5	0.7	**5.4**	0.7	0.4	2.4

* Average annual percentage changes over the period.
Source: Analytical Databank, OECD.

Table 3.   **General Government employment**
As a percentage of total employment

	1970	1975	1980	1985	1990	1991	1992	1993	1994	1995
Australia	12.1	15.7	16.3	**17.6**	16.2	16.7	16.6	16.5	15.6	..
Austria	13.3	15.6	17.2	19.6	20.7	20.9	21.1	21.9	**22.5**	..
Belgium	13.8	15.8	18.9	**20.4**	19.8	19.4	19.3	19.4	19.0	..
Canada	19.2	20.9	19.5	20.7	20.5	21.4	**21.9**	21.8	21.5	20.7
Czech Republic	..	..	..	..	..	5.0	5.1	5.2	**5.6**	5.4
Denmark	17.2	23.6	28.3	29.7	30.4	30.7	30.8	**31.4**	31.0	30.4
Finland	12.1	14.8	17.3	19.2	20.9	22.2	23.3	23.6	**23.8**	23.6
France	18.0	19.2	20.2	22.8	22.6	22.9	23.5	24.3	24.6	**24.7**
Germany	11.2	13.8	14.6	15.5	15.1	15.9	**16.1**	16.0	15.9	15.7
Greece	6.8	7.6	8.3	9.4	9.8	**10.3**	10.0	10.0	9.8	..
Iceland	12.4	13.9	15.7	16.5	18.3	18.7	19.1	**19.6**	..	..
Ireland	11.8	14.2	16.2	**18.5**	16.5	16.8	17.0	..	..	..
Italy	12.2	14.4	15.4	16.7	17.3	17.2	17.4	17.7	**17.9**	17.8
Japan	7.7	8.7	**8.8**	8.7	8.1	8.1	8.1	8.2	8.4	8.3
Luxembourg	9.3	9.7	10.8	**11.5**	11.1	11.0	..	..	..	..
Mexico	..	..	..	..	**27.2**	26.7	25.5	24.9	..	..
Netherlands	11.5	12.9	13.8	**14.8**	13.2	12.7	12.5	12.4	12.4	12.0
New-Zealand	15.7	17.1	**17.7**	16.2	16.5	16.4	15.9	15.8	15.1	..
Norway	17.4	21.1	24.6	25.3	28.0	29.1	30.1	30.8	**31.0**	..
Portugal	7.9	8.5	10.7	13.2	14.7	14.8	18.3	18.1	18.2	**18.4**
Spain	4.9	6.8	9.0	11.8	13.4	13.9	14.3	**14.8**	14.8	14.8
Sweden	20.9	25.7	30.7	33.3	32.0	32.5	32.6	**33.4**	32.7	..
Switzerland	9.9	12.0	13.4	13.3	12.9	13.1	13.7	14.0	**14.1**	..
Turkey	7.6	8.1	**9.2**	8.3	7.8	8.3	8.3	8.3	..	..
United Kingdom	18.1	20.8	21.2	**21.5**	19.4	19.5	19.2	17.0	15.0	14.4
United States	16.0	**17.1**	16.4	15.3	15.4	15.6	15.7	15.7	15.5	15.4

Source: Analytical Databank , OECD.

Table 4. **Changes in General Government employment**
Annual percentage changes from previous period

	1975-80*	1980-85*	1985-90*	1991	1992	1993	1994	1995
Australia	2.1	**3.1**	1.4	1.1	−1.3	−0.6	−2.4	..
Austria	2.6	2.3	2.0	2.8	2.4	**3.5**	2.9	..
Belgium	**4.0**	0.8	0.5	−1.9	−0.8	−0.7	−2.6	..
Canada	1.6	2.4	2.2	**2.6**	1.8	1.0	0.7	−2.1
Czech Republic	..	..	..	..	0.0	0.0	**8.6**	−6.6
Denmark	**5.0**	1.8	0.8	−0.5	−0.3	0.7	−1.7	−0.2
Finland	**4.5**	3.2	2.0	1.1	−2.6	−5.1	0.0	1.4
France	1.5	2.3	0.7	1.0	1.9	**2.5**	1.1	1.4
Germany	1.9	1.0	0.9	**35.0**	−1.0	−1.9	−1.3	−1.7
Greece	2.8	**4.3**	1.5	2.5	−1.1	1.2	0.0	..
Iceland	**5.2**	4.0	2.9	2.0	2.4	0.2	..	..
Ireland	**4.5**	1.4	−1.1	1.8	1.6	..	..	..
Italy	**2.4**	1.5	1.1	0.4	0.4	−0.7	−1.1	−0.7
Japan	1.5	0.7	0.2	1.2	1.2	**2.1**	1.9	−0.6
Luxembourg	2.4	1.5	2.5	**3.4**	..	..	..	..
Mexico	..	..	..	**3.7**	0.6	2.0	..	..
Netherlands	**2.3**	0.8	−0.1	−0.8	−0.5	0.0	0.3	−1.1
New-Zealand	**1.5**	−0.5	−0.4	−2.3	−2.8	1.5	−0.1	..
Norway	**5.6**	1.8	2.2	2.9	3.2	2.6	1.9	..
Portugal	6.5	5.6	4.5	3.9	**16.2**	−3.3	0.5	0.6
Spain	4.3	4.2	**6.2**	4.1	1.1	−0.8	−1.1	2.8
Sweden	**4.9**	1.7	0.3	−0.7	−3.8	−3.5	−3.1	..
Switzerland	2.9	1.0	2.0	2.5	**3.2**	1.9	0.2	..
Turkey	4.8	−0.8	0.9	**7.6**	1.3	0.5	..	..
United Kingdom	**0.5**	−0.1	−0.2	−2.7	−4.2	−12.0	−11.4	−3.3
United States	2.1	0.2	**2.3**	0.6	1.3	1.1	1.5	1.0

* Average annual percentage changes over the period.
Source: Analytical Databank, OECD.

Table 5. **Compensation of General Government employees**
As a percentage of nominal GDP

	1970	1975	1980	1985	1990	1991	1992	1993	1994	1995
Australia	9.9	**13.3**	13.0	12.6	11.6	12.3	12.4	12.2	12.0	11.8
Austria	10.2	11.5	12.0	12.7	12.1	12.3	12.5	**12.9**	12.7	..
Belgium	9.9	12.5	**13.7**	13.2	11.2	11.5	11.5	12.0	12.1	12.2
Canada	12.8	13.3	12.8	13.0	13.0	13.9	**14.3**	14.0	13.3	12.8
Czech Republic	..	..	..	..	..	7.0	**7.7**	..	..	..
Denmark	13.2	17.2	18.6	17.9	18.4	18.4	18.5	**18.7**	18.0	17.9
Finland	10.5	11.9	12.3	14.1	14.6	17.1	**17.6**	16.5	15.6	15.3
France	10.8	12.5	13.8	**14.6**	13.2	13.4	13.8	14.4	14.3	14.4
Germany	8.8	**11.4**	11.0	10.6	9.7	10.4	10.6	10.8	10.4	10.3
Greece	7.7	8.1	9.5	11.6	**12.7**	11.6	11.0	11.0	10.8	10.9
Iceland	..	..	10.3	9.9	11.5	12.3	**12.7**	..	..	..
Ireland	9.2	11.9	**12.3**	12.1	10.3	11.0	11.2	11.3	11.1	..
Italy	10.0	10.5	11.1	11.8	**12.8**	12.7	12.7	12.5	12.0	11.4
Japan	5.9	**8.4**	7.9	7.5	7.0	6.9	7.0	7.2	7.3	..
Luxembourg	6.5	9.4	**10.6**	10.2	10.1	10.5	..	..	..	..
Mexico	..	..	7.8	6.9	6.3	6.8	7.6	**8.3**	..	..
Netherlands	11.5	**13.2**	13.0	11.1	9.8	9.7	9.9	10.1	9.8	9.8
New-Zealand	10.3	13.0	**14.8**	11.8	11.9	11.9	11.7	11.1	10.6	..
Norway	10.1	12.0	11.7	11.7	13.6	13.8	**14.3**	14.1	..	..
Portugal	10.5	11.4	10.7	10.9	13.1	14.2	**15.3**	..	..	..
Spain	7.2	7.7	9.7	10.6	11.1	11.5	12.2	**12.3**	11.7	11.6
Sweden	14.5	16.4	**20.7**	18.9	18.8	18.9	19.4	19.2	18.4	17.3
Switzerland	6.8	9.3	9.9	10.3	10.3	10.7	11.1	**11.3**	11.2	..
Turkey	..	6.4	6.2	3.4	5.7	7.3	**8.0**	8.0	..	..
United Kingdom	10.4	**14.0**	12.7	12.1	11.6	11.9	12.0	10.9	9.5	9.0
United States	11.4	**11.6**	10.6	10.6	10.5	10.8	10.7	10.5	10.1	10.0

Source: Analytical Databank, OECD.

Table 6. **Changes in compensation of General Government employees**
Annual percentage changes from previous period in real terms

	1975-80*	1980-85*	1985-90*	1991	1992	1993	1994	1995
Australia	2.1	2.6	0.5	**3.9**	3.8	1.7	2.8	0.1
Austria	4.2	2.5	2.7	**5.0**	3.6	3.4	2.1	..
Belgium	4.1	−1.0	0.9	**4.4**	2.9	3.9	2.9	2.7
Canada	2.8	1.8	2.5	2.0	**3.5**	−1.2	−0.7	−2.1
Czech Republic	..	..	..	..	10.2	..	..	..
Denmark	**2.6**	1.7	1.9	1.4	1.5	1.8	0.6	1.7
Finland	3.0	5.8	4.8	**6.8**	−2.7	−7.3	−1.1	3.6
France	**5.1**	2.3	1.5	2.1	3.8	3.4	2.0	2.9
Germany	2.6	−0.3	2.6	**21.3**	4.7	0.1	−1.5	1.0
Greece	**7.2**	5.4	3.1	−5.1	−5.5	−1.3	−1.2	3.0
Iceland	..	0.1	7.2	**9.2**	−0.9	..	..	..
Ireland	6.0	0.8	1.3	6.7	4.9	**7.7**	2.6	..
Italy	**5.9**	3.2	5.9	2.2	−0.6	−2.6	−1.9	−2.5
Japan	2.2	2.0	**3.1**	1.7	2.5	1.8	1.5	..
Luxembourg	5.2	0.9	6.8	**7.9**	..	..	..	..
Mexico	..	−1.6	−0.8	10.8	**14.0**	11.0	..	..
Netherlands	2.5	−2.7	0.6	1.1	**3.2**	1.7	−0.6	1.7
New-Zealand	**3.7**	−1.5	1.0	−3.6	−0.3	0.7	−0.6	..
Norway	**4.6**	2.6	2.5	4.1	3.9	1.1	..	..
Portugal	3.3	0.1	11.0	13.4	**14.1**	..	..	..
Spain	6.1	2.6	6.4	7.1	**8.1**	−1.1	−3.4	2.2
Sweden	**6.2**	−0.7	3.0	−1.8	−0.5	−5.1	−0.8	−1.3
Switzerland	..	..	**4.1**	3.3	2.4	0.0	0.5	..
Turkey	1.6	−5.9	18.4	**22.9**	12.5	8.7	..	..
United Kingdom	0.4	0.8	**2.1**	1.2	1.3	−6.3	−9.7	−3.6
United States	0.4	**2.9**	2.4	1.7	1.0	0.2	−0.3	−0.1

* Average annual percentage changes over the period.
Source: Analytical Databank, OECD.

◆   Graph 1.   **General Government outlays and employment, 1994**

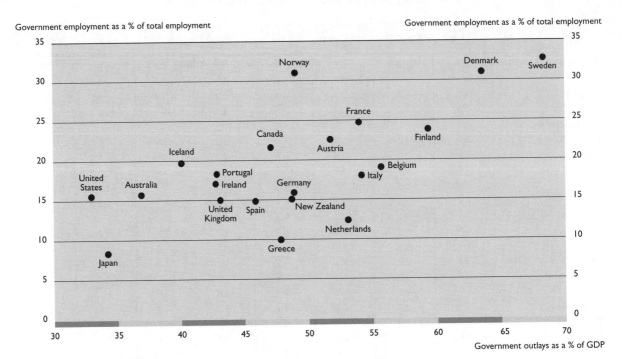

Government employment as a % of total employment

Government employment as a % of total employment

Government outlays as a % of GDP

Data for Ireland refer to 1993, data for Iceland refer to 1992.
Source: Analytical Databank, OECD.

Table 7. **General Government current receipts**
As a percentage of nominal GDP

	1970	1975	1980	1985	1990	1991	1992	1993	1994	1995	1996*	1997*	1998*
Australia	:	28.5	29.7	33.6	35.5	34.6	33.7	33.5	32.9	34.7	34.7	34.6	34.6
Austria	39.7	42.9	46.4	48.5	46.5	47.2	48.6	49.0	47.4	46.7*	47.9	48.4	47.8
Belgium	39.7	45.9	49.5	52.9	48.7	49.2	49.0	49.7	50.6	50.8	51.2	50.9	50.4
Canada	34.3	36.0	36.1	38.5	41.9	42.6	42.8	42.1	41.9	42.4	42.9	43.1	43.1
Czech Republic	:	:	:	:	:	:	51.4	:	:	:	:	:	:
Denmark	40.8	46.8	52.9	57.3	57.1	57.1	58.2	59.8	60.1	59.3	60.1	59.5	58.7
Finland	34.9	43.4	41.0	46.8	50.7	52.5	53.2	52.2	53.3	52.8*	54.3	53.3	53.1
France	39.4	41.0	46.1	49.3	48.3	48.3	48.2	49.0	48.4	48.9	50.0	49.8	49.7
Germany	38.5	42.8	45.0	45.8	43.0	44.5	45.7	46.0	46.5	46.0	45.5	45.5	45.6
Greece	23.7	24.6	27.8	31.5	32.1	32.9	33.7	34.4	35.9	37.6	38.0	38.6	39.0
Iceland	:	:	33.8	34.0	36.0	37.3	37.8	35.9	35.4	35.6*	35.9	36.3	36.3
Ireland	:	:	37.1	41.9	38.8	39.9	40.3	40.3	40.8	38.6*	38.2	37.9	37.7
Italy	29.0	28.7	33.6	38.6	42.4	43.4	44.3	47.4	45.2	44.8	46.7	48.0	47.1
Japan	20.6	24.0	27.6	30.8	34.2	33.8	33.1	32.1	32.2	32.1*	32.0	33.5	33.8
Luxembourg	:	:	:	:	:	:	:	:	:	:	:	:	:
Mexico	:	:	:	:	:	:	:	:	:	:	:	:	:
Netherlands	39.9	48.0	51.6	53.4	49.0	51.7	51.1	52.0	49.7	48.3	47.4	46.8	46.2
New-Zealand	:	:	:	:	52.6	50.9	51.3	50.7	51.4	51.1*	51.0	49.8	49.3
Norway	39.7	44.4	48.5	50.2	52.4	50.8	50.3	49.8	49.4*	50.2*	50.2	49.2	46.7
Portugal	22.7	23.1	29.4	33.7	36.4	37.5	40.0	37.1*	37.2*	38.2*	39.7	39.7	39.4
Spain	21.8	24.1	29.9	34.2	37.9	38.6	40.9	40.9*	39.6*	38.1*	38.3	38.2	37.7
Sweden	47.2	51.2	56.1	59.5	63.3	60.2	59.4	58.8	57.9	58.2*	61.6	60.2	60.3
Switzerland	32.3	39.0	40.3	42.5	42.7	42.6	43.8	45.8	46.5	46.9*	48.9	49.6	49.5
Turkey	:	:	21.3	18.3	:	:	:	:	:	:	:	:	:
United Kingdom	39.7	39.9	39.6	41.2	38.7	38.1	36.8	35.7	36.3	37.6	36.8	36.9	37.1
United States	28.9	28.7	30.0	29.7	30.1	30.1	30.0	30.3	30.7	31.3	31.7	31.5	31.5

* Estimates and projections. *Source: Economic Outlook No. 60, December 1996, OECD.*
Source: Analytical Databank, OECD.

Table 8. **General Government net lending**

As a percentage of nominal GDP

Net lending is often referred to as a measure of government deficits (–) or surpluses (+)

	1970	1975	1980	1985	1990	1991	1992	1993	1994	1995	1996*	1997*	1998*
Australia	:	–2.9	–1.7	–2.8	0.6	–2.7	**–4.0**	–3.7	–4.0	–2.2*	–1.7	–1.1	–0.1
Austria	1.2	–2.5	–1.7	–2.5	–2.2	–2.7	–1.9	–4.2	**–4.4**	–5.9*	–4.3	–3.0	–3.4
Belgium	–2.2	–5.0	–8.9	**–9.0**	–5.6	–6.5	–7.2	–7.5	–5.1	–4.1	–3.2	–2.9	–2.7
Canada	0.8	–2.5	–2.8	–6.8	–4.1	–6.6	**–7.4**	–7.3	–5.3	–4.1	–2.7	–1.5	–0.6
Czech Republic	:	:	:	:	:	:	:	:	:	:	:	:	:
Denmark	0.0	–1.4	–3.3	–2.0	–1.5	–2.1	–2.9	**–3.9**	–3.5	–1.6	–1.5	–0.4	0.3
Finland	4.9	5.8	2.9	3.0	5.4	–1.5	–5.8	**–8.0**	–6.2	–5.4*	–2.9	–1.7	–0.7
France	0.9	–2.4	0.0	–2.9	–1.6	–2.0	–3.8	**–5.6**	–5.6	–4.8	–4.1	–3.2	–3.0
Germany	0.2	**–5.6**	–2.9	–1.2	–2.1	–3.3	–2.8	–3.5	–2.4	–3.5	–4.1	–3.4	–2.6
Greece	:	:	:	–1.7	–3.3	–2.9	–2.8	–4.5	**–4.7**	–3.1*	–2.1	–1.0	–0.8
Iceland	:	:	1.3	–10.7	–2.3	–2.4	–2.5	–2.5	–2.0	–2.3*	–1.5	–1.1	–0.5
Ireland	:	**–12.8**	**–12.1**	–12.6	–11.0	–10.2	–9.5	–9.6	–9.0	–7.1	–6.7	–3.7	–3.4
Italy	–4.0	–2.8	–8.6	–12.6	2.9	2.9	1.4	–1.6	–2.1	–3.3*	–4.1	–2.6	–2.3
Japan	1.6	:	**–4.4**	–0.8	:	:	:	:	:	:	:	:	:
Luxembourg	:	:	:	:	:	:	:	:	:	:	:	:	:
Mexico	–1.7	–2.4	–4.3	–3.6	**–5.1**	–2.9	–3.9	–3.6	–3.4	–4.0	–2.6	–2.3	–2.1
Netherlands	3.0	3.0	5.2	**–7.9**	–5.3	–3.9	–3.2	–1.0	2.6	3.3*	3.0	2.6	2.8
New Zealand	2.7	–5.5	5.6	9.3	2.6	0.2	**–1.7**	–1.5*	0.3*	3.0*	5.4	5.0	4.1
Norway	0.2	–0.2	–2.2	**–7.5**	–5.5	–6.4	–3.3	–6.9*	–5.7*	–4.9*	–3.8	–2.9	–2.9
Portugal	4.4	2.8	–4.0	**–6.9**	–4.1	–4.9	–3.6	–6.8	–6.3	–6.6	–4.8	–3.4	–2.9
Spain	:	:	:	–3.8	4.2	–1.1	–7.8	**–12.3**	–10.3	–7.9*	–3.8	–2.5	–0.5
Sweden	:	:	:	:	:	:	:	:	:	:	:	:	:
Switzerland	3.0	–4.5	–3.4	–2.8	–1.2	–2.5	–6.3	**–7.8**	–6.8	–5.7	–4.8	–3.7	–3.0
Turkey	–1.1	–4.1	–1.4	–3.2	–2.7	–3.3	**–4.4**	–3.6	–2.3	–2.0	–1.6	–1.8	–1.8
United Kingdom													
United States													

* Estimates and projections. *Source: Economic Outlook No. 60, December 1996, OECD* .

Source: Analytical Databank, OECD.

◆   Graph 2.   **General Government outlays and net lending, 1994**

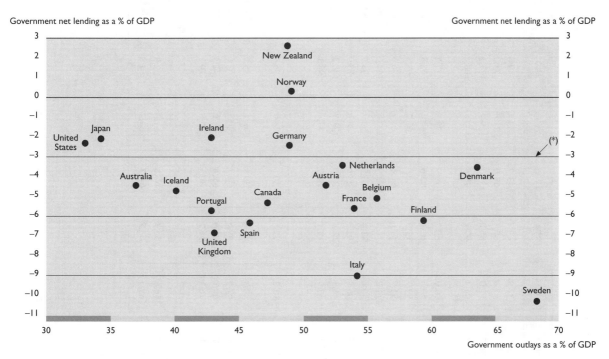

*Maastricht criterion to join the European Monetary Union.
Source: Analytical Databank, OECD.

◆   Graph 3.   **General Government gross public debt and outlays, 1994**

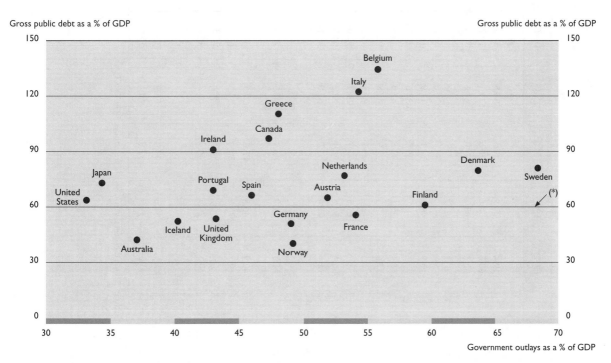

*Maastricht criterion to join the European Monetary Union.
Note: The definition of General Government gross debt used here is based on the system of National Account (SNA). It is slightly larger than the definition
              used to establish the convergence criteria applied under the Maastricht Treaty.
Source: Analytical Databank, OECD.

Table 9.   **General Government gross public debt**
As a percentage of nominal GDP

	1970	1975	1980	1985	1990	1991	1992	1993	1994	1995	1996*	1997*	1998*
Australia	..	..	..	0.0	21.3	22.9	27.7	31.8	42.7	**43.7**	43.4	42.6	40.6
Austria	19.4	23.9	37.3	50.5	58.3	58.7	58.3	62.8	65.1	**69.0**	71.8	73.3	74.7
Belgium	63.8	58.6	78.8	123.1	129.7	129.4	130.7	**137.0**	135.0	133.7	129.9	127.2	124.6
Canada	52.8	43.3	44.0	64.1	72.5	79.4	87.2	94.4	97.2	**99.6**	100.5	98.8	96.2
Czech Republic													
Denmark	..	..	44.7	76.6	68.0	69.1	73.2	**86.0**	80.2	79.9*	79.6	77.7	74.8
Finland	15.9	9.1	14.1	18.9	16.9	25.6	46.2	59.5	61.6	**62.6**	63.4	63.3	63.1
France	..	..	30.9	38.6	40.2	41.0	45.7	52.7	**55.9**	60.0*	62.2	63.3	64.2
Germany	18.4	25.1	32.8	42.5	45.5	44.4	45.8	51.9	51.6	**61.6**	64.7	66.5	67.2
Greece	17.6	18.5	22.9	47.8	90.2	92.4	99.3	111.8	110.4	**111.9**	108.6	104.5	100.7
Iceland	..	..	25.2	33.1	35.2	36.4	43.5	50.0	**52.4**	55.5*	54.9	53.7	52.5
Ireland	..	61.5	71.7	**103.2**	97.0	96.5	93.9	96.9	91.3	84.6*	80.0	75.9	70.8
Italy	38.1	57.6	58.1	82.3	104.5	108.4	114.8	116.3	**122.4**	122.0	121.7	120.3	117.9
Japan	11.5	22.4	51.2	67.0	65.1	62.3	63.5	67.9	**73.2**	80.7*	87.4	93.1	98.4
Luxembourg													
Mexico													
Netherlands	51.5	41.9	46.9	71.5	78.8	78.8	79.5	**80.8**	77.6	80.0	78.0	76.0	75.7
New-Zealand													
Norway	42.9	40.8	**47.6**	37.1	31.6	29.4	35.0	43.3	40.4*	39.9*	38.1	35.9	35.4
Portugal	19.1	23.2	33.0	58.5	65.5	**70.2**	62.4	67.3	69.6	71.7*	70.3	67.6	66.3
Spain	..	..	18.3	50.8	50.3	51.5	53.7	64.7	66.6	**69.6**	71.6	72.4	72.4
Sweden	30.5	29.5	44.3	66.7	44.3	53.2	71.1	76.3	**81.2**	80.5*	79.8	79.5	76.7
Switzerland													
Turkey													
United Kingdom	**77.1**	61.6	54.0	58.9	39.3	40.6	47.6	56.6	54.3	60.0	61.9	62.0	61.5
United States	41.5	39.9	37.0	49.1	55.6	59.6	62.0	63.5	63.7	**64.3**	64.2	64.0	63.8

* Estimates and projections. *Source: Economic Outlook No. 60, December 1996,* OECD.
Source: Analytical Databank, OECD.

Table 10. **Structure of General Government outlays by type of outlays**
As a percentage of total in each year

	1970					1980					1990					1994				
	Final consumption	Social security	Others transfers and subsidies	Investments	Debt interest	Final consumption	Social security	Others transfers and subsidies	Investments	Debt interest	Final consumption	Social security	Others transfers and subsidies	Investments	Debt interest	Final consumption	Social security	Others transfers and subsidies	Investments	Debt interest
Australia	51.9	—	27.1	14.2	6.8	52.5	—	33.2	8.0	6.3	46.7	—	35.7	6.2	11.4	45.5	—	39.1	5.2	10.3
Austria	38.5	20.8	25.7	12.2	2.8	38.1	20.1	27.7	8.9	5.3	37.1	21.9	25.9	6.6	8.5	37.0	21.4	27.6	6.0	8.0
Belgium	31.5	30.9	20.9	9.1	7.6	30.1	33.5	19.9	6.2	10.3	25.7	33.9	19.0	2.2	19.3	26.5	35.0	19.8	2.4	16.4
Canada	52.8	10.3	16.3	10.2	10.5	47.4	13.3	19.2	6.6	13.5	42.5	16.2	15.9	5.3	20.1	41.4	17.7	17.5	4.6	18.9
Czech Republic	..	..	..	..	..	..	..	..	..	..	..	..	..	..	..	..	..	..	..	..
Denmark	47.6	15.5	22.0	11.5	3.4	46.9	29.2	10.9	6.1	6.9	42.7	31.1	10.4	3.4	12.3	39.9	34.4	11.3	3.3	11.1
Finland	37.1	28.7	22.0	9.5	2.7	45.9	21.2	20.9	9.3	2.7	45.1	25.9	17.9	7.8	3.1	36.9	29.3	20.6	4.8	8.5
France	40.4	22.8	23.3	11.4	2.2	38.6	33.3	18.0	6.9	3.1	35.2	33.3	18.8	6.9	5.8	34.7	33.1	19.3	5.6	7.3
Germany	56.3	35.5	3.9	..	4.2	41.3	24.2	23.6	7.0	3.8	39.7	24.1	25.7	4.8	5.6	34.0	24.1	31.0	4.3	6.5
Greece	..	..	..	..	..	53.6	30.2	8.3	..	7.9	43.0	30.7	3.5	..	22.8	35.2	32.4	1.9	..	30.6
Iceland	..	..	..	..	..	49.6	9.7	25.2	10.8	4.8	48.0	9.9	23.4	9.9	8.8	50.3	11.2	19.1	9.9	9.5
Ireland	..	..	..	..	..	..	..	..	..	..	35.7	11.7	29.0	5.0	18.6	36.7	11.4	31.6	5.2	15.1¹
Italy	38.9	17.6	16.9	23.4	3.2	33.8	32.4	13.5	7.3	13.0	31.5	32.9	11.6	5.9	18.2	30.8	35.1	10.0	4.2	20.0
Japan	31.6	41.0	14.3	9.8	3.4	30.6	24.5	16.0	19.1	9.8	28.2	30.8	13.0	15.7	12.2	27.5	31.1	11.8	18.8	10.8
Luxembourg	..	..	..	..	..	30.4	41.4	15.2	11.5	1.5	..	..	..	..	..	..	..	..	..	..
Mexico	..	..	..	..	..	..	..	..	..	..	..	..	..	..	..	..	..	..	..	..
Netherlands	41.3	29.9	13.5	10.9	4.4	29.0	34.6	24.1	5.9	6.5	25.1	33.9	26.0	4.6	10.3	25.2	35.4	23.8	4.9	10.8
New-Zealand	..	..	..	..	..	37.5	22.7	25.8	7.8	6.2	41.6	32.1	12.0	7.2	7.2	42.7	32.7	11.9	6.5	6.2
Norway	..	..	..	..	..	..	..	..	..	..	35.5	19.8	17.4	7.7	19.6	38.5	23.7	17.8	5.3	14.7¹
Portugal	..	..	..	..	..	..	..	..	..	..	35.7	33.0	11.7	11.1	8.5	39.6	38.7	9.7	..	12.0
Spain	..	..	..	..	..	..	..	..	..	..	45.0	25.9	15.7	5.0	8.4	39.2	26.7	19.6	4.7	9.9
Sweden	49.3	29.4	14.5	..	6.9	47.9	22.6	15.6	7.0	6.7	43.5	34.6	17.3	..	4.6	38.2	37.8	18.3	..	5.8
Switzerland	..	..	..	..	..	43.5	35.2	15.0	..	6.3	..	..	..	..	..	..	..	..	..	..
Turkey	..	..	..	..	..	..	..	..	..	..	..	..	..	..	..	..	..	..	..	..
United Kingdom	45.3	13.6	19.2	12.0	9.9	48.1	14.2	21.8	5.5	10.5	48.3	13.4	24.8	5.5	8.0	47.8	13.7	27.1	4.1	7.3
United States	58.2	14.3	13.0	7.7	7.0	51.7	19.6	14.5	5.4	9.3	48.3	19.4	13.7	4.9	13.7	45.5	21.4	16.2	4.5	12.3¹

1. 1993

Source: *National Accounts*, OECD.

◆ Graph 4. **Structure of General Government outlays by type of outlay**
As a percentage of nominal GDP in 1980 and 1994 (or most recent available year)

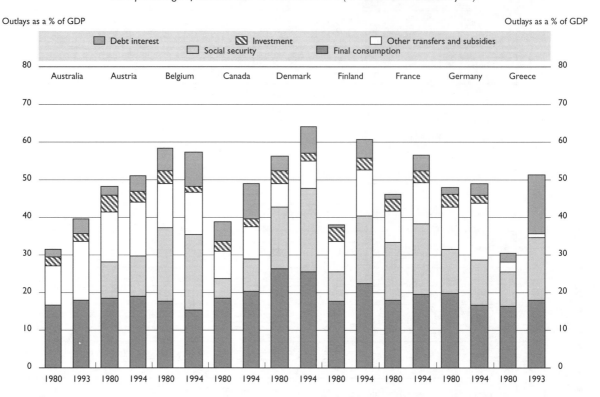

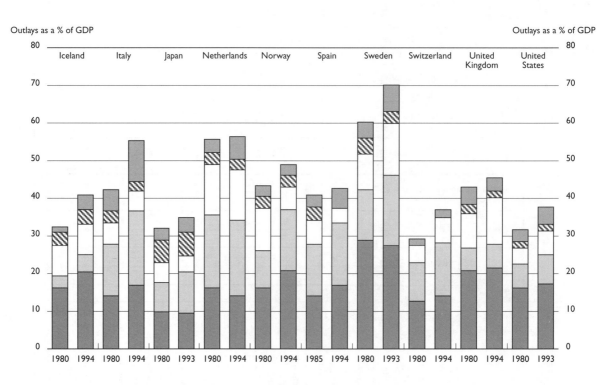

Source: National Accounts, OECD.

Table 11. **Structure of General Government outlays by level of government**
As a percentage of total in each year

	1970					1980					1990					1994				
	Central	Social security funds	Central and Social security*	State	Local	Central	Social security funds	Central and Social security*	State	Local	Central	Social security funds	Central and Social security*	State	Local	Central	Social security funds	Central and Social security*	State	Local
Australia**	55.4	–	55.4	–	44.6	52.1	–	52.1	–	47.9	50.9	–	50.9	–	49.1	54.6	–	54.6	–	45.4
Austria	46.3	33.9	80.2	8.1	11.7	40.5	33.8	74.3	13.6	12.1	41.1	34.1	75.2	13.6	11.3	41.6	33.2	74.8	13.9	11.3
Belgium	51.3	36.3	87.6	–	12.4	48.5	38.0	86.5	–	13.5	53.1	35.8	88.8	–	11.2	51.9	36.8	88.7	–	11.3
Canada	40.6	0.5	41.1	27.7	31.2	40.4	2.3	42.7	31.9	25.4	41.1	4.6	45.7	32.0	22.4	38.9	5.8	44.7	32.7	22.6
Czech Republic	..	..	..	..	..	..	..	..	..	..	..	..	..	..	..	..	..	..	..	..
Denmark	..	..	..	..	..	32.9	8.2	41.2	–	58.8	39.2	8.9	48.1	–	51.9	38.7	9.6	48.3	–	51.7
Finland	47.2	17.3	64.5	–	35.5	38.4	23.6	62.0	–	38.0	34.1	28.2	62.3	–	37.7	33.5	38.3	71.8	–	28.2
France	50.0	39.6	89.6	–	10.4	41.4	46.1	87.5	–	12.5	40.1	46.1	86.2	–	13.8	40.2	45.3	85.5	–	14.5
Germany	26.2	39.8	66.0	22.3	11.7	23.5	42.7	66.2	22.3	11.5	26.5	41.4	67.9	21.0	11.1	26.2	43.3	69.5	19.7	10.8
Greece	54.8	34.1	88.9	–	11.1	58.1	31.3	89.4	–	10.6	56.9	32.9	89.8	–	10.2	58.4	33.7	92.1	–	7.9
Iceland	..	..	..	..	..	58.7	25.3	83.9	–	16.1	64.2	20.2	84.4	–	15.6	60.2	20.4	80.6	–	19.4
Ireland	..	..	..	..	..	44.1	33.2	77.4	–	22.6	62.0	12.9	75.0	–	25.0	60.9	12.7	73.6	–	26.4[1]
Italy	27.1	25.4	52.5	–	47.5	44.1	33.2	77.4	–	22.6	48.1	27.2	75.3	–	24.7	48.4	28.5	76.9	–	23.1
Japan	44.8	43.5	88.3	–	11.7	26.9	32.4	59.3	–	40.7	25.2	38.4	63.6	–	36.4	22.3	41.1	63.4	–	36.6
Luxembourg	..	..	..	..	..	44.4	44.2	88.6	–	11.4	..	..	..	..	..	..	..	..	..	..
Mexico	..	..	..	..	..	..	..	..	..	..	..	..	..	..	..	..	..	..	..	..
Netherlands	..	..	..	..	..	30.3	39.0	69.2	–	30.8	35.7	37.2	72.9	–	27.1	35.3	38.9	74.3	–	25.7
New Zealand	..	..	..	..	..	..	..	..	..	..	..	..	..	..	..	..	..	..	..	..
Norway	..	..	..	..	..	38.3	31.2	69.5	–	30.5	39.8	27.3	67.1	–	32.9	39.2	27.9	67.1	–	32.9
Portugal	..	..	..	..	..	..	..	..	..	..	64.6	25.7	90.4	–	9.6	61.2	30.5	91.7	–	8.3[1]
Spain	..	..	..	..	..	..	..	..	..	..	34.3	45.4	79.7	–	20.3	33.4	46.2	79.6	–	20.4[1]
Sweden	20.5	31.9	52.4	23.7	23.9	44.5	14.6	59.1	–	40.9	41.8	19.0	60.8	–	39.2	45.3	20.3	65.5	–	34.5
Switzerland	..	..	..	..	..	17.4	38.4	55.8	24.9	19.3	17.0	38.2	55.2	26.3	18.4	14.6	41.7	56.4	26.1	17.5
Turkey	..	..	..	..	..	..	..	..	..	..	..	..	..	..	..	..	..	..	..	..
United Kingdom	54.1	16.7	70.7	–	29.3	57.3	15.7	73.0	–	27.0	58.2	15.1	73.2	–	26.8	59.7	15.0	74.7	–	25.3
United States**	46.5	16.2	62.6	–	37.4	40.6	21.2	61.8	–	38.2	41.4	20.8	62.3	–	37.7	38.4	22.9	61.3	–	38.7[1]

1. 1993.

* This column sums the two columns "central" and "social security funds"; total outlays is made up of central, social security funds, state plus local.

** Local Government includes State Government.

Source: National Accounts, OECD.

Table 12. **Changes in gross domestic product**
Percentage changes from previous period in real terms

	1975-80*	1980-85*	1985-90*	1991	1992	1993	1994	1995	1996**	1997**	1998**
Australia	3.1	3.4	3.5	-1.6	2.9	4.0	4.9	3.2	4.1	3.3	3.0
Austria	3.6	1.3	3.2	2.8	2.0	0.4	3.0	1.8	1.1	1.4	2.3
Belgium	3.2	0.8	3.3	1.6	1.7	-1.4	2.3	1.9	1.3	2.2	2.6
Canada	4.3	3.1	3.1	-1.8	0.8	2.2	4.1	2.3	1.5	3.3	3.3
Czech Republic	..	..	..	..	-6.4	-0.9	2.6	4.8	4.8	4.6	5.3
Denmark	2.6	2.8	1.5	1.3	0.2	1.5	4.4	2.8	1.9	2.9	3.1
Finland	3.2	3.1	3.6	-7.1	-3.6	-1.2	4.4	4.2	2.5	3.5	3.6
France	3.3	1.6	3.4	0.8	1.2	-1.3	2.8	2.2	1.3	2.5	2.6
Germany	3.5	1.2	3.6	13.2	2.2	-1.1	2.9	1.9	1.1	2.2	2.6
Greece	4.8	1.4	1.9	3.1	0.4	-1.0	1.5	2.0	2.2	2.5	2.8
Iceland	7.1	2.4	3.4	1.3	-3.3	0.8	3.5	2.1	5.4	3.3	2.9
Ireland	5.0	2.7	4.9	2.1	4.0	3.1	6.5	10.3	7.0	6.2	6.8
Italy	4.9	1.5	3.2	1.1	0.6	-1.2	2.1	3.0	0.8	1.2	2.1
Japan	4.8	3.6	5.1	4.0	1.1	0.1	0.5	0.9	3.6	1.6	3.7
Luxembourg	2.4	2.6	7.3	6.1	4.5	8.7	4.2	3.7	2.4	3.1	3.2
Mexico	7.6	2.0	1.4	3.6	2.8	0.6	3.5	-6.9	4.0	5.0	4.5
Netherlands	2.8	1.3	3.3	2.3	2.0	0.8	3.4	2.1	2.7	2.7	3.0
New-Zealand	-0.6	4.4	0.7	-2.5	0.8	4.4	5.0	1.9	1.2	2.9	2.9
Norway	5.4	3.6	1.5	2.9	3.4	2.1	5.0	3.3	5.1	3.0	2.3
Portugal	5.6	0.9	5.8	2.1	1.1	-1.2	0.8	2.4	2.6	2.9	3.2
Spain	1.8	1.6	4.9	2.3	0.7	-1.2	2.1	2.8	2.1	2.7	3.0
Sweden	1.4	1.8	2.4	-1.1	-1.4	-2.2	3.3	3.6	1.7	2.2	2.1
Switzerland	1.8	1.4	2.9	0.0	-0.3	-0.8	1.0	0.1	-0.3	0.8	2.0
Turkey	2.5	5.4	6.2	0.9	6.0	8.0	-5.5	7.3	7.5	5.7	5.0
United Kingdom	1.9	2.1	3.5	-2.0	-0.5	2.1	3.8	2.4	2.4	3.3	3.0
United States	3.9	3.1	3.0	-1.0	2.7	2.3	3.5	2.0	2.4	2.2	2.0

* Average annual percentage changes over the period.
**Estimates and projections. *Source: Economic Outlook No. 60, December 1996*, OECD.

Source: Analytical Databank, OECD.

Table 13. **Per capita gross domestic product**
At current prices and using purchasing power parities
(US dollars)

	1970	1975	1980	1985	1990	1991	1992	1993	1994	1995
Australia	3 665.4	5 940.8	9 208.7	12 852.2	16 029.7	16 339.5	17 035.9	18 017.4	19 004.9	..
Austria	3 048.1	5 138.1	8 849.6	12 278.3	16 623.3	17 294.8	18 822.3	19 166.8	20 224.8	..
Belgium	3 185.8	5 249.2	8 819.6	11 933.3	16 467.1	17 222.0	19 065.8	19 450.5	20 334.6	..
Canada	3 602.8	6 020.5	10 020.0	14 261.7	18 303.7	18 383.7	18 781.8	19 310.3	20 324.0	..
Czech Republic										
Denmark	3 551.0	5 379.3	8 745.8	12 996.8	16 548.3	17 418.2	18 338.7	19 190.8	20 460.3	..
Finland	2 884.7	4 861.2	8 004.3	11 681.9	16 192.9	15 443.6	15 078.9	15 645.7	16 288.5	..
France	3 480.7	5 612.9	9 318.3	12 743.9	17 347.3	18 156.2	19 259.0	18 675.7	19 251.2	..
Germany	4 044.1	6 233.0	10 693.0	15 097.8	20 063.7	16 962.0	17 747.0	16 891.0	17 590.0	..
Greece	1 484.3	2 603.8	4 401.1	5 940.2	7 427.2	7 802.0	8 559.9	8 759.4	9 212.3	..
Iceland	2 784.4	5 038.9	9 492.1	13 099.7	17 271.2	17 901.3	18 388.9	18 696.3	19 341.9	..
Ireland	1 871.0	3 115.5	5 290.5	7 501.2	11 244.9	11 976.2	13 412.4	13 790.9	15 223.4	..
Italy	2 993.6	4 690.9	8 415.2	11 654.9	16 256.6	17 113.1	18 353.5	17 710.5	18 665.1	..
Japan	2 908.6	4 765.6	8 203.5	12 188.0	17 823.7	19 122.7	20 324.6	20 691.5	21 170.5	..
Luxembourg	3 968.8	6 086.5	9 796.8	14 352.2	19 818.8	20 873.8	22 678.8	..	..	..
Mexico	1 282.1	..	3 640.0	4 720.8	5 493.2	5 754.1	7 319.4	7 359.4	7 617.6	..
Netherlands	3 469.0	5 467.4	8 750.0	11 839.4	15 958.2	16 408.2	17 687.8	17 817.2	18 741.8	..
New Zealand	3 386.4	5 370.2	7 711.3	11 184.9	13 483.8	13 603.2	14 307.7	15 206.5	16 247.6	..
Norway	2 974.0	5 097.0	9 205.0	13 898.0	17 497.0	18 547.0	20 612.0	21 328.0	21 968.0	..
Portugal	1 583.3	2 576.1	4 556.0	6 075.6	9 397.2	10 128.1	11 049.3	11 422.0	12 017.2	..
Spain	2 229.8	3 887.0	5 868.3	8 018.1	11 787.3	12 722.2	13 375.6	13 329.2	13 608.6	..
Sweden	3 837.0	6 038.5	9 250.3	13 057.0	17 004.4	16 808.9	17 200.0	16 870.2	17 525.1	..
Switzerland	5 139.5	7 387.8	11 719.8	15 968.8	21 283.2	21 719.0	23 081.4	23 182.7	24 027.7	..
Turkey	938.5	1 560.9	2 299.0	3 350.8	4 690.5	4 805.8	5 142.9	5 561.7	5 270.6	..
United Kingdom	3 262.2	5 063.8	8 041.3	11 462.2	15 888.0	15 550.3	16 885.5	16 913.4	17 654.3	..
United States	4 933.2	7 350.7	11 892.1	16 843.7	21 966.2	22 388.9	23 246.4	24 251.9	25 512.3	..

Source: National Accounts and Labour Force Statistics, OECD.

THE PUBLIC MANAGEMENT SERVICE (PUMA) OF THE OECD

The Public Management Service (PUMA) reports on, analyses and assesses information on public management developments in OECD Member countries. Through meetings of Member country officials and experts, exchanges of information and expertise, and reports, PUMA examines what governments do, and how they are seeking to improve public policy effectiveness, efficiency, responsiveness to citizens, and quality of services.

Its mission is to:

– provide information, analysis and assessment on public management for policy-makers in Member countries and for the OECD, and to develop the tools to do this;
– facilitate contact and exchange of experience on good practice amongst public management practitioners, particularly those working in central management agencies in government;
– report regularly on issues and developments in governance and public management, and on their relevance to economic and social development.

PUMA's work programme is shaped and directed by the Public Management Committee, and carried out by the PUMA Secretariat in collaboration with specialist groups of senior managers responsible for strategic management of policy-making, budgeting and financial management, performance management, regulatory management and human resources management. These specialist groups also meet regularly to exchange information and consider analysis of specific management issues.

PUMA's work currently covers the following areas and issues:

Governance and Public Management. This work addresses issues of governance and public management, and describes the range of techniques and strategies that are used to carry out governments' responsibilities, and the reforms being pursued in OECD Member countries. In addition to analysis and reporting on overall reform trends, issues and developments, this includes:

– **Strategic Management and Policy-Making**, which encompasses work to improve overall policy co-ordination and coherence, and draws upon experiences and information from centres of government;
– **Information Technology and Information Policy**, which refers to work on how governments manage programmes and information in the context of changing information technology.
– **Ethics in the Public Service**, which examines how governments are seeking to safeguard essential public service values and ensure high ethical standards.

Performance and the Management of Resources. This work addresses practical and specific issues of how to improve performance, issues related to redistribution of responsibilities, management of budgets and human resources. It includes:

– **Performance Management**, which examines issues of the measurement of the performance of public sector organisations, including their effectiveness, efficiency, service quality and responsiveness, and mechanisms to integrate performance issues into the management of these organisations.

- **Budgeting and Financial Management**, which addresses techniques aimed at increasing overall budgetary control.
- **Market-type Mechanisms**, which analyses government experiences in applying market-based mechanisms such as contracting out, user charging, increased choice, competition, corporatisation, and commercialisation.
- **Managing across Levels of Government**, which examines issues of co-ordination, performance and accountability related to redistributing responsibilities to different levels of government.
- **Human Resources Management**, which reports on management of public sector employees, including more flexible, performance-oriented, and cost-effective employment and pay practices.

Regulatory Management and Reform. This work addresses issues of improving regulatory quality, developing alternatives to traditional regulation, and reducing administrative burdens on private enterprises.

PUMA on the Internet

Further information on the Public Management Service can be found on the Internet. The PUMA Web Site is designed to help PUMA fulfil its mission by providing an up-to-date source for locating information on public management issues and developments. This information includes not only references to PUMA work, analysis, and publications, but also links to a growing range of sites and documents developed throughout the world. "**Focus On-Line**", the electronic version of *Focus*, PUMA's quarterly newsletter, can also be found on this site.

PUMA's Web address is: http: //www. oecd. org/puma.

GLOSSARY OF SELECTED TERMS

ACCOUNTABILITY *(responsabilité/obligation de rendre compte)* – Exists where there is a hierarchical relationship within which one party accounts to the other (a person or body) for the performance of tasks or functions conferred. Accountability goes hand in hand with devolution and flexibility: managers are held accountable for results once they are given the authority to make decisions that are part of producing those results. Another important aspect of accountability is the public accountability of those who govern to elected bodies and thence to the public at large.

CORPORATISATION *(constitution en société)* – The establishment of public units with commercial functions as separate legal entities similar to those operating in the private sector. It involves, among other things, identifying the property, rights, liabilities, and obligations of the business and establishing the capital structure and funding arrangements. Such state enterprises operate at arm's length from the ministers and parliament, within a framework of strategic objectives set by government.

DEPARTMENTS OR MINISTRIES AND AGENCIES *(départements ou ministères et agences)* – The meanings of these terms (and closely related ones) are specific to each OECD country. The broad distinction that is often made is between central management bodies such as the Ministry of Finance, the Budget Office, the Ministry of Public Administration, and the Prime Minister's Office, and operating units. The distinction may also be made between policy units and operational ones.

DEVOLUTION *(transfert de compétences)* – The granting of greater decision-making authority and autonomy:

a) by central management bodies to line departments and agencies;
b) by departments and agencies to independent subordinate bodies;
c) within departments and agencies to lower levels of management and to regional/local offices of central government; and
d) by central government to lower levels of government.

This single term may be used instead of several terms that have more precise meanings but that are used differently in different Member countries and therefore can be a source of confusion in an international context (such as decentralisation, deconcentration, delegation, and devolution itself).

MARKET-TYPE MECHANISMS *(mécanismes de type marché)* – All arrangements where at least one significant characteristic of markets is present (competition, choice, pricing, dispersed decision-making, monetary incentives, and so on). It excludes the two polar cases of traditional public delivery and complete privatisation.

PRIVATISATION *(privatisation)* – The transfer of a public enterprise from state to private ownership. It is generally *not* used to refer to the introduction of market-type mechanisms such as contracting out, or the private provision of public infrastructure, or the growth of private alternatives to public sector provision.

PUBLIC SECTOR *(secteur public)* – Central government departments and agencies, the wider public service (including defence forces, police, education, health), public enterprises, certain bodies funded from public monies, and subnational levels of government. The term corresponds roughly to the category of "general government" as defined in the System of National Accounts (SNA), plus public enterprises.

REGULATION (*réglementation*) – Includes the full range of legal instruments and decisions – constitutions, parliamentary laws, lower-level legislation, decrees, orders, norms, licenses, plans, codes, and often even "grey" regulations such as guidance and instructions – through which governments impose limits on the behaviour of citizens end enterprises. It should be noted that "laws" are a subset, although an important subset, of the set of regulations applied in a country.

SUBSIDIARITY (*subsidiarité*) – A paper on this subject by the Council of Europe states that "subsidiarity is a fashionable idea today, although its meaning remains unclear". It is not a term with a limited technical meaning applying to governmental structures. Rather, it conveys a political philosophy, which is the constant search for a decision-making level as close to the citizen as possible. For some, this also implies that the political power in a society rests inherently with the individual, not the state.

MAIN SALES OUTLETS OF OECD PUBLICATIONS
PRINCIPAUX POINTS DE VENTE DES PUBLICATIONS DE L'OCDE

AUSTRALIA – AUSTRALIE
D.A. Information Services
648 Whitehorse Road, P.O.B 163
Mitcham, Victoria 3132   Tel. (03) 9210.7777
                            Fax: (03) 9210.7788

AUSTRIA – AUTRICHE
Gerold & Co.
Graben 31
Wien I   Tel. (0222) 533.50.14
                            Fax: (0222) 512.47.31.29

BELGIUM – BELGIQUE
Jean De Lannoy
Avenue du Roi, Koningslaan 202
B-1060 Bruxelles   Tel. (02) 538.51.69/538.08.41
                            Fax: (02) 538.08.41

CANADA
Renouf Publishing Company Ltd.
5369 Canotek Road
Unit 1
Ottawa, Ont. K1J 9J3   Tel. (613) 745.2665
                            Fax: (613) 745.7660

Stores:
71 1/2 Sparks Street
Ottawa, Ont. K1P 5R1   Tel. (613) 238.8985
                            Fax: (613) 238.6041

12 Adelaide Street West
Toronto, QN M5H 1L6   Tel. (416) 363.3171
                            Fax: (416) 363.5963

Les Éditions La Liberté Inc.
3020 Chemin Sainte-Foy
Sainte-Foy, PQ G1X 3V6   Tel. (418) 658.3763
                            Fax: (418) 658.3763

Federal Publications Inc.
165 University Avenue, Suite 701
Toronto, ON M5H 3B8   Tel. (416) 860.1611
                            Fax: (416) 860.1608

Les Publications Fédérales
1185 Université
Montréal, QC H3B 3A7   Tel. (514) 954.1633
                            Fax: (514) 954.1635

CHINA – CHINE
Book Dept., China Natinal Publications
Import and Export Corporation (CNPIEC)
16 Gongti E. Road, Chaoyang District
Beijing 100020   Tel. (10) 6506-6688 Ext. 8402
                            (10) 6506-3101

CHINESE TAIPEI – TAIPEI CHINOIS
Good Faith Worldwide Int'l. Co. Ltd.
9th Floor, No. 118, Sec. 2
Chung Hsiao E. Road
Taipei   Tel. (02) 391.7396/391.7397
                            Fax: (02) 394.9176

**CZECH REPUBLIC –
RÉPUBLIQUE TCHÈQUE**
National Information Centre
NIS – prodejna
Konviktská 5
Praha 1 – 113 57   Tel. (02) 24.23.09.07
                            Fax: (02) 24.22.94.33
E-mail: nkposp@dec.niz.cz
Internet: http://www.nis.cz

DENMARK – DANEMARK
Munksgaard Book and Subscription Service
35, Nørre Søgade, P.O. Box 2148
DK-1016 København K   Tel. (33) 12.85.70
                            Fax: (33) 12.93.87

J. H. Schultz Information A/S,
Herstedvang 12,
DK – 2620 Albertslung   Tel. 43 63 23 00
                            Fax: 43 63 19 69
Internet: s-info@inet.uni-c.dk

EGYPT – ÉGYPTE
The Middle East Observer
41 Sherif Street
Cairo   Tel. (2) 392.6919
                            Fax: (2) 360.6804

FINLAND – FINLANDE
Akateeminen Kirjakauppa
Keskuskatu 1, P.O. Box 128
00100 Helsinki

Subscription Services/Agence d'abonnements :
P.O. Box 23
00100 Helsinki   Tel. (358) 9.121.4403
                            Fax: (358) 9.121.4450

*FRANCE
OECD/OCDE
Mail Orders/Commandes par correspondance :
2, rue André-Pascal
75775 Paris Cedex 16   Tel. 33 (0)1.45.24.82.00
                         Fax: 33 (0)1.49.10.42.76
                         Telex: 640048 OCDE
Internet: Compte.PUBSINQ@oecd.org

Orders via Minitel, France only/
Commandes par Minitel, France exclusivement :
36 15 OCDE

OECD Bookshop/Librairie de l'OCDE :
33, rue Octave-Feuillet
75016 Paris   Tel. 33 (0)1.45.24.81.81
                            33 (0)1.45.24.81.67

Dawson
B.P. 40
91121 Palaiseau Cedex   Tel. 01.89.10.47.00
                            Fax: 01.64.54.83.26

Documentation Française
29, quai Voltaire
75007 Paris   Tel. 01.40.15.70.00

Economica
49, rue Héricart
75015 Paris   Tel. 01.45.78.12.92
                            Fax: 01.45.75.05.67

Gibert Jeune (Droit-Économie)
6, place Saint-Michel
75006 Paris   Tel. 01.43.25.91.19

Librairie du Commerce International
10, avenue d'Iéna
75016 Paris   Tel. 01.40.73.34.60

Librairie Dunod
Université Paris-Dauphine
Place du Maréchal-de-Lattre-de-Tassigny
75016 Paris   Tel. 01.44.05.40.13

Librairie Lavoisier
11, rue Lavoisier
75008 Paris   Tel. 01.42.65.39.95

Librairie des Sciences Politiques
30, rue Saint-Guillaume
75007 Paris   Tel. 01.45.48.36.02

P.U.F.
49, boulevard Saint-Michel
75005 Paris   Tel. 01.43.25.83.40

Librairie de l'Université
12a, rue Nazareth
13100 Aix-en-Provence   Tel. 04.42.26.18.08

Documentation Française
165, rue Garibaldi
69003 Lyon   Tel. 04.78.63.32.23

Librairie Decitre
29, place Bellecour
69002 Lyon   Tel. 04.72.40.54.54

Librairie Sauramps
Le Triangle
34967 Montpellier Cedex 2   Tel. 04.67.58.85.15
                            Fax: 04.67.58.27.36

A la Sorbonne Actual
23, rue de l'Hôtel-des-Postes
06000 Nice   Tel. 04.93.13.77.75
                            Fax: 04.93.80.75.69

GERMANY – ALLEMAGNE
OECD Bonn Centre
August-Bebel-Allee 6
D-53175 Bonn   Tel. (0228) 959.120
                            Fax: (0228) 959.12.17

GREECE – GRÈCE
Librairie Kauffmann
Stadiou 28
10564 Athens   Tel. (01) 32.55.321
                            Fax: (01) 32.30.320

HONG-KONG
Swindon Book Co. Ltd.
Astoria Bldg. 3F
34 Ashley Road, Tsimshatsui
Kowloon, Hong Kong   Tel. 2376.2062
                            Fax: 2376.0685

HUNGARY – HONGRIE
Euro Info Service
Margitsziget, Európa Ház
1138 Budapest   Tel. (1) 111.60.61
                            Fax: (1) 302.50.35
E-mail: euroinfo@mail.matav.hu
Internet: http://www.euroinfo.hu//index.html

ICELAND – ISLANDE
Mál og Menning
Laugavegi 18, Pósthólf 392
121 Reykjavik   Tel. (1) 552.4240
                            Fax: (1) 562.3523

INDIA – INDE
Oxford Book and Stationery Co.
Scindia House
New Delhi 110001   Tel. (11) 331.5896/5308
                            Fax: (11) 332.2639
E-mail: oxford.publ@axcess.net.in

17 Park Street
Calcutta 700016   Tel. 240832

INDONESIA – INDONÉSIE
Pdii-Lipi
P.O. Box 4298
Jakarta 12042   Tel. (21) 573.34.67
                            Fax: (21) 573.34.67

IRELAND – IRLANDE
Government Supplies Agency
Publications Section
4/5 Harcourt Road
Dublin 2   Tel. 661.31.11
                            Fax: 475.27.60

ISRAEL – ISRAËL
Praedicta
5 Shatner Street
P.O. Box 34030
Jerusalem 91430   Tel. (2) 652.84.90/1/2
                            Fax: (2) 652.84.93

R.O.Y. International
P.O. Box 13056
Tel Aviv 61130   Tel. (3) 546 1423
                            Fax: (3) 546 1442
E-mail: royil@netvision.net.il

Palestinian Authority/Middle East:
INDEX Information Services
P.O.B. 19502
Jerusalem   Tel. (2) 627.16.34
                            Fax: (2) 627.12.19

ITALY – ITALIE
Libreria Commissionaria Sansoni
Via Duca di Calabria, 1/1
50125 Firenze   Tel. (055) 64.54.15
                            Fax: (055) 64.12.57
E-mail: licosa@ftbcc.it

Via Bartolini 29
20155 Milano   Tel. (02) 36.50.83

Editrice e Libreria Herder
Piazza Montecitorio 120
00186 Roma   Tel. 679.46.28
                            Fax: 678.47.51

Libreria Hoepli
Via Hoepli 5
20121 Milano   Tel. (02) 86.54.46
                            Fax: (02) 805.28.86

Libreria Scientifica
Dott. Lucio de Biasio 'Aeiou'
Via Coronelli, 6
20146 Milano   Tel. (02) 48.95.45.52
                                 Fax: (02) 48.95.45.48

JAPAN – JAPON
OECD Tokyo Centre
Landic Akasaka Building
2-3-4 Akasaka, Minato-ku
Tokyo 107   Tel. (81.3) 3586.2016
                                 Fax: (81.3) 3584.7929

KOREA – CORÉE
Kyobo Book Centre Co. Ltd.
P.O. Box 1658, Kwang Hwa Moon
Seoul   Tel. 730.78.91
                                 Fax: 735.00.30

MALAYSIA – MALAISIE
University of Malaya Bookshop
University of Malaya
P.O. Box 1127, Jalan Pantai Baru
59700 Kuala Lumpur
Malaysia   Tel. 756.5000/756.5425
                                 Fax: 756.3246

MEXICO – MEXIQUE
OECD Mexico Centre
Edificio INFOTEC
Av. San Fernando no. 37
Col. Toriello Guerra
Tlalpan C.P. 14050
Mexico D.F.   Tel. (525) 528.10.38
                                 Fax: (525) 606.13.07
E-mail: ocde@rtn.net.mx

NETHERLANDS – PAYS-BAS
SDU Uitgeverij Plantijnstraat
Externe Fondsen
Postbus 20014
2500 EA's-Gravenhage   Tel. (070) 37.89.880
Voor bestellingen: Fax: (070) 34.75.778

Subscription Agency/   Agence d'abonnements :
SWETS & ZEITLINGER BV
Heereweg 347B
P.O. Box 830
2160 SZ Lisse   Tel. 252.435.111
                                 Fax: 252.415.888

**NEW ZEALAND –
NOUVELLE-ZÉLANDE**
GPLegislation Services
P.O. Box 12418
Thorndon, Wellington   Tel. (04) 496.5655
                                 Fax: (04) 496.5698

NORWAY – NORVÈGE
NIC INFO A/S
Ostensjoveien 18
P.O. Box 6512 Etterstad
0606 Oslo   Tel. (22) 97.45.00
                                 Fax: (22) 97.45.45

PAKISTAN
Mirza Book Agency
65 Shahrah Quaid-E-Azam
Lahore 54000   Tel. (42) 735.36.01
                                 Fax: (42) 576.37.14

PHILIPPINE – PHILIPPINES
International Booksource Center Inc.
Rm 179/920 Cityland 10 Condo Tower 2
HV dela Costa Ext cor Valero St.
Makati Metro Manila   Tel. (632) 817 9676
                                 Fax: (632) 817 1741

POLAND – POLOGNE
Ars Polona
00-950 Warszawa
Krakowskie Prezdmiescie 7   Tel. (22) 264760
                                 Fax: (22) 265334

PORTUGAL
Livraria Portugal
Rua do Carmo 70-74
Apart. 2681
1200 Lisboa   Tel. (01) 347.49.82/5
                                 Fax: (01) 347.02.64

SINGAPORE – SINGAPOUR
Ashgate Publishing
Asia Pacific Pte. Ltd
Golden Wheel Building, 04-03
41, Kallang Pudding Road
Singapore 349316   Tel. 741.5166
                                 Fax: 742.9356

SPAIN – ESPAGNE
Mundi-Prensa Libros S.A.
Castelló 37, Apartado 1223
Madrid 28001   Tel. (91) 431.33.99
                                 Fax: (91) 575.39.98
E-mail: mundiprensa@tsai.es
Internet: http://www.mundiprensa.es

Mundi-Prensa Barcelona
Consell de Cent No. 391
08009 – Barcelona   Tel. (93) 488.34.92
                                 Fax: (93) 487.76.59

Libreria de la Generalitat
Palau Moja
Rambla dels Estudis, 118
08002 – Barcelona
                   (Suscripciones) Tel. (93) 318.80.12
                   (Publicaciones) Tel. (93) 302.67.23
                                 Fax: (93) 412.18.54

SRI LANKA
Centre for Policy Research
c/o Colombo Agencies Ltd.
No. 300-304, Galle Road
Colombo 3   Tel. (1) 574240, 573551-2
                   Fax: (1) 575394, 510711

SWEDEN – SUÈDE
CE Fritzes AB
S–106 47 Stockholm   Tel. (08) 690.90.90
                                 Fax: (08) 20.50.21

For electronic publications only/
Publications électroniques seulement
STATISTICS SWEDEN
Informationsservice
S-115 81 Stockholm   Tel. 8 783 5066
                                 Fax: 8 783 4045

Subscription Agency/Agence d'abonnements :
Wennergren-Williams Info AB
P.O. Box 1305
171 25 Solna   Tel. (08) 705.97.50
                                 Fax: (08) 27.00.71

Liber distribution
Internatinal organizations
Fagerstagatan 21
S-163 52 Spanga

SWITZERLAND – SUISSE
Maditec S.A. (Books and Periodicals/Livres
et périodiques)
Chemin des Palettes 4
Case postale 266
1020 Renens VD 1   Tel. (021) 635.08.65
                                 Fax: (021) 635.07.80

Librairie Payot S.A.
4, place Pépinet
CP 3212
1002 Lausanne   Tel. (021) 320.25.11
                                 Fax: (021) 320.25.14

Librairie Unilivres
6, rue de Candolle
1205 Genève   Tel. (022) 320.26.23
                                 Fax: (022) 329.73.18

Subscription Agency/Agence d'abonnements :
Dynapresse Marketing S.A.
38, avenue Vibert
1227 Carouge   Tel. (022) 308.08.70
                                 Fax: (022) 308.07.99

See also – Voir aussi :
OECD Bonn Centre
August-Bebel-Allee 6
D-53175 Bonn (Germany)   Tel. (0228) 959.120
                                 Fax: (0228) 959.12.17

THAILAND – THAÏLANDE
Suksit Siam Co. Ltd.
113, 115 Fuang Nakhon Rd.
Opp. Wat Rajbopith
Bangkok 10200   Tel. (662) 225.9531/2
                                 Fax: (662) 222.5188

**TRINIDAD & TOBAGO, CARIBBEAN
TRINITÉ-ET-TOBAGO, CARAÏBES**
Systematics Studies Limited
9 Watts Street
Curepe
Trinidad & Tobago, W.I.   Tel. (1809) 645.3475
                                 Fax: (1809) 662.5654
E-mail: tobe@trinidad.net

TUNISIA – TUNISIE
Grande Librairie Spécialisée
Fendri Ali
Avenue Haffouz Imm El-Intilaka
Bloc B 1 Sfax 3000   Tel. (216-4) 296 855
                                 Fax: (216-4) 298.270

TURKEY – TURQUIE
Kültür Yayinlari Is-Türk Ltd.
Atatürk Bulvari No. 191/Kat 13
06684 Kavaklidere/Ankara
                           Tel. (312) 428.11.40 Ext. 2458
                           Fax : (312) 417.24.90
Dolmabahce Cad. No. 29
Besiktas/Istanbul   Tel. (212) 260 7188

UNITED KINGDOM – ROYAUME-UNI
The Stationery Office Ltd.
Postal orders only:
P.O. Box 276, London SW8 5DT
Gen. enquiries   Tel. (171) 873 0011
                                 Fax: (171) 873 8463

The Stationery Office Ltd.
Postal orders only:
49 High Holborn, London WC1V 6HB
Branches at: Belfast, Birmingham, Bristol,
Edinburgh, Manchester

UNITED STATES – ÉTATS-UNIS
OECD Washington Center
2001 L Street N.W., Suite 650
Washington, D.C. 20036-4922 Tel. (202) 785.6323
                                 Fax: (202) 785.0350
Internet: washcont@oecd.org

Subscriptions to OECD periodicals may also be
placed through main subscription agencies.

Les abonnements aux publications périodiques de
l'OCDE peuvent être souscrits auprès des
principales agences d'abonnement.

Orders and inquiries from countries where Distribu-
tors have not yet been appointed should be sent to:
OECD Publications, 2, rue André-Pascal, 75775
Paris Cedex 16, France.

Les commandes provenant de pays où l'OCDE n'a
pas encore désigné de distributeur peuvent être
adressées aux Éditions de l'OCDE, 2, rue André-
Pascal, 75775 Paris Cedex 16, France.

12-1996

OECD PUBLICATIONS, 2, rue André-Pascal, 75775 PARIS CEDEX 16
PRINTED IN FRANCE
(42 97 01 1) ISBN 92-64-15452-3 – No. 49315 1997